LECTURES
ON THE
HISTORY OF PHILOSOPHY

LECTURES

ON THE

HISTORY OF PHILOSOPHY

GEORG WILHELM FRIEDRICH HEGEL

TRANSLATED FROM THE GERMAN BY

E. S. HALDANE AND FRANCES H. SIMSON, M. A.

IN THREE VOLUMES

VOL. III

GYAN

Published by

GYAN

Gyan Publishing House
5, Ansari Road
Daryaganj, New Delhi-110002
Phone: 011-47034999, 9811692060
E-mail: books@gyanbooks.com

Distribution Network
gyanbooks.com
India, USA, Canada, UK, Australia, France

ISBN: 978-81-212-8639-8 (Set)
978-81-212-8636 7 (PB)
First Published, 1896

2nd Impression 2023

Printed at: Gyan Press, Delhi.

LECTURES ON THE HISTORY OF PHILOSOPHY(VOL. III)
Author: GEORG WILHELM FRIEDRICH HEGEL, E. S. HALDANE AND FRANCES H. SIMSON

THE ENGLISH AND FOREIGN PHILOSOPHICAL LIBRARY

LECTURES

ON THE

HISTORY OF PHILOSOPHY

BY

GEORG WILHELM FRIEDRICH HEGEL

TRANSLATED FROM THE GERMAN BY

ELIZABETH S. HALDANE AND FRANCES H. SIMSON, M.A.

IN THREE VOLUMES

VOL. III.

1896

CONTENTS

PART TWO

PHILOSOPHY OF THE MIDDLE AGES

SECTION ONE

SECTION TWO

SECTION THREE

PART THREE

MODERN PHILOSOPHY

SECTION ONE

SECTION TWO

SECTION THREE

PART TWO

PHILOSOPHY OF THE MIDDLE AGES

INTRODUCTION

The first period embraces a space of one thousand years—from Thales, 550 B.C., to Proclus, who died 485 A.D., and until the disappearance of pagan philosophy as an outward institution, 529 A.D. The second period extends to the sixteenth century, and thus again embraces a thousand years, to pass over which we must provide ourselves with seven-leagued boots. While Philosophy has hitherto found its place in the religion of the heathen, from this time on it has its sphere within the Christian world; for Arabians and Jews have only to be noticed in an external and historic way.

1. Through the Neo-Platonic philosophy we have come into quite familiar acquaintance with the Idea of Christianity, as the new religion which has entered into the world. For the Neo-Platonic philosophy has as its essential principle the fact that the Absolute is determined as spirit in a concrete way, that God is not a mere conception. Although the Absolute is Thought, it must, in order to be true, be concrete in itself and not abstract; in what we have just seen we have, then, the first appearance of the

absolutely existent spirit. But in spite of their profound and true speculation, the Neo-Platonists still had not proved their doctrine that the Trinity is the truth, for there is lacking to it the form of inward necessity. The Neo-Platonists begin from the One that determines itself, that sets a limit to itself from which the determinate proceeds; this, however, is itself an immediate method of presentation, and it is this that makes such philosophers as Plotinus and Proclus so tiresome. Undoubtedly dialectic considerations enter in, in which the opposites which are conceived as absolute are shown to be null; but this dialectic is not methodical, but occurs only disconnectedly. The principle of retroversion and comprehension found with the Neo-Platonists is that of substantiality generally, but because subjectivity is lacking, this idea of Spirit is deficient in one moment, the moment of actuality, of the point which draws all moments into one, and which thereby becomes immediate unity, universality, and Being. To them spirit is thus not individual spirit; and this deficiency is made good through Christianity, in which spirit is found as actual, present spirit, immediately existent in the world here and now, and the absolute spirit is known in the immediate present as man.

In order to grasp and apply the Idea of Christianity, the philosophic Idea of which we have already spoken in connection with the Neo-Platonists must have been comprehended for itself; but within Christianity the basis of Philosophy is that in man has sprung up the consciousness of the truth, or of spirit in and for itself, and then that man requires to participate in this truth. Man must be qualified to have this truth present to him; he must further be convinced of this possibility. This is the absolute demand and necessity; the consciousness must be arrived at that this alone is true. The first point of interest in the Christian religion thus is that the content of the Idea should be revealed to man; more particularly that the unity of the divine and human nature should come to the consciousness of man, and that, indeed, on the one hand as an implicitly existent unity, and, on the other, in actuality as worship. The Christian life signifies that the culminating point of subjectivity is made familiar with this conception, the individual himself is laid claim to, is made worthy of attaining on his own account to this unity, which is to make himself worthy of the Spirit of God—Grace, as it is called—dwelling in him. Hence the doctrine of reconciliation is that God is known as reconciling Himself with the world, *i.e.* as we have seen in the Neo-Platonic philosophy, that He particularizes Himself and does not remain abstract. Not external nature alone, but the whole world pertains to the particular; above all must human individuality know itself in God. The interest of the subject is itself involved, and here it plays an essential rôle in order that God may be realized and may realize Himself in the consciousness of individuals who are spirit and implicitly free. Thus through the process these accomplish that reconciliation in themselves, actualize their freedom; that is to say, they attain to the consciousness of heaven upon earth, the elevation of man to God. Thus the true intellectual world is not a beyond, but the so-called finite is an element in it, and no division exists between this side and that. The real concrete in regard to the absolute Idea is the knowing of the mundane, the 'other' in God, as implicitly divine, as universal, as the world of intellect, as having its root in God, but only the root. In God man is accepted only in his truth, and not in his immediacy, and thus this doctrine is not what we call Pantheism, for that leaves the immediate just as it is. Man then has himself to accomplish the process of reconciliation in himself in order to attain to his truth. We have thus seen that man possesses the determination and attributes of God as the first begotten son, Adam Kadmon, the first man; we may call this unity the concrete Idea, which, however, is still only implicit.

But the fact that because man is capable of the divine, the identity of the divine and human nature must likewise be present for him, has in an immediate way become known to him in Christ, as one in whom the divine and human nature are implicitly one. In the world what has come to pass is that the Absolute has been revealed as the concrete, and, further, not only in thought in a general way as intelligible world, but because it has in itself proceeded to its ultimate point of intensity. Thus it is an actual self, an "I," the absolute universal, the concrete universal, that is God; and also the absolute opposite of this determination, the clearly finite as it exists in space and time, but this finite determined in unity with the eternal as self. The Absolute comprehended as concrete, the unity of these two absolutely different determinations, is the true God; each of them is abstract, and either of them taken by itself is thus not the true God. The fact that the concrete is thus known to men in this perfection as God, brings about the whole revolution that has taken place in the world's history. The Trinity is thereby not only present in conception, which would not yet constitute the perfect concrete, but actuality is perfectly united to it. In the consciousness of the world it has consequently broken in upon men that the Absolute has attained to this "culminating point" of immediate actuality, as Proclus says; and that is the manifestation of Christianity. The Greeks were anthropomorphic, their gods were humanly constituted; but the deficiency in them is that they were not anthropomorphic enough. Or rather the Greek religion is on the one hand too much, and, on the other hand, too little anthropomorphic —too much, because immediate qualities, forms, actions, are taken up into the divine; too little, because man is not divine as man, but only as a far-away form and not as 'this,' and subjective man.

Thus man reaches this truth, because for him it becomes a sure intuition that in Christ the λόγος has become

Flesh. We thus first have man through this process attaining to spirituality, and in the second place we have man as Christ, in whom this original identity of both natures is known. Now since man really is this process of being the negation of the immediate, and from this negation attaining to himself—to a unity with God—he must consequently renounce his natural will, knowledge, and existence. This giving up of his natural existence is witnessed in Christ's sufferings and death, and in His resurrection and elevation to the right hand of the Father. Christ became a perfect man, endured the lot of all men, death; as man He suffered, sacrificed Himself, gave up His natural existence, and thereby elevated Himself above it. In Him this process, this conversion of His other-being into spirit, and the necessity of pain in the renunciation of the natural man is witnessed; but this pain, the pain of feeling that God Himself is dead, is the starting point of holiness and of elevation to God. Thus what must come to pass in the subject—this process, this conversion of the finite—is known as implicitly accomplished in Christ. This constitutes the great leading Idea of Christianity.

From what has been said it follows, in the second place, that the world must not be left in its immediate naturalness. The original, implicitly existent, is found only in the strictest conception of mind, or as its determination: immediately, man is only a living being, who has indeed the capacity to become actual spirit—but spirit does not pertain to nature. Man is thus not by nature this particular in which the spirit of God lives and dwells: man is not by nature what he ought to be. The animal is by nature what it ought to be. But what has to be noticed in this respect is that natural things merely remain in their implicit Notion, or their truth does not enter into their sensuous life, for this their natural individuality is only a fleeting fact that cannot look back on itself. The misfortune in natural things is that they get no further, that their essential nature is not for itself and independent; from this it follows that they do not attain to infinitude, to liberation from their immediate individuality, *i.e.* they do not attain to freedom, but only remain in the necessity which is the connection of the "one" with an "other," so that when this other unites itself to natural things, these last perish because they cannot bear the contradiction. But because the truth exists for man as consciousness, and in it he has the qualities necessary for freedom, he is capable of perceiving the Absolute, of placing himself in a relation to the same, and having knowledge as an end; and the liberation of mind depends on the fact that consciousness does not remain in its natural condition, but becomes spiritual, *i.e.* that for it the eternal, that is the reconciliation of the finite as this subject with the infinite, exists. Thus consciousness does not signify remaining in the sphere of nature, but the existence of the process whereby the universal becomes object or end to man. Man makes himself divine, but in a spiritual, that is to say not in an immediate way. In the ancient religions the divine is also united to the natural or human; but this unity is no reconciliation, but an immediate, undeveloped, and thus unspiritual unity, just because it is merely natural. But because mind is not natural but only that into which it makes itself, the spiritual is first met with in this very process of producing unity. To this spiritual unity pertains the negation of nature, of the flesh, as that in which man must not rest; for nature is from the beginning evil. Man is likewise naturally evil, for all the wickedness that man does proceeds from a natural desire. Now because man is in himself the image of God, but in existence is only natural, that which is implicit must be evolved, while the first natural condition must be abrogated. So much the more is it true that man first becomes spiritual, and attains to truth through rising above the natural, inasmuch as God Himself is a spirit only in that He transformed the hidden unity into the other of Himself, in order from this other to turn back again into Himself.

Now the fact that this is given as, or asserted to be the fundamental Idea of Christianity, implies on the one hand an historic question; at different times this idea has been grasped in different ways, and now, for example, men again have their particular conceptions of it. In order to bring about the conclusion that this is the historic idea of Christianity, we should have to enter upon an historic disquisition; but because we cannot deal with this here, we must accept it as an historic axiom. On the other hand, in so far as this question falls within the history of Philosophy, the assertion that this is the idea of Christianity has another ground to stand on than that of history, and this constitutes the third point of interest. In connection with the preceding forms it has been shown that this Idea of Christianity must have now come forth, and indeed become the universal consciousness of the nations. The fact that it has come forth as the world-religion, is the content of history; it is this necessity in the Idea which has to be expounded more clearly in the philosophy of history. To this end the conception of mind must be made fundamental, and it must now be shown that history is the process of mind itself, the revelation of itself from its first superficial, enshrouded consciousness, and the attainment of this standpoint of its free self-consciousness, in order that the absolute command of mind, "Know thyself," may be fulfilled. The recognition of this necessity has been called the *à priori* construction of history; there is no good in decrying it as inadmissible, and indeed as arrogant. The development of history may be represented as contingent. Or, if the providence and government of God are seriously accepted, these are represented as though Christianity were so to speak ready made in the mind of God; then, when thrust into the world, it appears to be contingent. But the rationality and likewise the necessity of this decree of God's has now to be considered, and this may be called a theodicy, a justification of God, *i.e.* a vindication of our Idea. It is a demonstration that, as I have just said, things have happened rationally in the world, and it implies the fact that the world-history represents the process of mind partially as the history of mind, which has to be reflected into itself in order to come to a consciousness of what it is. It is this which is shown forth in temporal history, and as history, indeed, just because mind is the living movement, proceeding from its immediate existence to beget revolutions in the world, as well as in individuals.

Since it is hereby pre-supposed that this Idea must necessarily become universal religion, there is, in the fourth place, present in it the source of a method of knowledge proper to the particular consciousness. That is to say, the new religion has made the intelligible world of Philosophy the world of common consciousness. Tertullian hence says: "Even children in our day have a knowledge of God, which the wisest men of antiquity alone attained to." But in order that all may know the truth, this Idea must come to them as an object, not for the thinking, philosophic and cultured consciousness, but for the sensuous consciousness which still adheres to uncultured methods of regarding things. If this Idea were not to receive and to retain this form of outward consciousness, it would be a philosophy of the Christian religion; for the standpoint of Philosophy is the Idea in the form of the merely universal thought, and not the Idea as it is for the subject and directed to the subject. That through which this Idea appears as religion, belongs, however, to the history of religion, and this development of its form must here be passed over. Through these forms we must however not mistake the content, much less reject it altogether, for we must rather recognize its presence more completely; the forms must likewise not be held to be absolute, and we must not try to maintain the doctrines in this form alone, as was at one time done by an orthodoxy "of straw."

Only one example will here be given. The so-called doctrine of original sin implies that our first parents have sinned, that this sin has thus descended to all mankind as an hereditary disorder, and has come upon posterity in an external way as something inherent in their nature, which does not pertain to freedom of the mind, nor has its ground therein. Through this original sin, it is further signified, man has drawn upon himself the wrath of God. Now if these forms be adhered to, we have in the first place there the first parents in time, and not in thought; but the thought of these first parents is none other than man as he is in and for himself. What is said of him as such, what every member of the human race really is in himself, is represented here in the form of the first man, Adam; and in this first man sin manifests itself as something contingent, or, more particularly, in his allowing himself to be enticed into eating of the apple. But it is again not merely represented that he simply partook of the fruit, but that he ate of the tree of the knowledge of good and evil; it is as man that he must partake of it, and not as beast. The fundamental characteristic, however, through which he distinguishes himself from the animal, is the very fact that he knows what good and evil are. For God likewise says, "Behold, Adam has become as one of us, to know good and evil." But it is only through man's having the power of thinking that he can make this distinction between good and evil; in thought alone is there thus the source of good and evil, but the healing of the evil which is brought about through thought is also there. The second point is that man is by nature evil and transmits the evil, On the other hand, it is said: "Why should the sinner suffer punishment seeing that there is no responsibility for what is inborn in him?" As a matter of fact the statement that man is implicitly or by nature evil would seem to be a hard saying. But if we set aside this hard saying, and do not speak of a divine punishment, but make use of milder general expressions, in this idea of original sin the fact remains for us that man as he is by nature is not what he ought to be before God, but has the power of becoming explicitly what he only is implicitly; and the fact that this rests in the determination of man as such is represented as inheritance. The abrogation of mere naturalness is known to us simply as education, and arises of itself; through education subjection is brought about, and with that a capacity for becoming good is developed. Now if this appears to come to pass very easily, we must recollect that it is of infinite importance that the reconciliation of the world with itself, the making good, is brought about through the simple method of education.

2. What concerns us now is to make the Principle of Christianity, which has been explained at considerable length, into the principle of the world; the task set before the world is to bring this absolute Idea within itself, to actualize it in itself, and thereby to reconcile itself to God. This task once more falls into three separate divisions.

In the first place we have the dissemination of the Christian religion and the bringing of it within the hearts of men; this, however, lies outside the limits of our consideration. The heart signifies the subjective man as 'this,' and through this principle the latter has a different position from before; it is essential that this subject should be present. The individual subject is the object of divine grace; each subject, or man as man, has on his own account an infinite value, is destined to partake of this spirit which must, as God, be born within the heart of every man. Man is determined for freedom, he is here recognized as implicitly free; this freedom is, however, at first only formal, because it remains within the principle of subjectivity.

The second point is that the principle of the Christian religion should be worked out for thought, and be taken up into thinking knowledge, and realized in this; and thus that it should attain to reconciliation, having the divine Idea within itself, and that the riches of thought and culture belonging to the philosophic Idea should become united to the Christian principle. For the philosophic Idea is the Idea of God, and thought has the absolute right of reconciliation, or the right to claim that the Christian principle should correspond with thought. The Fathers have rendered the service of thus elaborating the Christian religion in thinking knowledge; but neither have we to consider further this development of the Christian principle, since it belongs to the history of the Church. We have only here to give the point of view adopted regarding the relation of the Fathers to Philosophy. They for the most part lived within the ancient Roman world and in Latin culture, though the Byzantines likewise are included with them. We know that the Fathers were men of great philosophic culture, and that they introduced Philosophy, and more especially Neo-Platonic philosophy, into the Church; in this way they worked out a Christian system by which the first mode in which Christianity was manifested in the world was supplemented, for system was not present in this first manifestation. The Fathers have dealt with all questions respecting the nature of God, the freedom of man, the relationship to God—who is the objective—the origin of evil, and so on; and whatever thought decided regarding these questions was by them brought into and incorporated with the Christian system. The nature of spirit, the way of salvation, *i.e.* the various stages in the spiritualizing of the subject, his growth, the process of spirit, whereby it is spirit, the changes it has undergone, they have likewise treated in its freedom, and recognized its moments in the depths to which it reaches.

We may thus describe the attitude of the Christian Fathers, and likewise remark that this first philosophic development of the Christian principle has been looked on as a crime on their part, and it has been said that they have thus corrupted the purity of Christianity as originally manifested. We must speak of the nature of this corruption. It is well known that Luther in his Reformation made his aim the bringing of the Church back to the purity of its first estate in the early centuries, but this first condition already shows the fabric of an extensive and closely interwoven system, an elaborate tissue of doctrines regarding what God is and what is man's relation to Him. Hence at the time of the Reformation no particular system was built up, but what was originally there was purified from later additions; it is a complicated erection, in which the most intricate pieces of workmanship are to be found. In modern times this elaborately woven system has been entirely pulled to pieces, because men have wished to bring Christianity back to the simple lines of the Word of God as found in the writings of the New Testament. Men have likewise given up the propagation of the system, the doctrine of Christianity as determined through the Idea and by the Idea, and have returned to the manner of its first appearance (and that, indeed, in eclectic fashion, and having regard to what will fit in with their own notions), so that now only the original Gospel narrative is regarded as forming the basis of Christianity. As regards the title of Philosophy and the Fathers to bring Philosophy into Christianity we have the following remarks to make.

Modern Theology on the one hand derives its formulas from the words of the Bible, which are made to form their basis, so that the whole business of the individual, as regards his thoughts and his conceptions, is merely exegetical; religion must be retained in its positive form, and thus it is from something received and given, something most evidently externally posited and revealed, that a beginning must be made. These words and this text are, however, of a nature such that they allow full latitude to the will of the interpreter; hence the other side is also present, or the application of the Bible saying: "The letter killeth, but the spirit giveth life." This must be assented to, and the spirit means none else than the power which dwells within those who apply themselves to the letter in order that they may spiritually apprehend and animate it. This signifies that it is the conceptions which we bring along with us which have in the letter to give efficacy to themselves. Now these reflections brought along with us may be grasped by the most ordinary human understanding, which is what is indicated in modern times when we say that dogmas must be popular. In that way the right to act upon the letter with the spirit is assumed, *i.e.* the right to approach it with our individual judgment; but to the Fathers this is forbidden. They did act upon it with the Spirit; and it is expressly said that the Spirit dwells within the Church, directs, teaches, and illuminates it. The Fathers have hence a similar right to relate themselves with the Spirit to the positive, to what is given by the senses. Only it will depend absolutely upon what the nature of the Spirit is, for spirits are very different.

The assertion that the spirit must give life to the mere letter is certainly more definitely stated as that spirit has only to expound what is given, *i.e.* it must leave the actual sense of what is immediately contained in the words. We must, however, be far behind in culture if we do not see the fallacy in the attitude here adopted. To expound without the individual spirit, as though the sense were one entirely given, is impossible. To elucidate signifies to make clear, and it must be made clear to me; this can be done by nothing excepting what was already present in me. It must be in conformity with my subjective judgment, the necessities of my knowledge, of my apprehension, of my heart, &c.; thus only is it for me. We find what we look for, and just because I make it clear to myself, I make my conception, my thought, a factor in it; otherwise it is a dead and external thing, which is not present for me at all. It is hence very difficult to make clear to ourselves those foreign religions which lie far below our spiritual needs; but yet they touch a side of my spiritual necessities and standpoints, although it is but a dim and sensuous side. Thus when we talk of "making clear," we conceal the real matter in a word; but if this word itself is made clear we find nothing in it but the fact that the spirit which is in man desires therein to recognize itself, and that it cannot know anything which does not rest in him. Thus have men made of the Bible what may be called a nose of wax. This man finds this thing, the other man that; what was secure now shows itself as insecure, because it is considered by the subjective spirit.

In this regard the nature of the text describing the method in which the first manifestation of Christianity took place, must be remarked upon; it cannot as yet expressly contain that which rests in the principle of Christianity, but only somewhat of an anticipation of what spirit is and will know as true. This also is expressly said in the text itself. Christ says: "If I depart, I will send the Comforter, the Holy Ghost . . . He will guide you into all truth," He—and not Christ's earthly presence nor His spoken words. It was only to be after Him, and after His teaching through the text, that the Spirit was to come into the Apostles, and that they were to become full of the Spirit. It might almost be said that when Christianity is carried back to its first appearing, it is brought down to the level of unspirituality, for Christ Himself says that the Spirit will not come until He Himself has departed. In the text of the first manifestation of Christianity we, on the other hand, see Christ only as the Messiah, or under the more explicit designation of a mere teacher; for His friends and apostles He is a present man whom they can perceive by the senses, and who does not yet hold to them the relationship of the Holy Ghost. His friends have seen Him, heard His doctrine, seen His miracles, and have thereby been brought to believe in Him. But Christ Himself sternly rebukes those who demand miracles of

Him; if He thus be made as God to man, God in the heart of man, He cannot have a sensuous and immediate presence. The Dalai-lama, in the form of a sensuous man, is God to the inhabitants of Thibet, but in the Christian principle, where God dwells in the hearts of men, He cannot be present to them in sensuous form.

The second point then is that the sensuous and present form must disappear, so that it may be taken into the Mnemosyne, into the realm of popular conception; then for the first time can the spiritual consciousness, the spiritual relation, enter in. To the question of whither Christ has gone, the answer is given, "He sits on the right hand of God," which signifies that it is only now that God can be known as this concrete One, as the One who has the other moment, His Son (λόγος, σοφία), in Himself. Thus to know what is the principle of Christianity as truth, the truth of the Idea of spirit must be known as concrete spirit, and this is the form peculiar to the Fathers of the Church. With this the idea that the abstractly divine breaks up and has broken up within itself, first began to appear. This other moment in the divine must not, however, be grasped in the mode of an intelligible world, or, as we certainly have it in the ordinary conception, of a kingdom of heaven with many angels, who are also finite, limited, thus approaching closer to humanity. But it is not sufficient that the concrete moment should be known in God, for the further knowledge is requisite that Christ is an actual present man. This moment of Christ's actual present humanity is of immense importance to Christianity, because it is the union of the most tremendous opposites. This higher conception could not have been present in the text, in the first manifestation; the greatness of the Idea could only come in later on, after the Spirit had perfected the Idea.

That the revelation of Christ has this significance is the

belief of Christians, while the profane, immediate and direct significance of this history is that Christ was a mere prophet and met the fate of all the prophets in being misunderstood. But the fact that it has the significance given by us is known through the Spirit, for the Spirit is revealed in this history. This history is the Notion, the Idea of Spirit itself, and the world-history has in it found its end, which is in this immediate way to know the truth. It is therefore the Spirit which so comprehends that history, and at the time of Pentecost this is shown in an immediate and evident manner. For before this time the Apostles did not know the infinite significance of Christ; they did not yet know that this is the infinite history of God; they had believed in Him, but not yet as seeing in Him this infinite truth.

This is the truth which the Fathers developed; the general relation of the first Christian Church to Philosophy is hereby given. On the one hand, the philosophic Idea has been transplanted into this religion; on the other, this moment in the Idea—according to which the latter breaks up within itself into wisdom, the active Logos, the Son of God, &c., but yet in so doing remains in universality —has been brought to a culmination in subjectivity, and further in the sensuous immediate individuality and present existence of a human individual appearing in time and space. These two elements are essentially intermingled in this Christian system, the Idea itself, and secondly the form as it presents itself through its connection with a single individuality present in time and space. To the Fathers this history had thus the Idea as its principle; the true Idea of the Spirit was consequently to them likewise in the determinate form of history. But the Idea was not yet, as such, separated from history; because the Church thus held to this Idea in historic form, it determined the doctrines. This, then, is the general character of the time.

From this Idea as comprehended through the Spirit,

many so-called heresies arose in the first centuries after Christ. Among such heretics must be included those of the Gnostics who take the Christian literature as their basis, but give a spiritual significance to everything therein present. For they did not remain at this historical form of the Idea of Spirit, since they interpreted the history and deprived it of its historical value. The reflections which they introduced are, as we have seen (Vol. II., pp. 396-399), to a greater or less extent such as are to be found in the philosophy of the Alexandrians or of Philo. In conformity with their principles they adopted a speculative attitude, but they proceeded into extravagances both of the imagination and morality, although in this dim fantastic region the elements which we found in history may always be recognized. But the form of immediate existence, an essential moment in Christ, is by them etherealized into a universal thought, so that the determination of the individual as a 'this' disappears. The Docetæ, for example, said that Christ had only a phantom body, a phantom life; yet in such assertions thought still constituted the background. The Gnostics were thus antagonistic to the Western Church, and, like Plotinus and the Neo-Platonists, this last strove hard against Gnosticism, because it remained in what is general, grasped the conception in the form of imagination, and because this conception was opposed to that of Christ in the Flesh (*Χριστὸς ἐν σαρκί*).[1] The Church, on the contrary, held to the definite form of personality as the principle of concrete actuality.

From the East other forms of opposition in the principles than those we mentioned in connection with the Gnostics have been introduced, namely, Light and Darkness, Good and Evil. But more particularly has this Parsee opposition emerged in Manichæism, in which God, as the Light opposes the evil, non-existent (*οὐκ ὄν*), the *ὕλη*, the

[1] Neander. Genet. Entwickelung d. vornehmsten gnost. Systeme, p. 43.

material, self-annihilating. Evil is that which contains contradiction in itself: the powers of evil (ὕλη), given over to themselves and raging in blind enmity against one another, were met by a gleam from the Kingdom of Light and thereby attracted, and this light pacified the powers of evil, so as to cause them to cease from strife and unite together in order to penetrate into the Kingdom of Light. As an inducement to make them so act, in order to weaken and mitigate their blind fury through a power operating irresistibly, and in order to bring about their final overthrow, and the universal supremacy of light, of life, of the soul, the Father of Light delivered over one of the powers of good. That is the world-soul (ψυχὴ ἁπάντων); it was swallowed up by the material, and this intermixture is the basis of the whole creation. Hence the soul is everywhere disseminated, and in the dead husk it is everywhere working and striving in man, the microcosm, as in the universe, the macrocosm, but with unequal power; for where beauty reveals itself, the Light-principle, the soul, obtains the mastery over matter, but in the ugly, the hateful, it is subordinate, and matter is the conqueror. This captive soul Mani likewise called the Son of Man—that is, of the primitive man, the heavenly man, of Adam Kadmon. But only a part of the Light-principle which was destined to strive with the Kingdom of Evil is in this manner delivered over; being too weak, it incurred the danger of being vanquished, and had to deliver over to matter a part of its armour, this soul. The part of the soul which had not suffered through such intermingling with matter, but had raised itself freely to heaven, works from above for the purification of the imprisoned souls, its kindred portions of light; and that is Jesus, the Son of Man, in so far as he has not suffered (ἀπαθής), as distinguished from the suffering Son of Man, the soul confined within the universe. But that delivering soul remains in the second and visible light which is still distinguished from the first and unapproachable, having its seat there, and by means of sun and moon exercising influence in the purification of nature. To Mani the whole course of the physical as of the spiritual world appears as a process of purification by means of this soul. The captive principle of Light required to be raised from the cycle of metempsychosis to an immediate re-union with the Kingdom of Light. Hence the pure heavenly soul came down to earth and appeared in the semblance of human form in order to reach to the suffering soul (to the *νοῦς παθητικός* of Aristotle?) a helping hand. The Manichæans also express themselves to the effect that God, the Good, goes forth, illumines, and thus produces an intelligible world. What comes third is Spirit as turning round, establishing the unity of the second and first, and experiencing feeling, and this feeling is Love. This heresy fully recognizes the Idea, but does away with the form of individual existence in which the Idea is presented in the Christian religion. The crucifixion of Christ is consequently taken as merely a semblance, as allegorical only, simply an image. That merely phantom crucifixion of the non-suffering Jesus, the fellow-suffering, only imaginary certainly, of the soul unmingled with matter, shows forth the actual suffering of the captive soul. Thus as the forces of Darkness could exercise no power over Christ, they must also show themselves powerless over the soul allied thereto. With the Manichæans originates the conception of a Jesus who is crucified in all the world and in the soul; the crucifixion of Christ thus mystically signifies only the wounds of our suffering souls. Through vegetation the particles of light were held fast, and thus held fast they were brought forth as plants. The earth becoming fruitful brings forth the suffering (*patibilis*) Jesus, who is the life and salvation of men and is crucified on every tree. The *νοῦς* which appeared in Jesus signifies all things.[1] The Church has

[1] Neander. Genetische Entwickelung, &c., pp. 87–91.

likewise made a principal point of asserting the unity of the divine and human nature. But because this unity in the Christian religion attained to conceiving consciousness, human nature was in its actuality taken as 'this,' and not merely in an allegorical or philosophic sense.

Now if, on the one hand, the essential matter with the orthodox Fathers who opposed themselves to these Gnostic speculations, is the fact that they held firmly to the definite form of an objectively conceived Christ, on the other hand they attacked the Arians and all that pertain to them; for these recognize the individual as manifested, but do not place the Person of Christ in connection with the separation, with the breaking up of the divine Idea. They took Christ to be a man, accorded to Him indeed a higher nature, not, however, making Him a moment of God, of Spirit itself. The Arians did not indeed go so far as the Socinians, who accepted Christ merely as a man of noble nature, a teacher, and so on; this sect hence did not form part of the Church at all, being simply heathen. But still the Arians, since they did not recognize God in Christ, did away with the idea of the Trinity, and consequently with the principle of all speculative philosophy. The according to Him of a higher nature is likewise a hollow mockery which cannot satisfy us; as against this the Fathers accordingly asserted the unity of the divine and human nature, which has come to consciousness in the individual members of the Church, and this is a point of fundamental importance. The Pelagians again, denied original sin, and maintained that man has by nature sufficient virtue and religion. But man should not be what he is by nature; he should be spiritual. And thus this doctrine is likewise excluded as heretical. Therefore the Church was ruled by Spirit, to enable it to hold to the determinations of the Idea, though always in the historic form. This is the philosophy of the Fathers; they produced the Church, as the developed Spirit required a developed doctrine, and nothing is so out of place as the endeavour or desire of some men of the present day to lead the Church back to her original form.

What follows thirdly is that the Idea permeates reality, is immanent therein, that not only is there a multitude of believing hearts, but that from the heart, just as the natural law rules over a sensuous world, a higher life of the world, a kingdom, is constituted—the reconciliation of God with Himself is accomplished in the world, and not as a heavenly kingdom that is beyond. This community is the kingdom of God upon earth in the Church; "Where two or three are gathered together in my name," says Christ, "there am I in the midst of them." The Idea is only for spirit, for subjective consciousness, in so far as it realizes itself in actuality, and thus it not only has to bring itself to perfection in the heart, but has to perfect itself also into a kingdom of actual consciousness. The Idea which man, self-consciousness, should recognize, must become altogether objective to him, so that he may truly apprehend himself as spirit and the Spirit, and then that he may be spiritual in a spiritual, and not in an emotional way. The first objectification is found in the first immediate consciousness of the Idea, where it appeared as an individual object, as the individual existence of a man. The second objectivity is the spiritual worship and communion extended to the Church. We might imagine a universal community of Love, a world of piety and holiness, a world of brotherly kindness, of innocent little lambs and pretty triflings with things spiritual, a divine republic, a heaven upon earth. But this is not supposed to come to pass on earth; that imagination is relegated to heaven, *i.e.* to some other place, that is to say, it is put off until death. Each living actuality directs his feelings, actions, and affairs in a very different way from this. On the appearance of Christianity it is first of all said: "My kingdom is not of this world;" but the realization has and ought to be in the present world. In other words the laws, customs, constitutions, and all that belongs to the actuality of spiritual consciousness should be rational. The kingdom of rational actuality is quite a different one, and must be organized and developed thinkingly and with understanding; the moment of the self-conscious freedom of the individual must maintain its rights against objective truth and objective command. This, then, is the true and actual objectivity of mind in the form of an actual temporal existence as state, just as Philosophy is the objectivity of thought which comes to us in the form of universality. Such objectivity cannot be in the beginning, but must come forth after being worked upon by mind and thought.

In Christianity these absolute claims of the intellectual world and of spirit had become the universal consciousness. Christianity proceeded from Judaism, from self-conscious abjectness and depression. This feeling of nothingness has from the beginning characterized the Jews; a sense of desolation, an abjectness where no reason was, has possession of their life and consciousness. This single point has later on, and in its proper time, become a matter of universal history, and into this element of the nullity of actuality the whole world has raised itself, passing out of this principle indeed, but also into the kingdom of Thought, because that nothingness has transformed itself into what is positively reconciled. This is a second creation which came to pass after the first; in it Mind became aware of itself as I = I, that is, as self-consciousness. This second creation has first of all appeared in self-consciousness equally directly in the form of a sensuous world, in the form of a sensuous consciousness. As much of the Notion as has entered in was adopted by the Fathers from the philosophers already mentioned; their Trinity, in so far as a rational thought, and not a mere ordinary conception, comes from these, and certain other ideas also.

But what mainly distinguishes them is the fact that for the Christian this intelligible world had likewise this immediate sensuous truth of an ordinary course of events—a form which it must have and retain for the majority of men.

3. This new world has therefore, however, to be adopted by a new race of men, by Barbarians; for it is characteristic of barbarians to apprehend the spiritual in a sensuous way. And it must be by northern barbarians, for it is the northern self-containedness alone that is the immediate principle of this new world-consciousness. With this self-consciousness of the intelligible world as a world immediately actual, mind, having regard to what it has in itself become, is higher than before, but, on the other side, in respect of its consciousness it is thrown quite back to the beginning of culture, and this consciousness had to commence from the beginning again. What it had to overcome was on the one hand this sensuous immediacy of its intelligible world, and secondly the opposed sensuous immediacy of actuality, by its consciousness held as null. It excludes the sun, replaces it with tapers, is furnished with images merely; it is in itself alone, and inward, not reconciled for consciousness—to self-consciousness a sinful, wicked world is present. For the intelligible world of Philosophy had not yet completed in itself the task of making itself the actual world—of recognizing the intelligible in the actual, as well as the actual in the intelligible. It is one thing to have the Idea of Philosophy, to recognize absolute essence as absolute essence, and quite another thing to recognize it as the system of the universe, of nature, and of individual self-consciousness, as the whole development of its reality. The Neo-Platonists had found that principle of realization—namely, this real substance which again places itself in quite opposed, though in themselves real determinations—but having got so far they did not find the form, the principle of self-consciousness.

On the Teutonic nations the world-spirit imposed the task of developing an embryo into the form of the thinking man. What comes first is the mind as apprehended, and to that is opposed the subjectivity of will which has not been taken up into mind ; the kingdom of truth and that of the world are bound together and at the same time evidently divided. An intelligible world has thus in the conception of men established itself in the mode of this same actuality, like a far-away land that is just as really conceived of by us, peopled and inhabited, as the world we see, but which is hidden from us as though by a mountain. It is not the Greek or any other world of gods and of mythology—a simple, undivided faith ; for there is likewise present in it the highest negativity, that is, the contradiction between actuality and that other world. This intellectual world expresses the nature of real absolute existence. It is on it that Philosophy tries its powers, and on it that thought also moils and toils. We have in general outline to deal with these not very pleasing manifestations.

Our first view of Philosophy, as revealed in Christianity(pp. 10-21) is that of a dim groping which is carried on within the depths of the Idea—as being the forms assumed by the same, which constitute its moments ; we see a hard struggle made by reason, which cannot force its way out of the imagination and popular conceptions to the Notion. There is no venture too rash for the imagination to undertake, because, impelled by reason, it cannot satisfy itself with beautiful images, but has to pass beyond them. There is likewise no extravagance of reason into which it does not fall, because it cannot obtain the mastery of the image, but within this element is merely in the act of warfare with it. Later on than this Western self-immersion, there arose in the East expansion, negation of all that is concrete, abstraction from all determinations ; this pure contemplation or pure thought present in Mohammedanism corresponds to the Christian descent into self. Within Christianity itself, however, the intellectual world is set in opposition to that first Cabalistic principle; in it pure conceptions rule which constitute the ideas present in thought, and with this we enter upon the Scholastic philosophy. Philosophy, like the arts and sciences, when, through the rule of the Barbarians of Germany, they became dumb and lifeless, took refuge with the Arabians, and there attained a wonderful development; they were the first sources from which the West obtained assistance. Through the pre-supposition of the immediately present and accepted truth, thought had lost its freedom and the truth its presence in conceiving consciousness; and philosophy sank into a metaphysics of the understanding and into a formal dialectic. We have thus in this period first of all to consider philosophy in the East, and secondly in the West; that is, the philosophy of the Arabians first, and subsequently the philosophy of the Schools. The Schoolmen are the principal figures in this period; they represent European philosophy in the European Middle Ages. The third stage is the dissolution of what is upheld in the scholastic philosophy; new meteor-like apparitions are now seen, which precede the third period, the genuine revival of free Philosophy.

SECTION ONE

Arabian Philosophy

In the West the Germanic tribes had obtained possession of what had hitherto formed a section of the Roman Empire, and their conquests were attaining to shape and solidity, when another religion dawned in the East, namely the Mohammedan. The East purified itself of all that was individual and definite, while the West descended into the depths and actual presence of spirit. As quickly as the Arabians with their fanaticism spread themselves over the Eastern and the Western world, so quickly were the various stages of culture passed through by them, and very shortly they advanced in culture much farther than the West. For in Mohammedanism, which quickly reached its culminating point, both as regards external power and dominion and also spiritual development, Philosophy, along with all the other arts and sciences, flourished to an extraordinary degree, in spite of its here not displaying any specially characteristic features. Philosophy was fostered and cherished among the Arabians; the philosophy of the Arabians must therefore be mentioned in the history of Philosophy. What we have to say, however, chiefly concerns the external preservation and propagation of Philosophy. The Arabians became acquainted with Greek philosophy mainly through the medium of the Syrians in Western Asia, who had imbibed Greek culture, and who were under the Arabian sway. In Syria, which formed a

Greek kingdom, at Antioch, especially in Berytus and Edessa, there were great institutes of learning; and thus the Syrians constituted the connecting link between Greek philosophy and the Arabians. Syrian was the language of the people even in Bagdad.[1]

Moses Maimonides, a learned Jew, gives further historical particulars in his *Doctor Perplexorum* of this transition of Philosophy to the Arabians. He says: "All that the Ishmaelites have written of the unity of God and other philosophic dogmas"—especially the sect of the Muatzali (מעתזלה, *i.e.* the Separated), who were the first to take an interest in the abstract intellectual knowledge of such subjects, while the sect Assaria (האשעריה) arose later—"is based upon arguments and propositions which have been taken from the books of the Greeks and Aramæans" (Syrians), "who strove to refute and deny the teachings of the philosophers. The cause of this is as follows: The Christian community came to include within it these nations also, and the Christians defended many dogmas which were contradictory of philosophic tenets; among these nations, however, the teachings of philosophers were very widely and generally diffused (for with them Philosophy had its origin), and kings arose who adopted the Christian religion. The Christian Greeks and learned Aramæans, therefore, when they perceived that their doctrines were so clearly and plainly refuted by the philosophers, thought out a wisdom of their own, the "Wisdom of the Words" (Devarim), and they themselves received on that account the name of the Speakers (Medabberim, מְדַבְּרִים). They set up principles which served the purpose both of confirming their faith and of refuting the opposite teaching of the philosophers. When the Ishmaelites followed and

[1] Tennemann, Vol. VIII. Section I. p. 366; Buhle: Lehrb. d. Gesch. d. Phil. Part V. p. 36; Brucker. Hist. crit. phil. T. III. pp. 23, 24; 28, 29.

attained supremacy, and the books of the philosophers themselves fell into their hands, and along with them the answers which "Christian Greeks and Aramæans had written against the philosophic books, as for instance the writings of Johannes Grammaticus, Aben Adi, and others, they eagerly laid hold of these and adopted them bodily."[1] Christians and Ishmaelites felt the same need of philosophy; the Ishmaelites, moreover, strove all the more eagerly after knowledge of this kind, because their first desire was to defend Mohammedanism against Christianity, which was the religion of a large proportion of the nations they had conquered.

The external sequence of events is this. Syriac versions of Greek works were to be had, and these were now translated into Arabic by the Arabians; or translations were made from the Greek directly into Arabic. In the reign of Harun-al-Raschid several Syrians are named who lived in Bagdad, and who had been called upon by the Caliphs to translate these works into Arabic. They were the first scientific teachers among the Arabians, and were chiefly physicians; hence the works they translated were on medicine. Among these translators was Johannes Mesue of Damascus, who lived in the reigns of Al-Raschid (*d.* A.D. 786), Al-Mamun (*d.* A.D. 833) and Al-Motawakkil (*d.* A.D. 847), rather earlier than the rise of the Turks to supremacy (A.D. 862); he was a hospital superintendent in Bagdad. Al-Raschid appointed him to make translations from Syriac into Arabic; he opened a public school for the study of medicine and all the sciences then known. Honain was a Christian, as was also his master Johannes, and belonged to the Arab tribe Ebadi; he applied himself to the study of Greek, and made a number of translations into Arabic, and also into Syriac, for example, Nicolaus *De summa philosophiæ Aristotelicæ*, Ptolemy, Hippo-

[1] Moses Maimonides: More Nevochim, P. I. c. 71, pp. 133, 134 (Basil. 1629).

crates and Galen. Another is Ebn Adda, an eminent dialectician, who is quoted by Abulfaraj.[1] Among the works of the Greek philosphers it was almost exclusively the writings of Aristotle which were translated by these Syrians, and the later commentaries on the same. It was thus not the Arabians themselves who translated the above works.

In the Arabic philosophy, which shows a free, brilliant and profound power of imagination, Philosophy and the sciences took the same bent that they had taken earlier among the Greeks. Plato with his Ideas or universals laid the foundation of the independent world of intellect, and established absolute existence as an existence which is manifestly present in the mode of thought; Aristotle developed, completed and peopled the realm of thought; the Neo-Platonic philosophy reached the further conception of the intelligible world as Idea of the existence which is independent in itself, of spirit; and then this first Idea, which we have already met with in connection with Proclus, passed over into a similar Aristotelian development and completion. Consequently it is the Alexandrian or Neo-Platonic Idea which forms the essential principle or basis of the Arabian as well as the Scholastic philosophy, and all that Christian philosophy offers; it is on it that the determinations of the Notion expend their strength, and around this that they career. A particular description of Arabian philosophy has in some parts but little interest; in other parts it will be found that the main dogmas of this philosophy have much in common with those of the Scholastics.

We may say of the Arabians that their philosophy constitutes no characteristic stage in the development of philosophy. The principal points in this, as in the later philosophy, were the question whether the world is

[1] Abulphar. Dynast. IX. pp. 153, 171, 208, 209; Brucker. Hist. crit. phil. T. III. pp. 27-29, 44.

eternal, and the task of proving the unity of God and similar dogmas. One great consideration in all this, however, was to defend the doctrines of Mohammedanism, and owing to this all philosophizing had to be carried on within the limits of these doctrines. The Arabians, like the Christians of the West, were restricted by the dogmas of their Church (if one may call it so), few though these dogmas were; yet this last circumstance of the small number of the dogmas certainly gave them greater liberty. But according to all that we know of them, they established no principle of self-conscious reason that was truly higher, and thus they brought Philosophy no further. They have no other principle than that of revelation, therefore only a principle that is external.

A. Philosophy of the Medabberim.

The Medabberim are specially mentioned by Moses Maimonides as a widely extended philosophic school or sect of considerable eminence. He speaks (More Nevochim, P. I. c. 71, pp. 134, 135) of the peculiarity of their method of philosophy somewhat as follows: "The Ishmaelites, however, have extended their discourses still further, and have aspired to other wonderful doctrines, of which none of the Greek Medabberim knew anything, because they were still on some points in agreement with the philosophers. The main point to be remarked is that all the Medabberim, whether among the Greeks who had become Christians, or among the Ishmaelites, in the building up of their principles did not follow the nature of the matter itself, or draw their arguments from it, but only had in view how the subject must be regarded in order to support their assertion, or at least not to refute it altogether: afterwards they boldly asserted that these were the circumstances of the case, and adduced further arguments and maxims in support of their object. They insisted on that, and that alone, which concurred with their opinions, even though it were in the most remote degree, through a hundred links of reasoning. The earliest of their learned men adopted this practice, though professing that they reached these reflections through speculation alone, without reference to any preconceived opinion. Their successors did not follow their example," &c.

In the pure philosophy of the so-called "Speakers" was expressed the principle, peculiar to the Oriental mind, of the dissolution of definite thought in all its consequences as the dissolution of all connection and relation. Maimonides says (P. I. c. 71, p. 135; c. 73, p. 149): "The ground-principle of the Medabberim is that men can have no certain knowledge of the nature of things, because in the understanding the contrary may ever exist and be thought. Besides this they in the majority of instances confound imagination with understanding, and give to the former the name of the latter. They adopted as a principle, atoms and empty space," where all connection appears as something contingent. "Production is nothing but a connection of atoms, and decay nothing but a separation of the same; and time consists of many 'nows.'" In this way nothing but the atom really exists. They have thus in the more advanced cultivation of thought brought to consciousness the main standpoint, then as now the standpoint of the Orientals—that of substance, the one substance. This pantheism, or Spinozism, if you like to call it so, is thus the universal view of Oriental poets, historians and philosophers.

The Medabberim go on to say: "Substances, *i.e.* individuals, which," for the rest, "are created by God, have many accidental qualities, as in snow every particle is white. But no quality can endure for two moments; as it comes, it goes again, and God creates another and yet another in its place." All determinations are thus fleeting or perishable; the individual alone is permanent. "If it pleases God to create another quality in a substance, it continues; but if He ceases to create, the substance perishes." Thereby all necessary connection is done away with, so that Nature has no meaning. "They therefore deny that anything exists by nature, likewise that the nature of this or that body necessitates that it should have certain qualities rather than others. But they say that God creates all qualities instantaneously, without natural means and without the help of anything else." General permanence is substance, and the particular is altered every moment, and so exists through the substance. "According to this principle they say, for instance, that when we think we have dyed a garment red with red dye we have not dyed it red at all; for God created the red colour in the garment at the very moment at which we thought we had brought about the result with the red dye. God observes the invariable custom of not permitting that the colour black should be produced except when the garment is dyed with that hue; and the first colour which comes to pass on the occasion of the connection is not permanent, but disappears on the instant, and every moment another appears which is created in its turn. In the same way knowledge also is an accident, which is created by God at every moment that I know anything; to-day we no longer possess the knowledge which we yesterday possessed. A man," when writing, "does not move the pen when he thinks he moves it, but the motion is an accident of the pen, created by God at the moment." In this way God alone is in truth the operative cause; but He might have made everything differently. "Their eighth proposition is to the effect that nothing but substance or accident exists, and natural forms are themselves accidents; substances alone are individuals. The ninth proposition is that accidents have nothing to do with one another; they have no causal connection or other relation; in every substance all accidents may exist. The tenth proposition is transition (אֶפְשָׁרוּת, *transitus, possibilitas*): " "All that we can fancy may also pass over into the understanding, *i.e.* be possible. But in this way everything is possible," since there are no laws of the understanding; this transition of thought is thus perfectly accidental. "A man as large as a mountain, a flea as large as an elephant, are possible. Everything may just as well be something else as what it is, and there is no reason at all why anything should be one way rather than another. They term it a mere habit that the earth revolves round a centre-point, that fire moves upward and that it is hot; it is just as possible, they say, that fire should be cold."[1]

We thus see an utter inconstancy of everything; and this whirl of all things is essentially Oriental. But at the same time this is certainly also a complete dissolution of all that pertains to reasonableness, in harmony of course with Eastern exaltation of spirit, which allows of nothing definite. God is in Himself the perfectly undefined, His activity is altogether abstract, and hence the particulars produced thereby are perfectly contingent; if we speak of the necessity of things, the term is meaningless and incomprehensible, and no attempt should be made to comprehend it. The activity of God is thus represented as perfectly devoid of reason. This abstract negativity, combined with the permanent unity, is thus a fundamental conception in the Oriental way of looking at things. Oriental poets are in a marked degree pantheists; the pantheistic is their ordinary point of view. Thus the Arabians developed the sciences and philosophy, without further defining the concrete Idea; their work is rather the dissolution of all that is definite in this substance, with which is associated mere changeableness as the abstract moment of negativity.

[1] Moses Maimonides: More Nevochim, P. I. c. 73, pp. 152–155, 157–159.

B. Commentators of Aristotle.

The Arabians, moreover, made a point for the most part of studying the writings of Aristotle very diligently, and of availing themselves more especially both of his metaphysical and logical writings, and also of his *Physics;* they occupied themselves particularly with multiplying commentaries on Aristotle, and developing still further the abstract logical element there present. Many of these commentaries are still extant. Works of this kind are known in the West, and have been even translated into Latin and printed; but much good is not to be got from them. The Arabians developed the metaphysics of the understanding and a formal logic. Some of the famous Arabians lived as early as the eighth and ninth centuries; their progress was therefore very rapid, for the West had as yet made very little advance in culture.

Alkendi, who wrote a commentary on the *Logic*, flourished in and about A.D. 800, under Almamun.[1] Alfarabi died in 966; he wrote commentaries on Aristotle's *Organon*, which were made diligent use of by the Scholastics, and was also author of a work "On the Origin and Division of the Sciences." It is related of him that he read through Aristotle's treatise *On Hearing* forty times, and his *Rhetoric* two hundred times, without getting at all tired of them;[2] he must have had a good stomach. The very physicians made a study of philosophy, and formulated theories; among them was Avicenna (*b.* A.D. 984, *d.* A.D. 1064), who belonged to Bokhara, to the east of the Caspian

[1] Pocock. Specim. hist. Arab. pp. 78, 79; Hottinger. Biblioth. orient. c. 2, p. 219; Brucker. Hist. cr. phil. T. III. pp. 65, 66; Tennemann, Vol. VIII. Section I. p. 374.

[2] Hottinger. Biblioth. orient. c. 2, p. 221; Gabriel Sionita: De moribus Orient. p. 16; Brucker. Hist. cr. phil. T. III. pp. 73, 74; Tennemann, Vol. VIII. Section I. pp. 374, 375.

Sea; he wrote a commentary on Aristotle.[1] Algazel (*d.* A.D. 1127 at Bagdad) wrote compendiums of logic and metaphysics; he was a sceptic of great ability, with a powerful mind of the Oriental cast; he held the words of the Prophet to be pure truth, and wrote *Destructio Philosophorum.*[2] Tofail died in Seville in A.D. 1193.[3] Averroës, who died A.D. 1217, was specially distinguished as the commentator of Aristotle.[4]

The acquaintance of the Arabians with Aristotle has this interest in history that it was thus that Aristotle first became known also in the West. The commentaries on Aristotle and the collections of passages from his writings become thus for the Western world a fountain of philosophy. Western nations long knew nothing of Aristotle, excepting through such retranslations of his works and translations of Arabian commentaries on them. For such translations were made from Arabic into Latin by Spanish Arabs, and especially by Jews in the south of Spain and Portugal and in Africa; there was often even a Hebrew translation between.

C. Jewish Philosophers.

With the Arabians are closely connected the Jewish philosophers, among whom the above-mentioned Moses Maimonides held a distinguished place. He was born at Cordova, in Spain, A.D. 1131 (Anno Mundi 4891, or,

[1] Leo Africanus: De illustrib. Arabum viris, c. 9, p. 268; Abulphar. Dynast. IX. p. 230; Tiedemann, Geist. d. spec. Phil. Vol. IV. p. 112, *sqq*; Brucker. Hist. cr. phil. T. III. pp. 80–84.

[2] Leo Afric. De illustrib. Arabum viris, c. 12, p. 274; Brucker. Hist. cr. phil. T. III. pp. 93–95; Tiedemann, Geist. d. spec. Phil. Vol. IV. pp. 120–126; Tennemann, Vol. VIII. Section I. pp. 383–396.

[3] Brucker. Hist. cr. phil. T. III. p. 97.

[4] Brucker. Hist. cr. phil. T. III. p. 101; Tennemann, Vol. III. Section I. pp. 420, 421.

according to others, 4895), and lived in Egypt.[1] Besides *More Nevochim*, which has been translated into Latin, he composed other works; of him and other Jews much more of a literary character might be said. In their philosophy a strong Cabalistic element, on the one hand, makes itself felt throughout, in astrology, geomancy, &c.; on the other hand, we find in Moses Maimonides, as in the Fathers, that the foundation is laid in history. He deals with this in a strictly abstract system of metaphysics, which is connected, in Philo's fashion, with the Mosaic books and their interpretation. We find in these Jewish philosophers proofs brought forward that God is One, that the world was created, and that matter is not eternal; Maimonides also speaks of the nature of God. The unity of God is dealt with as it was among the ancient Eleatics and the Neo-Platonists; to prove, namely, that not the Many, but the self-begetting and self-abrogating One is the truth.[2]

[1] Brucker. Hist. cr. phil. T. II. p. 857; Tennemann, Vol. VIII. Section I. pp. 446, 447.

[2] Moses Maimonides: More Nevochim, P. I. c. 51, pp. 76–78; c. 57, 58, pp. 93–98; II. c. 1, 2, pp. 184–193; III. c. 8, pp. 344–350; &c., &c.

SECTION TWO

The Scholastic Philosophy

All the Philosophy which we first encounter in the Middle Ages, when independent states begin to rise, consists of bare remnants of the Roman world, which on its Fall had sunk in all respects so low that the culture of the world seemed to have come entirely to an end. Thus in the West hardly anything was known beyond the Isagoge of Porphyry, the Latin Commentaries of Boethius on the Logical works of Aristotle, and extracts from the same by Cassiodorus—most barren compilations; there is also what is just as barren, the dissertations ascribed to Augustine *De dialectica* and *De categoriis*, which last is a paraphrase of the Aristotelian work upon the categories.[1] These were the first make-shifts or expedients for carrying on Philosophy; in them the most external and most formal reasoning is applied.

The whole effect of the scholastic philosophy is a monotonous one. In vain have men hitherto endeavoured to show in this theology, which reigned from the eighth or even sixth century almost to the sixteenth, particular distinctions and stages in development. In this case as in that of the Arabian philosophy, time does not allow—and if it did the nature of things would not allow—us to separate the scholastic philosophy into its individual systems or manifestations, but only to give a general sketch of the main elements present therein which it has actually

[1] Tennemann, Vol. VIII. Pt. I. p. 49.

taken up into thought. It is not interesting by reason of its matter, for we cannot remain at the consideration of this; it is not a philosophy. The name, however, properly speaking indicates a general manner rather than a system—if we may speak of a philosophic system. Scholasticism is not a fixed doctrine like Platonism or Scepticism, but a very indefinite name which comprehends the philosophic endeavours of Christendom for the greater part of a thousand years. However, this history which occupies nearly a thousand years is, as a matter of fact, comprised within one Notion which we propose to consider more closely; it has ever occupied the same standpoint, and been grounded on the same principle; for it is the faith of the Church that we catch sight of, and a formalism which is merely an eternal analysis and constant re-iteration within itself. The more general acceptance of the Aristotelian writings has merely brought forth a difference of degree and caused no real scientific progress. Here there is indeed a history of men, but speaking properly none of scientific knowledge; the men are noble, pious, and in all respects most distinguished.

The study of the scholastic philosophy is a difficult one, even if its language only be considered. The Scholastics certainly make use of a barbaric Latin, but this is not the fault of the Scholastics but of their Latin culture. Latin forms a quite unsuitable instrument for applying to philosophic categories such as these, because the terms which the new culture adopts could not possibly be expressed by this language without unduly straining it; the beautiful Latin of Cicero is not adapted for use in profound speculations. It cannot be expected of anyone to know at first hand this philosophy of the Middle Ages, for it is as comprehensive and voluminous as it is barren and ill-expressed.

Of the great schoolmen we still have many works left to us which are very lengthy, so that it is no easy task to study them: the later they are, the more formal do they become. The Schoolmen did not only write compendiums —for the writings of Duns Scotus amount to twelve, and those of Thomas Aquinas to eighteen folios. Abstracts of them are to be found in various works. The principal sources from which we obtain our knowledge are: 1, Lambertus Danæus in the Prolegomena to his *Commentarius in librum primum sententiarum Petri Lombardi, Genevæ*, 1580. (This is the best authority we have in abridged form): 2, Launoi: *De varia Aristotelis in Academia Parisiensi fortuna;* 3, Cramer: Continuation of Bossuet's History of the World, in the last two volumes; 4, the *Summa* of Thomas Aquinas. In Tiedemann's History of Philosophy extracts from the Scholastics are also to be found, as likewise in Tennemann; Rixner also makes judicious extracts.

We shall limit ourselves to general points of view. The name finds its origin in this way. From the time of Charles the Great it was only in two places—in the great schools attached to the great cathedral churches and monasteries—that a cleric, that is a canon who had the oversight of the instructors (*informatores*), was called *scholasticus;* he likewise gave lectures on the most important branch of science, theology. In the monasteries he who was the most advanced instructed the monks. We have not, properly speaking, to deal with these; but although scholastic philosophy was something altogether different, the name of Scholastics attached itself to those alone who propounded their theology scientifically and in a system. In place of the *patres ecclesiæ* there thus arose later on the *doctores*.

The scholastic philosophy is thus really theology, and this theology is nothing but philosophy. The further content of theology is merely that which is present in the ordinary conceptions of religion; theology, however, is the science of the system as it must necessarily be present within every Christian, every peasant, &c. The science of theology is often placed in an external historical content, in exegesis, in the enumeration of the various manuscripts of the New Testament, in considering whether these are written on parchment, cotton fabrics or paper, whether in uncial letters or otherwise, and which century they belong to; further matters for consideration are the Jewish conceptions of time, the history of the Popes, Bishops and Fathers, and what took place at the councils of the Church. All these matters, however, do not pertain to the nature of God and its relation to mankind. The one essential object of theology as the doctrine of God, is the nature of God, and this content is in its nature really speculative; those theologians who consider this are therefore nothing less than philosophers. The science of God is nothing but Philosophy. Philosophy and theology have hence here also been counted one, and it is their separation that constitutes the transition into modern times, seeing that men have thought that for thinking reason something could be true which is not true for theology. Down to the Middle Ages, on the contrary, it was held as fundamental that there should be but one truth. Thus the theology of the scholastics is not to be represented as though, as with us, it merely contained doctrines about God, &c., in historic guise, for in fact it also has within it the profoundest speculations of Aristotle and of the Neo-Platonists. Their philosophy, and much in them that is excellent, is found in Aristotle, only in a simpler and purer form; and to them too the whole lay beyond actuality and mingled with Christian actuality as it is represented to us.

From Christianity, within whose bounds we now have our place, Philosophy has to re-establish its position. In heathendom the root of knowledge was external nature as thought devoid of self, and subjective nature as the inward self. Both Nature and the natural self of mankind, and likewise thought, there possessed affirmative significance; hence all this was good. In Christianity the root of truth has, however, quite another meaning; it was not only the truth as against the heathen gods, but as against Philosophy also, against nature, against the immediate consciousness of man. Nature is there no longer good, but merely a negative; self-consciousness, the thought of man, his pure self, all this receives a negative position in Christianity. Nature has no validity, and affords no interest; its universal laws, as the reality under which the individual existences of nature are collected, have likewise no authority: the heavens, the sun, the whole of nature is a corpse. Nature is given over to the spiritual, and indeed to spiritual subjectivity; thus the course of nature is everywhere broken in upon by miracles. With this surrender of natural necessity we have the fact associated that all further content, all that truth which constitutes the universal of that nature, is given and revealed. The one starting-point, the contemplation of nature, is thus for knowledge undoubtedly not present. Then this fact is likewise set aside that I am present as a self. The self as this immediate certainty has to be abrogated; it must also merge itself in another self, but in one beyond, and only there does it have its value. This other self, in which the proper self is made to have its freedom, is first of all likewise a particular self, that has not the form of universality: it is determined and limited in time and space, and at the same time has the significance of an absolute in and for itself. A real sense of self is thus abandoned, but what self-consciousness on the other hand gains is not a universal, a thought. In thought I have real affirmative significance, not as an individual, but as universal 'I'; the content of truth is now, however, plainly individualized, and thus the thought of the 'I' falls away. Thereby, however, the highest concrete content of the absolute Idea is set forth, in which the opposites that are plainly infinite are united; it is the power which unites in itself what appears to consciousness infinitely removed from one another—the mortal and the absolute. This absolute is itself 'this first of all as this concrete, not as abstraction, but as the unity of universal and individual; this concrete consciousness is for the first time truth. The reason of the former content being also true, comes to me as something not pertaining to myself, but as a thing received outside of self. The testimony of spirit, indeed, pertains thereto, and my inmost self is present there; but the testimony of spirit is a thing concealed, which does not further reveal itself, does not beget the content from itself, but receives it. The Spirit which bears witness is further itself distinguished from me as an individual; my testifying spirit is another, and there only remains to me the empty shell of passivity. Conditioned by this inflexible standpoint, Philosophy had to go forth once more. The first working up of this content, the inward operation of universal thought in the same, is the task scholastic philosophy has to undertake. The opposition between faith and reason forms the end arrived at; reason, on the one hand, feels the necessity of setting to work on nature in order to obtain immediate certainty, and on the other hand of finding in genuine thought, in specific production out of self, this same satisfaction.

We must now speak of the methods and manners of the scholastics. In this scholastic activity thought pursues its work quite apart from all regard to experience; we no longer hear anything of taking up actuality and determining it through thought. Although the Notion came into recognition earlier than this, in Aristotle, in the first place, the Notion was not apprehended as the necessity of carrying the content further; for this was received in its succesive manifestations, and there was present merely an intermingling of actuality accepted as truth and of thought. Still less, in the second place, was the greater part of the content permeated by Notions, for this content was taken up superficially into the form of thought—more especially with the Stoics and Epicureans. The scholastic philosophy altogether dissociates itself from any such endeavours; it leaves actuality to exist alongside itself as if it were despised and had no interest. For reason found its true existence, its actualization, in another world and not in this; the whole progress of the cultivated world goes, however, to the re-instalment of a faith in the present world. Nevertheless, at first all knowledge and action, and whatever relates to an interest in this world, were entirely banished. Branches of knowledge that pertain to such ordinary matters as sight and hearing, restful contemplation and occupation with ordinary actuality here found no place; nor did such sciences as recognize a definite sphere of actuality after their own particular fashion, and constitute the material for genuine philosophy, nor arts which give to the Idea a sensuous existence. Likewise law and right, the recognition of the actual man, were not esteemed as pertaining to the social relationships of life, but to some other sphere. In this absence of rationality in the actual, or of rationality which has its actuality in ordinary existence, is found the utter barbarism of thought, in that it keeps to another world, and does not have the Notion of reason—the Notion that the certainty of self is all truth.

Now thought as sundered has a content, the intelligible world, as an actuality existent for itself, to which thought applies itself. Its conduct is here to be compared with that which takes place when the understanding applies itself to the sensuous and perceptible world, makes it as substance its basis, having a fixed object in it, and reasoning respecting it; it is then not the independent movement of Philosophy proper which penetrates existence and expresses it, for all it does is to find predicates regarding it. The scholastic philosophy has thus the intelligible world of the Christian religion, God and all His attributes and works therewith connected, as an independent object; and thought is directed to God's unchangeableness, to such questions as whether matter is eternal, whether man is free, &c.—just as the understanding passes to and fro over the phenomenal and perceived. Now the scholastic philosophy was here given over to the infinite movement of determinate Notions; the categories of possibility and actuality, freedom and necessity, constitution and substance, &c., are of this nature; they are not fixed, but pure movements. Anything whatever, determined as potential, transforms itself equally into the opposite, and must necessarily be surrendered; and determination can only save itself by a new distinction, because it must, on the one hand, be given up, and on the other retained. The scholastics are thus decried on account of the endless distinctions which they draw. For the sake of these determinations through the abstract Notion the Aristotelian philosophy was predominant, though not in its whole extent. It was the Aristotelian *Organon* that was held in such favour, and that indeed just as much for its laws of thought as for its metaphysical conceptions—the categories. These abstract Notions constituted in their determinateness the understanding of the scholastic philosophy, which could not pass beyond itself and attain to freedom, nor seize upon the freedom given by reason.

With this finite form a finite content is likewise directly associated. From one determination we pass on to another, and such determinations, as particular, are finite; the determination there relates itself externally and not as self-comprehensive and self-embracing. The result of this determination is that thought will really act as if it brought about conclusions, for to draw conclusions is the mode of formal logical progression. Philosophy thus consists of a methodical and syllogistic reasoning. Just as the Sophists of Greece wandered about amongst abstract conceptions on behalf of actuality, so did the scholastics on behalf of their intellectual world. To the former Being had validity; it they had rescued and delivered as against the negativity of the Notion, while along with that they had justified it through the same. The principal endeavour of the scholastics was in the same way to vindicate the Christian intellectual world as against the confusion of the Notion, and through the latter to demonstrate its conformity with the same. The universal form of the scholastic philosophy thus consisted in this—that a proposition was laid down, the objections to it brought forward, and these contradicted through counter-propositions and distinctions. Philosophy was hence not separated from theology, as it is not in itself, for Philosophy is the knowledge of absolute existence, that is to say, theology. But to that theology the Christian absolute world was a system which was held to be an actuality, as was ordinary actuality for the Greek sophists. Of Philosophy proper there thus remained only the laws of thought and abstractions.

A. Relationship of the Scholastic Philosophy to Christianity.

Philosophy with the scholastics had consequently the same quality of want of independence as it had before this with the Christian Fathers and the Arabians. The Church as already constituted established itself amongst the Teutonic nations, and through its constitution it conditioned philosophy. The Christian Church had indeed spread itself abroad throughout the Roman world, but, more especially in the beginning, it merely formed a community of its own, by whom the world was renounced, and which made no special claims to recognition—or if such claims were made they were merely negative, because the individuals in the world were simply martyrs, thus renouncing the world. But the Church in time became dominant, and the Roman emperors, both of the East and of the West, embraced Christianity. Thus the Church attained to a position openly recognized and undisturbed, from which it exercised much influence upon the world. The political world, however, fell into the hands of the Teutonic nations, and thereby a new form arose, and to this the scholastic philosophy pertains. We know the revolution by the name of the Migration of the Nations (*supra*, pp. 23, 24). Fresh races inundated the ancient Roman world and established themselves therein; they thus erected their new world on the ruins of the old—a picture which Rome in its present aspect still presents. There the splendour of the Christian temples is due in part to the remnants of the ancient, and new palaces are built on ruins and have ruins all around.

I. The principal feature in the Middle Ages is found in this disunion, the two sides here present; there are revealed in it two nations, two manners of speech. We see people who have hitherto ruled, a previous world having its own language, arts, and sciences, and on this to them foreign element the new nations grafted themselves, and these thus started upon their course internally dissevered. In this history we have thus before us not the development of a nation from itself, but one proceeding from its opposite, and one which is and remains burdened by this opposite, and which takes it up into itself and has to overcome it. Hence these people have in this way represented in themselves the nature of the spiritual process. Spirit is the making for itself a pre-supposition, the giving to itself the natural as a counterpoise, the separating itself therefrom, thus the making it an object, and then for the first time the working upon this hypothesis, formulating it, and from itself bringing it forth, begetting it, internally reconstructing it. Hence in the Roman as in the Byzantine world, Christianity has triumphed as a Church; but neither of these worlds was capable of effectuating the new religion in itself and of bringing forth a new world from this principle. For in both there was a character already present—customs, laws, a juridical system, a constitution (if it can be called constitution), a political condition, capacities, art, science, spiritual culture—in short, everything was there. The nature of spirit, on the contrary, requires that the world thus constituted should be begotten from it, and that this process of begetting should take place through the agency of reaction, through the assimilation of something which has gone before. These conquerors have thus established themselves in a foreign sphere, and have become the rulers over it; but at the same time they have come under the dominion of a new spirit which has been imposed upon them. Although on the one hand predominant, on the other they have come under the dominion of the spiritual element, because they conducted themselves passively in regard to it.

The spiritual Idea or spirituality has become imposed upon the dulness, both in mind and spirit, of these rough barbarians; their hearts were thereby pricked. The rough nature has in this way become immanent in the Idea as an eternal opposition, or there is kindled in them infinite pain, the most terrible suffering—such that it may even be represented as a crucified Christ. They had to sustain this conflict within themselves, and one side of it is found in the philosophy which later on made its appearance amongst them, and was first of all received as something given. They are still uncultured people, but for all their barbaric dulness they are deep in heart and mind; on them, then, has the principle of mind been bestowed, and along with it this pain, this war between spiritual and natural, has necessarily been instituted. Culture here begins from the most terrible contradiction, and this has to be by it resolved. It is a kingdom of pain, but of purgatory, for that which is in the pain is spirit and not animal, and spirit does not die, but goes forth from its grave. The two sides of this contradiction are really thus related to one another in such a way that it is the spiritual which has to reign over the barbarians.

The true dominion of spirit cannot, however, be a dominion in the sense that its opposite is in subjection to it; spirit in and for itself cannot have the subjective spirit to which it relates confronting it as an externally obedient slave, for this last is itself also spirit. The dominion that exists must take up this position, that spirit is in subjective spirit in harmony with itself. The universal is thus that opposition in which the one can only have supremacy by the subjection of the other, but which already contains the principle of resolution in itself because mind must necessarily bear rule. And hence the consequent development is only this, that mind as reconciliation attains the mastery. To this it pertains that not the subjective consciousness, mind and heart alone, but also the worldly rule, laws, institutions, the human life, in so far as these rest in mind, must become rational. In the Republic of Plato we have met with the idea that the philosophers are those who ought to reign. Now is the time in which it is said that the spiritual are to govern, but this talk about the spiritual has been made to bear the significance that ecclesiasticism and the ecclesiastics ought to govern. The spiritual is thus made a particular form, an individual, but the real meaning that it bears is that the spiritual as such ought to be the determining factor; and this has passed current until the present day. Thus in the French Revolution we see that abstract thought is made to rule; in accordance with it constitution and laws are determined, it forms the bond between man and man; and men come to have the consciousness that what is esteemed amongst them is abstract thought, and that liberty and equality are what ought to be regarded; in this the subject also has his real value, even in relation to actuality.

One form of this reconciliation is likewise this, that the subject is satisfied with himself and in himself as he stands and moves, with his thoughts, his desires, with his spirituality; and thus that his knowledge, his thought, his conviction, has come to be the highest, and has the determination of the divine, of what holds good as absolute. The divine and spiritual is thus implanted in my subjective spirit, is identical with me; I myself am the universal, and it has efficacy for me only as I directly know it. This form of reconciliation is the newest, but the most one-sided. For the spiritual is not there determined as objective, but is only comprehended as it is in my subjectivity, in my consciousness: my conviction as such is taken as ultimate, and that is the formal reconciliation of subjectivity with itself. If the reconciliation has this form, the point of view of which we spoke before has no longer any interest; it is past and a mere matter of history. If the conviction as it immediately reveals itself within every subject is the true, the absolute, this process of mediation between God, as the true and absolute, and mankind, is no longer in us a necessity. The doctrines of the Christian religion have likewise the position of something foreign, pertaining to a particular time, that with which certain men have occupied themselves. The conception that the Idea is absolutely concrete, and is as spirit in a relation of opposition to the subject, has disappeared, and only shows itself as having passed away. In so far that which I have said about the principle of the Christian system, and shall still say of the scholastics, has interest only from the standpoint which I have given, when the interest is in the Idea in its concrete determination, and not from the standpoint of the immediate reconciliation of the subject with himself.

2. We have now to consider further the character of the opposition to any agreement with Philosophy; and to do this we must shortly call to mind the historical aspect of the case, although we need only treat of the main points therein. The first matter to consider is the opposition that exists in the world. This form of opposition as it appears in history is as follows. Spirituality as such should be the spirituality of the heart; spirit, however, is one, and thus the communion of those who have this spirituality is asserted. Hence a community arises, which then becomes an external order, and thus, as we have seen

(pp. 21, 22), expands into a church. In as far as spirit is its principle, it is, as spiritual, immediately universal, for isolation in feeling, opinion, &c., is unspiritual. The Church organizes itself, but yet it goes forth into worldly existence, attains to riches, possesses goods, and even becomes worldly and imbued with all the brute passions; for the spiritual is merely the original principle. The heart that is set on ordinary existence, on the world, and the whole of such human relationships as are hereby involved, is guided by these inclinations, desires and passions, by all this grossness and vulgarity. Thus the Church merely has the spiritual principle within itself without its being truly real, and in such a way that its further relationships are not yet rational; for such is their character before the development of the spiritual principle in the world. The worldly element without being conformable to the spiritual, is present as existence, and is the immediately natural worldly element; in this way the Church comes to have in itself the immediately natural principle. All the passions it has within itself—arrogance, avarice, violence, deceit, rapacity, murder, envy, hatred—all these sins of barbarism are present in it, and indeed they belong to its scheme of government. This government is thus already a rule of passion, although it professes to be a spiritual rule, and thus the Church is for the most part wrong in its worldly principles, though right in its spiritual aspect.

Hence the new religion separated our whole conception of the world into two different worlds, the intellectual but not subjectively conceived world, and the temporal world. Therefore life as a whole fell into two parts, two kingdoms. Directly opposite the spiritual worldly kingdom there stands the independent worldly kingdom, emperor against pope, papacy and Church—not a state, but a worldly government; there the world beyond, here the world beside us. Two absolutely essential principles conflict with one another; the rude ways of the world, the ruggedness of the individual will, beget an opposition most terrible and severe. The culture which now begins to show itself is confronted by this incomplete reality, as an actual world in opposition to its world of thought; and it does not recognize the one as present in the other. It possesses two establishments, two standards of measure and of weight, and these it does not bring together but leaves mutually estranged.

The spiritual kingdom likewise has as Church an immediate present of ordinary actuality, but the worldly kingdom, both as external nature and as the real self of consciousness, has no truth or value in itself; for truth, as lying beyond it—the measure of truth that shines in it—is given to it from without as something inconceivable and in itself complete. The worldly kingdom must thus be subject to the spiritual become worldly; the emperor is hence defender and protector of the Church (*advocatus ecclesiæ*). The worldly element, in a certain sense, takes up a position of independence, no doubt, but it is still in unity with the other in such a way that it recognizes the spiritual as dominant. In this opposition a war must arise both on account of the worldly element which is present in the Church itself, and likewise on account of the directly worldly element of violence and of barbarism in worldly rule as it exists *per se*. The war must at first, however, prove disastrous to the worldly side, for just as its own position is asserted, the other is likewise recognized by it, and it is forced humbly to submit to this last, to the spiritual and its passions. The bravest, noblest emperors have been excommunicated by popes, cardinals, legates, and even by archbishops and bishops; and they could do nothing in self-defence, nor put their trust in outward power, for it was internally broken; and thus they were ever vanquished and finally forced to surrender.

In the second place, as regards morality in the individual, we see on the one hand religion in its truly noble and attractive form in a few isolated individuals alone. I refer to those solitary spirits who are dead to the world and far removed therefrom, who find in their emotions what satisfies them, and, living in a little circle, can limit themselves to the sphere of religion. This is the case with women in the Middle Ages, or with the monks or other solitaries who were able to preserve themselves in a restricted and contracted state of fervour such as this, in which the spiritual side makes itself infinitely felt, although it lacks actuality. The one truth stood isolated and alone in man, the whole actuality of mind was not yet penetrated by it. On the other hand it is, however, essential that mind as will, impulse and passion, should demand quite another position, another mode of venting and realizing itself, than any such solitary and contracted sphere affords, that the world should require a more extended sphere of existence, an actual association of individuals, reason and thought coming together in actual relations and actions. This circle in which mind is realized—the human life—is, however, at first separated from the spiritual region of truth. Subjective virtue partakes more of the character of suffering and privation on its own account, morality is just this renunciation and self-surrender, and virtue as regards others merely has the character of benevolence, a fleeting, accidental character destitute of relation. All that pertains to actuality is hence not perfected by the truth, which remains a heavenly truth alone, a Beyond. Actuality, the earthly element, is consequently God-forsaken and hence arbitrary; a few isolated individuals are holy, and the others are not holy. In these others we first see the holiness of a moment in the quarter of an hour of worship, and then for weeks a life of rudest selfishness and violence and the most ruthless passion. Individuals fall from one extreme into another, from the extreme of rude excess, lawlessness, barbarism, and self-will, into the renunciation of all things without exception, the conquest of all desires.

The great army of the Crusaders gives us the best example of this. They march forth on a holy errand, but on the way they give free vent to all the passions, and in this the leaders show the example; the individuals allow themselves to fall into violence and heinous sin. Their march accomplished, though with an utter lack of judgment and forethought, and with the loss of thousands on the way, Jerusalem is reached: it is beautiful when Jerusalem comes in view to see them all doing penance in contrition of heart, falling on their faces and reverently adoring. But this is only a moment which follows upon months of frenzy, foolishness and grossness, which everywhere displayed itself on their march. Animated by the loftiest bravery, they go on to storm and conquer the sacred citadel, and then they bathe themselves in blood, revel in endless cruelties, and rage with a brutal ferocity. From this they again pass on to contrition and penance; then they get up from their knees reconciled and sanctified, and once more they give themselves up to all the littleness of miserable passions, of selfishness and envy, of avarice and cupidity: their energies are directed to the satisfaction of their lusts, and they bring to nought the fair possession that their bravery had won. This comes to pass because the principle is only present in them in its implicitude as an abstract principle, and the actuality of man is not as yet spiritually formed and fashioned. This is the manner in which the opposition in actuality manifests itself.

In the third place, we reach the opposition existing in the content of religion, in the religious consciousness; this has many forms, though we have here only to call to mind those that are most inward. On the one hand, we have the Idea of God—that He is known as the Trinity; on the other, we have worship, *i.e.* the process of individuals making themselves conformable to spirit, to God, and reaching the certainty of entering the kingdom of God. A present and actual church is an actuality of the kingdom of God upon earth, in such a way that this last is present for every man—every individual lives and must live in the kingdom of God. In this disposition we have the reconciliation of every individual; thereby each becomes a citizen of this kingdom, and participates in the enjoyment of this certainty. But this reconciliation is allied to the fact that in Christ the unity of the divine and human nature is shown forth, that is to say, the way in which the spirit of God must be present in man. This Christ thus cannot be one who is past and gone, and the life of reconciliation cannot be a mere recollection of that past. For as the just behold Christ in heaven, so must Christ be an object on earth which may likewise be beheld. In that case this process must be present—the individual must be united to this to him objective form, and it becomes identical with him; the history of Christ, that God reveals Himself as man, sacrifices Himself, and through this sacrifice raises Himself to the right hand of God, is in the individual always being accomplished in the culminating point which is called the sacrifice of the mass. The mediating element to which the individual relates himself in worship, is ever present in the mass as the objective of which the individual must be made to partake, as the Host and the act of partaking of the same. This Host, on the one hand, as objective, is held to be divine, and, on the other, it is in form an unspiritual and external thing. But that is the lowest depth of externality reached in the Church; for in this perfect externality it is before the thing that the knee must be bowed, and not in as far as it is an object that may be partaken of. Luther changed this way of regarding matters; in what is called the Supper, he has retained the mystical fact that the subject receives the divine element into himself; but he maintains that it is only divine in so far as it is partaken of in this subjective spirituality of faith, and ceases to be an external thing. But in the Church of the Middle Ages, in the Catholic Church generally, the Host is honoured even as an external thing;

thus if a mouse eats of the Host, both it and its excrements are reverenced; there the divine element has altogether the form of externality. This is the central point of intense opposition which is on the one hand dissolved, and on the other remains in perfect contradiction, so that the Host, still held to be a merely external thing, must nevertheless be thus high and absolute.

With this externality the other side is connected—the consciousness of this relation—and here we then have the consciousness of what is spiritual, of what is the truth, in the possession of a priesthood. Thus as thing it is naturally also in the possession of another, from whom, since it is something distinguished by itself, it has to receive its distinction—or it must be consecrated—and this last is likewise an external action only, performed by individuals. The power to give this distinction to the thing is in the possession of the Church; from the Church the laity receive it.

But besides all this, the relationship of the subject in himself, the fact that he belongs to the Church and is a true member of the same, must be considered. After the admission of individuals into the Church their participation therein must likewise be brought about—that is, their purification from sin. To this it is, however, essential, in the first place, that it should be known what evil is, and secondly, that the individual should desire the good and that pertaining to religion; and thirdly, that sin should be committed from an innate and natural sinfulness. Now since what is inward, or conscience, must be of a right nature, the sins that are committed must be removed, and made as though they had not happened; man must ever be purified, baptized anew, so to speak, and received back again: the negation that shuts him out must ever be removed. Against this sinfulness positive commands and laws are now given, so that from the nature of spirit men cannot know what is good and evil. Thus the divine law is an external, which must hence be in someone's possession ; and priests are separated from others, so that they are exclusively acquainted both with the particular details of doctrine and the means of grace, *i.e.* the mode whereby the individual is religious in his worship and comes to know that he participates in the divine. In the same way that the administration of the means of grace belongs as an outward possession to the Church in relation to worship, so is the Church also in possession of a moral estimate for judging of the actions of individuals ; it is in the possession of the conscience, as of knowledge as a whole, so that man's inmost essence, his accountability, passes into other hands and to another person, and the subject is devoid of individuality even in his inmost self. The Church also knows what the individual ought to do; his faults must be known, and another, the Church, knows them; the sins must be taken away, and this also is effected in an external way, through purchase, fasting and stripes, through journeyings, pilgrimages, &c. Now this is a relation of self-suppression, unspirituality and deadness both of knowledge and will, in the highest things as well as in the most trivial actions.

These are the main facts as regards externality in religion itself, on which all further determinations depend.

3. We have now obtained a better idea of the elements present in this philosophy; but in barbaric nations Christianity could have this form of externality alone, and this pertains to history. For the dulness and frightful barbarism of such nations must be met by servitude, and through this service must their education be accomplished. Man serves under this yoke; this fearful discipline had to be gone through if the Teutonic nations were to be raised into spiritual life. But this severe and wearisome service has an end, an object; infinite spring and infinite elasticity, the freedom of spirit, is the prize. The Indians are in equal servitude, but they are irrevocably lost—identified and identical with nature, yet in themselves

opposed to nature. Knowledge is thus limited to the Church, but in this very knowledge a positive authority is firmly rooted, and it is a prominent feature of this philosophy, whose first quality is consequently that of lack of freedom. Thought thus does not appear as though it proceeded from itself and was grounded in itself, but as being really independent of self and depending on a given content, the doctrine of the Church—which, although speculative itself, also contains the mode of the immediate existence of external objects.

In theological form it may be said that, in general, the Middle Ages signify the dominion of the Son and not of Spirit; for this last is still in the possession of the priesthood. The Son has differentiated Himself from the Father, and is regarded as remaining in this differentiation, so that the Father in Him is only implicit; but in the unity of both we first reach Spirit, the Son as Love. If we remain a moment too long in the difference without likewise asserting the identity, the Son is the Other; and in this we find the Middle Ages defined and characterized. The character of Philosophy in the Middle Ages is thus in the second place an attempt to think, to conceive, to philosophize under the burden of absolute hypotheses; for it is not the thinking Idea in its freedom, but set forth in the form of an externality. We thus find here in Philosophy the same character as is present in the general condition of things, and for this reason I before called to mind the concrete character that prevails; for on every period of time one special characteristic is always imprinted. The philosophy of the Middle Ages thus contains the Christian principle, which is the highest incentive to thought, because the Ideas therein present are thoroughly speculative. Of this one side is that the Idea is grasped by the heart, if we call the individual man the heart. The identity of the immediate individuality with the Idea rests in this, that the Son, the mediator, is known as *this* man; this is the identity of spirit with God for the heart as such. But the connection itself, since it is likewise a connection with God in God, is hence immediately mystical and speculative; thus here there is the call to thought which was first of all responded to by the Fathers, and then by the scholastics.

But since, in the third place, there exists the opposition between the doctrine of the Church and the worldly man—who has indeed through thought worked his way out of this same barbarism, but who in his healthy human understanding has not yet penetrated to reason—the mode in which Philosophy was treated at this time for the setting forth of formal thought, has still no concrete content. We may appeal to the human concrete mind; in it we have a living present as thinking and feeling; a concrete content such as this has its root in the thought of man, and constitutes the material for his independent consciousness. Formal thought directs its course by this; the wanderings of abstract reflection have in such consciousness an aim, which sets a limit upon them, and leads them back to a human concrete. But the reflections of the scholastics on such a content depend unsupported on the determinations of formal thought, on formal conclusions; and all the determinations regarding natural relationships, laws of nature, &c., that may issue, receive as yet no sustenance from experience; they are not yet determined by the healthy human understanding. In this respect the content likewise is unspiritual, and these unspiritual relationships are inverted and carried into the spiritual in so far as advance is made to determinateness of a higher kind. These three points constitute the main characteristics of this philosophy.

More particularly we would shortly deal with the chief representatives of this philosophy. Scholastic philosophy is considered to begin with John Scotus Erigena who flourished about the year 860, and who must not be confused with the Duns Scotus of a later date. We do not quite know whether he belonged to Ireland or to Scotland, for Scotus points to Scotland, and Erigena to Ireland. With him true philosophy first begins, and his philosophy in the main coincides with the idealism of the Neo-Platonists. Here and there stray works of Aristotle were likewise known, even to John Scotus, but the knowledge of Greek was very limited and rare. He shows some knowledge of the Greek and Hebrew tongues, and even of Arabic as well; but we do not know how he attained to this. He also translated from Greek to Latin writings of Dionysius the Areopagite, a later Greek philosopher of the Alexandrian school, who more especially followed Proclus: namely, *De cœlesti hierarchia*, and others which Brucker calls (Hist. crit. phil. T. III. p. 521), *nugæ et deliria Platonica*. Michael Balbus, Emperor of Constantinople, had in the year 824 made a present of these works to the Emperor Louis the Pious; Charles the Bald caused them to be translated by Scotus, who long resided at his court. In this way something of the Alexandrian philosophy became known in the West. The Pope quarrelled with Charles, and complained to him of the translator, against whom he made the reproach that "he should have first sent the book to him in conformity with the general usage, and asked his approval." John Scotus afterwards lived in England as head of a school at Oxford, which had been founded by King Alfred.[1]

Scotus was also the author of some original works, which are not without depth and penetration, upon nature and its various orders (*De naturæ divisione*), &c. Dr. Hjort, of Copenhagen, published an epitome of the writings of Scotus Erigena, in 1823. Scotus Erigena sets to work philosophically, expressing himself in the manner of the Neo-Platonists, and not freely, and as from himself. Thus in the method of expression adopted by Plato, and also by Aristotle, we

[1] Brucker. Hist. crit. phil. T. III. pp. 614-617; Bulæus: Hist. Universitatis Parisiensis; T. I. p. 184.

are rejoiced to find a new conception, and on bringing it to the test of philosophy, to find it both correct and profound; but here everything is ready to hand, cut and dry. Yet, with Scotus, theology is not yet built on exegesis, and on the authority of the Church; the Church in many cases rejected his writings. Thus Scotus is reproached by a Lyons church council in these words: "There have come to us the writings of a boastful, chattering man, who disputes about divine providence and predestination, in human fashion, or, as he himself boasts, with philosophic arguments, and without relying on the holy scriptures and bringing forward the authority of the Fathers. And he dares to defend this on its own merit, and to establish it on its own laws, without submitting himself to the holy scriptures and the authority of the Fathers."[1] Scotus Erigena hence even said: "The true Philosophy is the true Religion, and the true Religion is the true Philosophy."[2] The separation came later on. Scotus then made a beginning, but properly he does not belong to the scholastics.

B. General Historical Points of View.

All further scholastic philosophy attaches itself more to the doctrines of the Christian Church; the ecclesiastical system which it thereby made its necessary basis, became early established through church councils, while the faith of the Evangelical Church already prevailed before the time of these councils from which the Catholic Church derives its support. The most important and most interesting thoughts which pertain to the scholastics, are, on the one

[1] Bulæus: Hist. Univ. Paris. T. I. p. 182. (Tennemann, Vol. VIII. pp. 71, 72.)

[2] De prædestinatione. Proœmium (Veterum auctorum, qui IX. sæculo de prædestinatione et gratia scripserunt, opera et fragmenta, cura Gilb. Mauguin. Paris, 1650. T. I. p. 103.)

hand, the strife between nominalism and realism; and, on the other, the proof of the existence of God—quite a new manifestation.

1. The Building up of Dogmas on Metaphysical Grounds.

The efforts of the scholastics were further directed, firstly, to the building up of the dogmas of the Christian Church on metaphysical bases. After this, the collected doctrines of the Church were systematically treated. Then the scholastics had branches or modifications of these dogmas, which were not determined by the doctrinal system. Those grounds themselves, and then these further and special points of view, were objects handed over for free discussion. Neo-Platonic philosophy was what lay before the theologians first of all; the manner of this school is recognized in the older and purer scholastics. Anselm and Abelard are the more distinguished of those who follow later.

a. Anselm.

Amongst those who wished to give additional proof of the doctrines of the Church through thought, is Anselm, a man of great distinction and high repute. He was born at Aosta, in Piedmont, about 1034; in 1060 he became a monk at Bec, and in 1093 was raised to the rank of Archbishop of Canterbury; in 1109 he died.[1] He sought to consider and prove philosophically the doctrines of the Church, and it has even been said of him that he laid the basis for scholastic philosophy.

He speaks as follows of the relation of faith to thought: "Our faith must be defended by reason against the godless, and not against those who glory in the name of Christian; for of these we may rightly demand that they should hold firm to the obligations which they came under in baptism. Those others must be shown through reason how

[1] Tennemann, Vol. VIII. Sec. I. pp. 115, 117.

irrationally they strive against us. The Christian must go on through faith to reason, and not come from reason to faith; but if he cannot attain to comprehension, he must still less depart from faith. For if he is able to press on to knowledge, he rejoices therein; when he is unable so to do, he humbly adores."[1] He makes a noteworthy remark, which contains his whole philosophy, in his work *Cur Deus homo* (I. 2), which is rich in speculative thought: "It appears to me great negligence if we are firm in the faith, and do not seek also to comprehend what we believe." Now this is declared to be arrogance; immediate knowledge, faith, is held to be higher than knowledge. But Anselm and the scholastics maintained the opposite view.

Anselm may be regarded from this point of view as quite specially the founder of scholastic theology. For the thought of proving through a simple chain of reasoning what was believed—that God exists—left him no rest day and night, and tortured him for long. At first he believed his desire to prove the divine truths through reason to be a temptation of the devil, and he was in great anxiety and distress on that account; finally, however, success came to him by the grace of God in his *Proslogium*.[2] This is the so-called ontological proof of the existence of God which he set forth, and which made him specially famous. This proof was included among the various proofs up to the time of Kant, and—by some who have not yet reached the Kantian standpoint—it is so included even to the present day. It is different from what we find and read of amongst the ancients. For it was said that God is absolute thought as objective; for because things in the world are contingent, they are not the truth in and for itself—but this is found

[1] Anselmi Epistol. XLI. I. 11 (Tennemann, Vol. VIII. Sec. I. pp. 159, 160.)

[2] Tennemann, Vol. VIII. Sec. I. p. 116; Eadmerus: De vita Anselmi (subjuncta operibus Anselmi editis a Gabr. Gerberon. 1721. Fol.), p. 6.

in the infinite. The scholastics also knew well from the Aristotelian philosophy the metaphysical proposition that potentiality is nothing by itself, but is clearly one with actuality. Later, on the other hand, the opposition between thought itself and Being began to appear with Anselm. It is noteworthy that only now for the first time through the Middle Ages and in Christianity, the universal Notion and Being, as it is to ordinary conception, became established in this pure abstraction as these infinite extremes; and thus the highest law has come to consciousness. But we reach our profoundest depths in bringing the highest opposition into consciousness. Only no advance was made beyond the division as such, although Anselm also tried to find the connection between the sides. But while hitherto God appeared as the absolute existent, and the universal was attributed to Him as predicate, an opposite order begins with Anselm—Being becomes predicate, and the absolute Idea is first of all established as the subject, but the subject of thought. Thus if the existence of God is once abandoned as the first hypothesis, and established as a result of thought, self-consciousness is on the way to turn back within itself. Then we have the question coming in, Does God exist? while on the other side the question of most importance was, What is God?

The ontological proof, which is the first properly metaphysical proof of the existence of God, consequently came to mean that God as the Idea of existence which unites all reality in itself, also has the reality of existence within Himself; this proof thus follows from the Notion of God, that He is the universal essence of all essence. The drift of this reasoning is, according to Anselm (Proslogium, c. 2), as follows: "It is one thing to say that a thing is in the understanding, and quite another to perceive that it exists. Even an ignorant person (*insipiens*) will thus be quite convinced that in thought there is something beyond which nothing greater can be thought; for when he hears this he understands it, and everything that is understood is in the understanding. But that beyond which nothing greater can be thought cannot certainly be in the understanding alone. For if it is accepted as in thought alone, we may go on farther to accept it as existent; that, however, is something greater" than what is merely thought. "Thus were that beyond which nothing greater can be thought merely in the understanding, that beyond which nothing greater can be thought would be something beyond which something greater can be thought. But that is truly impossible; there thus without doubt exists both in the understanding and in reality something beyond which nothing greater can be thought." The highest conception cannot be in the understanding alone; it is essential that it should exist. Thus it is made clear that Being is in a superficial way subsumed under the universal of reality, that to this extent Being does not enter into opposition with the Notion. That is quite right; only the transition is not demonstrated—that the subjective understanding abrogates itself. This, however, is just the question which gives the whole interest to the matter. When reality or completion is expressed in such a way that it is not yet posited as existent, it is something thought, and rather opposed to Being than that this is subsumed under it.

This mode of arguing held good until the time of Kant; and we see in it the endeavour to apprehend the doctrine of the Church through reason. This opposition between Being and thought is the starting point in philosophy, the absolute that contains the two opposites within itself—a conception, according to Spinoza, which involves its existence likewise. Of Anselm it is however to be remarked that the formal logical mode of the understanding, the process of scholastic reasoning is to be found in him; the content indeed is right, but the form faulty. For in the first place the expression "the thought of a Highest" is assumed as the *prius*. Secondly, there are two sorts of objects of thought—one that is and another that is not; the object that is only thought and does not exist, is as imperfect as that which only is without being thought. The third point is that what is highest must likewise exist. But what is highest, the standard to which all else must conform, must be no mere hypothesis, as we find it represented in the conception of a highest acme of perfection, as a content which is thought and likewise *is*. This very content, the unity of Being and thought, is thus indeed the true content; but because Anselm has it before him only in the form of the understanding, the opposites are identical and conformable to unity in a third determination only—the Highest—which, in as far as it is regulative, is outside of them. In this it is involved that we should first of all have subjective thought, and then distinguished from that, Being. We allow that if we think a content (and it is apparently indifferent whether this is God or any other), it may be the case that this content does not exist. The assertion "Something that is thought does not exist" is now subsumed under the above standard and is not conformable to it. We grant that the truth is that which is not merely thought but which likewise is. But of this opposition nothing here is said. Undoubtedly God would be imperfect, if He were merely thought and did not also have the determination of Being. But in relation to God we must not take thought as merely subjective; thought here signifies the absolute, pure thought, and thus we must ascribe to Him the quality of Being. On the other hand if God were merely Being, if He were not conscious of Himself as self-consciousness, He would not be Spirit, a thought that thinks itself.

Kant, on the other hand, attacked and rejected Anselm's proof—which rejection the whole world afterwards followed up—on the ground of its being an assumption that the unity of Being and thought is the highest perfection. What Kant thus demonstrates in the present day—that

Being is different from thought and that Being is not by any means posited with thought—was a criticism offered even in that time by a monk named Gaunilo. He combated this proof of Anselm's in a *Liber pro insipiente* to which Anselm himself directed a reply in his *Liber apologeticus adversus insipientem*.[1] Thus Kant says (Kritik der reinen Vernunft, p. 464 of the sixth edition): If we think a hundred dollars, this conception does not involve existence. That is certainly true: what is only a conception does not exist, but it is likewise not a true content, for what does not exist, is merely an untrue conception. Of such we do not however here speak, but of pure thought; it is nothing new to say they are different—Anselm knew this just as well as we do. God is the infinite, just as body and soul, Being and thought are eternally united; this is the speculative, true definition of God. To the proof which Kant criticizes in a manner which it is the fashion to follow now-a-days, there is thus lacking only the perception of the unity of thought and of existence in the infinite; and this alone must form the commencement.

Other proofs such, for example, as the cosmological, which argues from the contingency of the world to an absolute existence, have thereby not reached the idea of absolute essence as spirit, and are without consciousness of the fact that it is an object of thought. The old physico-theological proof, which even Socrates possessed, from beauty, order, organic ends, indeed implies an understanding, a richer thought of absolute existence, and not alone an indeterminate Being, but in this proof it likewise remains unknown that God is the Idea. And then what sort of an understanding is God? A different and immediate one; then this spirit is independent. Further, disorder likewise exists, and thus there must be something else conceived of than this apparent order of nature only.

[1] Gaunilo: Liber pro insipiente, c. 5; Tennemann, Vol. VIII. Sec. I. p. 139; Brucker, Hist. crit. phil. T. III. p. 665.

But from asking about the existence of God, from making his objective mode a predicate and thus knowing that God is Idea, to pass to making the absolute existence I=I, thinking self-consciousness, not as predicate but in such a way that each thinking I is the moment of this self-consciousness—is still a long stride. Here, where we see this form first emerge, absolute existence is clearly to be taken as the Beyond of finite consciousness; this is to itself the null and void, and it has not yet grasped its sense of self. Its thoughts regarding things are manifold, and the mere fact of being a thing is to it likewise just such a predicate as the rest; but it is thereby not yet turned back within itself, it knows of existence, but not of itself.

In this, says Tennemann (Vol. VIII. Sec. I. p. 121), "Anselm has laid the first formal ground of scholastic theology;" but even before this the same was present, only to a more limited extent, and merely for individual dogmas—as is also the case with Anselm. His writings bear witness of great penetration and mental ability; and he gave rise to the philosophy of the scholastics, inasmuch as he united theology to philosophy. The theology of the Middle Ages thus stands much higher than that of modern times; never have Catholics been such barbarians as to say that there should not be knowledge of the eternal truth, and that it should not be philosophically comprehended. This is one point which has to be specially noted in Anselm, the other is that he apprehended in its unity that highest opposition between thought and Being spoken of above.

b. Abelard.

With Anselm Peter Abelard is associated, both being mainly concerned in the introduction of philosophy into theology. Abelard lived about 1100—from 1079 to 1142—and is famed for his learning, but still more famed in the world of sentiment and passion for his love to Heloise and his after fate.[1] After the days of Anselm he attained to great repute, and he followed him in his treatment of the doctrines of the Church, more especially seeking to give a philosophic proof of the Trinity. He taught at Paris. Paris about this time was to the theologians what Bologna was to the jurists, the central point of the sciences; it was at that time the seat of philosophizing theology. Abelard often delivered his lectures there before a thousand listeners. Theological science and philosophizing regarding it, was in France (as was jurisprudence in Italy) a matter of great importance, which, as most significant in the development of France, has hitherto been too much neglected. The conception prevailed that philosophy and religion were one and the same; which they absolutely speaking are. But the distinction was soon reached, "that much may be true in philosophy and false in theology:" this the Church denied. Tennemann (Vol. VIII. Sec. II. pp. 460, 461) quotes as follows from a rescript of the Bishop Stephen: "They say that this is true according to philosophy, and not according to the Catholic faith, just as if there were two contradictory truths, and as if in the doctrines of the accursed heathen a truth contradictory to the truth of the holy scriptures could be present." While then undoubtedly, through the separation of the four faculties in the University of Paris which came about in 1270, philosophy became separated from theology, it was yet forbidden to it to subject theological beliefs and dogmas to disputation.[2]

2. Methodical Representation of the Doctrinal System of the Church.

We now go on to the more definite form which the

[1] Tiedemann: Geist d. specul. Philos. Vol. IV. p. 277; Brucker. Hist. crit. phil. T. III. p. 762.

[2] Tennemann, Vol. VIII. Sec. II. pp. 457, 458.

scholastic theology reached; for in a second development of scholastic philosophy the main endeavour became to make the teaching of the Christian Church methodical, while still keeping its connection with all previous metaphysical arguments. These and their counter-arguments were placed side by side in stating every dogma, so that theology became represented in a scientific system, while before this the ecclesiastical teaching in the general education of the clergy was limited to the propounding of successive dogmas, and the writing down of passages from Augustine and other Fathers bearing on each proposition.

a. Peter Lombard.

Peter of Novara in Lombardy was the first of those who brought this to pass; he dates from the middle of the twelfth century, and was the originator of this method. He died in the year 1164. Petrus Lombardus set forth a whole system of scholastic theology which remained for several centuries the basis of the doctrine of the Church. He composed to that end his *Quatuor libros sententiarum*, and hence he likewise received the name *Magister sententiarum*. For in those times every learned schoolman had some predicate such as *Doctor acutus, invincibilis, sententiosus, angelicus*, &c. Others also availed themselves of the same title for their works; thus Robert Pulleyn wrote *Sententiarum libros octo*.[1]

Lombard collected the principal points in church doctrines from councils and Fathers, and then added subtle questions respecting particular items; with these the schools occupied themselves, and they became a subject of disputation. He himself, indeed, answered these questions, but he caused counter-arguments to follow, and his answer often left the whole matter problematical, so that the questions were not properly decided. The arguments are

[1] Brucker. Hist. crit. phil. T. III. pp. 764-768.

thus enumerated on either side; even the Fathers contradicted themselves, and numerous passages from them were quoted by both the opposed sides in support of their respective views. In this way *theses* arose, then *quæstiones*, in reply to these *argumenta*, then again *positiones*, and finally *dùbia*; according as men chose to take the words in this sense or that, and followed this or that authority. Yet a certain degree of method began to enter in.

Speaking generally, this middle of the twelfth century forms the epoch in which scholasticism became more universal as a learned theology. The book of Lombard was all through the Middle Ages commentated by the *doctores theologicæ dogmaticæ*, who were now held to be the recognized guardians of ecclesiastical doctrine, while the clergy had charge of the soul. Those doctors had great authority, they held synods, criticized and condemned this or that doctrine and book as heretical, &c., in synods or as the Sorbonne, a society of such doctors in the University of Paris. They took the place of assemblages of the Church, and were something like the Fathers in reference to the Christian doctrine. In particular they rejected the writings of the mystics like Amalrich and his disciple David of Dinant, who, resembling Proclus in their point of view, went back to unity. Amalrich, who was attacked as a heretic in 1204, for instance said, "God is all, God and the Creature are not different, in God all things are, God is the one universal substance." David asserted, "God is the first matter and everything is one in matter, and God is just this unity." He divided everything into three classes, bodies, souls, eternal immaterial substances or spirits. "The indivisible principle of souls is the νοῦς, and that of spirits is God. These three principles are identical and hence all things in essence are one." His books were burned.[1]

[1] Tennemann, Vol. VIII. Sec. I. pp. 317, 325; Brucker, Hist. crit. phil. T. III. p. 688; Thomas Aquinas: in IV. libros sentent. L. II. Dist. 17, Qu. I. Art. I; Alberti Magni: Summa Theol. P. I. Tract. IV. Qu. 20 (Oper. T. XVII. p. 76).

b. Thomas Aquinas.

The other individual who was equally famous with Peter Lombard, was Thomas Aquinas, born in 1224 of the noble race Aquino, in his paternal castle Roccasicca, in the province of Naples. He entered the Order of Dominicans, and died in 1274 on a journey to a church council at Lyons. He possessed a very extensive knowledge of theology, and also of Aristotle; he was likewise called *Doctor angelicus* and *communis*, a second Augustine. Thomas Aquinas was a disciple of Albertus Magnus, he wrote commentaries on Aristotle and on Petrus Lombardus; and he also himself composed a *summa theologiæ* (that is, a system) which with his other writings obtained for him the greatest honour, and which became one of the principal text-books in scholastic theology.[1] In this book there are found, indeed, logical formalities—not, however, dialectical subtleties, but fundamental metaphysical thoughts regarding the whole range of theology and philosophy.

Thomas Aquinas likewise added questions, answers and doubts, and he gave the point on which the solution depended. The main business of scholastic theology consisted in working out the *summa* of Thomas. The principal point was to make theology philosophic and more widely systematic; Peter Lombard and Thomas Aquinas are best known in respect of this endeavour, and for long their works formed the basis of all further learned elaborations of doctrine. With Thomas, Aristotelian forms constitute the basis—that of substance (*forma substantialis*) is, for instance, analogous to the entelechy (*ἐνέργεια*) of Aristotle. He said of the doctrine of knowledge, that material things consist of form and matter; the soul has the substantial form of the stone in itself.[2]

[1] Tennemann, Vol. VIII. Sec. II. pp. 550-553; Brucker, Hist. crit. phil. T. III. p. 802.

[2] Tennemann, Vol. VIII. Sec. II. pp. 554-561.

c. JOHN DUNS SCOTUS.

In respect of the formal development of philosophic theology a third individual is famous, namely, Duns Scotus, *Doctor subtilis*, a Franciscan, who was born at Dunston in the county of Northumberland, and who little by little obtained thirty thousand disciples. In the year 1304 he came to Paris, and in 1308 to Cologne, as a doctor in the university newly instituted there. He was received with great rejoicings, but he died there of apoplexy soon after his arrival, and is said to have been buried alive. He is supposed to have been only 34, according to others 43, and according to others again 63 years old, for the year of his birth is not known.[1] He wrote commentaries on the *Magister sententiarum*, which procured for him the fame of a very keen thinker, following the order of beginning with the proof of the necessity of a supernatural revelation as against the mere light of reason.[2] On account of his power of penetration he has been likewise called the *Deus inter philosophos*. He was accorded the most excessive praise. It was said of him: "He developed philosophy to such an extent that he himself might have been its discoverer if it had not already been discovered; he *knew* the mysteries of the faith so well that he can scarcely be said to have *believed* them; he knew the secrets of providence as though he had penetrated them, and the qualities of angels as though he were himself an angel; he wrote so much in a few years that scarcely one man could read it all, and hardly any were able to understand it."[3]

According to all testimony it appears that Scotus helped the scholastic method of disputation to reach its height,

[1] Brucker. Hist. crit. phil. T. III. pp. 825-828; Bulæus: Hist. Univ. Paris. T. IV. p. 970.

[2] Duns Scotus in Magistrum sententiarum. Procemium (Tennemann, Vol. VIII. Sec. II. p. 706).

[3] Brucker. Hist. crit. phil. T. III. p. 828; et not. from Sancrutius.

finding the material for the same in arguments and counter-arguments arranged in syllogisms; his manner was to add to each *sententia* a long succession of *distinctiones, quæstiones, problemata, solutiones, argumenta pro et contra*. Because he also refuted his arguments in a similar series, everything fell once more asunder; hence he was held to be the originator of the quodlibetan method. The *Quodlibeta* signified collections of miscellaneous dissertations on individual objects in the every-day manner of disputation, which speaks of everything, but without systematic order and without any consistent whole being worked out and set forth; others, on the other hand, wrote *summas*. The Latin of Scotus is exceedingly barbarous, but well suited for exact philosophic expression; he invented an endless number of new propositions, terms and syntheses.

3. Acquaintanceship with Aristotelian Writings.

We must further remark a third development, which proceeded from the external historical circumstance that in the end of the twelfth and in the thirteenth century the Western theologians became more generally acquainted with the Aristotelian writings and their Greek and Arabian commentators, in Latin translations from the Arabic. These now became much used by them, and were made the subject of further commentaries and discussions. The veneration, admiration and respect which Aristotle received, now reached its height.

a. Alexander of Hales.

The familiar acquaintance with Aristotle and the Arabians became first evident in Alexander of Hales (died 1245), the *Doctor irrefragabilis*. The earlier stages by which this familiarity came about has been shown above (p. 35). Hitherto the acquaintance with Aristotle was very slight, and through many centuries it was limited, as we saw above (p. 37), more especially to his Logic, which had survived from the earliest times and was transmitted in the works of Boethius, Augustine and Cassiodorus. It was only when we came to Scotus Erigena that we found (p. 59) a knowledge of Greek, although it was quite unusual in his day. In Spain, under the Arabians, the sciences flourished greatly. In particular the university of Cordova in Andalusia was a centre-point of learning; many from the lands of the West journeyed thither, just as even the Pope Sylvester II., so well known in his earlier days as Gerbert, escaped as a monk to Spain for the purpose of studying with the Arabs.[1] The sciences of medicine and alchemy were diligently pursued. Christian doctors there studied medicine under the Jewish-Arabian teachers. It was principally the Aristotelian metaphysics and physics which were then known, and from these abstracts (*summæ*) were constructed. The logic and metaphysics of Aristotle were spun out with extreme fineness into endless distinctions, and brought into genuine syllogistic forms of the understanding, which constituted for the most part the principle for the treatment of the subject dealt with. In this way dialectic subtlety was much increased, while the properly speculative side in Aristotle remained for the spirit of externality, and consequently also of irrationality, in the back-ground.

The Hohenstaufen emperor Frederick II. then sent for Aristotelian books from Constantinople and had them translated into Latin. At first, indeed, on the first appearance of the Aristotelian writings, the Church made difficulties; the reading of his metaphysics and physics and the abstracts prepared therefrom, as also the exposition of the same, was forbidden by a church synod held at Paris 1209. Likewise in 1215 the cardinal Robert Corceo came to Paris and there held a visitation of the university, on

[1] Trithemius: Annal. Hirsaugiens, T. I. p. 135.

which occasion he ordained that regular lectures on the dialectical writings of Aristotle should be held while he forbade the reading of and lecturing on the metaphysics and natural philosophy of Aristotle, and the abstracts prepared from them; he also condemned the doctrines of the heretics David of Dinant and Amalrich and likewise the Spaniard Mauritius. Pope Gregory, in a bull issued to the University of Paris in 1231, without mentioning metaphysics, forbade the books of the Physics to be read until they had been examined and purified from all suspicion of error. But later on, in 1366, it was on the other hand ordained by two cardinals that no one could be made a *magister* unless he had studied the prescribed books of Aristotle—amongst which were the Metaphysics and some of the Physics—and had proved himself capable of explaining them.[1] It was only much later on, however, when Greek literature in general had again become widely diffused, that men became better acquainted with the Greek text of the Aristotelian writings.

b. Albertus Magnus.

Amongst those who distinguished themselves through their commentaries on Aristotle's writings, we must specially mention Albertus Magnus, the most celebrated German schoolman, of the noble race of Bollstädt. Magnus either was his family name, or it was given him on account of his fame. He was born in 1193 or 1205 at Lauingen on the Danube in Swabia, and began by studying at Padua, where his study is still shown to travellers. In the year 1221 he became a Dominican friar, and afterwards lived at Cologne as Provincial of his Order in Germany:

[1] Brucker. Hist. crit. phil. T. III. pp. 779, 697; Tennemann, Vol. VIII. Sec. I. pp. 353–359, and in the same place, note 3 (cf. Jourdain, Gesch. d. Arist. Schriften im Mittelalter, übersetzt von Stahr pp. 165–176); Bulæus: Hist. Univers. Paris, T. III. pp. 82, 142; Launoius, De varia Arist. fortuna in Academ. Paris, c. IX. p. 210.

in 1280 he died. It is said of him that in his youth he showed himself very dull and stupid, until, according to a legend, the Virgin Mary appeared to him in company with three other beautiful women, incited him to the study of Philosophy, liberated him from his dulness of understanding, and promised him that he should enlighten the Church, and, in spite of his science, should still die in the faith. What happened was in accordance with this prophecy, for five years before his death he forgot all his philosophy as quickly as he learned it, and then actually died in the dulness and orthodoxy of his earlier years. Hence there is current regarding him an old saying: "Albert changed quickly from an ass into a philosopher, and from a philosopher into an ass." His learning was generally understood to consist largely of magic. For although natural objects have nothing to do with scholasticism proper, which was really perfectly blind to nature, he occupied himself much therewith; and amongst other devices he manufactured a talking machine which alarmed his pupil Thomas of Aquino, who even aimed a blow at it, thinking he saw therein a work of the devil. Likewise the fact that he received and entertained William of Holland[1] in the middle of winter in a garden full of blossom, is counted as magic.[2] While as for us—we find the winter-garden in Faust quite natural.

Albert wrote a great deal, and twenty-one folios remain to us of his writings. He wrote on Dionysius the Areopagite, commentated the *Magister sententiarum*, was specially conversant with the Arabians and the Rabbis, as he was also well acquainted with the works of Aristotle, although he himself understood neither Greek nor Arabic. He likewise wrote on the Physics of Aristotle. There is

[1] Hegel erroneously mentions this event as occurring to "William of England" instead of to William of Holland, King of the Romans. [Translator's note.]

[2] Brucker. Hist. cr. phil. T. III. pp. 788–798.

found in him a remarkable instance of deficient knowledge of the history of Philosophy. He derived the name Epicurean (Opera, T.V. pp. 530, 531) from the fact that they idled away their time [auf der faulen Haut lägen] (*ἐπὶ cutem*) or else from *cura* because they concerned themselves with many useless things (*supercurantes*). He represents the Stoics as being something like our choir-boys; he says that they were people who made songs (*facientes cantilenas*), and roamed about in porticoes. For, as he here remarks in a very learned way, the first philosophers clothed their philosophy in verses, and then sang them in halls and porches, and hence they are called standers in the porch (*Stoici*). Gassendi relates (*Vita Epicuri*, I. c. 11, p. 51) that Albertus Magnus mentioned as the first Epicureans, Hesiodus, Athalius or Achalius (of whom we know nothing), Cæcina, or, as others call him, Tetinnus, a friend of Cicero, and Isaacus, the Jewish philosopher. How that is arrived at we do not know at all. Of the Stoics Albertus, on the contrary, mentions Speusippus, Plato, Socrates and Pythagoras. These anecdotes give us a picture of the condition of culture in these times.

4. Opposition between Realism and Nominalism.

In the fourth place we must mention an important matter, to which much attention was devoted in the Middle Ages, namely that particular philosophic question which formed the subject of controversy between the Realists and the Nominalists, and the discussion of which was continued through very nearly the whole of the Scholastic period. Speaking generally, this controversy is concerned with the metaphysical opposition between the universal and the individual; it occupies the attention of Scholastic philosophy for several centuries, and reflects great credit upon it. A distinction is drawn between the earlier and later Nominalists and Realists, but otherwise their history is very obscure; and we know more of the theological aspect of the subject than of this.

a. Roscelinus.

The beginning of the controversy dates back to the eleventh century, Roscelinus being the earliest Nominalist. The famous Abelard, although he professes to be an opponent of Roscelinus, is himself nothing more or less than a Nominalist. Roscelinus wrote also against the doctrine of the Trinity, and was pronounced guilty of heresy in 1092 at an ecclesiastical council which met at Soissons. His influence was, however, but small.[1]

The matter in question is the universal as such (*universale*), or the genus, the essence of things, what in Plato was called the Idea—for instance, Being, humanity, the animal. The followers of Plato asserted that these universals exist; their existence was individualized, and thus 'tableness' was said to be also a real existence (*supra*, Vol. II. p. 29). We make representations of a thing to ourselves, and say "it is blue;" this is a universal. The question now is whether such universals are something real in and for themselves, apart from the thinking subject, and independent of the individual existing thing, so that they exist in the individual things independently of the individuality of the thing and of each other; or whether the universal is only nominal, only in the subjective representation, a thing of thought. Those who maintained that the universals had a real existence apart from the thinking subject and distinct from the individual thing, and that the Idea alone constitutes the essence of things, were termed Realists—a use of the term in quite an opposite sense to that which passes current now. I mean that this expression has for us the signification that things as they are in their immediacy have an actual existence; and to this idealism is opposed, that being a name which was given

[1] Anselmus: De fide trinitatis, c. 2, 3; Epist. XLI. l. 11; Tennemann, Vol. VIII. Section I. p. 158.

later to the philosophy which ascribes reality to ideas alone, and asserts that things as they appear in their individuality have no truth. The realism of the Scholastics in the same way maintained that the Universal has an independent, absolute existence, for Ideas are not liable to destruction, like natural things, therefore they are immutable and the only true existence. In opposition to this, the others, the Nominalists or Formalists, asserted that if generals or universals are formed, these are only names, matters of form, representations which we make to ourselves, a subjective generalization, a product of the thinking mind; the individual alone is the real.

This is then the matter in question; it is of great interest, and is founded upon a much higher opposition than any the ancients knew of. Roscelinus made universal conceptions arise only from the necessities of language. He maintained that ideas or universals, like Being, life, reason, are in themselves nothing but mere abstract notions or generic names, which, as such, have in and for themselves no universal reality of their own: that which has Being and life is found in the individual alone. Against these assertions arguments are brought forward by which one can see that the manner in which the Christian world was taken as basis, often became in the highest degree ridiculous. For instance, Abelard reproaches Roscelinus for having asserted that no thing has parts, that only the words which denote the things are divisible. Abelard proved that according to Roscelinus, Christ did not eat a real part of the broiled fish, but only a part—I do not know which—of the word "broiled fish," since according to him there were no parts—which interpretation would be preposterous and highly blasphemous.[1] Our way of

[1] Rixner: Handbuch der Geschichte der Philos., Vol. II. p. 26 (1st ed.); Anselmus: De fide trinitatis, c. 2; Buhle: Lehrbuch d. Geschichte d. Philosoph., Part V. p. 184; Abælard, Epist. XXI.; Tennemann, Vol. VIII. Section I. pp. 162, 163.

reasoning from "healthy human understanding," is not much better.

b. Walter of Mortagne.

Walter of Mortagne (d. 1174) aimed at the union of the particular and the universal, saying that the universal must be individual, that universals must be united with individuals in accordance with their essence.[1] In later times the two rival factions were known to fame as Thomists, from the Dominican Thomas Aquinas, and Scotists, from the Franciscan Johannes Duns Scotus. Nevertheless, the original question as to whether universal notions have reality, and, if so, to what extent they have it, underwent a great variety of modifications and gradations, just as the opposing parties received very various names. Nominalism, in its crude form, declared universal notions to be mere names, which have reality only in speech, and it ascribed reality to individuals alone; Realism followed the exactly opposite course of attributing reality only to universals, while it considered that what distinguished individual things was an accident only or a pure difference. Neither of these two theories was correct in the manner of passing from the universal to the particular. There were some, however, among the Schoolmen who grasped the true conception that individuation, the limitation of the universal, and indeed of what is most universal, Being and entity, is a negation. Others said that the limit is itself something positive, but that it is not one with the universal by union with it, for it rather stands in a metaphysical connection with it, that is, in a connection such as that which binds thought with thought. This implies that the individual is only a clearer expression of what is already contained in the general conception; so that these conceptions, in spite of their being divided into parts and differentiated, still

[1] Tennemann, Vol. VIII. Section I. p. 339; Joh. Sarisberiensis: Metalogicus, L. II. c. 17.

remain simple; Being or entity, moreover, really is a Notion.[1]

Thomas, who was a Realist, declared the universal Idea to be indeterminate, and placed individuation in determinate matter (*materia signata*), *i.e.* matter in its dimensions or determinations. According to him, the original principle is the universal Idea; the form, as *actus purus*, may, as with Aristotle, exist on its own account; the identity of matter and form, the forms of matter, as such, are further removed from the original principle,—while thinking substances are mere forms.[2] But for Scotus the universal is rather the individual One, the one he thinks may appear also in the other; he maintained therefore the principle of individuation, and the formal character of the universal. In his view indeterminate matter becomes individual through an inward positive addition; the substantial forms of things are their real essence. Occam thus represents the views of Scotus: "In the thing that exists outside of the soul the same Nature exists *realiter* with the difference limiting (*contrahente*) it to a determinate individual, being only formally distinguished, and in itself neither universal nor individual, but incompletely universal in the thing, and completely universal in the understanding."[3] Scotus racked his brains much over this subject. To universals the Formalists allowed only an ideal reality in the divine and human intellect beholding them.[4] We thus see how closely connected with this is

[1] Tiedemann: Geist d. specul. Philos. Vol. V. pp. 401, 402; Suarez: Disputationes metaphysicæ, Disp. I. Sectio 6.

[2] Tiedemann; Geist d. specul. Philos. Vol. IV. pp. 490, 491; Thomas Aquinas: De ente et essent. c. 3 et 5.

[3] Tiedemann: Geist d. spec. Philos. Vol. IV. pp. 609-613; Scotus: in Magistrum sententiar. L. II. Dist., 3. Qu. 1–6; Occam: in libr. I. sentent. Dist. II. Quæst. 6 (Tennemann, Vol. VIII. Section II. pp. 852, 853.

[4] Rixner: Handbuch der Geschichte der Philos. Vol. II. p. 110.

the thought which we first meet with in the Scholastics, namely the seeking and giving of so-called proofs of God's existence (*supra*, pp. 62-67).

c. William Occam.

The opposition between Idealists and Realists appeared at an early stage, it is true, but it was not until later, after the time of Abelard, that it became the order of the day, and was invested with general interest. This was brought about chiefly by the Franciscan William Occam, of the village of Occam in the county of Surrey in England, who was surnamed *Doctor invincibilis*, and flourished in the beginning of the fourteenth century: the year of his birth is unknown. He is greatly celebrated for his skill in handling the weapons of logic; he is keen in discrimination and fertile in devising arguments and counter-arguments. Occam was a leading champion of Nominalism, which up to this time had found only here and there a defender, like Roscelinus and Abelard; his numerous followers received the name of Occamists and were Franciscans, while the Dominicans retained the name of Thomists. The conflict between Nominalists and Realists raged with a burning vehemence, and was carried to the greatest extremes; a pulpit is still shown which was separated by a wooden partition from the platform of the opponent, in order that the disputants might not come to blows. Henceforth theology was taught under two forms (*theologia scholastica secundum utramque partem*). Owing to the civil wars in France, politics also began gradually to affect the relationship between the orders, and this lent increased importance to the conflict into which jealousy had plunged the rival factions. In 1322, at a convention of his order, and also on other occasions, Occam and his order defended to the utmost of their power the claims of the different princes, such as the King of France and the Emperor of Germany, Louis of Bavaria, against the pretensions of the Pope.

Among the words of William to the Emperor were these, "Do thou defend me with the sword, and I will defend thee with the pen." Interdicts of the Paris University and Papal bulls were issued against Occam. The Paris University forbade his doctrines to be taught or his works quoted. A special prohibition was issued in 1340: "No teacher shall venture to assert plainly, or in so many words, that some familiar maxim of the author on whom he is lecturing is false, but shall either assent to it, or distinguish the true and the false significance; otherwise the dangerous result is to be apprehended that the truths of the Bible might be in like manner rejected. No teacher shall assert that a maxim cannot be thus explained or further defined." Occam was excommunicated in 1328, and died at Munich in 1343.[1]

Occam asks in one of his writings (*in libr. I. Sentent. Dist. II. Quæst.* 4), "Whether what is immediately and proximately denoted by the universal and by the generic name is a real thing outside of the soul, something intrinsic and essential in the things to which it is common and which are called by its name, and yet in reality distinguished from them." This definition of the Realists is given more in detail by Occam as follows: "As to this question, one opinion is that each generic designation or universal is a thing really existing outside of the soul in each and every individual, and that the Being (*essentia*) of each individual is really distinguished from each individual" (*i.e.* from its individuality), "and from each universal. Thus man, the universal, is a true thing outside of the soul, which exists in reality in each human being, but is distinguished from each human being, from universal living nature, and from the universal substance, and in this way from all species and genera, those that are subordinate as well as those that are

[1] Brucker. Hist. crit. phil. T. III. pp. 846–848, 911, 912; Tennemann, Vol. VIII. Section II. pp. 903, 944, 945, 925, 939, 940; Bulæus: Hist. Univers. Paris, T. IV. pp. 257, 265.

not subordinate." The universal, the common designation of all the individuals, is therefore, according to this, not identical with the Self, the ultimate point of subjectivity. "As many universal predicables as there are of any individual thing"—*e.g.* humanity, reason, Being, life, quality, &c. —"so many really different things there are in nature, each of which is really distinct from the other and from that individual, and all these things are in no wise multiplied in themselves, however much the separate predicables are multiplied, which are in every individual of the same kind." That is the most uncompromising way of stating the independence and isolation of every universal quality in a thing. Occam refutes this, saying: "Nothing which is one in number can, without being changed or multiplied, be present in several subjects or individuals. Science invariably restricts itself to propositions regarding the known; it is, therefore, a matter of no moment whether the terms of the propositions are known things outside of the soul, or only in the soul; and therefore it is not necessary for the sake of science to assume universal things, really distinct from individual things."

Occam proceeds to state other opinions opposed to that first given; he does not exactly give his own decision, yet in this same passage (Quæst. 8) he, in the main, argues in favour of the opinion "that the universal is not something real that has explicit subjectivity (*esse subjectivum*) neitner in the soul nor in the thing. It is something conceived, which, however, has objective reality (*esse objectivum*) in the soul, while the external thing has this objective reality as an explicitly existent subject (*in esse subjectivo*). This comes to pass in the following manner. The understanding, which perceives a thing outside the soul, forms the mental image of a similar thing, so that, if it had productive power, it would, like an artist, exhibit it in an absolutely existing subject, as numerically an individual distinct from any preceding. Should anyone be displeased by this manner of speaking of the mental image as being *formed*, it may be said that the mental image and every universal conception is a quality existing subjectively in the mind, which by its nature is the sign of a thing outside of the soul, just as the spoken word is a sign of the thing, arbitrarily instituted for marking out that thing." Tennemann says (Vol. VIII. Section II. p. 864): "One result of this theory was that the principle of individuation, which had occupied to such an extent the attention of the Scholastics, was cast aside as utterly unnecessary." Thus the main question with the Scholastics concerns the definition of the universal, and this was in itself highly important and significant for the culture of more modern times. The universal is the One, but not abstract; it is conceived or thought of as comprehending all things in itself. With Aristotle the universal was, in a judgment, the predicate of the subject in question; in a syllogism it was the *terminus major*. With Plotinus, and especially with Proclus, the One is still incommunicable, and is known only by its subordinate forms. But because the Christian religion is a revelation, God is no longer therein the unapproachable, incommunicable, a hidden mystery: for the various stages of the progression from Him are verily His manifestation, and the Trinity is thus the revealed. In this way the triads and the One are not distinguished, but these three Persons in the Godhead are themselves God and One, *i.e.* One as it is for another, as in itself relative. The Father, the God of Israel, is this One; the moment of the Son and of the Spirit is the Most High in spiritual and bodily presence, the former in the Church, the latter in Nature. With the Neo-Platonists the universal is, on the contrary, only the first condition of things which then merely opens out and develops; with Plato and Aristotle it is rather the Whole, the All, the All in One.

d. Buridan.

Buridan, a Nominalist, inclines to the view of the Determinists that the will is determined by circumstances. Against him is cited the case of the ass which, being placed between two equal bundles of hay, perforce perished from hunger.

Louis XI., in 1473, confiscated the books of the Nominalists and interdicted the teaching of their doctrines, but in the year 1481 this interdict was removed. In the theological and philosophical faculty Aristotle is said to have been interpreted and studied, as were also his commentators, Averroës, Albertus Magnus, and Thomas Aquinas.[1]

5. Formal Dialectic.

The study of dialectics was carried to a very great height, but it was quite formal in character; this constitutes the fifth point for consideration. With this is closely connected the interminable finding out of *termini technici*. This formal dialectic was very ingenious in devising objects, problems and questions, destitute of all religious and philosophic interest, on which to practise its method of procedure. The last remark that we have, however, in this connection to make regarding the Scholastics is this, that it was not only into the ecclesiastical system that they introduced all possible formal relations of the understanding, but that also objects intelligible in themselves—the intellectual conceptions and religious ideas—they represented as immediately and sensuously real, as brought down into the externality of altogether sensuous relations, and in these relations subjected to systematic investigation. Originally, it is true, the basis was spiritual, but the externality in which it was at once comprehended, made of the spiritual something perfectly unspiritual. It may therefore be said that, on the one hand, the Scholastics showed great profundity in their treatment of Church dogma; and, on the other hand,

[1] Tennemann, Vol. VIII. Section II. pp. 914—919, 945—947; Bulæus: Hist. Univ. Paris. T.V. pp. 706, 739, 740.

that they secularized it by placing it in quite inappropriate external relations; thus here we have the worst kind of secularity. For the dogma of the Church explicitly contains, in the historical form of the Christian religion, a number of ordinary conceptions determined in an external way, which are connected with the spiritual, it is true, but trench upon sensuous relationships. If a network of such relationships is then contrived, there arises a host of oppositions, contrasts, contradictions, which have not the very slightest interest for us. It is this aspect of the matter that the Scholastics have taken up and handled with finite dialectic; and it is on this account that the Scholastics in later times were so much ridiculed. Of this I have some examples to give.

a. JULIAN, ARCHBISHOP OF TOLEDO.

Julian, Archbishop of Toledo, sought, with as great earnestness as if the salvation of the human race depended on it, to answer questions which contain an absurd assumption. In doing so he no less gives himself up to petty triflings than do the philologists when they institute investigations regarding Greek accents, metres, and verse-divisions. For instance, there arises a question of this kind as to the dead. It is a dogma of the Church, that man will rise again; now if to this it be added that he will be clothed with the body, we thereby enter the sensuous sphere. The following were inquiries which arose in connection with this question: "What will be the age of the dead when they rise? Will they rise as children, youths, grown men, or aged? In what form will they rise? What will be the constitution of their bodies? Will the fat be again fat, and the lean again lean? Will the distinction of sex continue in that future life? Will those who rise again recover all that they lost here in the way of nails and hair?"[1] Thus a special distinction was drawn between the actual dogma, which was indisputable, and the various aspects of the supersensuous world which are connected with that dogma. These were regarded, though often only for the time being, as detached from the doctrinal system of the Church. For the system was not so definitely formulated but that anything in it might have to be proved from the Fathers, until a council or a special synod decided the point. Disputes were also possible regarding the proofs which were given of the content of this system; and besides there was quite a large amount of matter which was open to discussion, and respecting which the Scholastics—with the exception, of course, of the noble men, renowned as *Doctores* and writers,—expressed themselves in finite syllogisms and forms, which degenerated into an utterly empty and formal craze for disputation. The Scholastic Philosophy is thus the direct opposite of the empirical science of the understanding, with which curiosity is largely mingled, and which, careless of the Notion, follows after facts alone.

b. PASCHASIUS RADBERTUS.

About 840 another subject of discussion was raised, namely, the birth of Christ, whether it was natural or supernatural. This led to a protracted controversy. Paschasius Radbertus wrote two volumes, *De partu beatæ virginis*; and many others wrote and argued on the same topic.[2] They went so far as even to speak of an accoucheur, and to discuss this subject; and many questions were raised, to which our sense of what is fitting forbids us even to turn our thoughts.

[1] Tennemann, Vol. VIII. Section I. p. 61; Cramer, Fortsetzung von Bossnet, Part V. Vol. II. p. 88.

[2] Tennemann, Vol. VIII. Section I. p. 61; Bulæus: Hist. Univ. Paris. T. I. p. 169.

God's wisdom, omnipotence, foresight, and predetermination led in the same way to a host of contradictions in abstract, meaningless, local and trivial particulars, which concern not God. In the works of Petrus Lombardus, where the Trinity, the Creation, and the Fall are dealt with, as also angels and their orders and ranks, questions are found such as whether God's providence and predetermination would have been possible, had nothing been created; and where God was before the Creation. Thomas of Strasburg answered: *Tunc ubi nunc, in se, quoniam sibi sufficit ipse.*[1]

Lombardus goes on to ask "If God can know more than He knows?" as if potentiality and actuality still remained distinguished; "If God retains at all times all power that He has once possessed? Where the angels were after their creation? If the angels have always existed?" A multitude of other questions of this kind are raised regarding the angels. Then he asks: "At what age was Adam created? Why was Eve made from the rib, and not from some other part of the man? Why during sleep, and not when the man was awake? Why did the first human pair not have intercourse in Paradise? How the human race would have been propagated, if man had not sinned? If in Paradise children would have been born with limbs fully grown, and the complete use of their senses? Why it was the Son, and not the Father or the Holy Ghost, who became man?" To do this rests in the very Notion of the Son. "If God could not have also become incarnate in female form?"[2]

Additional examples of *quæstiones* of this kind are given by those who ridiculed such dialectic, for instance by Erasmus in his *Encomium moriæ:* "Could there be several sonships (*filiationes*) in Christ? Is the proposition possible that God the Father hates the Son? Might God not have also taken the form of a woman, or have passed into the

[1] Rixner: Handbuch d. Gesch. d. Phil. Vol. II. p. 153.

[2] Tennemann, Vol. VIII. Section I, pp. 236, 237.

devil? Might He not also have appeared in the form of an ass or of a pumpkin? In what manner would the pumpkin have preached and wrought miracles, and how would it have been crucified?"[1] Thus were intellectual determinations combined and distinguished in a manner altogether without sense or thought. The main point is that the Scholastics were like barbarians in their way of handling divine things and bringing them into sensuous determinations and relations. They thus introduced a completely sensuous rigidity and these altogether external and senseless forms into the purely spiritual, thus bringing it to a lower and unspiritual level; Hans Sachs similarly made a Nürnberg version of sacred history [die göttliche Geschichte vernürnbergert]. In such representations as are given in the Bible of the wrath of God, or of the history of God's work of creation, it is said that God did this or that, naming some human and homely action. God is certainly not to be looked on as something alien and unapproachable; on the contrary, we are to come to Him with courage and with all our heart. But to bring Him into the province of thought, and strive in earnest after a knowledge of Him, is a very different matter. The reverse of this is to bring forward arguments *pro* and *contra*, for they decide nothing, and are of no use; they are no more than the assumptions which are only sensuous and finite determinations, and therefore infinite differences and distinctions. This barbarous use of the understanding is utterly irrational; it is like putting a golden necklace on a sow. The One is the Idea of the Christian religion, and it is also the philosophy of the great and noble Aristotle; neither of the two could have been more bedraggled and besmirched, to so low a pass had the Christians brought their spiritual Idea.

[1] Brucker. Hist. crit. phil. T. III. p. 878.

6. Mystics.

In the above sketch we have mentioned the principal heads which come under our consideration in studying Scholastic philosophy. With regard to this intrusion of distinctions of the understanding and sensuous relations into that which in and for itself and by virtue of its very nature is spiritual, absolute and infinite, it is to be remarked that to this craze for reducing everything to the finite, some noble spirits here and there opposed themselves. As such we must here, in the sixth place, make honourable mention of the many great Scholastics who have been named Mystics, for although they are to be distinguished from the real ecclesiastical Scholastics, they followed upon identical lines, and are closely connected with them. They took but little interest in these discussions and arguments, and maintained their purity in regard to Church doctrines and philosophic speculation. Some of them were pious and spiritual men, who carried on their philosophic studies upon the lines of the Neo-Platonic philosophy, as Scotus Erigena had done in earlier times. Among them genuine philosophy is to be found—termed also Mysticism; it tends to inwardness and bears a great resemblance to Spinozism. They also derived morality and the religious sentiment from actual feelings, and the meditations and maxims we have from them embody these views.

a. John Charlier.

John Charlier, more generally known as Von Jerson or Gerson, was born in 1363; he wrote a *theologia mystica*.[1]

b. Raymundus of Sabunde.

Very similar were the views expressed by Raymundus of Sabunde or Sabeyde, a Spaniard of the fifteenth century,

[1] Tennemann, Vol. VIII. Section II. pp. 955, 956.

and professor at Toulouse about the year 1437. In his *theologia naturalis*, which he handled in a speculative spirit, he dealt with the Nature of things, and with the revelation of God in Nature and in the history of the God-man. He sought to prove to unbelievers the Being, the trinity, the incarnation, the life, and the revelation of God in Nature, and in the history of the God-man, basing his arguments on Reason. From the contemplation of Nature he rises to God; and in the same way he reaches morality from observation of man's inner nature.[1] This purer and simpler style must be set off against the other, if we are to do justice to the Scholastic theologians in their turn.

c. Roger Bacon.

Roger Bacon treated more especially of physics, but remained without influence. He invented gunpowder, mirrors, telescopes, and died in 1294.[2]

d. Raymundus Lullus.

Raymundus Lullus, the *Doctor illuminatus*, made himself famous chiefly by the art of thinking which he invented, which was called the *ars magna*. He was born at Majorca in 1234, and was one of those eccentric, unsettled natures whose activity finds vent in all directions. He had a strong inclination towards alchemy and great enthusiasm for the sciences in general, as well as a fiery, restless power of imagination. In his youth he led a reckless life, throwing himself headlong into a round of pleasures; then he retreated to a desert, and had there many visions of Jesus. At this time the impulse shaped itself in his ardent nature to dedicate his life to spreading the blessings of Chris-

[1] Rixner: Handbuch d. Geschichte d. Philos. Vol. II. p. 157; Tennemann, Vol. VIII. Section II. p. 964 seq.; Tiedemann: Geist d. spec. Phil. Vol. V. p. 290 seq.

[2] Tennemann, Vol. VIII. Section II. pp. 824-829.

tianity among the Mohammedans in Asia and Africa. In order to carry on this work of conversion he learned Arabic, travelled through Europe and Asia, sought for assistance from the Pope and all the crowned heads of Europe, without giving up, for all that, his interest in his 'Art.' He suffered persecution and passed through many hardships and strange adventures, perils of death, imprisonments, cruelties. He lived long in Paris at the beginning of the fourteenth century, and was the author of well-nigh four hundred works. After a life of the utmost restlessness, he died in 1315, revered as a saint and martyr, his death being the result of cruel treatment which he had suffered in Africa.[1]

The chief object aimed at in this man's 'Art' was an enumeration and arrangement of the various concepts under which all objects fall, or of the pure categories according to which they can be determined, so that it may be possible in regard to every object to indicate with ease the conceptions applicable to it. Lullus is so systematic that he becomes at times mechanical. He constructed a diagram in circles, on which were marked triangles through which the circles pass. In these circles he arranged the various concepts, and strove to give a complete catalogue of them. Some of the circles were fixed, others movable, and they were six in number, two of them indicating the subjects, three the predicates, while the outermost circle represented possible questions. For each class he had nine qualities, to indicate which he chose nine letters, B C D E F G H I K. Thus in the first place he wrote round the diagram nine absolute predicates, goodness, greatness, duration, power, wisdom, volition, virtue, truth, splendour; then he wrote nine relative predicates, diversity, unanimity, opposition, beginning, middle, end, the qualities of being greater, equal, or less; in the third place he set down the questions

[1] Rixner: Lehrbuch d. Gesch. d. Philos. Vol. II. p. 126; Tennemann, Vol. VIII. Section II. pp. 829, 833.

Whether? What? Whence? Why? How great? Of what nature? When? Where? How and wherewith? the ninth of which contains two determinations; in the fourth place he put nine substances (*esse*), viz. God (*divinum*), angel (*angelicum*), heaven (*cœleste*), man (*humanum*), *imaginativum, sensitivum, vegetativum, elementativum, instrumentativum;* in the fifth place were nine accidents, *i.e.* natural relations, viz. quantity, quality, relation, activity, passivity, possession, position, time, place; and sixthly nine moral relations, the virtues, viz. justice, prudence, courage, temperance, faith, hope, love, patience, piety; and the vices, viz. envy, wrath, inconstancy, covetousness, falsehood, gluttony, riotousness, pride, sluggishness (*acedia*). These circles had to be placed in a certain way, in order to give proper combinations. By turning them round according to certain rules, by which all substances received the absolute and relative predicates which fitted them, it was supposed that there would be obtained in every possible combination universal science, truth, and the knowledge of concrete objects in general.[1]

C. General Standpoint of the Scholastics.

After thus dealing with the subject in detail, we must pronounce judgment on the Scholastics, and give an estimate of them. Though the subjects which they investigated were lofty, and though there were noble, earnest and learned individuals in their ranks, yet this Scholasticism on the whole is a barbarous philosophy of the finite understanding, without real content, which awakens no true

[1] Tennemann, Vol. VIII. Section II. pp. 834-836; Rixner: Handb. d. Gesch. d. Phil. Vol. II. Appendix, pp. 86-89; Jordanus Brunus Nolanus: De compendiosa architectura et complemento artis Lullii, Sectio II. (Bruni scripta, quæ latine confecit, omnia; ed Gfrörer, Stuttgardiæ 1835, Fasciculus II. pp. 243-264).

interest in us, and to which we cannot return. For although religion is its subject matter, thought here reached such an excessive point of subtlety that, as a form of the mere empty understanding, it does nothing but wander amongst baseless combinations of categories. Scholastic philosophy is this utter confusion of the barren understanding in the rugged North German nature. We see here two different worlds, a kingdom of life and a kingdom of death. The intellectual kingdom, which is outside and above, while in the popular conception, is thereby brought within the sphere of the mere understanding and the senses, even though by nature it is purely peculative; and this does not take place as in art, but, on the contrary, after the fashion of ordinary reality. As the relationship of Father and Son, to begin with, appealed to the senses, so the divine world was furnished for the imaginative faculty and for purposes of devotion (in a way unknown to the disciples of Plato) with angels, saints and martyrs, instead of with thoughts;—or the thoughts are nothing but a rubbishy metaphysic of the understanding. In the supersensuous world there was no reality of the thinking, universal, rational self-consciousness to be met with: in the immediate world of sensuous nature, on the other hand, there was no divinity, because nature was but the grave of God, in the same way that God was outside of nature. The existence of the Church, as the government of Christ upon earth, is higher, it is true, than the external existence which stands in contrast to it; for religion must rule our temporal affairs, and through the subjection of worldly power the Church became a theocracy. But the divine kingdom, the dwelling-place of the dead, was to be reached only through the gate of death; yet the natural world was dead to an equal degree—all that lived in it was the vision of that other world, and hope—it had no present. It was of no avail to introduce mediators as a connecting link, the Virgin Mary, or the dead in a world beyond. The reconciliation was formal, not absolute; for it was nothing but the longing of man for a satisfaction to be found only in another world. What purpose does all this serve? It lies behind us as a thing of the past, and must continue useless to us on its own merits. There is no good, however, in calling the Middle Ages a barbarous period. It is a singular kind of barbarism, and is not simple and rude; for the absolute Idea and the highest culture have sunk into barbarism, and that through the agency of thought. Thus we have here, on the one hand, the most hideous form of barbarism and perversion, but, on the other hand, the never-failing source of a higher reconciliation.

If we seek an immediate contrast to scholastic philosophy and theology and their methods, we may say that it is to be found in the "healthy human understanding," in outward and inward experience, in the contemplation of nature, and in humanity. The character of Greek humanity, for instance, was that everything concrete, everything that possessed interest for mind, had its place in the human breast, and its root in the feelings and thoughts of man. Intelligent consciousness, cultured science, has in such content its real material—that in which it is and remains at home with itself; knowledge busies itself on all sides with that which concerns it, and remains true to itself, while both on its serious and its playful side it finds in this material, in Nature and its uniform laws, a standard and a guide by which to direct its course aright. Even should we go astray on ground like this, our errors keep in view the fixed centre-point of the self-consciousness of the human mind, and as errors even they have a root therein, which as such forms the justification for them. It is only a one-sided withdrawal from the unity of this root with the altogether concrete groundwork and original, that is really faulty. What we see here, in contrast with the above, is the infinite truth, expressed as spirit, committed to a nation of barbarians who have not the self-consciousness of their spiritual humanity—they have a human breast, it is true, but not yet a human spirit. The absolute truth does not yet make itself real and present in actual consciousness, but men are torn out of themselves. They still find this content of spirit within themselves, introduced as into a strange vessel full of the most intense impulses and desires of physical and intellectual life, but it is like a ponderous stone, whose enormous pressure they only feel, but which they neither digest nor assimilate with their own impulses or desires. Thus they can only find rest and reconciliation when they come absolutely out of themselves, and they have become fierce and savage in the very circumstances and by the very means which ought to have rendered their spirit peaceable and mild.

Just as truth was not yet the foundation of reality, so science was likewise destitute of firm basis. The understanding, when it comes to think, applies itself, it is true, in the first place to the mysteries of religion, which, as an altogether speculative content, exist for the rational Notion only. But as Spirit, the rational element in question, has not yet taken its place in thought, thought is still God-forsaken, it is still only abstract, finite understanding, a manner of thinking which is in itself quite formal and devoid of content, which is a stranger to subjects of such profundity as this, even when it is ostensibly occupying itself with the same. This understanding therefore draws its content entirely from things to which it remains altogether alien, and which remain altogether alien to it; yet it is not thereby at all circumscribed, for it observes no bounds in its determinations and distinctions. It is just as if one were to arbitrarily form and connect propositions, words and tones—without making the presupposition that they should by themselves express a concrete sense—which need be only capable of being uttered, without having any restriction except possibility, that is, that they must not contradict each other.

In the second place, in so far as the understanding keeps to the given religious content, it can prove this content; one can demonstrate that it must be so, just as if it were a geometrical proposition. But there still remains something to be desired, in order that the satisfaction may be complete; the content is proved, but I nevertheless do not understand it. Thus Anselm's excellent proposition (*supra*, pp. 63, 64) in which we may perceive the general character of the scholastic understanding, is a proof, it may be admitted, of the existence of God, but it shows no comprehension of it. Though I see the truth of the proposition, I have not attained to the final point, the object of my desire; for there is lacking the I, the inner bond, as inwardness of thought. This lies only in the Notion, in the unity of the particular and the universal, of Being and thought. For the comprehension of this unity, without which there could be no true proof, it was implied that further progress should not take place after the manner of the understanding. It was necessary that from the nature of thought itself it should become evident how, taken on its own account, it negates itself, and how the determination of Being itself rests therein, or that the manner in which thought determines itself into Being should be shown forth. On the other hand it must in like manner be demonstrated in the case of Being that it is its peculiar dialectic to abrogate itself, and from itself to make itself a universal Notion. The determination of itself into Being is certainly an object of thought, whose content is thought itself. This is inwardness, not a mere conclusion drawn from pre-suppositions. Here in scholastic philosophy, however, the object is not the nature of thought and Being, for what they are is a mere matter of assumption.

The understanding may take its start from experience, a given concrete content, a determinate contemplation of nature, the human heart, right, duty, which are just exactly what inwardness means. It may find its determinations, so to speak, on behalf of this content, and starting from this point it may come to abstractions, such as matter and force in physics. In this case, although a general form such as this does not satisfy the content, it has at any rate therein a fixed point, by which it can regulate itself, and a boundary line for speculation, which would otherwise have no limit set to its roaming. Or when we have the concrete perception of state and family, reasoning has in this content a fixed point which gives it guidance—a conception, which is the main thing; the deficiency in its form becomes concealed and forgotten, and emphasis is not laid on it. But in scholastic philosophy, in the third place, a basis was not sought in such objects as direct the course of reflection; with this understanding of the Scholastics it was rather the case that they received in the categories the external culture of the understanding as tradition, and enlarged upon it. Because there was no standard set up for this scholastic understanding, either by concrete intuition or by the pure Notion, it remained unregulated in its externality. In later times this spirit-forsaken understanding came across the philosophy of Aristotle, in an external way; but that philosophy is a two-edged sword, a highly determinate, clear understanding, which is at the same time speculative Notion; in it the abstract determinations of the understanding, taken by themselves, and powerless thus to stand, pass away by means of dialectic, and have truth only when taken in their connexion. The speculation that we find in Aristotle has this condition, that such thought never abandons itself to free reflection, but keeps ever before it the concrete nature of the object; this nature is the Notion of the thing, and this speculative essence of the thing is the ruling spirit, which does not leave the determinations of reflection free on their own account. But the Scholastics laid down hard and fast the abstract determinations of the understanding, which are always inadequate to their absolute subject, and in like manner they took every example from life as subject, and since the concrete contradicts them, they could hold fast by these determinations of the understanding only by defining and limiting. In so doing, however, they involved themselves in an endless web of distinctions, which could themselves be held in the concrete, and maintained thereby alone. There is thus no "healthy human understanding" in such procedure of the Scholastics; the former cannot oppose itself to speculation, but it can very well take up a position hostile to ungrounded reflection, seeing that it contains a basis and a rule of guidance for abstract determinations of the understanding. The Aristotelian philosophy is quite opposed to this Scholastic procedure, but it became therein alienated from itself. The fixed conception of the supersensuous world with its angels and so on was a subject which the Scholastics elaborated without any regulating standard, in barbaric fashion, and they enriched and embellished it with the finite understanding and with the finite relationships of the same. There is present no immanent principle in the thinking itself, but the understanding of the Scholastics got into its possession a ready-made metaphysic, without the need of making it relate to the concrete; this metaphysic was killed, and its parts in their lifelessness were separated and parcelled out. It might be said of the Scholastics that they philosophized without conception, that is, without a concrete; for *esse reale, esse formale, esse objectivum, quidditas* (τὸ τί ἦν εἶναι) they made their subjects of discussion.

This crude understanding, in the fourth place, made everything equal, reduced it all to the same level, and that in virtue of its abstract universality, which was held to be valid. In politics also the understanding aims at making all alike equal. This crude understanding did not make away with itself and its finitude, but in its dealings with them simply reduced to finite relations Heaven, the Idea, the intellectual, mystic, speculative world; for it makes no difference (and can make none) whether its finite determinations are valid here or not. Hence arose these senseless questions, and the endeavours to decide them; for it is senseless, I may even say it is distasteful and revolting, although it may be logically correct, to carry over determinations into a field where they are utterly out of place, as soon as it comes to be a matter of comprehending a concrete content in its universality. This understanding in its operations furnishes no bridge from the universal to the particular, and the conclusions which it draws it leaves up in the clouds as conceptions of its fancy. If, for instance, law is divided into canonical law, criminal law, and so on, the ground of division is not taken from the universal itself; and it is thus left vague which particular determination is in accordance with the universal object. If this object is God,—for instance, such a determination as that He became man—the relation between God and man is not derived from their nature. Because God only manifests Himself, He can do so in any way whatever; then, because nothing is impossible with God, the pumpkin idea is easily introduced (p. 90), since it is a matter of indifference in which determination the Universal is supposed to be. Regarding the apple in Paradise the understanding asks to what species of apple it belonged.

We must go on to indicate the principles which have been adopted and stand opposed to one other, and the development of the same, in order to comprehend the transition into modern history and the present standpoint of philosophy. For this reason we must speak of the further progress of universal spirit. For thought was distorted by reason of its being bound to an externality, and spirit was in it no longer acting for spirit. Because then in this and similar ways the Idea of spirit had, as it were, its heart pierced through, the parts remained without spirit and life, and were worked upon by the understanding. Amongst the learned ignorance of the rational was displayed, a complete and unnatural lack of spirituality; and in the same way there was the most utter and terrible ignorance amongst the others, the monks. This destruction of knowledge brought about the transition to a different state of affairs; while heaven and the divine were thus degraded, the lofty aspirations and high spiritual claims of the clerical element rose above the secular. For we saw that the supersensuous world of truth, as the world of religious conceptions, was ruined by the understanding making all things equal. We saw, on the one hand, a handling of dogma in philosophic fashion, but we saw also a development of formal logical thought, the secularization of the absolutely existent content. In the same way the existing Church, this presence of heaven upon earth, brought itself down to the level of the secular, by entering upon the possession of riches and lands. In this way the distinction between the world and the Church is blotted out, not in a rational manner as regards the Church, but in a way that is altogether revolting, and which amounts to destruction: it is a reality, I grant, but one most terrible and barbarous. For state, government, right, property, civil order, all these enter into religion as rational differences, that is, laws on their own account fixed. The acknowledgment of ranks, classes, divisions, their different occupations, the stages and degrees of evil, as well as of good, are an entering into the form of finitude, actuality, existence of the subjective will, while what is religious has only the form of infinity. But the Church in its outward existence is inviolable, it can throw over all the laws of the good; every offence against it is a violation of sanctity. Evil and its penalties are made eternal, divergences of opinion are punished even with death: so are heresy and also heterodoxy in respect of the most abstract and empty determinations of an endless system of dogmas. Abominable practices and evil passions, utter wantonness, voluptuousness, bribery, dissoluteness, avarice, crimes of all kinds found their way into the Church, because it was unrestrained by laws; and it founded and maintained the system of government. The secular ought to be only secular; but this whole secular government of the Church claims at the same time the dignity and authority of the divine. This mingling of the sacred, divine, inviolable, with temporal interests, begets, on the one hand, fanaticism, as among the Turks, and on the other hand, the humility and *obedientia passiva* of the laity against this dread power. It was this ruin of the supersensuous world, as represented in knowledge and as the actual Church, that inevitably forced man out of a temple such as this, the Holy of Holies degraded into finitude.

Against this disunion, on the other hand, the secular element has spiritualized itself in itself; or it has established itself firmly in itself, and that in a manner which the Spirit justifies. To religion was lacking the presence of its culminating point, the present reality of its head; to the present secularity there is lacking the presence in it of thought, reason, spirit. In the tenth century there was manifested in Christendom a general impulse to build churches, although it was not possible to regard God Himself as present therein. It was thus that Christianity rose up, in her longing to take to herself the principle of reality as absolutely her own. But neither these buildings, nor external wealth, nor the power and dominion of the Church, nor monks, nor clergy, nor Pope, are the principle of real actual presence in her; they were insufficient for the spiritual. The Pope or the Emperor is not Dalai-lama, the Pope is only the Vicar of Christ; Christ, as a past existence, is in memory and hope alone. Impatient at the lack of reality and at the want of holiness, Christendom goes to seek this true Head; and this is the ruling motive of the Crusades. Christendom sought Christ's outward presence in the land of Canaan, the traces of Him, the mount where He suffered, His grave; they took possession of the Holy Sepulchre. What they represent to themselves as real they also take possession of in fact as real; but a grave is a grave—all that they find is a grave, and even that is torn from them. "Because Thou wilt not leave my soul in hell, neither wilt Thou suffer Thine Holy One to see corruption." Christians made the mistake of thinking that they would find satisfaction in this; this was the true object of their search; but they did not understand themselves. These holy spots, the Mount of Olives, the Jordan, Nazareth, as external sensuous presence of place without presence of time, are things of the past, a mere memory, no perception of the immediate present; the Christians found only their loss, their grave, in this present. Barbarians all the time, they did not seek the universal, the world-controlling position of Syria and Egypt, this central point of the earth, the free connection of commerce; Bonaparte did this when mankind became rational. The Crusaders were by the Saracens and by their own violence and repulsiveness, as also by their own misery (p. 53), brought to confess that they had in this deceived themselves. This experience taught them that they must hold to the actual reality which they despised, and seek in this the realization of their intelligible world. What they sought for they were to find in themselves, in the present of the understanding; thought, personal knowledge and will constitute this present. Because their acts, their aims and their interests are upright, and thus are constituted the Universal, the present is rational. What pertains to the world has thus become fixed in itself, that is, it has received into itself thought, justice, reason.

With reference to the general aspect of the period, from an historical point of view, it may be remarked that as on the one side we see the selflessness of spirit, the fact that spirit is not at home with itself, the torn and rent condition of man, on the other side we see the political condition becoming more consolidated, in the establishment of an independence which is no longer merely selfish. In the first indcpondonoo there is contained the moment of barbarism, which has need of fear in order to be held within bounds. Now, however, we see justice and order enter in; it is true that the ruling order is the feudal system with its servitude, but everything therein has certainly a firm basis in justice. Justice, however, has its root in freedom, and thus the individual therein brings himself into existence, and is recognized; nevertheless relationships which properly belong to the state are here still made the concern of private individuals. Feudal monarchy, which now emerges in opposition to the self-abnegation of the Church, determines essential rights, it is true, according to birth; ranks are not, however, like the system of caste among the Indians, for in the ecclesiastical hierarchy, for instance, anyone might from the lowest class rise to the very highest position. Even under the feudal system, moreover, justice, civil order, legal freedom gradually emerged. In Italy and Germany cities obtained their rights as citizen republics, and caused these to be recognized by the temporal and ecclesiastical power; wealth displayed itself in the Netherlands, Florence and the free cities on the Rhine. In this way men gradually began to emerge from the feudal system; an example of this is seen in the case of the Capitani. The fact that the *lingua volgare* became the language used may also be looked on as a springing up of self-abnegation of spirit: as in Dante's *Divina Commedia*.

The spirit of the times took this new direction; it forsook the intellectual world, and looked upon its present world, this hither side. The finite heaven, the content which had lost its religious character, drove it to the finite present. With this revolution the scholastic philosophy sinks and is lost, as its thoughts are outside of reality. While the Church heretofore believed itself to be in possession of divine truth, so now the temporal government, as it received into itself order and right, and worked its way out through the hard discipline of service, felt itself to be a divine institution, and consequently considered that it had the divine element here present in it, and that it was justified in having an independent existence in opposition to the divine element in the Church, which takes up an exclusive position as regards the laity. Since in this way the temporal power, the worldly life, self-consciousness, has taken into itself the higher and more divine ecclesiastical principle, the harsh contrast has disappeared. The power of the Church appeared as the violence of the Church, not aiming at operating in accordance with reality and in reality, but at being mighty in the spirit. There at once came into the secular element the consciousness that abstract Notions were filled with the reality of the present, so that this was no longer a nullity, but had truth also in itself.

With this commerce and the arts are associated. It is implied in the arts that man brings what is divine out of himself; as artists were at one time so pious that as individuals they had self-abnegation as their principle, it was they from whose subjective abilities these representations were produced. With this is connected the circumstance that the secular knew that it had in itself the right to hold to such determinations as are founded on subjective freedom. In his handicraft the individual is taken in reference to his work, and is himself the producer. Thus men came to the point of knowing that they were free, and insisting on the recognition of that freedom, and having the power of exercising their activity for their own objects and interests. Thus spirit came again to itself; it drew itself together again, and looked into its reason, as if looking into its own hands. This new birth is pointed out as the revival of the arts and sciences which were concerned with present matter, the epoch when the spirit gains confidence in itself and in its existence, and finds its interest in its present. It is in reality reconciled with the world, not implicitly, far away in mere thought, at the last day, at the world's transfiguration, *i.e.* when the world is reality no more, but it has to do with the world as not by any means annihilated. The man who was moved to seek what was moral and right, could no longer find it on such soil, but looked round about him to seek it elsewhere. The place which was pointed out to him is himself, his inner life, and external Nature; in the contemplation of Nature the spirit begins to have a sense of being present therein.

SECTION THREE

REVIVAL OF THE SCIENCES

THE deeper interest of the subject had been lost sight of, as we have seen, in the dryness and dulness of the content of thought, and in speculations which went wandering off into endless details. But now spirit gathered itself together, and rose to claim the right to find and know itself as actual self-consciousness, both in the supersensuous world and in immediate nature. This awakening of the selfhood of spirit brought with it the revival of the arts and sciences of the ancient world. This looked like a falling back into childhood, but it was really a spontaneous ascent into the Idea, a movement originating with self—while up to this time the intellectual world had been rather something given from without. From this proceeded all efforts and all inventions, the discovery of America and of the way to the East Indies. Thus in a very special way the love for the old, so-called heathen sciences once more awoke, for men turned to the works of the ancients, which had now become objects of study, as *studia humaniora*, where man is recognized in what concerns himself and in what he effects. These sciences, though at first they were placed in opposition to the divine, are rather themselves the divine, as living, however, in the reality of spirit. Men, because they are men, find it interesting to study men as men. With this a further consideration is intimately connected, namely, that when the formal culture of the mind, found among the Scholastics, became transformed into the Universal, the result necessarily was that thought knew and found itself in itself; from this the antithesis between the finite understanding and ecclesiastical dogma or faith consequently arose. The idea became prevalent that the understanding can recognize something to be false which the Church affirms to be true; and it was of importance that the understanding did so apprehend itself, although it was in opposition to the positive in general.

A. Study of the Ancients.

The first way in which the desire to find the human element in reference to what pertains to science manifested itself, was that an interest in such matters sprang up in the West, a receptive power where the ancients in their definiteness and beauty are concerned. But the revival of the arts and sciences, and especially of the study of ancient literature bearing on Philosophy, was at first in some measure a simple revival of the old philosophy in its earlier and original form, without anything new being added; this working up of old philosophies, to which a great number of writings were devoted, was thus the restoration of something forgotten only. The study of the Greeks was more especially revived; the knowledge of the Greek originals which the West acquired is connected with external political events. The West kept up constant intercourse with the Greeks through the Crusades, and Italy did so by means of commerce; yet there were no special diplomatic relations. Even the Roman laws were brought back from the East, until a code of the *corpus juris* was by chance discovered. But the West was again, and more effectually, brought into touch with the Greek East when, on the disastrous fall of the Byzantine Empire, the noblest and most distinguished of the Greeks fled to Italy. Earlier than this even, when the Greek Empire was being harassed by the Turks, ambassadors had been sent to the West in order to solicit help. These ambassadors were men of learning, and by their means—for as a rule they settled in the West—there was transplanted thither that love for antiquity to which we have referred. Petrarch in this way learned Greek from Barlaam, a monk in Calabria, where dwelt many belonging to the order of St. Basil; this order had monasteries in the south of Italy, and used Greek ritual. In Constantinople Barlaam had made the acquaintance of Greeks, particularly of Chrysoloras, who from 1395 chose Italy as his permanent dwelling-place. These Greeks made the West familiar with the works of the ancients, especially of Plato.[1] Too much honour is done to the monks when it is asserted that they preserved for us the writings of the ancients; these works, at least such as were in Greek, came rather from Constantinople, while the Latin portion of them, it is true, were preserved in the West. Acquaintance was now also for the first time made with Aristotle's own writings (*supra*, p. 75), and thereby the old philosophies were again revived, although mingled with intellectual vagaries of the utmost wildness.

Thus it was partly the old Platonic philosophy that was sought out, and partly the Neo-Platonic, as also the Aristotelian and Stoic, the Epicurean as far as it regarded physics, and the popular philosophy of Cicero in its first form; these were brought forward as authorities against Scholasticism, being in direct contradiction to it. Such endeavours are, however, connected rather with the history of literature and culture, and with the advancement of the same; we do not find originality in this philosophic work, nor can we recognize therein any forward step. We have still writings of that period, by which we find that each school of the Greeks found its adherents, and that Aristo-

[1] Buhle: Lehrb. d. Gesch. d. Phil., Part VI. Section I. pp. 125–128; Tennemann, Vol. IX. pp. 22, 23.

telians, Platonists, and so on appeared on the scenes, though they were of a very different stamp from those of olden times. For true instruction in philosophy we must, however, go to the original sources, the ancients.

1. Pomponatius.

Pomponatius was one of the most remarkable of these Aristotelians; among other subjects he wrote in 1534 on the immortality of the soul, and in so doing he showed—following a practice which was specially in vogue at that time—that this dogma, which he believed as a Christian, was according to Aristotle and reason incapable of proof.[1] The disciples of Averroës alleged that the universal νοῦς, which is present in thought, is immaterial and immortal, while the soul as numerically one is mortal; and Alexander Aphrodisiensis also maintained its mortality. Both of these opinions were condemned in 1513 at the Council of Benevento, under Leo X.[2] The vegetative and sensitive soul Pomponatius asserted to be mortal (c. VIII. p. 36; c. IX. pp. 51, 62–65): and he maintained that it is only through thought and reason that man partakes of immortality. Pomponatius was summoned before the Inquisition; but as cardinals protected him, no further notice was taken of the matter.[3] There were many other pure Aristotelians; especially among the Protestants at a later time were they general. The Scholastics were erroneously termed Aristotelians; therefore the Reformation was opposed to Aristotle only in appearance, but to the Scholastics it was opposed in fact.

[1] Pomponatius: Tractatus de immortalitate animæ, c. VII., VIII. p. 35; c. IX. pp. 57, 58; c. XII. pp. 89, 90; c. XV. p. 142.

[2] Ficinus: Prooemium in Plotinum, p. 2; Pomponatius, l. l. c. III. p. 9; c. IV. 12; Tennemann, Vol. IX. pp. 65–67.

[3] Bruck. Hist. crit. phil. T. IV. P. I. p. 164.

2. Bessarion, Ficinus, Picus.

Men now began to form acquaintance more especially with Plato, when manuscripts of his works were brought from Greece; Greeks, refugees from Constantinople, gave lectures on Plato's philosophy. Cardinal Bessarion of Trapezunt, at one time Patriarch of Constantinople, was specially active in making Plato known in the West.[1]

Ficinus, who was born in Florence in 1433, and died in 1499, the accomplished translator of Plato, was a man of note; it was mainly due to him that the study of Neo-Platonism, as presented by Proclus and Plotinus, was again revived. Ficinus wrote also a Platonic Theology. One of the Medici in Florence, Cosmo II., went so far as to found a Platonic Academy even in the fifteenth century. These Medici, the elder Cosmo, Lorenzo, Leo X., Clement VII., were patrons of all the arts and sciences, and made their court the resort of classical Greek scholars.[2]

Two counts of the name of Pico della Mirandola—Giovanni, and Giovanni Francesco, his nephew—were influential rather by virtue of their marked personality and their originality; the elder propounded nine hundred theses, fifty-five of which were taken from Proclus, and invited philosophers one and all to a solemn discussion of the same; he also in princely fashion undertook to pay the travelling expenses of those at a distance.[3]

3. Gassendi, Lipsius, Reuchlin, Helmont.

Somewhat later, and specially by Gassendi, the opponent of Descartes, the atom theory of Epicurus was again re-

[1] Brucker. Hist. crit. phil. T. IV. P. I. pp. 44, 45.

[2] Ficinus: Procemium in Plotinum, p. 1; Brucker. l. l. p. 49, 55, 48.

[3] Proclus: Theologia Platonis, Appendix, pp. 503–505; Tennemann, Vol. IX. p. 149.

vived. As a development therefrom the theory of molecules maintained its place thenceforth in physical science.

The revival of Stoic philosophy due to Lipsius was not so clearly evidenced.

In Reuchlin (Καπνίο), who was born at Pforzheim in Swabia in 1455, and who was himself the translator of several comedies of Aristophanes, the Cabalistic philosophy found a defender. He endeavoured also to reconstruct the Pythagorean philosophy proper; but he mingled with it much that is vague and mysterious. There was in hand a project to destroy all Hebrew books in Germany by an imperial decree, as had been done in Spain; Reuchlin deserves great credit for having prevented this.[1] On account of the entire lack of dictionaries, the study of the Greek language was rendered so difficult that Reuchlin travelled to Vienna for the purpose of learning Greek from a Greek.

Later on we find many profound thoughts in Helmont, an Englishman, who was born in 1618, and died in 1699.[2]

All these philosophies were carried on side by side with belief in Church dogmas, and without prejudice thereto; not in the sense in which the ancients conceived them. A mass of literature exists on this subject, containing the names of a multitude of philosophers, but it is a literature of the past, without the vitality characteristic of higher principles; it is in fact not a true philosophy at all, and I shall therefore not dwell any longer upon it.

4. Ciceronian Popular Philosophy.

Cicero's mode of philosophizing, a very general mode, was revived in an especial degree. It is a popular

[1] Tennemann, Vol. IX. pp. 164, 165; Tiedemann: Geist d. Spec. Phil. Vol. V. p. 483; Brucker. Hist. crit. phil. T. IV. P. I. pp. 358, 365, 366; Rixner: Handbuch d. Gesch. d. Phil. Vol. II. p. 206.

[2] Tennemann, Vol. IX. pp. 228–230; Brucker. l. l. p. 721.

style of philosophizing, which has no real speculative value, but in regard to general culture it has this importance, that in it man derives more from himself as a whole, from his outer and inner experience, and speaks altogether from the standpoint of the present. He is a man of understanding who says,—

"What helps a man in life, is what life itself has taught him."

The feelings, &c., of man obtained due recognition, we must observe, as against the principle of self-abnegation. A very large number of writings of this kind were issued, some of them simply on their own account, others aimed against the Scholastics. Although all that great mass of philosophical writings—much, for instance, that Erasmus wrote on similar subjects—has been forgotten, and though it possesses little intrinsic value, it was still of very great service, as succeeding the barrenness of the Scholastics and their groundless maunderings in abstractions:—groundless I say, for they had not even self-consciousness as their basis. Petrarch was one of those who wrote from himself, from his heart, as a thinking man.

This new departure in Philosophy applies in this regard to the reform of the Church by Protestantism also. Its principle is simply this, that it led man back to himself, and removed what was alien to him, in language especially. To have translated for German Christians the book on which their faith is grounded, into their mother-tongue, is one of the greatest revolutions which could have happened. Italy in the same way obtained grand poetic works when the vernacular came to be employed by such writers as Dante, Boccaccio and Petrarch; Petrarch's political works were however written in Latin. It is not until a thing is expressed in my mother tongue that it becomes my own possession. Luther and Melancthon cast the Scholastic element quite aside, and drew their conclusions from the Bible, from faith, from the human heart. Melancthon presents to us a calm popular philosophy, in which the human element makes itself felt, and which therefore forms the most striking contrast to the lifeless and jejune Scholasticism. This attack against the Scholastic method was made in the most different directions and in the most various forms. But all this belongs rather to the history of Religion than to that of Philosophy.

B. Certain Attempts in Philosophy.

A second series of writers who now appeared have mainly to do with particular attempts made in Philosophy which remained attempts merely, and are only found while this terrible time of upheaval lasted. Many individuals of that period saw themselves forsaken by what had hitherto been accepted by them as content, by the object which up to this time had formed the stay and support of their consciousness—by faith. Side by side with the peaceful re-appearance of the ancient philosophy there displayed itself, on the other hand, a multitude of individuals in whom a burning desire after the conscious knowledge of what is deepest and most concrete was violently manifested. It was spoilt, however, by endless fancies, extravagances of the imagination and a craze for secret, astrological, geomantic and other knowledge. These men felt themselves dominated, as they really were, by the impulse to create existence and to derive truth from their very selves. They were men of vehement nature, of wild and restless character, of enthusiastic temperament, who could not attain to the calm of knowledge. Though it cannot be denied that there was in them a wonderful insight into what was true and great, there is no doubt on the other hand that they revelled in all manner of corruption in thought and heart as well as in their outer life. There is thus to be found in them great originality and subjective energy of spirit; at the same time the content is heterogeneous and unequal, and their confusion of mind is great. Their fate, their lives, their writings—which often fill many volumes—manifest only this restlessness of their being, this tearing asunder, the revolt of their inner being against present existence and the longing to get out of it and reach certainty. These remarkable individuals really resemble the upheavals; tremblings and eruptions of a volcano which has become worked up in its depths and has brought forth new developments, which as yet are wild and uncontrolled. The most outstanding men of this nature are Cardanus, Bruno, Vanini, Campanella, and lastly Ramus. They are representative of the character of the time in this interval of transition, and fall within the period of the Reformation.

1. Cardanus.

Hieronymus Cardanus is of their number; he was remarkable as an individual of world-wide reputation, in whom the upheaval and fermentation of his time manifested itself in its utmost violence. His writings fill ten folio volumes. Cardanus was born in 1501 at Pavia, and died at Rome in 1575. He recounted his own history and described his character in his book *De vita propria*, where he makes an extraordinary confession of his sins, passing the severest possible judgment upon them. The following may serve to give a picture of these contradictions. His life was a series of the most varied misfortunes, external and domestic. He speaks first of his pre-natal history. He relates that his mother, when pregnant with him, drank potions in order to produce abortion. When he was still at the breast, there was an outbreak of the plague; the nurse who suckled him died of the pestilence, he survived. His father was very severe in his treatment of him. He lived sometimes in the most crushing poverty and the utmost want, sometimes in the greatest luxury. Afterwards he applied himself to science, became a Doctor of Medicine, and travelled much. He was celebrated far and wide; summons came to him from every quarter, several times he was called to Scotland. He writes that he cannot tell the sums of money that were offered to him. He was professor at Milan, first of mathematics and then of medicine; after that he lay for two years in Bologna in the strictest imprisonment, and had to undergo the most frightful tortures. He was a profound astrologer, and predicted the future for many princes, who on that account held him in the greatest awe and reverence.[1] He is a name of note in mathematics; we have from him still the *regula Cardani* for the solution of equations of the third degree, the only rule we have had up to this time.

He lived his whole life in perpetual inward and outward storms. He says that he suffered the greatest torments in his soul. In this inward agony he found the greatest delight in inflicting torture both on himself and others. He scourged himself, bit his lips, pinched himself violently, distorted his fingers, in order to free himself from the tortures of his spiritual disquietude and induce weeping, which brought him relief. The same contradictions were to be seen in his outward demeanour, which was sometimes quiet and decorous, while at other times he behaved as if he were crazy and demented, and that without any external provocation whatever, and in matters the most indifferent. Sometimes he put on decent clothes and made himself neat and trim, at other times he went in rags. He would be reserved, diligent, persevering in his work, and then would break out into excesses, wasting and squandering all that he had, his household goods and his wife's jewels. Sometimes he would walk quietly along, like other men; at other times he would rush on as if he were mad. The upbringing

[1] Brucker. Hist. crit. phil. T. IV. P. II. pp. 63, 64, 66-68; Buhle: Lehrb. d. Gesch. d. Phil. Part VI. Section I. pp. 360, 362; Cardanus: De vita propria, c. 4, pp. 9-11; Tiedemann, Geist d. spec. Philosophie, Vol. V. pp. 563, 564.

of his children, as was quite to be expected under the circumstances, was very bad. He had the unhappiness of seeing his sons turn out ill; one of them poisoned his own wife and was executed with the sword; he had his second son's ears cut off, to chastise him for being dissipated.[1]

He himself was of the wildest temperament, brooding deeply within himself, and yet breaking out into violence in the most contradictory manner; within him there also raged a consuming restlessness. I have epitomized the description which he gives of his own character, and now quote it: "I have by nature a mind of philosophic and scientific cast; I am witty, elegant, well-bred, fond of luxury, cheerful, pious, faithful, a lover of wisdom, reflective, enterprising, studious, obliging, emulous, inventive, self-taught. I have a longing to perform prodigies, I am crafty, cunning, bitter, versed in secrets, sober, diligent, careless, talkative, contemptuous of religion, vindictive, envious, melancholy, malicious, treacherous, a sorcerer, a magician, unhappy; I am surly to my family, ascetic, difficult to deal with, harsh, a soothsayer, jealous, a ribald talker, a slanderer, compliant, inconstant; such contradictoriness of nature and manners is to be found in me."[2]

His writings are in parts just as utterly unequal as his character. In them he gave vent to the wild vehemence of his nature; they are disconnected and contradictory, and were often written in the direst poverty. They contain a medley of all kinds of astrological and chiromantic superstition, yet lit up here and there with profound and brilliant flashes; there are Alexandrine and Cabalistic mysteries side

[1] Buhle: Lehrb. d. Gesch. d. Phil. Part VI. Section I. pp. 362-365; Tiedemann, Geist d. Spec. Phil. Vol. V. p. 565; Brucker. Hist. crit. phil. T. IV. P. II. pp. 71-74; Cardanus: De vita propria, c. 26, p. 70.

[2] Cardanus: De genitur. XII. p. 84; Buhle: Lehrbuch d. Gesch. d. Phil. Part VI. Section I. pp. 363, 364; Tiedemann: Geist. d. Spec. Phil. Vol. V. pp. 564, 565.

by side with perfectly lucid psychological observations of his own. He treated astrologically the life and deeds of Christ. His positive merit consists, however, rather in the stimulus which he gave to original production, and in this direction he exercised an important influence on his times. He boasted of the originality and novelty of his ideas, and the craze to be original drove him to the strangest devices. This represents the first form taken by the newly awakened and energizing reason in its spontaneous activity; to be new and different from others was regarded as tantamount to possessing a private claim to science.

2. Campanella.

Tommaso Campanella, a student of Aristotle, represents just such another medley of all possible dispositions. He was born at Stilo, in Calabria, in 1568, and died at Paris in 1639. Many of his writings still remain to us. For seven-and-twenty years of his life he was kept in strict imprisonment at Naples.[1] Such men as he aroused enormous interest and gave great offence, but on their own account they were productive of very little result. We have still to make special mention of Giordano Bruno and Vanini as belonging to this period.

3. Bruno.

Giordano Bruno was of an equally restless and effervescent temperament, and we see in him a bold rejection of all Catholic beliefs resting on mere authority. In modern times he has again been brought into remembrance by Jacobi (Werke, Vol. IV. Section II. pp. 5-46), who appended to his letters on Spinoza an abstract of one of Bruno's works.[2] Jacobi caused great attention to be paid to Bruno,

[1] Brucker. Hist. crit. phil. T. IV. P. II. pp. 108, 114-120; Tennemann, Vol. IX. pp. 290-295.

[2] Giordano Bruno: De la causa, principio et uno, Venetia 1584, 8,

more especially by his assertion that the sum of Bruno's teaching was the One and All of Spinoza, or really Pantheism; on account of the drawing of this parallel Bruno obtained a reputation which passes his deserts. He was less restless than Cardanus; but he had no fixed habitation on the earth. He was born at Nola in the province of Naples, and lived in the sixteenth century; the year of his birth is not known with certainty. He roamed about in most of the European states, in Italy, France, England, Germany, as a teacher of philosophy: he forsook Italy, where at one time he had been a Dominican friar, and where he had made bitter reflections both upon various Catholic dogmas—for instance, on transubstantiation and the immaculate conception of the Virgin—and upon the gross ignorance and scandalous lives of the monks. He then lived in Geneva in 1582, but there he fell out in the same way with Calvin and Beza, and could not live with them: he made some stay in several other French cities, such as Lyons; and after a time he came to Paris, where in 1585 he formally challenged the adherents of Aristotle, by following a practice greatly in favour in those days (*supra*, p. 112), and proposing for public disputation a series of philosophic theses, which were specially directed against Aristotle. They appeared under the title *Jord. Bruni Nol. Rationes articulorum physicorum adversus Peripateticos Parisiis propositorum, Vitebergæ apud Zachariam Cratonem*, 1588; he was not successful in them, however, as the position of the Aristotelians was still too well assured. Bruno was also in London; he visited Wittenberg in the year 1586; he likewise stayed in Prague and other universities and towns. In Helmstedt he was high in the favour of the Dukes of Brunswick-Lüneburg in 1589; after that he went to Frankfort-on-Main, where he had several of his works printed. He was a wandering professor and

which was certainly not really printed at Venice, since both it and the following work, De l'infinito, Universo e Mondi, Venetia 1584, 8, appeared at Paris. Both these works are dialogues.

author. Finally he came back to Italy in 1592, and lived in Padua for some time undisturbed, but at last he was seized in Venice by the Inquisition, cast into prison, sent on to Rome, and there in the year 1600, refusing to recant, he was burned at the stake as a heretic. Eye-witnesses, and amongst them Scioppius, recount that he met death with the most unflinching courage. He had become a Protestant when in Germany, and had broken the vows of his order.[1]

Among both Catholics and Protestants his writings were held to be heretical and atheistic, and therefore they were burned and destroyed, or kept in concealment. His complete works are hence very seldom met with; the greatest number of them are to be found in the University Library at Göttingen; the fullest account of them is given in Buhle's History of Philosophy (*supra*, Vol. I. p. 113). His works are for the most part rare, and in many cases interdicted; in Dresden they are still included among prohibited writings, and are therefore not to be seen there. Lately[2] an edition of them in the Italian language was prepared,[3] which possibly has never yet been issued. Bruno also wrote a great deal in Latin. Wherever he took up his abode for a time, he gave public lectures, wrote and published works; and this increases the difficulty of making complete acquaintance with his books. Many of his writings are for the above reason very similar in their matter, the form only being different, and in the evolution of his thoughts he never consequently advanced very much nor attained to any results. But the leading characteristic of his various writings is really to some extent the grand enthusiasm of a noble soul, which has a sense of indwelling

[1] Brucker. Hist. crit. phil. T. IV. P. II. pp. 15-29.

[2] Lectures of 1829–30.

[3] Opere di Giordano Bruno Nolano, ora per la prima volta raccolte e pubblicate da Adolfo Wagner in due volumi. Lipsia, Weidmann 1830.

spirit, and knows the unity of its own Being and all Being to be the whole life of thought. There is something bacchantic in his way of apprehending this deep consciousness; it overflows in becoming thus an object of thought, and in the expression of its riches. But it is only in knowledge that spirit can bring itself forth as a whole; when it has not yet attained to this point of scientific culture, it reaches out after all forms, without bringing them first into due order. Bruno displays just such an unregulated and multiform profusion; and on that account his expositions have frequently a dreamy, confused, allegorical appearance of mystical enthusiasm. Many of his writings are in verse, and much that is fantastic finds a place in them, as for instance when he says in one of his works, entitled *La Bestia Trionfante*, that something else must be put in place of the stars.[1] He sacrificed his personal welfare to the great enthusiasm which filled him, and which left him no peace. It is easy to say that he was "a restless being, who could get on with nobody." But whence did this restlessness come to him? What he could not get on with was the finite, the evil, the ignoble. Thence arose his restlessness. He rose to the one universal substantiality by putting an end to this separation of self-consciousness and nature, whereby both alike are degraded. God was in self-consciousness, it was admitted, but externally, and as remaining something different from self-consciousness, another reality; while Nature was made by God, being His creature, not an image of Him. The goodness of God displayed itself only in final causes, finite ends, as when it is said: "Bees make honey for man's food; the cork tree grows to provide stoppers for bottles."[2]

As to his reflections, Jacobi has by his recent[3] exposition

[1] Cf. Opere di Giordano Bruno pubbl. da Wagner. Introduzione, pp. xxiv., xxv.

[2] v. Hegel's Werke, Vol. VII. Section II. p. 10.

[3] Lectures of 1805–6.

of them made it seem as if it were a theory specially characteristic of Bruno that one living Being, one World-Soul, should penetrate all existence, and should be the life of all. Bruno asserted, in the first place, the unity of life and the universality of the World-Soul, and, in the second place, the indwelling presence of reason; but Bruno in so saying is far from being original, and in fact this doctrine is a mere echo of the Alexandrian. But in his writings there are two specially marked features. The first is the nature of his system, based as it is on his leading thoughts, or his philosophic principles generally, namely the Idea as substantial unity. The second, which is closely connected with the first, is his use of the *Art* of Lullius; this is specially emphasized and highly esteemed by him, the art of finding differences in the Idea: it he wished to bring into special recognition.

a. His philosophic thoughts, to express which he sometimes made use of Aristotle's concepts, give evidence of a peculiar, highly strung and very original mind. The substance of his general reflections is found in the greatest enthusiasm for the above-mentioned vitality of Nature, divinity, the presence of reason in Nature. His philosophy is thus on the whole certainly Spinozism, Pantheism. The separation of man from God or the world, all such relations of externality, have been superadded to his living idea of the absolute, universal unity of all things, for the expression of which idea Bruno has been so greatly admired. In his conception of things the main points are that, on the one hand, he gives the universal determination of matter, and, on the other hand, that of form.

α. The unity of life he thus determines as the universal, active understanding (*νοῦς*), which manifests itself as the universal form of all the world, and comprehends all forms in itself; it bears the same relation to the production of natural objects as does the understanding of man, and moulds and systematizes them, as the human understanding moulds the multitude of its concepts. It is the artist within, who shapes and forms the material without. From within the root or the seed-grain it makes the shoot come forth; from this again it brings the branches, and from them the twigs, and from out of the twigs it calls forth the buds, and leaves, and flowers. All is planned, prepared and perfected within. In the same way this universal reason within calls back their saps from the fruits and blossoms to the twigs, and so on. The universe is thus an infinite animal, in which all things live and move and have their being in modes the most diverse. The formal understanding is thus in no wise different from the Final Cause (the Notion of end, the entelechy, the unmoved principle, which we meet with in Aristotle); but these are just as truly also active understanding, the efficient cause (*causa efficiens*), this same producing force. Nature and Spirit are not separated; their unity is the formal understanding, in which is contained the pure Notion, not as in consciousness, but as free and independent, remaining within itself, and at the same time exercising activity and passing beyond itself. The understanding working towards one particular end is the inward form of the thing itself, an inward principle of the understanding. What is continually produced is in accordance with this form, and contained within it; what appears is determined as the form is in itself determined.[1] With Proclus in the same way the understanding, as substantial, is that which includes all things in its unity: life is the outgoing, the producing force: and the understanding as such similarly includes the returning force, which brings all things back into unity. In dealing with Kant's philosophy we shall have again to mention this determination of final purpose.

[1] Jacobi: Werke, Vol. IV. Section II. pp. 7–18; Tennemann, Vol. IX. pp. 391–394; Giordano Bruno: De la causa, principio et uno, Dialog. II. (Opere pubbl. da Ad. Wagner, Vol. I.), pp. 235–243.

That which has organic life, whose principle is formative, which has its efficacy in itself, and in the same only remains at home with itself and maintains itself, is nothing but the end, the activity determined in itself, which in its relation to what is different does not comport itself as mere cause, but returns upon itself.

β. Bruno, who asserts the final cause to be immediately operative, and the life immanent in the universe, asserts it also to be existent, as substance; he is therefore opposed to the conception of a merely extra-mundane understanding. To a certain extent Bruno distinguishes form and matter in substance, which itself, as the aforesaid activity of the Idea, is the unity of form and matter; thus matter has life in itself. The permanent element in the endless changes of existence is, he says, the first and absolute matter; although without form, it is nevertheless the mother of all forms, and receptive of all forms. Because matter is not without the first universal form, it is itself principle or in itself final cause. Form is immanent in matter; the one simply cannot exist without the other; thus matter itself brings about these changes of form, and the same matter runs through them all. What was at first seed becomes blade, then ear, then bread, chyle, blood, seed of animal, an embryo, a human being, a corpse, then once more earth, stone, or other substance; from sand and water frogs are produced. Here then we can perceive something which, although it transforms itself into all these things in turn, yet still in itself remains one and the same. This matter cannot be a body, for bodies have form; nor can it belong to the class which we term properties, attributes, or qualities, for these are liable to change. Thus nothing seems to be eternal and worthy of the name of a principle, except matter. Many have for this reason held matter to be the only reality, and all forms to be accidental. This error arises from the fact of their recognizing only a form of the second kind, and not that necessary first and eternal form, which is the form and source of all forms. In the same way the aforesaid matter, on account of its identity with the understanding which causes form beforehand, is itself intelligible, as the universal presupposition of all corporeality. Because it is everything in general, it is nothing in particular, neither air nor water, nor anything else, abstract or otherwise; it has no dimensions, in order to have all dimensions. The forms of matter are the inward power of matter itself; it is, as intelligible, the very totality of form.[1] This system of Bruno's is thus objective Spinozism, and nothing else; one can see how deeply he penetrated.

Bruno here asks the question: "But this first universal form and that first universal matter, how are they united, inseparable? Different—and yet one Being?" He answers by making use of the Aristotelian forms of δύναμις and ἐνέργεια: Matter is to be regarded as potentiality; in this way all possible forms of existence in a certain sense are included in the Notion of it. The passivity of matter must be regarded as pure and absolute. Now it is impossible to attribute existence to a thing which lacks the power to exist. Existence has, however, such an express reference to the active mode, that it is at once clear that the one cannot exist without the other, but that each of them pre-supposes the other. If therefore at all times a capacity of working, producing, creating, was there, so must there also have been at all times a capacity of being worked upon, produced, created. The perfect potentiality of the existence of things (matter) cannot precede their actual existence, and just as little can it remain

[1] Jacobi: Werke, Vol. IV. Section II. pp. 19–23, 28–31; Tennemann, Vol. IX. pp. 394–396, 398, 399; Giordano Bruno: De la causa, principio et uno, Dial. III. pp. 251–257; Dial. IV. pp. 269–274.

after that is past. The first and most perfect principle includes all existence in itself, can be all things, and is all things. Active power and potentiality, possibility and actuality are therefore in it one undivided and indivisible principle.[1] This simultaneousness of acting and being acted upon is a very important determination; matter is nothing without activity, form is therefore the power and inward life of matter. If matter were nothing but indeterminate potentiality, how would the determinate be arrived at? This simplicity of matter is itself only one moment of form: in wishing therefore to tear asunder matter and form, matter is at once established in one determination of form, but in so doing there is immediately established also the existence of the Other.

Thus the Absolute is determined for Bruno: it is not so with other things, which may exist and also may not exist, and which may be determined in one way or in another way. In regard to finite things and in finite determinations of the understanding the distinction between form and matter is thus present. The individual man is at every moment what he may be at that moment, but not everything which he may be in general and with reference to substance. The things which appear to be different are only modifications of one single thing which includes in its existence all other existence. The universe, unbegotten Nature, is, however, everything which it can be in reality and at one time, because it includes in itself the whole of matter, as well as the eternal, unchangeable form of its changing forms. But in its developments from moment to moment, its particular parts, qualities, individual existences, in its externality as a whole, it is no more what it is and may be; but a part such as this is only a shadow of the

[1] Jacobi: Werke, Vol. IV. Section II. pp. 23–25; Tennemann, Vol. IX. p. 396; Giordano Bruno: De la causa, principio et uno, Dial III. pp. 260, 261.

image of the first principle.[1] Thus Bruno wrote also a book, *De umbris idearum.*

γ. This is Bruno's fundamental idea. He says: "To recognize this unity of form and matter in all things, is what reason is striving to attain to. But in order to penetrate to this unity, in order to investigate all the secrets of Nature, we must search into the opposed and contradictory extremes of things, the maximum and the minimum." It is in these very extremes that they are intelligible, and become united in the Notion; and this union of them is infinite Nature. "To find the point of union is not the greatest matter; but to develop from the same its very opposite, this is the real and the deepest secret of the art."[2] It is saying much if we speak of knowing the development of the Idea as a necessity of determinations; we shall see later how Bruno proceeded to do this. He represents the original principle, which is elsewhere known as the form, under the Notion of the minimum, which is at the same time the maximum—One, which at the same time is All; the universe is this One in All. In the universe, he says, the body is not distinguished from the point, nor the centre from the circumference, nor the finite from the infinite, nor the maximum from the minimum. There is nothing but centre point; or the centre point is everywhere and in everything. The ancients expressed the same by saying of the Father of the gods, that he really had his dwelling-place in every point of the universe. It is the universe that first gives to things true reality; it is the substance of all things, the monad, the atom, the spirit poured out on all things, the innermost essence, the pure form.[3]

[1] Jacobi: Werke, Vol. IV. Section II. pp. 25, 26; Tennemann, Vol. IX. p. 397; Giordano Bruno: De la causa, principio et uno, Dial. III. p. 261.

[2] Jacobi: Werke, Vol. IV. Section II. pp. 32, 45; Tennemann, Vol. IX. pp. 399, 403, 404; Giordano Bruno: De la causa, principio et uno, Dial. IV. p. 275; Dial. V. p. 291.

[3] Jordanus Brunus: De Minimo, pp. 10, 16–18; Jacobi: Werke,

b. The second object to which Bruno devoted himself was the so-called Lullian Art, which received its name from its first inventor, the Scholastic Raymundus Lullus (*supra*, pp. 92-94). Bruno adopted this and carried it to completion; he termed it also his *ars combinatoria*. This art is in some respects like what we met with in Aristotle under the name of the Topics (Vol. II. pp. 217, 218), seeing that both give an immense number of "places" and determinations which were fixed in the conception like a table with its divisions, in order that these headings might be applied to all that came to hand. But the Topics of Aristotle did this in order to apprehend and determine an object in its various aspects, while Bruno rather worked for the sake of lightening the task of memory. He thus really connected the Lullian Art with the art of mnemonics as practised by the ancients, which has come into notice again in recent times, and which will be found described in greater detail in the *Auctor ad Herennium* (Libr. III. c. 17, sqq.). To give an example: one establishes for oneself a certain number of different departments in the imagination, which are to be chosen at pleasure; there may be perhaps twelve of these, arranged in sets of three, and indicated by certain words, such as Aaron, Abimelech, Achilles, Berg, Baum, Baruch, etc., into which divisions one inserts, as it were, what has to be learnt by heart, and forms it into a succession of pictures. In this way when we repeat it, we have not to say it from memory or out of our head, as we are accustomed to do, but

Vol. IV. Section II. pp. 34–39; Tennemann, Vol. IX. pp. 400–402; Giordano Bruno: De la causa, principio et uno, Dial. V. pp. 281–284.—On this opposition of the minimum and the maximum Bruno wrote several special works, for example, De triplici Minimo et Mensura libri V. Francofurti apud Wechelium et Fischer, 1591, 8; the text is hexameters, with notes and scholia; Buhle gives the title as De Minimo libri V. Another work bears the title: De Monade, Numero et figura liber; Item De Innumerabilibus, Immenso et Infigurabili: seu de Universo et Mundis libri VIII. Francof. 1591, 8.

we have only to read it off as if from a table. The only difficulty lies in making some ingenious connection between the content in question and the picture ; that gives rise to the most unholy combinations, and the art is therefore not one to be commended. Bruno also soon abandoned it, since what had been a matter of memory became a matter of imagination ; which was, of course, a descent. But since with Bruno the diagram is not only a picture of external images, but a system of universal determinations of thought, he certainly gave to this art a deeper inward meaning.[1]

a. Bruno passes over to this art from universal ideas which are given. Since namely one life, one understanding is in all things, Bruno had the dim hope of apprehending this universal understanding in the totality of its determinations, and of subsuming all things under it—of setting up a logical philosophy by its means, and making it applicable in all directions.[2] He says : The object of considera-

[1] Bruno wrote many such topico-mnemonic works, of which the earliest are the following : Philotheus Jordanus Brunus Nolanus De compendiosa architectura et complemento artis Lullii, Paris. ap. Æg. Gorbinum, 1582. 12.—J. Brunus Nol. De Umbris idearum, implicantibus Artem quærendi, &c., Paris. ap. eund. 1582. 8. The second part has the title : Ars memoriæ.—Ph. Jord. Bruni Explicatio XXX sigillorum &c. Quibus adjectus est Sigillus sigillorum, &c. It is evident from the dedication that Bruno published this work in England, therefore between 1582 and 1585.—Jordanus Brunus De Lampade combinatoria Lulliana, Vitebergæ 1587. 8. In the same place he wrote De Progressu et lampade venatoria Logicorum, Anno 1587, which he dedicated to the Chancellor of the Wittenberg University.—Jordanus Brunus De Specierum scrutinio et lampade combinatoria Raym. Lullii, Pragæ, exc. Georg. Nigrinus 1588. 8 ; also printed in the works of Raymund Lullius.—Also De imaginum, signorum et idearum compositione Libri III. Francofurti ap. Jo. Wechel. et Petr. Fischer. 1591. 8.

[2] Buhle : Geschichte der neuern Philos. Vol. II. Section II. p. 715 (717) ; Jordanus Brunus : De compendiosa architectura et complemento artis Lullii (Jordani Bruni Nolani scripta, quæ latine confecit, omnia, ed. A. Fr. Gfrörer, Stuttgard, 1835, Fasc. II.), c. 1, p. 238.

tion therein is the universe, in so far as it enters into the relation of the true, the knowable and the rational. Like Spinoza he distinguishes between the intelligible thing of reason and the actual thing: As metaphysics has for object the universal thing, which is divided into substance and accident, so the chief matter is that there is a single and more universal art which knits together and compasses round the thing of reason and the actual thing, and recognizes them both as harmonizing with one another, so that the many, be they of what kind they may, are led back to simple unity.[1]

β. For Bruno the principle in all this is the understanding generally: None other than the understanding whose activity extends beyond itself, which brings into existence the sensuous world. It is related to the illumination of the spirit as the sun is related to the eye: it relates therefore to a phenomenal manifold, illuminating this, not itself. The Other is the active understanding in itself, which is related to the objects of thought in their various classes, as the eye is to things visible.[2] The infinite form, the active understanding which dwells in reason, is the first, the principle, which develops; the process in some respects resembles what was met with in the Neo-Platonists. Bruno's great endeavour is really now to apprehend and demonstrate the modes of organizing this active understanding.

γ. This is presented more in detail as follows: To the pure truth itself, the absolute light, man approaches only; his Being is not absolute Being itself, which alone is the One and First. He rests only under the shadow of the Idea, whose purity is the light, but which at the same time partakes of the darkness. The light of substance emanates from this pure First Light, the light of accident emanates

[1] Buhle: Geschichte der neuern Philos. Vol. II. Section II. pp. 717, 718 (719, a-718, b); Jord. Brunus: De compend. architect. c. 5, p. 239.

[2] Buhle: Gesch. d. neuern Philos. Vol. II. Section II. p. 717 (719, a); Jord. Brun. De compend. architect. c. 2, 3, pp. 238, 239.

from the light of substance. This we met with also in Proclus (*supra*, Vol. II. p. 446) as the third moment in the first triad. This absolute principle in its unity is for Bruno the first matter, and the first act of this principle he names the original light (*actus primus lucis*). But substances and accidents, which are many, cannot receive the full light, they are therefore only included in the shadow of the light; in like manner the ideas also are only shadows thereof.[1] The development of Nature goes on from moment to moment; created things are only a shadow of the first principle, not the first principle itself.

δ. Bruno continues: From this super-essential (*superessentiale*)—an expression which is also met with in Proclus (*supra*, Vol. II. p. 441)—advance is made to the essences, from the essences to that which is, from that which is to their traces, images and shadows, and that in a double direction: both towards matter, in order to be produced within her (these shadows are then present in natural fashion), and also towards sensation and reason, in order to be known by means of these. Things withdraw themselves from the First Light towards the darkness. But since all things in the universe are in close connection, the lower with the middle, and those with the upper, the compound with the simple, the simple with those which are more simple, the material with the spiritual, in order that there may be one universe, one order and government of the same, one principle and aim, one first and last; so, following the sound of the lyre of the universal Apollo (an expression which we saw used by Heraclitus, Vol. I. pp. 284, 285), the lower can be led back

[1] Buhle: Gesch. d. neuern Philos. Vol. II. Section II. pp. 723, 724; Jordani Bruni De Umbris idearum (Jord. Bruni Nolani scripta, ed. A. Fr. Gfrörer, Fasc. II.): Triginta intentiones umbrarum, Intentio I-IV. pp. 300-302.

step by step to the higher, as fire was condensed and transformed into air, air into water, water into earth. Thus One Being is in all. That process is the same as this return, and they form a circle. Nature within her limits can produce all from all, and so the understanding can also know all from all.[1]

ε. The unity of opposites is explained more in detail as follows: The diversity of shadows is no real opposition. In the same conception the opposites are known, the beautiful and the ugly, the appropriate and the inappropriate, the perfect and the imperfect, the good and the evil. Imperfection, evil, ugliness, do not rest upon special ideas of their own; they become known in another conception, not in one peculiar to themselves, which is nothing. For this that is peculiarly theirs is the non-existent in the existent, the defect in the effect. The first understanding is the original light; it streams its light out of the innermost to the outermost, and draws it again from the outermost to itself. Every Being can, according to its capacity, appropriate somewhat of this light.[2]

ζ. The real element in things is just that which is intelligible, not that which is perceived or felt, or what is peculiar to the individual; whatever else is termed real, the sensuous, is non-Being. All that comes to pass beneath the sun, all that dwells in the region of matter, falls under the notion of vanity (finitude). Seek to take from Ideas a firm basis for thy conceptions, if thou art wise. The pure light of things is nothing but this knowableness, which proceeds from the first understanding and is directed towards it; the non-existent is not known. What is here

[1] Buhle: Gesch. d. neuern Philos. Vol. II. Section II. pp. 724-726; Jordanus Brunus: De Umbris idearum, Intentio V-IX. pp. 302-305.

[2] Buhle: Gesch. d. neuern Philos. Vol. II. Section II. pp. 727, 731; Jordanus Brunus: De Umbris idearum, Intentio XXI. p. 310; De triginta idearum conceptibus: Conceptus X. p. 319.

contrast and diversity, is in the first understanding harmony and unity. Try therefore if thou canst identify the images thou hast received, if thou canst harmonize and unite them; thus thou wilt not render thy mind weary, thy thoughts obscure, and thy memory confused. Through the idea which is in the understanding a better conception of anything will be formed than by means of the form of the natural thing in itself, because this last is more material: but that conception is reached in a supreme degree through the idea of the object as it exists in the divine understanding.[1] The differences which are here given, are therefore no differences at all; but all is harmony. To develop this was therefore Bruno's endeavour; and the determinations, as natural in that divine understanding, correspond with those which appear in the subjective understanding. Bruno's art consists only in determining the universal scheme of form, which includes all things within itself, and in showing how its moments express themselves in the different spheres of existence.

η. The main endeavour of Bruno was thus to represent the All and One, after the method of Lullus, as a system of classes of regular determinations. Hence in the manner of Proclus he specifies the three spheres: First, the original form (ὑπερουσία) as the originator of all forms; secondly, the physical world, which impresses the traces of the Ideas on the surface of matter, and multiplies the original picture in countless mirrors set face to face; thirdly, the form of the rational world, which individualizes numerically for the senses the shadows of the Ideas, brings them into one, and raises them to general conceptions for the understanding. The moments of the original form itself are termed Being,

[1] Buhle: Gesch. d. neuern Philos. Vol. II. Section II. pp. 730-734; Jordani Bruni De Umbris idearum: De triginta idearum conceptibus, Conceptus VII. X. XIII. XXVI. pp. 318-320, 323, 324.

goodness (nature or life), and unity. (Something similar to this we also met with in Proclus, Vol. II. p. 445.) In the metaphysical world the original form is thing, good, principle of plurality (*ante multa*); in the physical world it manifests itself in things, goods, individuals; in the rational world of knowledge it is derived from things, goods and individuals.[1] Unity is the agent that brings them back once more; and Bruno, while distinguishing the natural and metaphysical world, seeks to set up the system of the above determinations, in order to show at once how the same thing is in one way a natural appearance, and in another way an object existing for thought.

Since Bruno sought to apprehend this connection more closely, he considers thinking as a subjective art and activity of the soul, representing inwardly and in accordance with the ordinary conception, as it were through an inward writing, what Nature represents externally, as it were, through an outward writing. Thinking, he says, is the capability both of receiving into one's self this external writing of nature and of imagining and substantiating the inward writing in the outward. This art of thinking inwardly and organizing outwardly in accordance with the same, and the capacity to reverse the process—an art possessed by the soul of man—Bruno places in the closest connection with the art of the nature of the universe, with the energy of the absolute World-principle, by means of which all is formed and fashioned. It is one form which develops; it is the same world-principle which causes form in metals, plants and animals, and which in man thinks and organizes outside himself, only that it expresses itself in its operations in an endlessly varied manner throughout the entire world. Inwardly and outwardly there is con-

[1] Buhle: Gesch. d. neuern Philos. Vol. II. Section II. p. 745; Jordani Bruni Explicatio triginta sigillorum: Sigillus Sigillorum, P. II. § 11.

sequently one and the same development of one and the same principle.[1]

In his *Ars Lulliana* Bruno made the attempt to determine and systematize these various writings of the soul, by means of which also the organizing world-principle reveals itself. He assumes therein twelve principal kinds of writing, or classes of natural forms, to form a starting-point: "*Species, Formæ, Simulacra, Imagines, Spectra, Exemplaria, Indicia, Signa, Notæ, Characteres et Sigilli*. Some kinds of writing are connected with the external sense, like external forms, pictures and ideals (*extrinseca forma, imago, exemplar*); these painting and other plastic arts represent, by imitating Mother Nature. Some are connected with the inner sense, where—with regard to mass, duration, number—they are magnified, extended in time and multiplied; such are the products of fancy. Some are connected with a common point of similarity in several things; some are so divergent from the objective nature of things that they are quite imaginary. Finally, some appear to be peculiar to art, as *signa, notæ, characteres et sigilli*; by means of these the powers of art are so great that it seems to be able to act independently of Nature, beyond Nature, and, when the matter in question involves it, even against Nature."[2]

So far all, on the whole, goes well; it is the carrying out of the same scheme in all directions. All respect is due to this attempt to represent the logical system of the inward artist, the producing thought, in such a way that the forms of external Nature correspond thereto. But while the system of Bruno is otherwise a grand one, in it the

[1] Buhle: Gesch. d. neuern Philos. Vol. II. Section II. p. 734; cf. Jordan. Brun. De Umbris Idearum: Ars Memoriæ, I.–XI. pp. 326–330.

[2] Buhle: Gesch. d. neuern Philos. Vol. II. Section II. pp. 734, 735; Jordan. Brun. De Umbris Idearum: Ars Memoriæ, XII. pp. 330, 331.

determinations of thought nevertheless at once become superficial, or mere dead types, as in later times was the case with the classification of natural philosophy; for Bruno merely enumerates the moments and contrasts of the system, just as the natural philosophers developed the threefold character in every sphere, regarded as absolute. Further or more determinate moments Bruno has done nothing more than collect together; when he tries to represent them by figures and classifications, the result is confusion. The twelve forms laid down as basis neither have their derivation traced nor are they united in one entire system, nor is the further multiplication deduced. To this part of his subject he devoted several of his writings (*De sigillis*), and in different works it is presented in different ways; the appearances of things are as letters, or symbols, which correspond with thoughts. The idea is on the whole praiseworthy compared with the fragmentariness of Aristotle and the Scholastics, according to whom every determination is fixed once for all. But the carrying out of the idea is in part allied with the Pythagorean numbers, and consequently unmethodical and arbitrary; and in part we find metaphorical, allegorical combinations and couplings, where we cannot follow Bruno; in this attempt to introduce order, all things are mingled together in the wildest disorder.

It is a great beginning, to have the thought of unity; and the other point is this attempt to grasp the universe in its development, in the system of its determinations, and to show how the outward appearance is a symbol of ideas. These are the two aspects of Bruno's teaching which had to be taken into consideration.

4. Vanini.

Julius Cæsar Vanini has also to be mentioned as belonging to this period; his first name was really Lucilius. He has many points of similarity with Bruno, and, like him, he suffered as a martyr on account of philosophy; for he shared Bruno's fate, which was to be burned at the stake. He was born in 1586 at Taurozano in the province of Naples. He wandered from country to country; we find him in Geneva, and then in Lyons, whence he fled to England in order to save himself from the Inquisition. After two years he returned to Italy. In Genoa he taught Natural Philosophy on the system of Averroës, but did not bring himself into favour. In his travels he met with all manner of strange adventures, and engaged in many and various disputations on philosophy and theology. He became more and more an object of suspicion, and fled from Paris; he was summoned before the tribunal on a charge of impiety, not of heresy. Franconus, his accuser, stated on oath that Vanini had uttered blasphemies. Vanini protested that he had remained faithful to the Catholic Church, and to his belief in the Trinity; and in answer to the charge of atheism he took up a straw from the ground in the presence of his judges, and said that even this straw would convince him of the existence of God. But it was of no avail; in 1619 at Toulouse in France he was condemned to the stake, and before the carrying out of this sentence his tongue was torn out by the executioner. How the case was proved against him is not, however, clear; the proceedings seem to have been in great part due to personal enmity, and to the zeal for persecution which filled the clergy in Toulouse.[1]

Vanini derived his chief stimulus from the originality of Cardanus. In him we see reason and philosophy taking a direction hostile to theology, while Scholastic philosophy went hand in hand with theology, and theology was sup-

[1] Brucker. Hist. crit. phil. T. IV. P. II. pp. 671-677; Buhle: Gesch. d. neuern Phil. Vol. II. Section II. pp. 866-869.

posed to be confirmed thereby. Art developed in the Catholic Church, but free thought broke off from, and remained alien to it. In Bruno and Vanini the Church took her revenge for this; she renounced science, and took up a position of hostility to it.

Vanini's philosophy does not go very far; he admires the living energy of Nature; his reasonings were not deep, but were more of the nature of fanciful ideas. He always chose the dialogue form; and it is not evident which of the opinions stated are his own. He wrote commentaries on Aristotle's works on Physics. We have two other works by Vanini, which are very rare. The one is styled: *Amphitheatrum æternæ providentiæ divino-magicum, christiano-physicum, nec non astrologo-catholicum, adversus veteres philosophos, Atheos, Epicureos, Peripateticos et Stoicos. Auctore Julio Cæsare Vanino, Lugd.* 1615; in this he gives a very eloquent account of all these philosophies and their principles, but the manner in which he refutes them is rather feeble. The second work is entitled: "On the Wonderful Secrets of Nature, the Queen and Goddess of Mortals" (*De admirandis Naturæ, reginæ Deæque mortalium, arcanis libr. IV., Lutetiæ* 1616); it was printed "with the approval of the Sorbonne," which at first found in it nothing "which contradicted and was hostile to the Catholic Apostolic and Roman religion." It contains scientific investigations into various matters belonging to physics and natural history, and is also in dialogue form, without definite indication being given as to which of the characters is made the mouthpiece of Vanini's own opinions. What one finds is assurances from him that he would believe this or that doctrine if he had not received Christian teaching. Vanini's tendency, however, was towards naturalism; he showed that it is Nature that is the Deity, that all things had a mechanical genesis. He therefore explained the whole universe in its connection by efficient causes alone, not by final causes; but the statement of this is made in such a way that the writer does not give it as his own conclusion.[1]

Thus Vanini placed reason in opposition to faith and church dogma, as had already been done by Pomponatius (*supra*, p. 111) and others. Yet all the time that they were proving by reason this or that dogma which is in direct contradiction to the Christian belief, they were declaring that they submitted their conviction to the Church—a course which was always adopted by Bayle afterwards in the reformed church. Another practice of these philosophers was to bring forward all sorts of arguments and theories contradictory of theological dogmas, as so many insoluble difficulties and contradictions brought about by reason, which were, however, by them submitted to faith. Thus, for instance, Bayle says in the article "Manichæans" found in his critical *Dictionnaire*—in which he touches on many philosophic conceptions—that the assertion of the existence of two principles cannot be disproved, but that we must submit herein to the Church. In this fashion all possible arguments were advanced against the Church. Vanini thus states objections against the Atonement, and brings forward arguments to prove that Nature is God. Now men were convinced that reason could not be contradictory of the Christian dogmas, and no faith was placed in the sincerity of a submission which consisted in giving up what one was convinced of by reason; therefore Galileo, because he defended the system of Copernicus, had to recant on his knees, and Vanini was burned at the stake. Both of them had in vain chosen the dialogue form for their writings.

Vanini certainly made one of the speakers in the Dialogues prove (*De naturæ arcanis*, p. 420) even "out of the text of the Bible, that the devil is mightier than God," and that

[1] Buhle: Lehrbuch. d. Gesch. d. Phil. Part VI. Section I. pp. 410-415; Brucker. Hist. crit. phil. T. IV. P. II. pp. 677-680; Buhle: Gesch. d. neuern Philos. Vol. II. Section II. pp. 870-878.

therefore God does not rule the world. Among his arguments are the following: It was against the will of God that Adam and Eve sinned, and thus brought the whole human race to ruin (*ad interitum*): Christ also was crucified by the powers of darkness. Moreover it is the will of God that all men should be saved. But of Catholics there are very few in comparison with the rest of the world, and the Jews often fell away from their faith; the Catholic religion extends only over Spain, France, Italy, Poland and a part of Germany. If there were to be deducted also the atheists, blasphemers, heretics, whoremongers, adulterers, and so on, there would be still fewer left. Consequently the devil is mightier than God. These are arguments of reason; they are not to be refuted; but he submitted himself to the faith. It is remarkable that no one believed this of him; the reason thereof being that it was impossible for him to be in earnest with the refutation of what he asserted to be rational. That the refutation was but weak and subjective does not justify anyone in doubting Vanini's sincerity; for poor reasons may be convincing for the subject, just as the subject holds to his own rights in respect of objective matters. What lies at the bottom of the proceedings against Vanini is this, that when a man by means of his reason has come to perceive something which seems to him incontrovertible, he cannot but adhere to these definite perceptions, he cannot believe what is opposed to them. It is impossible to believe that faith is stronger in him than this power of perception.

The Church in this way fell into the strange contradiction of condemning Vanini, because he did not find her doctrines in accordance with reason, and yet submitted himself to them; she thus appeared to demand—a demand which she emphasized with the burning pile—not that her doctrines should be considered above reason, but in accordance with it, and that reason should have merely the formal function of explaining the content of theology, without adding anything of her own. This susceptibility of the Church is inconsistent, and entangled her in contradictions. For in earlier times she certainly admitted that reason could not grasp what was revealed, and that it was consequently a matter of little importance to refute and solve by reason the objections which reason itself brought forward. But as she now would not permit the contradiction of faith and reason to be taken seriously, but burned Vanini at the stake as an atheist for professing so to do, it was implied that the doctrine of the Church cannot contradict reason, while man has yet to submit reason to the Church.

There is kindled here the strife between so-called revelation and reason, in which the latter emerges independently, and the former is separated from it. Up to this time both were one, or the light of man was the light of God; man had not a light of his own, but his light was held to be the divine. The Scholastics had no knowledge having a content of its own beyond the content of religion; philosophy remained entirely formal. But now it came to have a content of its own, which was opposed to the content of religion; or reason felt at least that it had its own content, or was opposing the form of reasonableness to the immediate content of the other.

This opposition had a different meaning in former times from what it bears now-a-days; the earlier meaning is this, that faith is the doctrine of Christianity, which is given as truth, and by which as truth man has to remain. We have here faith in this content, and opposed to this stands conviction by means of reason. But now this faith is transferred into the thinking consciousness itself; it is a relation of self-consciousness itself to the facts which it finds within itself, not to the objective content of the doctrine. In respect to the earlier opposition a distinction must be drawn in the objective creed; the one part of it is the teaching of the Church as dogma, the teaching as to the nature of God, that He is Three in One; to this pertains the appearing of God in the world, in the flesh, the relation of man to this divine nature, His holiness and divinity. That is the part which has to do with the eternal verities, the part which is of absolute interest for men; this part is in its content essentially speculative, and can be object only for the speculative Notion. The other part, belief in which is also required, has reference to other external conceptions, which are connected with that content; to this pertains the whole extent of what belongs to history, in the Old and New Testament as well as in the Church. A belief in all this finite element may be demanded also. If a man, for instance, did not believe in ghosts, he would be taken for a free-thinker, an atheist: it would be just the same if a man did not believe that Adam in Paradise ate of the forbidden fruit. Both parts are placed upon the one level; but it tends to the destruction of Church and faith, when belief is demanded for these parts alike. It is to the external conceptions that attention has been chiefly directed by those who have been decried as opponents of Christianity and as atheists, down to the time of Voltaire. When external conceptions such as these are held to firmly, it is inevitable that contradictions should be pointed out.

5. Petrus Ramus.

Pierre de la Ramée was born in 1515 in Vermandois, where his father worked as a day-labourer. He early betook himself to Paris, in order to satisfy his desire for learning: he was, however, obliged on two occasions to leave it on account of the difficulty he experienced in procuring a subsistence, before he obtained employment as a servant at the *Collége de Navarre.* Here he found an opportunity of extending his knowledge; he occupied himself with the Aristotelian philosophy and with mathematics, and he distinguished himself in disputation by extraordinary oratorical and dialectical readiness. In a disputation for obtaining the degree of *magister*, he came publicly forward with a thesis that caused a great sensation: "All that Aristotle taught is not true;" and the honour fell to him. Having became *magister*, he attacked so bitterly and violently the Aristotelian logic and dialectic, that the government took notice of it. He was now accused of undermining by his anti-Aristotelian opinions the foundations of religion and science; this accusation was brought before the parliament of Paris by the enemies of Ramus, as a criminal case. But because the parliament appeared disposed to act in a judicial way, and seemed favourably inclined to Ramus, the complaint was withdrawn, and brought before the council of the king. The latter decided that Ramus should hold a disputation with his opponent Goveanus before a special commission of five judges, two of whom Goveanus was to choose, and two Ramus, while the king was to appoint the president; these judges were to lay their opinion of the result before the king. The interest of the public was intense, but the contest was conducted in the most pedantic way. On the first day Ramus maintained that the Aristotelian logic and dialectic were imperfect and faulty, because the *Organon* did not begin with a definition. The commission decided that a disputation or a dissertation requires indeed a definition, but in dialectic it is not necessary. On the second day Ramus criticized the Aristotelian logic for its want of arrangement; this, he asserted, is essential. The majority of the judges, consisting of the commissioner of the king and the two nominees of the opponent Goveanus, now wished to annul the investigation as far as it had gone, and to set to work in another way, since the assertions of Ramus put them in a difficulty. He appealed to the king, who, however, refused to hear him, and decided that the decision of the judges should be considered final. Ramus was hence condemned, but the other two took no share in the matter, and, indeed, resigned. The decision was publicly placarded in all the streets of Paris, and sent to all the academies of learning throughout Europe. Plays aimed against Ramus were performed in the theatres, greatly to the delight of the Aristotelians. The public generally took a very lively interest in such disputes, and a number of contests of this kind had already taken place on similar questions of the schools. For example, the professors in a royal *Collége* disputed with the theologians of the Sorbonne whether *quidam, quisquis, quoniam* should be said or *kidem, kiskis, koniam,* and from this dispute a case before parliament arose, because the doctors took away his benefice from a theologian who said *quisquis*. Another hot and bitter controversy came before the magistrates as to whether *ego amat* was as correct as *ego amo*, and this dispute had to be suppressed by them. Finally Ramus obtained a public educational appointment, a professorship in Paris; but because he had become a Huguenot he had to vacate this office several times in the internal disquietude that prevailed; on one occasion he even went to travel in Germany. On St. Bartholomew's Eve in 1572, Ramus finally fell, murdered through the instrumentality of his enemies; one of his colleagues who was among his bitterest enemies, Charpentier, had engaged assassins for the purpose, by whom Ramus was frightfully maltreated, and then thrown down from an upper window.[1]

Ramus aroused great interest, more especially by his attacks on the Aristotelian dialectic as it had hitherto existed, and he contributed very greatly to the simplification of the formal nature of the rules of dialectic. He is specially famed for his extreme hostility to the scholastic logic, and for having set up in opposition to it a logic of Ramus—an opposition which has spread so far that even in the history of literature in Germany we find various factions of Ramists and anti-Ramists and semi-Ramists mentioned.

[1] Buhle: Gesch. d. neuern Philos. Vol. II. Sec. II. pp. 670-680; Brucker. Hist. crit. phil. T. IV. P. II. pp. 548-562.

There are many other remarkable men who come within this period and who are usually mentioned in the history of Philosophy, such as Michael of Montaigne, Charron, Macchiavelli, etc. The popular writings of the first two contain pleasing, refined and spiritual thoughts on human life, social relationships, the right and good. The efforts of such men are counted as philosophy in as far as they have drawn from their consciousness, from the sphere of human experience, from observation, from what takes place in the world and in the heart. It is in a philosophy of life that they have comprehended and imparted such experiences; they are thus both entertaining and instructive. In accordance with the principle on which they worked, they entirely forsook the sources from which Scholastic knowledge had up to this time been derived, and also the methods hitherto prevalent of acquiring it. But because they do not make the question of highest interest to Philosophy the object of their investigation, and do not reason from thought, they do not properly belong to the history of Philosophy, but to general culture and to the healthy human understanding. They have contributed to man's taking a greater interest in his own affairs, to his obtaining confidence in himself; and this is their main service. Man has looked within his heart again and given to it its proper value; then he has restored to his own heart and understanding, to his faith, the essence of the relationship of the individual to absolute existence. Although still a divided heart, this division, this yearning, has become a disunion within itself; and man feels this disunion within himself, and along with that his rest in himself. But here we must notice a transition, with which we are concerned, on account of the universal principle which in it is known in a higher way and in its true authority.

C. The Reformation.

It was in the Lutheran Reformation that the great revolution appeared, as, after the eternal conflicts and the terrible discipline which the stiff-necked Germanic character had undergone and which it had to undergo, mind came to the consciousness of reconciliation with itself, a reconciliation whose form required that it should be brought about within the mind. From the Beyond man was thus called into the presence of spirit, as earth and her bodily objects, human virtues and morality, the individual heart and conscience, began to have some value to him. In the church, if marriage was not held to be immoral, self-restraint and celibacy were considered higher, but now marriage came to be looked on as a divine institution. Then poverty was esteemed better than possession, and to live on alms was considered higher than to support oneself honestly by the work of one's hands; now, however, it becomes known that poverty is not the most moral life, for this last consists in living by one's work and taking pleasure in the fruits thereof. The blind obedience by which human freedom was suppressed, was the third vow taken by the monks, as against which freedom, like marriage and property, was now also recognized as divine. Similarly on the side of knowledge man turned back into himself from the Beyond of authority; and reason was recognized as the absolutely universal, and hence as divine. Now it was perceived that it is in the mind of man that religion must have its place, and the whole process of salvation be gone through—that man's salvation is his own affair, and that by it he enters into relationship with his conscience and into immediate connection with God, requiring no mediation of priests having the so-called means of grace within their hands. There is indeed a mediation present still by means of doctrine, perception, the observation of self and of one's actions; but that is a mediation without a separating wall, while formerly a brazen wall of division was present separating the laity from the church. It is thus the spirit of God that must dwell within the heart of man, and this indwelling spirit must operate in him.

Although Wycliffe, Huss, and Arnold of Brescia had started from scholastic philosophy with similar ends in view, they did not possess the character requisite to enable them modestly, and without any learned scholastic convictions, to set aside everything but mind and spirit. It was with Luther first of all that freedom of spirit began to exist in embryo, and its form indicated that it would remain in embryo. This beginning of the reconciliation of man with himself, whereby divinity is brought into man's actuality, is thus at first principle alone. The unfolding of this freedom and the self-reflecting grasp of the same was a subsequent step, in the same way as was the working out of the Christian doctrine in the Church in its time. The subjective thought and knowledge of man, which enables him, being satisfied in his activity, to have joy in his work and to consider his work as something both permissible and justifiable —this value accorded to subjectivity now required a higher confirmation, and the highest confirmation, in order to be made perfectly legitimate, and even to become absolute duty; and to be able to receive this confirmation it had to be taken in its purest form. The mere subjectivity of man, the fact that he has a will, and with it directs his actions this way or that, does not constitute any justification: for else the barbarous will, which fulfils itself in subjective ends alone, such as cannot subsist before reason, would be justified. If, further, self-will obtains the form of universality, if its ends are conformable to reason, and it is apprehended as the freedom of mankind, as legal right which likewise belongs to others, there is therein only indeed the element of permission, but still there is much in the end being recognized as permitted, and not as absolutely sinful. Art and industry receive through this principle new activity, since now their activity is justified. But we always find the principle of personal spirituality and independence at first limited to particular spheres of objects merely, in accordance with its content. Not until this principle is known and recognized in relation to the absolutely existent object, *i.e.* in relation to God, and is likewise grasped in its perfect purity, free from desires and finite ends, does it receive its highest confirmation, and that is its sanctification through religion.

This, then, is the Lutheran faith, in accordance with which man stands in a relation to God which involves his personal existence: that is, his piety and the hope of his salvation and the like all demand that his heart, his subjectivity, should be present in them. His feelings, his faith, the inmost certainty of himself, in short, all that belongs to him is laid claim to, and this alone can truly come under consideration: man must himself repent from his heart and experience contrition; his own heart must be filled with the Holy Ghost. Thus here the principle of subjectivity, of pure relation to me personally, *i.e.* freedom, is recognized, and not merely so, but it is clearly demanded that in religious worship this alone should be considered. The highest confirmation of the principle is that it alone has value in the eyes of God, that faith and the subjection of the individual heart are alone essential: in this way this principle of Christian freedom is first presented and brought to a true consciousness. Thereby a place has been set apart in the depths of man's inmost nature, in which alone he is at home with himself and at home with God; and with God alone is he really himself, in the conscience he can be said to be at home with himself. This sense of being at home should not be capable of being destroyed through others; no one should presume to have a place therein. All externality in relation to me is thereby banished, just as is the externality of the Host; it is only in communion and faith that I stand in relation to God. The distinction between the laity and the priests is by it removed; there are no longer any laymen, for in religion each by himself is enjoined to know personally what it is. Responsibility is not to be avoided; good works without spiritual reality in them are no longer of avail; there must be the heart which relates itself directly to God without mediation, without the Virgin, and without the Saints.

This is the great principle—that all externality disappears in the point of the absolute relation to God; along with this externality, this estrangement of self, all servitude has also disappeared. With it is connected our ceasing to tolerate prayer in foreign tongues, or to study the sciences in such. In speech man is productive; it is the first externality that he gives himself, the simplest form of existence which he reaches in consciousness. What man represents to himself, he inwardly places before himself as spoken. This first form is broken up and rendered foreign if man is in an alien tongue to express or conceive to himself what concerns his highest interest. This breach with the first entrance into consciousness is accordingly removed; to have one's own right to speak and think in one's own language really belongs to liberty. This is of infinite importance, and without this form of being-at-home-with-self subjective freedom could not have existed; Luther could not have accomplished his Reformation without translating the Bible into German. Now the principle of subjectivity has thus become a moment in religion itself, and in this way it has received its absolute recognition, and has been grasped as a whole in the form in which it can only be a moment in religion. The injunction to worship God in spirit is now fulfilled. Spirit, however, is merely conditioned by the free spirituality of the subject. For it is this alone which can be related to spirit; a subject who is not free does not stand in an attitude of spirituality, does not worship God in spirit. This is the general signification of the principle.

Now this principle was at first grasped in relation to religious objects only, and thereby it has indeed received its absolute justification, but still it has not been extended to the further development of the subjective principle itself. Yet in so far as man has come to the consciousness of being reconciled to himself, and of only being able to reconcile himself in his personal existence, he has in his actuality likewise attained another form. The otherwise hearty and vigorous man may also, in as far as he enjoys, do so with a good conscience; the enjoyment of life for its own sake is no longer regarded as something which is to be given up, for monkish renunciation is renounced. But to any other content the principle did not at first extend. Yet further, the religious content has more specially been apprehended as concrete, as it is for the recollection, and into this spiritual freedom the beginning and the possibility of an unspiritual mode of regarding things has thus entered. The content of the *Credo*, speculative as it is in itself, has, that is to say, an historical side. Within this barren form the old faith of the church has been admitted and allowed to exist, so that in this form it has to be regarded by the subject as the highest truth. The result then follows that all development of the dogmatic content in a speculative manner is quite set aside. What was required is man's inward assurance of his deliverance, of his salvation—the relation of the subjective spirit to the absolute, the form of subjectivity as aspiration, repentance, conversion. This new principle has been laid down as paramount, so that the content of truth is clearly of importance; but the teaching respecting the nature and the process of God is grasped in the form in which it at first appears for the ordinary conception. Not only have all this finality, externality, unspirituality, this formalism of scholastic philosophy, been on the one hand discarded, and with justice, but, on the other, the philosophic development of the doctrines of the church has been also set aside, and this is done in connection with the very fact that the subject is immersed in his own heart. This immersion, his penitence, contrition, conversion, this occupation of the subject with himself, has become the moment of first importance; but the subject has not immersed himself in the content, and the earlier immersion of spirit therein has also been rejected. Even to this present day we shall find in the Catholic Church and in her dogmas the echoes, and so to speak the heritage of the philosophy of the Alexandrian school; in it there is much more that is philosophic and speculative than in the dogmatism of Protestantism, even if there is still in this an objective element and if it has not been made perfectly barren, as though the content were really retained only in the form of history. The connection of Philosophy with the theology of the Middle Ages has thus in the Catholic Church been retained in its essentials; in Protestantism, on the contrary, the subjective religious principle has been separated from Philosophy, and it is only in Philosophy that it has arisen in its true form again. In this principle the religious content of the Christian Church is thus retained, and it obtains its confirmation through the testimony of spirit that this content shall only hold good for me in as far as it makes its influence felt in my conscience and heart. This is the meaning of the words: "If any man will do his will, he shall know of the doctrine whether it be of God." The criterion of truth is how it is confirmed in my heart; the fact that I judge and know rightly—or that what I hold to be true is the truth—must be revealed to my heart. Truth is what it is in *my* mind; and, on the other hand, my spirit is only then in its proper attitude to truth when truth is within it, when the spirit and its content are related thus. One cannot be isolated from the other The content has not thus the confirmation in itself which was given to it by philosophical theology in the fact that the speculative Idea made itself therein effectual; neither has it the historic confirmation which is given to a content in so far as it has an outward and historic side in which historic witnesses are heard in evidence, and in which its correctness is determined by their testimony. The doctrine has to prove itself by the condition of my heart, by penitence, conversion and joy in God. In doctrine we begin with the external content, and thus it is external only; but taken thus, independently of the state of my mind, it properly speaking has no significance. Now this beginning is, as Christian baptism and education, a working upon the nature in addition to an acquaintance with externals. The truth of the gospel and of Christian doctrines only, however, exists in true relation to the same; it is really so to speak a use of the content to make it educative. And this is just what has been said, that the nature is reconstructed and sanctified in itself, and it is this sanctification for which the content is a true one. No further use can be made of the content than to build up and edify the mind, and awaken it to assurance, joy, penitence, conversion. Another and wrong relation to the content is to take it in an external way, *e.g.* according to the great new principle of exegesis, and to treat the writings of the New Testament like those of a Greek, Latin or other author, critically, philologically, historically. Spirit is alone in true relation to spirit; and it is a wrong beginning of a wooden and unyielding exegesis to prove in such an external and philological way the truth of the Christian religion. This has been done by orthodoxy, which thereby renders the content devoid of spirituality. This, then, is the first relation of spirit to this content; here the content is indeed essential, but it is as essential that the holy and sanctifying spirit should bear a relation to it.

This spirit is, however, in the second place really thinking spirit likewise. Thought as such must also develop itself therein, and that really as this form of inmost unity of spirit with itself; thought must come to the distinction and contemplation of this content, and pass over into this form of the purest unity of spirit with itself. At first thought, however, reveals itself as abstract thought alone, and it possesses as such a relation to theology and religion. The content which is here in question, even in so far as it is historic merely and externally accepted, must yet be religious; the unfolding of the nature of God must be present therein. In this we have the further demand that the thought, for which the inward nature of God is, should also set itself in relation to this content. But inasmuch as thought is at first understanding and the metaphysic of the understanding, it will remove from the content the rational Idea and make it so empty that only external history remains, which is devoid of interest.

The third position arrived at is that of concrete speculative thought. According to the standpoint which has just been given, and as religious feeling and its form are here determined, all speculative content as such, as well as its developments, are at first rejected. And as for the enrichment of the Christian conceptions through the treasures of the philosophy of the ancient world, and through the profound ideas of all earlier oriental religions, and the like,—all this is set aside. The content had objectivity; but this merely signified that the objective content, without subsisting for itself, was to constitute the beginning only, on which the mind had spiritually to build up and sanctify itself. All the enrichment of the content, whereby it became philosophic, is thus abandoned, and what follows later simply is that the mind, as thinking, again immerses itself in itself, in order to be concrete and rational. What forms the basis of the Reformation is the abstract moment of a mind being within self, of freedom, of coming to self; freedom signifies the life of the spirit in being turned back within itself in the particular content which appears as another; while spirit is not free if it allows this other-being, either unassimilated or dead, to exist in it as something foreign. In as far as spirit now goes on to knowledge, to spiritual determinations, and as it looks around and comes forth as a content, so far will it conduct itself therein as in its own domain, as in its concrete world, so to speak—and it will there really assert and possess its own. This concrete form of knowledge which, however, in the beginning remains but dim, we have now to consider, and it forms the third period of our treatise, into which we properly step with the Reformation, although Bruno, Vanini and Ramus, who lived later, still belong to the Middle Ages.

PART THREE

MODERN PHILOSOPHY

INTRODUCTION

If we cast a glance back over the period just traversed, we find that in it a turning-point had been reached, that the Christian religion had placed its absolute content in the mind and will of man, and that it was thus, as a divine and supersensuous content, separated from the world and shut up within itself in the centre-point of the individual. Over against the religious life an external world stood as a natural world—a world of heart or feeling, of desire, of human nature—which had value only in as far as it was overcome. This mutual independence of the two worlds had much attention bestowed on it throughout the Middle Ages; the opposition was attacked on all quarters and in the end overcome. But since the relation of mankind to the divine life exists upon earth, this conquest at first presented the appearance of bringing with it the destruction of the church and of the eternal through the sensuous desires of man. The eternal truth was likewise grafted upon the dry, formal understanding, so that we might say that the separation of self-consciousness has in itself disappeared, and thereby a possibility has been given of obtaining reconciliation. But because this implicit union of the Beyond and the Here was of so unsatisfactory a nature that the better feelings were aroused and forced to turn against it, the Reformation made its appearance, partly, no doubt, as a separation from the Catholic Church, but partly as a reformation from within. There is a mistaken idea that the Reformation only effected a separation from the Catholic Church; Luther just as truly reformed the Catholic Church, the corruption of which one learns from his writings, and from the reports of the emperors and of the empire to the Pope; if further evidence be required, we need only read the accounts given even by the Catholic bishops, the Fathers of the councils at Constance, Basle, &c., of the condition of the Catholic priesthood and of the Roman Court. The principle of the inward reconciliation of spirit, which was in itself the very Idea of Christianity, was thus again estranged, and appeared as a condition of external, unreconciled alienation and discord; this gives us an example of the slow operation of the world-spirit in overcoming this externality. It eats away the inward substance, but the appearance, the outward form, still remains; at the end, however, it is an empty shell, the new form breaks forth. In such times this spirit appears as if it—having so far proceeded in its development at a snail's pace, and having even retrograded and become estranged from itself—had suddenly adopted seven-leagued boots.

Since thus the reconciliation of self-consciousness with the present is implicitly accomplished, man has attained to confidence in himself and in his thought, in sensuous nature outside of and within him; he has discovered an interest and pleasure in making discoveries both in nature and the arts. In the affairs of this world the understanding developed; man became conscious of his will and his achievements, took pleasure in the earth and its soil, as also in his occupations, because right and understanding were there present. With the discovery of gunpowder the individual passion of battle was lost. The romantic impulse towards a casual kind of bravery passed into other adventures, not of hate or revenge, or the so-called deliverance from what men considered the wrongs of innocence, but more harmless adventures, the exploration of the earth, or the discovery of the passage to the East Indies. America was discovered, its treasures and people—nature, man himself; navigation was the higher romance of commerce. The present world was again present to man as worthy of the interests of mind; thinking mind was again capable of action. Now the Reformation of Luther had inevitably to come—the appeal to the *sensus communis* which does not recognize the authority of the Fathers or of Aristotle, but only the inward personal spirit which quickens and animates, in contradistinction to works. In this way the Church lost her power against it, for her principle was within it and no longer lacking to it. To the finite and present due honour is accorded; from this honour the work of science proceeds. We thus see that the finite, the inward and outward present, becomes a matter of experience, and through the understanding is elevated into universality; men desire to understand laws and forces, *i.e.* to transform the individual of perceptions into the form of universality. Worldly matters demand to be judged of in a worldly way; the judge is thinking understanding. The other side is that the eternal, which is in and for itself true, is also known and comprehended through the pure heart itself; the individual mind appropriates to itself the eternal. This is the Lutheran faith without any other accessories—works, as they were called. Everything had value only as it was grasped by the heart, and not as a mere thing. The content ceases to be an objective thing; God is thus in spirit alone, He is not a beyond but the truest reality of the individual.

Pure thought is likewise one form of inwardness; it also approaches absolute existence and finds itself justified in apprehending the same. The philosophy of modern times proceeds from the principle which ancient philosophy had reached, the standpoint of actual self-consciousness—it has as principle the spirit that is present to itself; it brings the standpoint of the Middle Ages, the diversity between what is thought and the existent universe, into opposition, and it has to do with the dissolution of this same opposition. The main interest hence is, not so much the thinking of the objects in their truth, as the thinking and understanding of the objects, the thinking this unity itself, which is really the being conscious of a pre-supposed object. The getting rid of the formal culture of the logical understanding and the monstrosities of which it was composed, was more essential than the extension of it: investigation in such a case becomes dissipated and diffused, and passes into the false infinite. The general points of view which in modern philosophy we reach are hence somewhat as follows :—

1. The concrete form of thought which we have here to consider on its own account, really appears as subjective with the reflection of implicitude, so that this has an antithesis in existence; and the interest is then altogether found in grasping the reconciliation of this opposition in its highest existence, *i.e.* in the most abstract extremes. This highest severance is the opposition between thought and Being, the comprehending of whose unity from this time forward constitutes the interest of all philosophies. Here thought is more independent, and thus we now abandon its unity with theology; it separates itself therefrom, just as with the Greeks it separated itself from mythology, the popular religion, and did not until the time of the Alexandrians seek out these forms again and fill the mythological conceptions with the form of thought. The bond remains, but for this reason it is clearly implicit: theology throughout is merely what philosophy is, for this last is simply thought respecting it. It does not help theology to strive against philosophy, or to say that it wishes to know nothing about it, and that philosophic maxims are thus to be set aside. It has always to do with the thought that it brings along with it, and these its subjective

conceptions, its home and private metaphysics, are thus frequently a quite uncultured, uncritical thought—the thought of the street. These general conceptions are, indeed, connected with particular subjective conviction, and this last is said to prove the Christian content to be true in a sense all its own; but these thoughts which constitute the criterion are merely the reflections and opinions which float about the surface of the time. Thus, when thought comes forth on its own account, we thereby separate ourselves from theology; we shall, however, consider one other in whom both are still in unity. This individual is Jacob Boehme, for since mind now moves in its own domains, it is found partly in the natural and finite world, and partly in the inward, and this at first is the Christian.

While earlier than this, moreover, the spirit, distracted by outward things, had to make its influence felt in religion and in the secular life, and came to be known in the popular philosophy so-called, it was only in the sixteenth and seventeenth centuries that the genuine Philosophy re-appeared, which seeks to grasp the truth as truth because man in thought is infinitely free to comprehend himself and nature, and along with that seeks to understand the present of rationality, reality, universal law itself. For this is ours, since it is subjectivity. The principle of modern philosophy is hence not a free and natural thought, because it has the opposition of thought and nature before it as a fact of which it is conscious. Spirit and nature, thought and Being, are the two infinite sides of the Idea, which can for the first time truly make its appearance when its sides are grasped for themselves in their abstraction and totality. Plato comprehended it as the bond, as limiting and as infinite, as one and many, simple and diverse, but not as thought and Being; when we first thinkingly overcome this opposition it signifies comprehending the unity. This is the standpoint of philosophic consciousness generally; but the way in which this unity must be thinkingly developed is a double one. Philosophy hence falls into the two main forms in which the opposition is resolved, into a realistic and an idealistic system of philosophy, *i.e.* into one which makes objectivity and the content of thought to arise from the perceptions, and one which proceeds to truth from the independence of thought.

a. Experience constitutes the first of these methods, viz. Realism. Philosophy now signified, or had as its main attribute, self-thought and the acceptance of the present as that in which truth lay, and which was thereby knowable. All that is speculative is pared and smoothed down in order to bring it under experience. This present is the existent external nature, and spiritual activity as the political world and as subjective activity. The way to truth was to begin from this hypothesis, but not to remain with it in its external self-isolating actuality, but to lead it to the universal.

α. The activities of that first method operate, to begin with, on physical nature, from the observation of which men derive universal laws, and on this basis their knowledge is founded; the science of nature, however, only reaches to the stage of reflection. This kind of experimental physics was once called, and is still called philosophy, as Newton's *Principia philosophiæ naturalis* (Vol. I. p. 59) show. This work is one in which the methods of the finite sciences through observation and deduction are alone present—those sciences which the French still call the *sciences exactes*. To this, the understanding of the individual, piety was opposed, and hence in this respect philosophy was termed worldly wisdom (Vol. I. p. 60). Here the Idea in its infinitude is not itself the object of knowledge; but a determinate content is raised into the universal, or this last in its determinateness for the understanding is derived from observation, just as is, for instance, done in Keppler's Laws. In Scholastic philosophy, on the other hand, man's power of observation was set aside, and disputations respecting nature at that time proceeded from abstruse hypotheses.

β. In the second place, the spiritual was observed as in its realization it constitutes the spiritual world of states, in order thus to investigate from experience the rights of individuals as regards one another, and as regards rulers, and the rights of states against states. Before this popes anointed kings, just as was done in Old Testament times to those appointed by God; it was in the Old Testament that the tithe was commanded; the forbidden degrees of relationship in marriage were also adopted from the Mosaic laws. What was right and permissible for kings was demonstrated from Saul's and David's histories, the rights of priesthood from Samuel—in short, the Old Testament was the source of all the principles of public law, and it is in this way even now that all papal bulls have their deliverances confirmed. It may easily be conceived how much nonsense was in this manner concocted. Now, however, right was sought for in man himself, and in history, and what had been accounted right both in peace and in war was explained. In this way books were composed which even now are constantly quoted in the Parliament of England. Men further observed the desires which could be satisfied in the state and the manner in which satisfaction could be given to them, in order thus from man himself, from man of the past as well as of the present, to learn what is right.

b. The second method, that of Idealism, proceeds from what is inward; according to it everything is in thought, mind itself is all content. Here the Idea itself is made the object; that signifies the thinking it and from it proceeding to the determinate. What Realism draws from experience is now derived from thought *à priori*; or the determinate is also comprehended but not led back to the universal merely, but to the Idea.

The two methods overlap one another, however, because experience on its side desires to derive universal laws from observations, while, on the other side, thought proceeding from abstract universality must still give itself a determinate content; thus *a priori* and *a posteriori* methods are mingled. In France abstract universality was the more predominant; from England experience took its rise, and even now it is there held in the greatest respect; Germany proceeded from the concrete Idea, from the inwardness of mind and spirit.

2. The questions of present philosophy, the opposites, the content which occupies the attention of these modern times, are as follows:—

a. The first form of the opposition which we have already touched upon in the Middle Ages is the Idea of God and His Being, and the task imposed is to deduce the existence of God, as pure spirit, from thought. Both sides must be comprehended through thought as absolute unity; the extremest opposition is apprehended as gathered into one unity. Other subjects which engage our attention are connected with the same general aim, namely, the bringing about of the inward reconciliation in the opposition which exists between knowledge and its object.

b. The second form of opposition is that of Good and Evil—the opposition of the assertion of independent will to the positive and universal; the origin of evil must be known. Evil is plainly the "other," the negation of God as Holiness; because He is, because He is wise, good, and at the same time almighty, evil is contradictory to Him; an endeavour is made to reconcile this contradiction.

c. The third form of opposition is that of the freedom of man and necessity.

α. The individual is clearly not determined in any other way than from himself, he is the absolute beginning of determination; in the 'I,' in the self, a power of decision is clearly to be found. This freedom is in opposition to the theory that God alone is really absolutely determining. Further, when that which happens is in futurity, the determining of it through God is regarded as Providence and the foreknowledge of God. In this, however, a new contradiction is involved, inasmuch as because God's knowledge is not merely subjective, that which God knows likewise *is*.

β. Further still, human freedom is in opposition to necessity as the determinateness of nature; man is dependent on nature, and the external as well as the inward nature of man is his necessity as against his freedom.

γ. Considered objectively, this opposition is that between final causes and efficient causes, *i.e.* between the acts of freedom and the acts of necessity.

δ. This opposition between the freedom of man and natural necessity has finally likewise the further form of community of soul and body, of *commercium animi cum corpore*, as it has been called, wherein the soul appears as the simple, ideal, and free, and the body as the manifold, material and necessary.

These matters occupy the attention of science, and they are of a completely different nature from the interests of ancient philosophy. The difference is this, that here there is a consciousness of an opposition, which is certainly likewise contained in the subjects with which the learning of the ancients was occupied, but which had not come to consciousness. This consciousness of the opposition, this 'Fall,' is the main point of interest in the conception of the Christian religion. The bringing about in thought of the reconciliation which is accepted in belief, now constitutes the whole interest of knowledge. Implicitly it has come to pass; for knowledge considers itself qualified to bring about in itself this recognition of the reconciliation. The philosophic systems are therefore no more than modes of this absolute unity, and only the concrete unity of those opposites is the truth.

3. As regards the stages which were reached in the pro-

gress of this knowledge we have to mention three of the principal.

a. First of all we find the union of those opposites stated; and to prove it genuine attempts are made, though not yet determined in purity.

b. The second stage is the metaphysical union; and here, with Descartes, the philosophy of modern times as abstract thought properly speaking begins.

α. Thinking understanding seeks to bring to pass the union, inasmuch as it investigates with its pure thought-determinations; this is in the first place the standpoint of metaphysics as such.

β. In the second place, we have to consider negation, the destruction of this metaphysics—the attempt to consider knowledge on its own account, and the determinations which proceed from it.

c. The third stage is that this union itself which is to be brought about, and which is the only subject of interest, comes to consciousness and becomes an object. As principle the union has the form of the relationship of knowledge to the content, and thus this question has been put: 'How is, and how can thought be identical with the objective?' With this the inward element which lies at the basis of this metaphysic is raised into explicitude and made an object; and this includes all modern philosophy in its range.

4. In respect to the external history and the lives of the philosophers, it will strike us that from this time on, these appear to be very different from those of the philosophers of ancient times, whom we regarded as self-sufficing individualities. It is required that a philosopher should live as he teaches, that he should despise the world and not enter into connection with it; this the ancients have accomplished, and they are such plastic individualities just because the inward spiritual aim of philosophy has likewise frequently determined their external relations and conditions. The object of their knowledge was to take a thoughtful view of

the universe; they kept the external connection with the world all the further removed from themselves because they did not greatly approve of much therein present; or, at least, it ever proceeds on its way, according to its own particular laws, on which the individual is dependent. The individual likewise participates in the present interests of external life, in order to satisfy his personal ends, and through them to attain to honour, wealth, respect, and distinction; the ancient philosophers, however, because they remained in the Idea, did not concern themselves with things that were not the objects of their thought. Hence with the Greeks and Romans the philosophers lived in an independent fashion peculiar to themselves, and in an external mode of life which appeared suitable to and worthy of the science they professed; they conducted themselves independently as private persons, unfettered by outside trammels, and they may be compared to the monks who renounced all temporal goods.

In the Middle Ages it was chiefly the clergy, doctors of theology, who occupied themselves with philosophy. In the transition period the philosophers showed themselves to be in an inward warfare with themselves and in an external warfare with their surroundings, and their lives were spent in a wild, unsettled fashion.

In modern times things are very different; now we no longer see philosophic individuals who constitute a class by themselves. With the present day all difference has disappeared; philosophers are not monks, for we find them generally in connection with the world, participating with others in some common work or calling. They live, not independently, but in the relation of citizens, or they occupy public offices and take part in the life of the state. Certainly they may be private persons, but if so, their position as such does not in any way isolate them from their other relationships. They are involved in present conditions, in the world and its work and progress.

Thus their philosophy is only by the way, a sort of luxury and superfluity. This difference is really to be found in the manner in which outward conditions have taken shape after the building up of the inward world of religion. In modern times, namely, on account of the reconciliation of the worldly principle with itself, the external world is at rest, is brought into order—worldly relationships, conditions, modes of life, have become constituted and organized in a manner which is conformable to nature and rational. We see a universal, comprehensible connection, and with that individuality likewise attains another character and nature, for it is no longer the plastic individuality of the ancients. This connection is of such power that every individuality is under its dominion, and yet at the same time can construct for itself an inward world. The external has thus been reconciled with itself in such a way that both inward and outward may be self-sufficing and remain independent of one another; and the individual is in the condition of being able to leave his external side to external order, while in the case of those plastic forms the external could only be determined entirely from within. Now, on the contrary, with the higher degree of strength attained by the inward side of the individual, he may hand the external over to chance; just as he leaves clothing to the contingencies of fashion, not considering it worth while to exert his understanding upon it. The external he leaves to be determined by the order which is present in the particular sphere in which his lot is cast. The circumstances of life are, in the true sense, private affairs, determined by outward conditions, and do not contain anything worthy of our notice. Life becomes scholarly, uniform, commonplace, it connects itself with outwardly given relationships and cannot represent or set itself forth as a form pertaining only to itself. Man must not take up the character of showing himself an independent form, and giving himself a position in the world created by himself. Because the objective power of external relationships is infinitely great, and for that reason the way in which I perforce am placed in them has become a matter of indifference to me, personality and the individual life generally are equally indifferent. A philosopher, it is said, should live as a philosopher, *i.e.*, should be independent of the external relationships of the world, and should give up occupying himself with and troubling himself concerning them. But thus circumscribed in respect of all necessities, more especially of culture, no one can suffice for himself; he must seek to act in connection with others. The modern world is this essential power of connection, and it implies the fact that it is clearly necessary for the individual to enter into these relations of external existence; only a common mode of existence is possible in any calling or condition, and to this Spinoza forms the solitary exception. Thus in earlier times bravery was individual; while modern bravery consists in each not acting after his own fashion, but relying on his connection with others—and this constitutes his whole merit. The calling of philosopher is not, like that of the monks, an organized condition. Members of academies of learning are no doubt organized in part, but even a special calling like theirs sinks into the ordinary commonplace of state or class relationships, because admission thereinto is outwardly determined. The real matter is to remain faithful to one's aims.

SECTION ONE

Modern Philosophy in its First Statement

The first two philosophers whom we have to consider are Bacon and Boehme; there is as complete a disparity between these individuals as between their systems of philosophy. None the less both agree that mind operates in the content of its knowledge as in its own domain, and this consequently appears as concrete Being. This domain in Bacon is the finite, natural world; in Boehme it is the inward, mystical, godly Christian life and existence; for the former starts from experience and induction, the latter from God and the pantheism of the Trinity.

A. Bacon.

There was already being accomplished the abandonment of the content which lies beyond us, and which through its form has lost the merit it possessed of being true, and is become of no significance to self-consciousness or the certainty of self and of its actuality; this we see for the first time consciously expressed, though not as yet in a very perfect form, by Francis Bacon, Baron Verulam, Viscount St. Albans. He is therefore instanced as in the fore-front of all this empirical philosophy, and even now our countrymen like to adorn their works with sententious sayings culled from him. Baconian philosophy thus usually means a philosophy which is founded on the observation of the external or spiritual nature of man in his inclinations, desires, rational and judicial qualities. From these conclusions are drawn, and general conceptions, laws pertaining to this domain, are thus discovered. Bacon has entirely set aside and rejected the scholastic method of reasoning from remote abstractions and being blind to what lies before one's eyes. He takes as his standpoint the sensuous manifestation as it appears to the cultured man, as the latter reflects upon it; and this is conformable to the principle of accepting the finite and worldly as such.

Bacon was born in London in 1561. His progenitors and relatives held high office in the state, and his father was Keeper of the Great Seal to Queen Elizabeth. He in his turn, having been educated to follow the same vocation, at once devoted himself to the business of the state, and entered upon an important career. He early displayed great talent, and at the age of nineteen he produced a work on the condition of Europe (*De statu Europæ*). Bacon in his youth attached himself to the Earl of Essex, the favourite of Elizabeth, through whose support he, who as a younger son had to see his paternal estate pass to his elder brother, soon attained to better circumstances, and was elevated to a higher position. Bacon, however, sullied his fame by the utmost ingratitude and faithlessness towards his protector; for he is accused of having been prevailed upon by the enemies of the Earl after his fall to charge him publicly with High Treason. Under James I., the father of Charles I. who was beheaded, a weak man, to whom he recommended himself by his work *De augmentis scientiarum*, he received the most honourable offices of state by attaching himself to Buckingham: he was made Keeper of the Great Seal, Lord Chancellor of England, Baron Verulam. He likewise made a rich marriage, though he soon squandered all his means, and high though his position was, he stooped to intrigues and was guilty of accepting bribes in the most barefaced manner. Thereby he brought upon himself the ill-will both of people and of nobles, so that he was prosecuted, and his case was tried before Parliament. He was fined 40,000*l.*, thrown into the Tower, and his name was struck out of the list of peers; during the trial and while he was in prison he showed the greatest weakness of character. He was, however, liberated from prison, and his trial was annulled, owing to the even greater hatred of the king and his minister Buckingham, under whose administration Bacon had filled these offices, and whose victim he appeared to have been; for he fell earlier than his comrade Buckingham, and was deserted and condemned by him. It was not so much his innocence as the fact that those who ruined him had made themselves hated to an equal degree through their rule, that caused the hatred and indignation against Bacon to be somewhat mitigated. But he neither recovered his own sense of self-respect nor the personal esteem of others, which he had lost through his former conduct. He retired into private life, lived in poverty, had to beg sustenance from the king, occupied himself during the remainder of his life with science only, and died in 1626.[1]

Since Bacon has ever been esteemed as the man who directed knowledge to its true source, to experience, he is, in fact, the special leader and representative of what is in England called Philosophy, and beyond which the English have not yet advanced. For they appear to constitute that people in Europe which, limited to the understanding of actuality, is destined, like the class of shopkeepers and workmen in the State, to live always immersed in matter, and to have actuality but not reason as object. Bacon won great praise by showing how attention is to be paid to the outward and inward manifestations of Nature, and the esteem in which his name is thus held is greater than can

[1] Buhle: Gesch. d. neuern Philos. Vol. II. Section II. pp. 950–954; Brucker. Hist. crit. phil. T. IV. P. II. pp. 91–95.

be ascribed directly to his merit. It has become the universal tendency of the time and of the English mode of reasoning, to proceed from facts, and to judge in accordance with them. Because Bacon gave expression to the tendency, and men require to have a leader and originator for any particular manner of thinking, he is credited with having given to knowledge this impulse towards experimental philosophy generally. But many cultured men have spoken and thought regarding what concerns and interests mankind, regarding state affairs, mind, heart, external nature, &c., in accordance with experience and in accordance with a cultured knowledge of the world. Bacon was just such a cultured man of the world, who had seen life in its great relations, had engaged in state affairs, had dealt practically with actual life, had observed men, their circumstances and relations, and had worked with them as cultured, reflecting, and, we may even say, philosophical men of the world. He thus did not escape the corruption of those who stood at the helm of the state. With all the depravity of his character he was a man of mind and clear perception; he did not, however, possess the power of reasoning through thoughts and notions that are universal. We do not find in him a methodical or scientific manner of regarding things, but only the external reasoning of a man of the world. Knowledge of the world he possessed in the highest degree: "rich imagination, powerful wit, and the penetrating wisdom which he displays upon that most interesting of all subjects, commonly called the world. This last appears to us to have been the characteristical quality of Bacon's genius. . . It was men rather than things that he had studied, the mistakes of philosophers rather than the errors of philosophy. In fact he was no lover of abstract reasoning;" and although it pertains to philosophy, we find as little as possible of it in him. "His writings are indeed full of refined and most acute observations, but it seldom requires any effort on our part to apprehend their wisdom." Hence mottoes are often derived from him. "His judgments," however, "are commonly given *ex cathedra*, or, if he endeavours to elucidate them, it is by similes and illustrations and pointed animadversions more than by direct and appropriate arguments. General reasoning is absolutely essential in philosophy; the want of it is marked in Bacon's writings."[1] His practical writings are specially interesting; but we do not find the bright flashes of genius that we expected. As during his career in the state he acted in accordance with practical utility, he now, at its conclusion, likewise applied himself in a practical way to scientific endeavours, and considered and treated the sciences in accordance with concrete experience and investigation. His is a consideration of the present, he makes the most of, and ascribes value to it as it appears; the existent is thus regarded with open eyes, respect is paid to it as to what reigns preeminent, and this sensuous perception is reverenced and recognized. Here a confidence on the part of reason in itself and in nature is awakened; it thinkingly applies itself to nature, certain of finding the truth in it, since both are in themselves harmonious.

Bacon likewise treated the sciences methodically; he did not merely bring forward opinions and sentiments, he did not merely express himself regarding the sciences dogmatically, as a fine gentleman might, but he went into the matter closely, and established a method in respect of scientific knowledge. It is only through this method of investigation introduced by him that he is noteworthy— it is in that way alone that he can be considered to belong to the history of the sciences and of philosophy. And through this principle of methodical knowledge he has likewise produced a great effect upon his times, by drawing attention to what was lacking in the sciences, both in their

[1] The *Quarterly Review*, Vol. XVII., April, 1817, p. 53.

methods and in their content. He set forth the general principles of procedure in an empirical philosophy. The spirit of the philosophy of Bacon is to take experience as the true and only source of knowledge, and then to regulate the thought concerning it. Knowledge from experience stands in opposition to knowledge arising from the speculative Notion, and the opposition is apprehended in so acute a manner that the knowledge proceeding from the Notion is ashamed of the knowledge from experience, just as this again takes up a position of antagonism to the knowledge through the Notion. What Cicero says of Socrates may be said of Bacon, that he brought Philosophy down to the world, to the homes and every-day lives of men (Vol. I. p. 389). To a certain extent knowledge from the absolute Notion may assume an air of superiority over this knowledge; but it is essential, as far as the Idea is concerned, that the particularity of the content should be developed. The Notion is an essential matter, but as such its finite side is just as essential. Mind gives presence, external existence, to itself; to come to understand this extension, the world as it is, the sensuous universe, to understand itself as this, *i.e.* with its manifest, sensuous extension, is one side of things. The other side is the relation to the Idea. Abstraction in and for itself must determine and particularize itself. The Idea is concrete, self-determining, it has the principle of development; and perfect knowledge is always developed. A conditional knowledge in respect of the Idea merely signifies that the working out of the development has not yet advanced very far. But we have to deal with this development; and for this development and determination of the particular from the Idea, so that the knowledge of the universe, of nature, may be cultivated—for this, the knowledge of the particular is necessary. This particularity must be worked out on its own account; we must become acquainted with empirical nature, both with the physical and with the human. The merit of modern times is to have accomplished or furthered these ends; it was in the highest degree unsatisfactory when the ancients attempted the work. Empiricism is not merely an observing, hearing, feeling, etc., a perception of the individual; for it really sets to work to find the species, the universal, to discover laws. Now because it does this, it comes within the territory of the Notion—it begets what pertains to the region of the Idea; it thus prepares the empirical material for the Notion, so that the latter can then receive it ready for its use. If the science is perfected the Idea must certainly issue forth of itself; science as such no longer commences from the empiric. But in order that this science may come into existence, we must have the progression from the individual and particular to the universal—an activity which is a re-action on the given material of empiricism in order to bring about its reconstruction. The demand of *a priori* knowledge, which seems to imply that the Idea should construct from itself, is thus a reconstruction only, or what is in religion accomplished through sentiment and feeling. Without the working out of the empirical sciences on their own account, Philosophy could not have reached further than with the ancients. The whole of the Idea in itself is science as perfected and complete; but the other side is the beginning, the process of its origination. This process of the origination of science is different from its process in itself when it is complete, just as is the process of the history of Philosophy and that of Philosophy itself. In every science principles are commenced with; at the first these are the results of the particular, but if the science is completed they are made the beginning. The case is similar with Philosophy; the working out of the empirical side has really become the conditioning of the Idea, so that this last may reach its full development and determination. For instance, in order that the history of the Philosophy of modern times may exist, we must have a history of Philosophy in general, the process of Philosophy during so many thousand years; mind must have followed this long road in order that the Philosophy may be produced. In consciousness it then adopts the attitude of having cut away the bridge from behind it; it appears to be free to launch forth in its ether only, and to develop without resistance in this medium; but it is another matter to attain to this ether and to development in it. We must not overlook the fact that Philosophy would not have come into existence without this process, for mind is essentially a working upon something different.

1. Bacon's fame rests on two works. In the first place, he has the merit of having in his work *De augmentis scientiarum* presented to us a systematic encyclopedia of the sciences, an outline which must undoubtedly have caused a sensation amongst his contemporaries. It is important to set before men's eyes a well arranged picture such as this of the whole, when that whole has not been grasped in thought. This encyclopedia gives a general classification of the sciences; the principles of the classification are regulated in accordance with the differences in the intellectual capacities. Bacon thus divides human learning according to the faculties of memory, imagination, and reason, for he distinguishes what pertains (1) to memory; (2) to imagination; (3) to reason. Under memory he considered history; under imagination, poetry, and art; and finally, under reason, philosophy.[1] According to his favourite method of division these again are further divided, since he brings all else under these same heads; this is, however, unsatisfactory. To history belong the works of God—sacred, prophetic, ecclesiastical history; the works of men—civil and literary history; and likewise the works of nature, and so on.[2] He goes through these topics after

[1] Bacon. De augmentis scientiarum, II. c. 1 (Lugd. Batavor, 1652. 12), pp. 108-110 (Operum omnium, pp. 43, 44, Lipsiæ, 1694).

[2] Ibidem, c. 2, p. 111 (Operum, p. 44); c. 4, pp. 123, 124 (p. 49); c. 11, pp. 145-147 (pp. 57, 58).

the manner of his time, a main characteristic of which is that anything can be made plausible through examples, *e.g.* from the Bible. Thus, in treating of *Cosmetica*, he says in regard to paint that "He is surprised that this depraved custom of painting has been by the penal laws both ecclesiastical and civil so long overlooked. In the Bible we read indeed of Jezebel that she painted her face; but nothing of the kind is said of Esther or Judith."[1] If kings, popes, etc., are being discussed, such examples as those of Ahab and Solomon must be brought forward. As formerly in civil laws—those respecting marriage, for instance—the Jewish forms held good, in Philosophy, too, the same are still to be found. In this work theology likewise appears, as also magic; there is contained in it a comprehensive system of knowledge and of the sciences.

The arrangement of the sciences is the least significant part of the work *De augmentis scientiarum*. It was by its criticism that its value was established and its effect produced, as also by the number of instructive remarks contained in it; all this was at that time lacking in the particular varieties of learning and modes of discipline, especially in as far as the methods hitherto adopted were faulty, and unsuitable to the ends in view: in them the Aristotelian conceptions of the schools were spun out by the understanding as though they were realities. As it was with the Schoolmen and with the ancients, this classification is still the mode adopted in the sciences, in which the nature of knowledge is unknown. In them the idea of the science is advanced beforehand, and to this idea a principle foreign to it is added, as a basis of division, just as here is added the distinction between memory, imagination and reason. The true method of division is found in the self-division of the Notion, its separating itself from

[1] Bacon. De augmentis scientiarum, IV. c. 2, pp. 294, 295 (p. 213) (Ellis and Spedding's translation, Vol. IV. p. 394).

itself. In knowledge the moment of self-consciousness is undoubtedly found, and the real self-consciousness has in it the moments of memory, imagination and reason. But this division is certainly not taken from the Notion of self-consciousness, but from experience, in which self-consciousness finds itself possessed of these capacities.

2. The other remarkable feature in Bacon is that in his second work, his *Organon*, he sought at great length to establish a new method in learning; in this regard his name is still held greatly in honour by many. What chiefly distinguishes his system is his polemical attitude towards scholastic methods as they had hitherto existed, towards syllogistic forms. He calls these methods *anticipationes naturæ*; in them men begin with pre-suppositions, definitions, accepted ideas, with a scholastic abstraction, and reason further from these without regarding that which is present in actuality. Thus regarding God and His methods of operating in nature, regarding devils, &c., they make use of passages from the Bible, such as "Sun, stand thou still," in order to deduce therefrom certain metaphysical propositions from which they go further still. It was against this *a priori* method that Bacon directed his polemic; as against t ese anticipations of nature he called attention to the explanation, the interpretation of nature.[1] "The same action of mind," he says, "which discovers a thing in question, judges it; and the operation is not performed by the help of any middle term, but directly, almost in the same manner as by the sense. For the sense in its primary objects at once apprehends the appearance of the object, and consents to the truth thereof."[2] The syllogism is altogether rejected by Bacon. As a matter of fact, this Aristotelian deduction is not a

[1] Bacon. Novum Organon, L. I. Aphor. 11-34, pp. 280-282 (Operum).

[2] Bacon. De augm. scient. V. c. 4, p. 358 (p. 137). (Ellis and Spelding's translation. Vol. IV. p. 428.

knowledge through itself in accordance with its content: it requires a foreign universal as its basis, and for that reason its movement is in its form contingent. The content is not in unity with the form, and this form is hence in itself contingent, because it, considered on its own account, is the movement onwards in a foreign content. The major premise is the content existent for itself, the minor is likewise the content not through itself, for it goes back into the infinite, *i.e.* it has not the form in itself; the form is not the content. The opposite may always be made out equally well through the syllogism, for it is a matter of indifference to this form what content is made its basis. "Dialectic does not assist in the discovery of the arts; many arts were found out by chance." [1]

It was not against this syllogism generally, *i.e.* not against the Notion of it (for Bacon did not possess this), but against deduction as it was put into operation, as it was to the scholastics—the deduction which took an assumed content as its basis—that Bacon declaimed, urging that the content of experience should be made the basis, and the method of induction pursued. He demanded that observations on nature and experiments should be made fundamental, and pointed out the objects whose investigation was of special importance in the interests of human society, and so on. From this there then resulted the establishment of conclusions through induction and analogy.[2] In fact it was only to an alteration in the content that, without being aware of it, Bacon was impelled. For though he rejected the syllogism and only permitted conclusions to be reached through induction, he unconsciously himself drew deductions; likewise all these champions of empiricism, who followed after him, and who put into

[1] Bacon. De augmentis scientiarum, V. c. 2, pp. 320, 321 (pp. 122, 123).

[2] Bacon. Novum Organon, L. I. Aphor. 105, p. 313; De augmentis scientiarum, V. c. 2, pp. 326, 327 (pp. 124, 125).

practice what he demanded, and thought they could by observations, experiments and experiences, keep the matter in question pure, could neither so do without drawing deductions, nor without introducing conceptions; and they drew their deductions and formed their notions and conceptions all the more freely because they thought that they had nothing to do with conceptions at all; nor did they go forth from deduction to immanent, true knowledge. Thus when Bacon set up induction in opposition to the syllogism, this opposition is formal; each induction is also a deduction, which fact was known even to Aristotle. For if a universal is deduced from a number of things, the first proposition reads, "These bodies have these qualities;" the second, "All these bodies belong to one class;" and thus, in the third place, this class has these qualities. That is a perfect syllogism. Induction always signifies that observations are instituted, experiments made, experience regarded, and from this the universal determination is derived.

We have already called to mind how important it is to lead on to the content as the content of actuality, of the present; for the rational must have objective truth. The reconciliation of spirit with the world, the glorification of nature and of all actuality, must not be a Beyond, a Futurity, but must be accomplished now and here. It is this moment of the now and here which thereby comes into self-consciousness. But those who make experiments and observations, do not realize what they are really doing, for the sole interest taken by them in things, is owing to the inward and unconscious certainty which reason has of finding itself in actuality; and observations and experiments, if entered upon in a right way, result in showing that the Notion is the only objective existence. The sensuous individual eludes the experiments even while it is being operated upon, and becomes a universal; the best known example of this is to be found in positive and negative electricity in so far as it is positive and negative. There is another shortcoming of a formal nature, and one of which all empiricists partake,—that is that they believe themselves to be keeping to experience alone; it is to them an unknown fact that in receiving these perceptions they are indulging in metaphysics. Man does not stop short at the individual, nor can he do so. He seeks the universal, but thoughts, even if not Notions likewise, are what constitute the same. The most remarkable thought-form is that of force; we thus speak of the force of electricity, of magnetism, of gravity. Force, however, is a universal and not a perceptible; quite uncritically and unconsciously the empiricists thus permit of determinations such as these.

3. Bacon finally gives the objects with which Philosophy mainly has to deal. These objects contrast much with that which we derive from perception and experience. "In the summary which Bacon gives of what he conceives ought to be the objects of philosophical inquiry, are the following; and we select those which he principally dwells upon in his works: 'The prolongation of life; the restitution of youth in some degree; the retardation of old age, and the altering of statures; the altering of features; versions of bodies into other bodies; making of new species; impression of the air and raising tempests; greater pleasures of the senses, &c.'" He likewise deals with objects such as these, and he seeks to direct attention upon whether in their regard the means could not be found to carry out their ends; in such powers we should be able to make some progress. "He complains that such investigations have been neglected by those whom he designates *ignavi regionum exploratores*. In his Natural History he gives formal receipts for making gold, and performing many wonders."[1] Bacon thus does not by any means take

[1] The *Quarterly Review*, Vol. XVII., April, 1817, pp. 50, 51: cf. Bacon silva silvarum sive historia naturalis, Cent. IV., Sect. 326, 327 (Operum, pp. 822, 823).

the intelligent standpoint of an investigation of nature, being still involved in the grossest superstition, false magic, &c. This we find to be on the whole propounded in an intelligent way, and Bacon thus remains within the conceptions of his time. "The conversion of silver, quicksilver, or any other metal into gold is a thing difficult to believe, yet it is far more probable that a man who knows clearly the natures of weight, of the colour of yellow, of malleability and extension, of volatility and fixedness, and who has also made diligent search into the first seeds and menstruums of minerals, may at last by much and sagacious endeavour produce gold, than that a few grains of an elixir may so do. . . . So again a man who knows well the nature of rarefaction, of assimilation, and of alimentation, shall by diets, bathings, and the like prolong life, or in some degree renew the vigour of youth."[1] These assertions are thus not as crude as they at first appear. In dealing with Medicine Bacon speaks amongst other things of maceration (*Malacissatio per exterius*)[2] and so forth.

Bacon emphasizes what has reference to the formal aspect of investigation. For he says, "Natural philosophy is divided into two parts, the first consists in the investigation of causes; the second in the production of effects; the causes to be investigated are either final or formal causes, or else material or efficient causes. The former constitutes metaphysics; the latter physics. This last Bacon looks upon as a branch of philosophy very inferior in point of dignity and importance to the other and accordingly to ascertain the most probable means of improving our knowledge of metaphysics is the great object of his *Organon*."[3] He himself says: "It is a correct

[1] Bacon. De augmentis scientiarum, III. c. 5, pp. 245, 246 (p. 95).

[2] Ibid. IV. c. 2, p. 293 (p. 112).

[3] The *Quarterly Review*, Vol. XVII., April, 1817, pp. 51, 52; cf. Bacon. De augmentis scientiarum, III. c. 3, 4, pp. 200-206 (pp. 78-80).

position that 'true knowledge is knowledge by causes. And causes, again, are not improperly distributed into four kinds: the material, the formal, the efficient, and the final.'"[1] (Vol. I. p. 174, Vol. II. p. 138.)

But in this connection an important point is that Bacon has turned against the teleological investigation of nature, against the investigation into final causes. "The investigation of final causes is useless; they corrupt rather than advance the sciences except such as have to do with human action."[2] To Bacon the important matter is to investigate by the study of *causæ efficientes*. To the consideration of final causes such assertions as these belong: "That the hairs of the eyelids are for a protection to the eyes; that the thick skins and hides of living creatures are to defend them from heat and cold; that the trees have leaves so that the fruit may not suffer from sun and wind"[3]: the hair is on the head on account of warmth; thunder and lightning are the punishment of God, or else they make fruitful the earth; marmots sleep during the winter because they can find nothing to eat; snails have a shell in order that they may be secure against attacks; the bee is provided with a sting. According to Bacon this has been worked out in innumerable different ways. The negative and external side of utility is turned round, and the lack of this adaptation to end is likewise drawn within the same embrace. It may, for example, be said that if sun or moon were to shine at all times, the police might save much money, and this would provide men with food and drink for whole months together. It was right that Bacon should set himself to oppose this investigation into final causes, because it relates to external expediency, just as Kant was right in distin-

[1] Bacon. Novum Organon, L. II. Aphor. 2. (Ellis and Spedding's translation, Vol. IV. p. 119.)

[2] Bacon. Novum Organon, L. II. Aphor. 2; cf. the *Quarterly Review*, Vol. XVII. April, 1817, p. 52.

[3] Bacon. De augmentis scientiarum, III. c. 4; p. 237 (p. 92).

guishing the inward teleology from the outward. As against the external end, there is, in fact, the inward end, *i.e.* the inward Notion of the thing itself, as we found it earlier in Aristotle (Vol. II. pp. 156–163). Because the organism possesses an inward adaptation to its ends, its members are indeed likewise externally adapted as regards one another; but the ends, as external ends, are heterogeneous to the individual, are unconnected with the object which is investigated. Speaking generally, the Notion of nature is not in nature itself, which would mean that the end was in nature itself; but as teleological, the Notion is something foreign to it. It does not have the end in itself in such a way that we have to accord respect to it—as the individual man has his end in himself and hence has to be respected. But even the individual man as individual has only a right to respect from the individual as such, and not from the universal. He who acts in the name of the universal, of the state, as a general does for instance, does not require to respect the individual at all; for the latter, although an end in himself, does not cease to be relative. He is this end in himself, not as excluding himself and setting himself in opposition, but only in so far as his true reality is the universal Notion. The end of the animal in itself as an individual is its own self-preservation; but its true end in itself is the species. Its self-preservation is not involved in this; for the self-preservation of its individuality is disadvantageous to the species, while the abrogation of itself is favourable thereto.

Now Bacon separates the universal principle and the efficient cause, and for that reason he removes investigation into ends from physics to metaphysics. Or he recognizes the Notion, not as universal in nature, but only as necessity, *i.e.* as a universal which presents itself in the opposition of its moments, not one which has bound them into a unity—in other words he only acknowledges a comprehension of one determinate from another determinate going on into infinity, and not of both from their Notion. Bacon has thus made investigation into the efficient cause more general, and he asserts that this investigation alone belongs to physics, although he allows that both kinds of investigation may exist side by side.[1] Through that view he effected a great deal, and in so far as it has counteracted the senseless superstition which in the Germanic nations far exceeded in its horrors and absurdity that of the ancient world, it has the very merit which we met with in the Epicurean philosophy. That philosophy opposed itself to the superstitious Stoics and to superstition generally—which last makes any existence that we set before ourselves into a cause (a Beyond which is made to exist in a sensuous way and to operate as a cause), or makes two sensuous things which have no relation operate on one another. This polemic of Bacon's against spectres, astrology, magic, &c.,[2] can certainly not be regarded exactly as Philosophy like his other reflections, but it is at least of service to culture.

He also advises that attention should be directed to formal causes, the forms of things, and that they should be recognized.[3] "But to give an exact definition of the meaning which Bacon attaches to the phrase formal causes is rather difficult; because his language upon this subject is uncertain in a very remarkable degree."[4] It may be thought that he understood by this the immanent determinations of things, the laws of nature; as a matter of fact the forms are none else than universal determinations, species, &c.[5]

[1] Bacon. De augm. scient. III. c. 4, p. 239 (p. 92).

[2] Bacon. De augmentis scientiarum, I. p. 46 (p. 19); III. c. 4, pp. 211–213 (pp. 82, 83); Novum Organon, L. I. Aphor. 85, p. 304.

[3] Bacon. De augmentis scientiarum, III. c. 4, pp. 231–234 (pp. 89, 90).

[4] The *Quarterly Review*, Vol. XVII. April, 1817, p. 52.

[5] Bacon. Novum Organon, L. II. Aphor. 17, pp. 345, 346.

He says: "The discovery of the formal is despaired of. The efficient and the material (as they are investigated and received, that is as remote causes, without reference to the latent process leading to the forms) are but slight and superficial, and contribute little, if anything, to true and active science. For though in nature nothing really exists beside individual bodies, performing pure individual acts according to a fixed law, yet in philosophy this very law, and the investigation, discovery and explanation of it, is the foundation as well of knowledge as of operation. And it is this law, with its clauses, that I mean when I speak of Forms . . . Let the investigation of Forms which are eternal and immutable constitute metaphysics. Whosoever is acquainted with Forms embraces the unity of nature in substances the most unlike."[1] He goes through this in detail, and quotes many examples to illustrate it, such as that of Heat. "Mind must raise itself from differences to species. The warmth of the sun and that of the fire are diverse. We see that grapes ripen by the warmth of the sun. But to see whether the warmth of the sun is specific, we also observe other warmth, and we find that grapes likewise ripen in a warm room; this proves that the warmth of the sun is not specific."[2]

"Physic," he says, "directs us through narrow rugged paths in imitation of the crooked ways of nature. But he that understands a form knows the ultimate possibility of superinducing that nature upon all kinds of matter; that is to say, as he himself interprets this last expression, is able to superinduce the nature of gold upon silver," that is to say to make gold from silver, "and to perform all those other marvels to which the alchymists pretended. The error of these last consisted alone in

[1] Bacon. Novum Organon, L. II. Aphor. II. pp. 325, 326. (Tennemann, Vol. X. pp. 35, 36); Lib. I. Aphor. 51, p. 286; L. II. Aphor. 9; Aphor. 3, p. 326.

[2] Bacon. Novum Organon, L. II. Aphor. 35, p. 366.

hoping to arrive at these ends by fabulous and fantastical methods;" the true method is to recognize these forms. "One leading object of the *Instauratio Magna* and of the *Novum Organon* is to point out the necessity of ascertaining the formal causes and logical rules."[1] They are good rules, but not adapted to attain that end.

This is all that we have to say of Bacon. In dealing with Locke we shall have more to say of these empirical methods which were adopted by the English.

B. Jacob Boehme.

We now pass on from this English Lord Chancellor, the leader of the external, sensuous method in Philosophy, to the *philosophus teutonicus*, as he is called—to the German cobbler of Lusatia, of whom we have no reason to be ashamed. It was, in fact, through him that Philosophy first appeared in Germany with a character peculiar to itself: Boehme stands in exact antithesis to Bacon. He was also called *theosophus teutonicus*, just as even before this *philosophia teutonica* was the name given to mysticism.[2] This Jacob Boehme was for long forgotten and decried as being simply a pious visionary; the so-called period of enlightenment, more particularly, helped to render his public extremely limited. Leibnitz thought very highly of him, but it is in modern times that his profundity has for the first time been recognized, and that he has been once more restored to honour. It is certain, on the one hand, that he did not merit the disdain accorded him; on the

[1] The *Quarterly Review*, Vol. XVII. April, 1817, p. 52. Cf. Bacon. De augmentis scientiarum, III. c. 4, p. 236 (p. 91).

[2] Jacob Böhme's Leben und Schriften (in his Works, Hamburg, 1715, 4), No. I. § 18, pp. 11, 12; No. V., § 2, p. 54 and the title-page; No. I. § 57, pp. 27, 28.

other, however, he did not deserve the high honour into which he was elevated. To call him an enthusiast signifies nothing at all. For if we will, all philosophers may be so termed, even the Epicureans and Bacon; for they all have held that man finds his truth in something else than eating and drinking, or in the common-sense every-day life of wood-cutting, tailoring, trading, or other business, private or official. But Boehme has to attribute the high honour to which he was raised mainly to the garb of sensuous feeling and perception which he adopted; for ordinary sensuous perception and inward feeling, praying and yearning, and the pictorial element in thought, allegories and such like, are in some measure held to be essential in Philosophy. But it is only in the Notion, in thought, that Philosophy can find its truth, and that the Absolute can be expressed and likewise is as it is in itself. Looked at from this point of view, Boehme is a complete barbarian, and yet he is a man who, along with his rude method of presentation, possesses a deep, concrete heart. But because no method or order is to be found in him, it is difficult to give an account of his philosophy.

Jacob Boehme was born in 1575 of poor parents, at Altseidenburg, near Görlitz, in Upper Lusatia. In his youth he was a peasant boy who tended the cattle. He was brought up as a Lutheran, and always remained such. The account of his life which is given with his works was drawn up by a clergyman who knew him personally, from information given by Boehme himself. Much is there related as to how he attained to more profound knowledge and wisdom by means of certain experiences through which he passed. Even when a herd tending the cattle, as he tells of himself, he had these wonderful manifestations. The first marvellous awakening that occurred to him took place in a thicket in which he saw a cavern and a vessel of gold. Startled by the splendour of this sight he was inwardly awakened from a dull stupor, but afterwards he found it was impossible for him to discover the objects of his vision. Subsequently he was bound apprentice to a shoemaker. More especially "was he spiritually awakened by the words: 'Your heavenly Father will give the Holy Spirit to them that ask Him' (Luke xi. 13), so that, desiring to come to a knowledge of the truth, and yet retaining the simplicity of his mind, he prayed and sought, and knocked, fervently and earnestly, until, while travelling about with his master, he was, through the influence of the Father in the Son, spiritually transported into the glorious peace and the Sabbath of the soul, and thus his request was granted. According to his own account, he was then surrounded with divine light, and for seven days he remained in the supremest divine contemplation and joy." His master for this dismissed him, saying he could not keep in his service "house-prophets such as he was." After that he lived at Görlitz. In 1594 he rose in his trade to be master, and married. Later on, "in the year 1600, and in the twenty-fifth year of his age, once more" the light broke upon him in a second vision of the same kind. He tells that he saw a brightly scoured pewter dish in the room, and "by the sudden sight of this shining metal with its brilliant radiance" he was brought (into a meditation and a breaking free of his astral mind) "into the central point of secret nature," and into the light of divine essence. "He went out into the open air in order that he might rid his brain of this hallucination, and none the less did he continue all the more clearly as time went on to experience the vision in this way received. Thus by means of the signatures or figures, lineaments, and colours which were depicted, he could, so to speak, look into the heart and inmost nature of all creatures (in his book *De signatura rerum* this reason which was impressed upon him is found and fully explained); and for this he was overwhelmed with joy, thanked God, and went peacefully about his affairs." Later on he wrote several works. He continued to pursue his handicraft at Görlitz, and died at the same place in 1624, being then a master shoemaker.[1]

His works are especially popular with the Dutch, and for that reason most of the editions are issued from Amsterdam, though they were also surreptitiously printed in Hamburg. His first writing is the "Aurora" or "Morgenröthe im Aufgange," and this was followed by others; the work "Von den drei Principien," and another "Vom dreifachen Leben des Menschen," are, along with several others, the most noteworthy. Boehme constantly read the Bible, but what other works he read is not known. A number of passages in his works, however, prove that he read much—evidently mystical, theosophic, and alchemistic writings for the most part, and he must certainly have included in his reading the works of Theophrastus Bombastus von Hohenheim, known as Paracelsus, a philosopher of a somewhat similar calibre, but much more confused, and without Boehme's profundity of mind. He met with much persecution at the hands of the clergy, but he aroused less attention in Germany than in Holland and England, where his writings have been often printed.[2] In reading his works we are struck with wonder, and one must be familiar with his ideas in order to discover the truth in this most confused method of expression.

The matter of Jacob Boehme's philosophy is genuinely German; for what marks him out and makes him noteworthy is the Protestant principle already mentioned of placing the intellectual world within one's own mind and heart, and of experiencing and knowing and feeling in one's own self-consciousness all that formerly was conceived as a Beyond. Boehme's general conceptions thus on the one hand reveal themselves as both deep and sound,

[1] Jacob Böhme's Leben und Schriften, No. I. 2-4, pp. 3, 4; § 6, 7, p. 5; § 10, 11, pp. 7, 8; § 28, 29, pp. 17, 18.

[2] Jacob Böhme's Leben und Schriften, No. VI. § 3-8, pp. 81-87; No. I. § 12-17, pp. 8-11.

but on the other, with all his need for and struggle after determination and distinction in the development of his divine intuitions of the universe, he does not attain either to clearness or order. There is no systematic connection but the greatest confusion in his divisions—and this exists even in his tables,[1] in which three numbers are made use of.

I.

What God is beside nature and creation.

II.

Separability: God in Love.	*Mysterium magnum.*	The first *Principium.* God in Wrath.

III.

God in wrath and love.

Here nothing definite to hold the moments asunder is shown, and we have the sense of merely doing it by effort; now these and now other distinctions are set forth, and as they are laid down disconnectedly, they again come into confusion.

The manner and system which Boehme adopts must accordingly be termed barbarous; the expressions used in his works prove this, as when, for example, he speaks of the divine Salitter, Marcurius, &c. As Boehme places the life, the movement of absolute existence in the heart, so does he regard all conceptions as being in a condition of actuality; or he makes use of actuality as Notion, that is to say he forcibly takes natural things and sensuous qualities to express his ideas rather than the determinations of the Notion. For instance, sulphur and such like are not to him the things that we so name, but their essence; or the

[1] Theosophische Sendbriefe, 47th Letter (Werke, Hamburg, 1715, 4), p. 3879.

Notion has this form of actuality. Boehme's profoundest interest is in the Idea, and he struggles hard to express it. The speculative truth which he desires to expound really requires, in order to be comprehended, thought and the form of thought. Only in thought can this unity be comprehended, in the central point of which his mind has its place; but it is just the form of thought that is lacking to him. The forms that he employs are really no longer determinations of the Notion at all. They are on the one hand sensuous, chemical determinations, such qualities as acid, sweet, sour, fierce; and, on the other, emotions such as wrath and love; and, further, tincture, essence, anguish, &c. For him these sensuous forms do not, however, possess the sensuous significance which belongs to them, but he uses them in order to find expression for his thought. It is, however, at once clear to us how the form of manifestation must necessarily appear forced, since thought alone is capable of unity. It thus appears strange to read of the bitterness of God, of the *Flagrat*, and of lightning; we first require to have the Idea, and then we certainly discern its presence here. But the other side is that Boehme utilizes the Christian form which lies nearest to him, and more especially that of the Trinity, as the form of the Idea: he intermingles the sensuous mode and the mode of popularly conceived religion, sensuous images and conceptions. However rude and barbarous this may on the one hand be, and however impossible it is to read Boehme continuously, or to take a firm grasp of his thoughts (for all these qualities, spirits and angels make one's head swim), we must on the other hand recognize that he speaks of everything as it is in its actuality, and that he does this from his heart. This solid, deep, German mind which has intercourse with what is most inward, thus really exercises an immense power and force in order to make use of actuality as Notion, and to have what takes place in heaven around and within it. Just as Hans Sachs represented God, Christ and the Holy Ghost, as well as patriarchs and angels, in his own particular manner and as ordinary people like himself, not looking upon them as past and historic, so was it with Boehme.

To faith spirit has truth, but in this truth the moment of certainty of self is lacking. We have seen that the object of Christianity is the truth, the Spirit; it is given to faith as immediate truth. Faith possesses the truth, but unconsciously, without knowledge, without knowing it as its self-consciousness; and seeing that thought, the Notion, is necessarily in self-consciousness—the unity of opposites with Bruno—this unity is what is pre-eminently lacking to faith. Its moments as particular forms fall apart, more especially the highest moments—good and evil, or God and the Devil. God is, and the Devil likewise; both exist for themselves. But if God is absolute existence, the question may be asked, What absolute existence is this which has not all actuality, and more particularly evil within it? Boehme is hence on one side intent on leading the soul of man to the divine life, on inducing the soul to pay attention to the strife within itself, and make this the object of all its work and efforts; and then in respect of this content he strives to make out how evil is present in good—a question of the present day. But because Boehme does not possess the Notion and is so far back in intellectual culture, there ensues a most frightful and painful struggle between his mind and consciousness and his powers of expression, and the import of this struggle is the profoundest Idea of God which seeks to bring the most absolute opposites into unity, and to bind them together—but not for thinking reason. Thus if we would comprehend the matter, Boehme's great struggle has been—since to him God is everything—to grasp the negative, evil, the devil, in and from God, to grasp God as absolute; and this struggle characterizes all his writings and brings about the torture of his mind. It requires a great and severe mental effort to bring together in one what in shape and form lie so far asunder; with all the strength that he possesses Boehme brings the two together, and therein shatters all the immediate significance of actuality possessed by both. But when thus he grasps this movement, this essence of spirit in himself, in his inward nature, the determination of the moments simply approaches more nearly to the form of self-consciousness, to the formless, or to the Notion. In the background, indeed, there stands the purest speculative thought, but it does not attain to an adequate representation. Homely, popular modes of conception likewise appear, a free out-spokenness which to us seems too familiar. With the devil, particularly, he has great dealings, and him he frequently addresses. "Come here," he says, "thou black wretch, what dost thou want? I will give thee a potion."[1] As Prospero in Shakespeare's "Tempest"[2] threatens Ariel that he will "rend an oak and peg him in his knotty entrails . . . twelve winters," Boehme's great mind is confined in the hard knotty oak of the senses—in the gnarled concretion of the ordinary conception—and is not able to arrive at a free presentation of the Idea.

I shall shortly give Boehme's main conceptions, and then several particular forms which he in turn adopts; for he does not remain at one form, because neither the sensuous nor the religious can suffice. Now even though this brings about the result that he frequently repeats himself, the forms of his main conceptions are still in every respect very different, and he who would try to give a consistent explanation of Boehme's ideas, particularly when they pass into further developments, would only delude himself in making the attempt. Hence we must neither expect to

[1] Trostschrift von vier Complexionen, § 43-63, pp. 1602-1607.

[2] Act I. Scene 2.

find in Boehme a systematic presentation nor a true method of passing over into the individual. Of his thoughts we cannot say much without adopting his manner of expression, and quoting the particular passages themselves, for they cannot otherwise be expressed. The fundamental idea in Jacob Boehme is the effort to comprise everything in an absolute unity, for he desires to demonstrate the absolute divine unity and the union of all opposites in God. Boehme's chief, and one may even say, his only thought—the thought that permeates all his works—is that of perceiving the holy Trinity in everything, and recognizing everything as its revelation and manifestation, so that it is the universal principle in which and through which everything exists; in such a way, moreover, that all things have this divine Trinity in themselves, not as a Trinity pertaining to the ordinary conception, but as the real Trinity of the absolute Idea. Everything that exists is, according to Boehme, this three-fold alone, and this three-fold is everything.[1] To him the universe is thus one divine life and revelation of God in all things, so that when examined more closely, from the one reality of God, the sum and substance of all powers and qualities, the Son who shines forth from these powers is eternally born; the inward unity of this light with the substance of the powers is Spirit. Sometimes the presentation is vague, and then again it is clearer. What comes next is the explanation of this Trinity, and here the different forms which he uses to indicate the difference becoming evident in the same, more especially appear.

In the *Aurora*, the "Root or Mother of Philosophy, Astrology and Theology," he gives a method of division in which he places these sciences in proximity, and yet appears merely to pass from one to the other without any clear

[1] Von Christi Testament der heiligen Taufe, Book II. chap. i. § 4-5, pp. 2653, 2654.

definition or determination. "(1) In Philosophy divine power is treated of, what God is, and how in the Being of God nature, stars and *Elementa* are constituted; whence all things have their origin, what is the nature of heaven and earth, as also of angels, men and devils, heaven and hell and all that is creaturely, likewise what the two qualities in nature are, and this is dealt with out of a right ground in the knowledge of spirit, by the impulse and motion of God (2) In astrology the powers of nature, of the stars and elements, are treated of, and how all creatures proceed from them, how evil and good are through them effected in men and animals. (3) In theology the kingdom of Christ is dealt with, as also its nature, and how it is set in opposition to hell, and how in nature it wars with the kingdom of darkness."[1]

1. What comes first is God the Father; this first is at once divided in itself and the unity of both its parts. "God is all," he says, "He is the Darkness and the Light, Love and Anger, Fire and Light, but He calls Himself God only as to the light of His love. There is an eternal *Contrarium* between darkness and light; neither comprehends the other and neither is the other, and yet there is but one essence or substance, though separated by pain; it is likewise so with the will, and yet there is no separable essence. One single principle is divided in this way, that one is in the other as a nothing which yet exists; but it is not manifest in the property of that thing in which it is."[2] By anguish is expressed that which we know as the absolute negativity—that is the self-conscious, self-experienced, the self-relating negativity which is therefore absolute affirmation. All Boehme's efforts were directed towards this point; the principle of the Notion is living in him, only he cannot express it in the form of thought. That is to say, all

[1] Morgenröthe im Anfgang, Preface, § 84, 85, 88, p. 18.

[2] Von wahrer Gelassenheit, chap. ii. § 9, 10, p. 1673.

depends on thinking of the negative as simple, since it is at the same time an opposite; thus anguish [Qual] is the inward tearing asunder and yet likewise the simple. From this Boehme derives sources or springs [Quellen], a good play on the words. For pain [die Qual], this negativity, passes into life, activity, and thus he likewise connects it with quality [Qualität], which he makes into Quallity.[1] The absolute identity of difference is all through present to him.

a. Boehme thus represents God not as the empty unity, but as this self-separating unity of absolute opposites; one must not, however, here expect a clearly defined distinction. The first, the one, the Father, has likewise the mode of natural existence; thus, like Proclus, he speaks of this God being simple essence. This simple essence he calls the hidden; and he therefore names it the *Temperamentum*, this unity of what is different, in which all is tempered. We find him also calling it the great Salitter—now the divine and now the natural Salitter—as well as Salniter. When he talks of this great salitter as of something known to us, we cannot first of all conceive what it means. But it is a vulgar corruption of the word *sal nitri*, saltpetre (which is still called salniter in Austria), *i.e.* just the neutral and in truth universal existence. The divine pomp and state is this, that in God a more glorious nature dwells, trees, plants, &c. "In the divine pomp or state two things have principally to be considered; salitter or the divine power, which brings forth all fruits, and marcurius or the sound."[2] This great salitter is the unrevealed existence, just as the Neo-Platonic unity is without knowledge of itself and likewise unrecognized.

[1] Von den drei Principien göttlichen Wesens, chap. x. § 42, p. 470.

[2] Von der Gnadenwahl, chap. i. § 3-10, pp. 2408-2410; chap. ii. § 9, p. 2418; § 19, 20, p. 2420; Schlüssel der vornehmsten Puncten und Wörter, § 2, p. 3668; § 145, 146, pp. 3696, 3697; Morgenröthe, chap. iv. § 9-21, pp. 49-51; chap. xi. § 47, pp. 126, 127, etc.

b. This first substance contains all powers or qualities as not yet separated; thus this salitter likewise appears as the body of God, who embraces all qualities in Himself. Quality thus becomes an important conception, the first determination with Boehme; and he begins with qualities in his work "Morgenröthe im Aufgang." He afterwards associates with this the conferring of quality, and in the same place says: "Quality is the mobility, boiling, springing, and driving of a thing." These qualities he then tries to define, but the account he gives of them is vague. "As for example heat which burns, consumes and drives forth all whatsoever comes into it which is not of the same property; and again it enlightens and warms all cold, wet, and dark things; it compacts and hardens soft things. It contains likewise two other kinds in it, namely Light and Fierceness" (Negativity); "of which the light or the heart of the heat is in itself a pleasant, joyful glance or lustre, a power of life . . . and a source of the heavenly kingdom of joy. For it makes all things in this world living and moving; all flesh, trees, leaves, and grass grow in this world, as in the power of the light, and have their light therein, viz. in the good. Again, it contains also a fierceness or wrath which burns, consumes and spoils. This wrath or fierceness springs, drives, and elevates itself in the light, and makes the light movable. It wrestles and fights together in its two-fold source. The light subsists in God without heat, but it does not subsist so in nature. For all qualities in nature are one in another, in the same manner as God is all. For God" (the Father) "is the Heart." On another occasion (Vom dreifachen Leben des Menschen, chap. iv. § 68, p. 881) the Son is the heart of God; and yet again the Spirit is called the heart (Morgenröthe, chap. ii. § 13, p. 29) "or fountain of nature, and from Him comes all. Now heat reigns and predominates in all powers in nature and warms all, and is one source or spring in all. But the light in the heat gives power to all qualities, for that all grow pleasant and joyful." Boehme goes over quite a list of qualities: cold, hot, bitter, sweet, fierce, acid, hard, dense, soft qualities, sound, etc. "The bitter quality is in God also, but not in that manner as the gall is in man, but it is an everlasting power, in an elevating, triumphing spring or source of joy. All the creatures are made from these qualities, and live therein as in their mother."[1]

"The virtues of the stars are nature itself. Everything in this world proceeds from the stars. That I shall prove to you if you are not a blockhead and have a little reason. If the whole *Curriculum* or the whole circumference of the stars is considered, we soon find that this is the mother of all things, or the nature from which all things have arisen and in which all things stand and live, and through which all things move. And all things are formed from these same powers and remain eternally therein." Thus it is said that God is the reality of all realities. Boehme continues: "You must, however, elevate your mind in the Spirit, and consider how the whole of nature, with all the powers which are in nature, also extension, depth and height, also heaven and earth and all whatsoever is therein, and all that is above the heavens, is together the Body and Corporeity of God; and the powers of the stars are the fountain veins in the natural Body of God, in this world. You must not conceive that in the Body of the stars is the whole triumphing Holy Trinity, God the Father, Son, and Holy Ghost. But we must not so conceive as if God was not at all in the *Corpus* or Body of the stars, and in this world. . . . Here now the question is, From whence has heaven, or whence borrows it this power, that it causes such mobility in nature? Here you must lift up your eyes beyond nature into the light, holy, triumphing, divine

[1] Morgenröthe, chap. i. § 3-7, 9-24, pp. 23-27; chap. ii. § 38-40, pp. 34, 35; § i. p. 28 [see Law's translation].

power, into the unchangeable holy Trinity, which is a triumphing, springing, movable Being, and all powers are therein, as in nature: of this heaven, earth, stars, elements, devils, angels, men, beasts, and all have their Being; and therein all stands. When we nominate heaven and earth, stars and elements, and all that is therein, and all whatsoever is above the heaven, then thereby is nominated the total God, who has made Himself creaturely in these abovementioned " many " Beings, in His power which proceedeth forth from Him."[1]

c. Boehme further defines God the Father as follows: "When we consider the whole nature and its property, then we see the Father: when we behold heaven and the stars, then we behold His eternal power and wisdom. So many stars as stand in the whole heaven, which are innumerable, so manifold and various is the power and wisdom of God the Father. Every star differs in its quality." But "you must not conceive here that every power which is in the Father stands in a peculiar severed or divided part and place in the Father, as the stars do in heaven. No, but the Spirit shows that all the powers in the Father," as the fountainhead, "are one in another as one power." This whole is the universal power which exists as God the Father, wherein all differences are united; " creaturely " it, however, exists as the totality of stars, and thus as separation into the different qualities. "You must not think that God who is in heaven and above the heaven does there stand and hover like a power and quality which has in it neither reason nor knowledge, as the sun which turns round in its circle and shoots forth from itself heat and light, whether it be for benefit or hurt to the earth and creatures. No, the Father is not so, but He is an All-mighty, All-wise, All-knowing, All-seeing, All-

[1] Morgenröthe, chap. ii. § 8, 14-18, 31-33, pp. 29-34 [see Laws' translation].

hearing, All-smelling, All-tasting God, who in Himself is meek, friendly, gracious, merciful, and full of joy, yea Joy itself."[1]

Since Boehme calls the Father all powers, he again distinguishes these as the seven first originating spirits.[2] But there is a certain confusion in this and no thought-determination, no definite reason for there being exactly seven—such precision and certainty is not to be found in Boehme. These seven qualities are likewise the seven planets which move and work in the great Salitter of God; "the seven planets signify the seven spirits of God or the princes of the angels." But they are in the Father as one unity, and this unity is an inward spring and fermentation. "In God all spirits triumph as one spirit, and a spirit ever calms and loves the others, and nothing exists excepting mere joy and rapture. One spirit does not stand alongside the others like stars in heaven, for all seven are contained within one another as one spirit. Each spirit in the seven spirits of God is pregnant with all seven spirits of God;" thus each is in God itself a totality. "One brings forth the other in and through itself;" this is the flashing forth of the life of all qualities.[3]

2. As what came first was the source and germ of all powers and qualities, what comes second is process. This second principle is a very important conception, which with Boehme appears under very many aspects and forms, viz. as the Word, the Separator, Revelation—speaking generally the "I," the source of all difference, and of the will and implicit Being which are in the powers of natural things; but in such a way that the light therein likewise breaks forth which leads them back to rest.

[1] Morgenröthe, chap. iii. § 2, 8-11, pp. 36-38.

[2] Morgenröthe, chap. iv. § 5, 6, p. 48; chap. viii. § 15—chap. xi. 46, pp. 78-126.

[3] Morgenröthe, chap. iii. § 18, p. 40; chap. x. § 54, p. 115; § 39, 40, p. 112; chap. xi. § 7-12, pp. 119, 120.

a. God as the simple absolute existence is not God absolutely; in Him nothing can be known. What we know is something different—but this "different" is itself contained in God as the perception and knowledge of God. Hence of the second step Boehme says that a separation must have taken place in this temperament. "No thing can become manifest to itself without opposition; for if it has nothing to withstand it, it always goes forward on its own account and does not go back within itself. But if it does not go back into itself as into that from which it originally arose, it knows nothing of its original state." Original state [Urstand] he makes use of for substance; and it is a pity that we cannot use this and many other striking expressions. "Without adversity life would have no sensibility nor will nor efficacy, neither understanding nor science. Had the hidden God who is one solitary existence and will not of His own will brought Himself out of Himself, out of the eternal knowledge in the *Temperamento,* into divisibility of will, and introduced this same element of divisibility into an inclusiveness" (Identity) "so as to constitute it a natural and creaturely life, and had this element of separation in life not come into warfare, how was the will of God which is only one to be revealed to Himself? How could a knowledge of itself be present in a solitary will?"[1] We see that Boehme is elevated infinitely above the empty abstraction of the highest reality, etc.

Boehme continues: "The commencement of all Beings is the Word as the breath of God, and God has become the eternal One of eternity and likewise remains so in eternity. The Word is the eternal beginning and remains so eternally, for it is the revelation of the eternal One through and by which the divine power is brought into one knowledge of somewhat. By the Word we understand

[1] Von göttlicher Beschaulichkeit, chap. i. § 8-10, p. 1739.

the revealed will of God: by the Word we mean God the hidden God, from whom the Word eternally springs forth. The Word is the efflux of the divine One, and yet God Himself as His revelation." Λόγος is more definite than Word, and there is a delightful double significance in the Greek expression indicating as it does both reason and speech. For speech is the pure existence of spirit; it is a thing which when once heard goes back within itself. "What has flowed out is wisdom, beginning and cause of all powers, colours, virtue and qualities."[1]

Of the Son Boehme says: "The Son is" of the Father and "in the Father, the heart of the Father or light, and the Father beareth him ever, from eternity to eternity." Thus "the Son is" indeed "another Person from the Father, though no other," but the same "God as the Father," whose image he is.[2] "The Son is the Heart" or the pulsating element "in the Father; all the powers which are in the Father are the propriety of the Father; and the Son is the heart or the kernel in all the powers in the whole Father, and he is the cause of the springing joy in all powers in the whole Father. From the Son the eternal joy rises and springs in all the powers of the Father, as the sun does in the heart of the stars. It signifies the Son, as the circle of the stars signifies the manifold powers of the Father; it lightens the heavens, the stars and the deep above the earth, working in all things that are in this world; it enlightens and gives power to all the stars and tempers their power. The Son of God is continually generated from all the powers of his Father from eternity, just as the sun is born of the stars; He is ever born and is not made, and is the heart and lustre shining forth from all powers. He shines in all powers of the Father, and his power is the moving, spring-

[1] Von göttlicher Beschaulichkeit, chap. iii. § 1-3, pp. 1755, 1756.

[2] Morgenröthe, chap. iii. § 33-35, p. 44 (cf. Rixner: Handbuch d. Gesch. d. Philos. Vol. II. Appendix, p. 106, § 7).

ing joy in all the powers of the Father, and shines in the whole Father as the sun does in the whole world. For if the Son did not shine in the Father, the Father would be a dark valley; for the Father's power would not rise from eternity to eternity, and so the divine Being would not subsist."[1] This life of the Son is an important matter; and in regard to this issuing forth and manifestation Boehme has likewise brought forward the most important assertions.

b. "From such a revelation of powers in which the will of the eternal One contemplates itself, flows the understanding and the knowledge of the something [Ichts], since the eternal will contemplates itself in the something [Ichts]." "Ichts" is a play upon the word "Nichts" (nothing), for it is simply the negative; yet it is at the same time the opposite of nothing, since the Ich (Ego) of self-consciousness is contained in it. The Son, the something, is thus "I," consciousness, self-consciousness: God is not only the abstract neutral but likewise the gathering together of Himself into the point of Being-for-self. The "other" of God is thus the image of God. "This similitude is the *Mysterium magnum*, viz. the creator of all beings and creatures; for it is the separator" (of the whole) "in the efflux of the will which makes the will of the eternal One separable—the separability in the will from which powers and qualities take their rise." This separator is "constituted the steward of nature, by whom the eternal will rules, makes, forms and constitutes all things." The separator is effectuating and self-differentiating, and Boehme calls this "Ichts," likewise Lucifer, the first-born Son of God, the creaturely first-born angel who was one of the seven spirits. "But this Lucifer has fallen and Christ has come in his place."[2] This is the connection of the devil

[1] Morgenröthe, chap. iii. § 15, 18-22, pp. 39-41.
[2] Von göttlicher Beschaulichkeit, chap. iii. § 4, 5, p. 1756, § 12,

with God, namely other-Being and then Being-for-self or Being-for-one, in such a way that the other is for one; and this is the origin of evil in God and out of God. This is the furthest point of thought reached by Jacob Boehme. He represents this Fall of Lucifer as that the "Ichts," i.e. self-knowledge, the "I" [Ichheit] (a word which we find used by him), the inward imagining of self, the inward fashioning of self (the being-for-self), is the fire which absorbs all things. This is the negative side in the separator, the anguish; or it is the wrath of God. This divine wrath is hell and the devil, who through himself imagines himself into himself. This is very bold and speculative; Boehme here seeks to show in God Himself the sources of the divine anger. He also calls the will of the something ["Ichts"] self-hood; it is the passing over of the something ["Ichts"] into the nothing [Nichts], the "I" imagining itself within itself. He says: "Heaven and hell are as far removed from one another as day and night, as something and nothing." Boehme has really here penetrated into the utmost depths of divine essence; evil, matter, or whatever it has been called, is the I = I, the Being-for-self, the true negativity. Before this it was the *nonens* which is itself positive, the darkness; but the true negativity is the "I." It is not anything bad because it is called the evil; it is in mind alone that evil exists, because it is conceived therein as it is in itself. "Where the will of God willeth in anything, there God is manifested, and in that manifestation the angels also dwell; but where God in any thing willeth not with the will of the thing, there God is not manifested to it, but dwelleth" (there) "in Himself without the co-operating of the thing;" in that

p. 1758; Morgenröthe, chap. xii. § 99-107, p. 149, 150; chap. xiii. § 92-104, 31-52, pp. 166-168, 157-160; chap. xiv. § 36, p. 178; Von den drei Principien göttlichen Wesens, chap. iv. § 69, p. 406; chap. xv. § 5, pp. 543, 544.

case "in that thing is its own will, and there the devil dwelleth and all whatever is without God." [1]

Boehme in his own way sets forth the form further assumed in this process in a pictorial manner. This "*Separator* deduces qualities from itself, from which the infinite manifold arises, and through which the eternal One makes itself perceptible" (so that it is for others) "not according to the unity, but in accordance with the efflux of the unity." Implicit Being and the manifold are absolutely opposed through the Notion, which Boehme did not have: Being-for-self implies Being-for-another and retrogression into the opposite. Boehme sways backwards and forwards in apparent contradictions, and does not well know how to find a way out of the difficulty. "But the efflux is carried on to the greatest extreme possible, to the generation of fire"—dark fire without light, darkness, the hidden, the self; [2]—"in which fiery nature," however, since this fire rises and shoots up, "the eternal One becomes majestic and a light," and this light which there breaks forth is the form which the other principle assumes. This is the return to the One. "Thereby" (through fire) "the eternal power becomes desirous and effectual and" (fire) "is the original condition" (essence) "of the sensitive" (feeling) "life, where in the Word of power an eternal sensitive life first takes its origin. For if life had no sensitiveness, it would have no will nor efficacy; but pain"—anguish, suffering—first "makes it" (all life) "effectual and endows

[1] Morgenröthe, chap. xiii. § 53-64, pp. 160-162; Vierzig Fragen von der Seele, XII. § 4, p. 1201; Von sechs theosophischen Puncten, V. 7, § 3, p. 1537; Von wahrer Gelassenheit, chap. i. § 1-7, pp. 1661-1663; Von göttlicher Beschaulichkeit, chap. i. § 23-26, pp. 1742, 1743; Von der Geburt und Bezeichnung aller Wesen, chap. xvi. § 49, p. 2391; Vom übersinnlichen Leben, § 41, 42, p. 1696 [see Law's translation].

[2] Von der Menschwerdung Jesu Christi, Pt. I. chap. v. § 14 p. 1323; Von den drei Principien göttlichen Wesens, chap. x. § 43, p. 470.

it with will. And the light of such kindling through fire makes it joyous, for it is an anointment," joy and loveliness "of painfulness."[1]

Boehme turns this round in many ways in order to grasp the something [Ichts], the Separator, as it "rises"[2] from the Father. The qualities rise in the great Salitter, stir, raise, and move [rügen] themselves. Boehme has there the quality of astringency in the Father, and he then represents the process of the something [Ichts] as a sharpness, a drawing together, as a flash of lightning that breaks forth. This light is Lucifer. The Being-for-self, the self-perception, is by Boehme called the drawing together into a point. That is astringency, sharpness, penetration, fierceness; to this pertains the wrath of God, and here Boehme in this manner grasps the "other" of God in God Himself. "This source can be kindled through great motion or elevation. Through the contraction the creaturely Being is formed so that a heavenly *Corpus* may be" intelligibly "formed. But if it"—the sharpness—" be kindled through elevation, which those creatures only can do which are created out of the divine Salitter, then it is a burning source-vein of the wrath of God. The flash is the mother of light; for the flash generates the light, and is the Father of the fierceness; for the fierceness abides in the flash as a seed in the father, and that flash generates also the tone or sound"—the flash is, speaking generally, the absolute generator. The flash is still connected with pain; light is what brings intelligence. The divine birth is the going forth of the flash, of the life of all qualities.[3] This is all from the Aurora.

In the *Quæstionibus theosophicis* Boehme makes particular use of the form of Yes and No for the separator, for

[1] Von göttlicher Beschaulichkeit, chap. iii. § 11, p. 1757.

[2] *Infra*, p. 213.

[3] Morgenröthe, chap. viii. § 15-20, pp. 78, 79; chap. x. § 38, p. 112; chap. xiii. § 69-91, pp. 162-166; chap xi. § 5-13, pp. 119, 120.

this opposition. He says: "The reader must know that in Yes and No all things consist, whether divine, devilish, earthly, or what they may be called. The One as the Yes is pure power and life, and it is the truth of God or God Himself. He would be unknowable in Himself, and in Him there would be no joy nor elevation, nor feeling" —life—"without the No. The No is a counter-stroke of the Yes, or of the truth" (this negativity is the principle of all knowledge, comprehension), "that the truth may be manifest and be a something wherein there is a *contrarium* in which there is the eternal love, moving, feeling, and willing, and demanding to be loved. And yet we cannot say that the Yes is separated from the No, and that they are two things in proximity; for they are only one thing, but they separate themselves into two beginnings and make two *centra*, where each works and wills in itself. Without those two, which are continually in strife, all things would be a nothing, and would stand still without movement. If the eternal will did not itself flow from itself and introduce itself into receptibility, there would be no form nor distinction, for all powers would" then "be one power. Neither could there be understanding in that case, for the understanding arises" (has its substance) "in the differentiation of the manifold, where one property sees, proves and wills the others. The will which has flowed out wills dissimilarity, so that it may be distinguished from similarity and be its own something—and that something may exist, that the eternal seeing may see and feel. And from the individual will arises the No, for it brings itself into ownness, *i.e.* receptivity of self. It desires to be something and does not make itself in accordance with unity; for unity is a Yes which flows forth, which ever stands thus in the breathing forth of itself, being imperceptible; for it has nothing in which it can find itself excepting in the receptivity of the dissentient will, as in the No which is counterstroke to the Yes, in which the Yes is indeed revealed, and in which it possesses something which it can will. And the No is therefore called a No, because it is a desire turned inwards on itself, as if it were a shutting up into negativity. The emanated seeking will is absorbent and comprehends itself within itself, from it come forms and qualities: (1) Sharpness, (2) Motion, (3) Feeling. (4) The fourth property is Fire as the flash of light; this rises in the bringing together of the great and terrible sharpness and the unity. Thus in the contact a *Flagrat* [Schrack] results, and in this *Flagrat* [Schrack] unity is apprehended as being a Flash or Gleam, an exulting joy." That is the bursting forth of the unity. "For thus the light arises in the midst of the darkness, for the unity becomes a light, and the receptivity of the carnal will in the qualities becomes a Spirit-fire which has its source and origin out of the sharp, cold astringency. And according to that, God is an angry" and "jealous God," and in this we have evil. "(*a*) The first quality of the absorption is the No; (*b*) Sharpness; (*c*) Hardness; (*d*) Feeling; (*e*) the source of fire, hell or hollowness, Hiddenness. (5) The fifth quality, Love, makes in the fire, as in pain, another *Principium* as a great fire of love."[1] These are the main points under the second head. In such depths Boehme keeps struggling on, for to him conceptions are lacking, and there are only religious and chemical forms to be found; and because he uses these in a forced sense in order to express his ideas, not only does barbarism of expression result, but incomprehensibility as well.

c. "From this eternal operation of the sensation the visible world sprang; the world is the Word which has flowed forth and has disposed itself into qualities, since in qualities the particular will has arisen. The *Separator*

[1] 177 Fragen von göttlicher Offenbarung, III. § 2-5, 10-16, pp. 3591-3595.

has made it a will of its own after such a fashion."[1] The world is none other than the essence of God made creaturely.[2] Hence "If thou beholdest the Deep" of the heavens, "the Stars, the Elements and the Earth," and what they have brought forth, "then thou" certainly "comprehendest not with thy eyes the bright and clear Deity, though indeed it is" likewise "there and in them." Thou seest only their creaturely manifestation. "But if thou raisest thy thoughts and considerest . . . God who rules in holiness in this government or dominion, then thou breakest through the heaven of heavens and apprehendest God at His holy heart. The powers of heaven ever operate in images, growths and colours, in order to reveal the holy God, so that He may be in all things known."[3]

3. Finally what comes third in these threefold forms is the unity of the light, of the separator and power: this is the spirit, which is already partially implied in what has preceded. "All the stars signify the power of the Father, and from them issues the sun" (they make themselves a counterstroke to unity). "And from all the stars there goes forth the power which is in every star, into the Deep, and the power, heat and shining of the sun goes likewise into the Deep"—back to the stars, into the power of the Father. "And in the Deep the power of all stars, together with the heat and lustre of the sun, are all but one thing, a moving, boiling Hovering, like a spirit or matter. Now in the whole deep of the Father, externally without the Son, there is nothing but the manifold and unmeasurable

[1] Von göttlicher Beschaulichkeit, chap. iii. § 12, 14, pp. 1757, 1758.

[2] Rixner: Handbuch d. Gesch. d. Philos. Vol. II. Appendix, p. 108, § 5 (from Boehme's Morgenröthe, chap. ii. § 16, pp. 30, 31; § 33, p. 34).

[3] Morgenröthe, chap. xxiii. § 11, 12, pp. 307, 308 (cf. Rixner: Handb. d. Gesch. d. Philos. Vol. II. Appendix, p. 108, § 5); Theosophische Sendbriefe, I. § 5, p. 3710.

or unsearchable power of the Father and the Light of the Son. The Light of the Son is in the Deep of the Father a living, all-powerful, all-knowing, all-hearing, all-seeing, all-smelling, all-tasting, all-feeling Spirit, wherein is all power, splendour, and wisdom, as in the Father and the Son."[1] That is Love, the softener of all powers through the light of the Son. We see that the sensuous element thus pertains to this.

Boehme really has the idea that "God's essence" (which has proceeded from the eternal deep as world) "is thus not something far away which possesses a particular position or place, for" essence, "the abyss of nature and creation, is God Himself. Thou must not think that in heaven there was some manner of *Corpus*"—the seven spirits generate this *Corpus* or heart—"which above all other things is called God. No; but the whole divine power which itself is heaven and the heaven of all heavens, is so generated, and that is called God the Father; of whom all the holy angels are generated, in like manner also the spirit of all men. Thou canst name no place, either in heaven or in this world, where the divine birth is not. The birth of the divine Trinity likewise takes place in thine own heart; all three persons are generated in thy heart, God the Father, Son and Holy Ghost. In the divine power everywhere we find the fountain spring of the divine birth; and there already are all the seven qualifying or fountain spirits of God, as if thou wouldst make a spacious creaturely circumscribed circle and hadst the deity therein."[2] In every spirit all are contained.

To Boehme this trinity is the complete universal life in each individual, it is absolute substance. He says: "All things in this world are according to the similitude of this

[1] Morgenröthe, chap. iii. § 29, 30, p. 43 [see Law's translation].

[2] Von göttlicher Beschaulichkeit, chap. iii. § 13, p. 1758; Morgenröthe, chap. x. § 55, 60, 58, pp. 115, 116 (chap. xi. § 4, p. 118).

ternary. Ye blind Jews, Turks, and Heathens, open wide the eyes of your mind: I will show you, in your body, and in every natural thing, in men, beasts, fowls, and worms, also in wood, stone, leaves, and grass, the likeness of the holy ternary in God. You say, there is but one Being in God, and that God has no Son. Open your eyes and consider your selves: man is made according to the similitude and out of the power of God in his ternary. Behold thy inward man, and then thou wilt see it most plainly and clearly, if thou art not a fool and an irrational beast. Therefore observe, in thy heart, in thy veins, and in thy brain, thou hast thy spirit; and all the powers which move in thy heart, in thy veins, and in thy brain, wherein thy life consists, signify God the Father. From that power springs up [gebäret] thy light, so that thou seest, understandest, and knowest in the same power what thou art to do; for that light glimmers in thy whole body; and the whole body moves in the power and knowledge of the light; this is the Son which is born in thee." This light, this seeing and understanding, is the second determination; it is the relationship to itself. "Out of thy light goes forth into the same power, reason, understanding, skill, and wisdom, to govern the whole body, and to distinguish all whatsoever is externally without the body. And both these are but one in the government of thy mind, viz. thy spirit, which signifies God the Holy Ghost. And the Holy Ghost from God rules in this spirit in thee, if thou art a child of light and not of darkness. Now observe: in either wood, stone, or herbs there are three things contained, neither can anything be generated or grow, if but one of the three should be left out. First, there is the power, from which a body comes to be, whether wood, stone, or herbs; after that there is in that" thing "a sap which is the heart of the thing. And thirdly there is in it a springing, flowing power, smell, or taste, which is the spirit of the thing whereby it grows and increases.

Now if any of these three fail, the thing cannot subsist."[1] Thus Boehme regards everything as this ternary.

When he comes into particulars we see that he is obscure; from his detailed explanations there is therefore not much to be derived. As showing his manner of apprehending natural things I shall give one more example of the manner in which, in the further working out of the existence of nature as a counterstroke to the divine knowledge, he makes use of what we call things as Notions (*supra*, p. 192). The creaturely, he says, has "three kinds of powers or *Spiritus* in different *Centris*, but in one *Corpore*. (*a*) The first and external *Spiritus* is the coarse sulphur, salt and *Mercurius*, which is a substance of four elements" (fire, water, earth, air) "or of the stars. It forms the visible *Corpus* according to the constellation of the stars or property of the planets and now enkindled elements—the greatest power of the *Spiritus mundi*. The *Separator* makes the signature or sign"—the self. The salt, the salitter, is approximately the neutral: mercury [Merk or Mark] the operating, unrest as against nourishment; the coarse sulphur, the negative unity. (*β*) "The other *Spiritus* is found in the oil of sulphur, the fifth essence, viz. a root of the four elements. That is the softening and joy of the coarse, painful spirit of sulphur and salt; the real cause of growing life, a joy of nature as is the sun in the elements"—the direct principle of life. "In the inward ground of that coarse spirit we see a beautiful, clear *Corpus* in which the ideal light of nature shines from the divine efflux." The outward separator signs what is taken up with the shape and form of the plant which receives into itself this coarse nourishment. (*γ*) "What comes third is the tincture, a spiritual fire and light; the highest reason for which the first separation of qualities takes place in the existence of this world. *Fiat* is the

[1] Morgenröthe, chap. iii. § 36-38, 47, pp. 44-46 [see Law's translation].

Word of each thing and belongs according to its peculiar quality to eternity. Its origin is the holy power of God. Smell [Ruch] is the sensation of this tincture. The elements are only a mansion and counterstroke of the inward power, a cause of the movement of the tincture."[1] Sensuous things entirely lose the force of sensuous conceptions. Boehme uses them, though not as such, as thought-determinations; that constitutes the hard and barbarous element in Boehme's representations, yet at the same time this unity with actuality and this present of infinite existence.

Boehme describes the opposition in creation in the following way. If nature is the first efflux of the *Separator*, two kinds of life must yet be understood as in the counterstroke of the divine essence; beyond that temporal one there is an eternal, to which the divine understanding is given. It stands at the basis of the eternal, spiritual world, in the *Mysterium Magnum* of the divine counterstroke (personality)—a mansion of divine will through which it reveals itself and is revealed to no peculiarity of personal will. In this *centrum* man has both lives in himself, he belongs to time and eternity. He is (*a*) universal in the "eternal understanding of the one good will which is a temperament; (*β*) the original will of nature, viz. the comprehensibility of the *Centra*, where each *centrum* in the divisibility shuts itself in one place to egotism and self-will as a personal *Mysterium* or mind. The former only requires a counterstroke to its similarity; this latter, the self-generated natural will also requires in the place of the egotism of the dark impression a likeness, that is a counterstroke through its own comprehensibility; through which comprehension it requires nothing but its corporality as a natural ground."

[1] Von göttlicher Beschaulichkeit, chap. i. § 33, p. 1745; chap. ii. § 29, p. 1754; chap. iii. § 15, 18-24, 27, 29, pp. 1758-1761; Von den drei Principien göttlichen Wesens, chap. viii. § 5, p. 433; Mysterium Magnum, oder Erklärung des ersten Buchs Mosis, chap. xix. § 28, pp. 2830, 2831.

Now it is this "I," the dark, pain, fire, the wrath of God, implicitude, self-comprehension, which is broken up in regeneration; the I is shattered, painfulness brought into true rest—just as the dark fire breaks into light.[1]

Now these are the principal ideas found in Boehme; those most profound are (*a*) the generating of Light as the Son of God from qualities, through the most living dialectic; (*β*) God's diremption of Himself. Barbarism in the working out of his system can no more fail to be recognized than can the great depths into which he has plunged by the union of the most absolute opposites. Boehme grasps the opposites in the crudest, harshest way, but he does not allow himself through their unworkableness to be prevented from asserting the unity. This rude and barbarous depth which is devoid of Notion, is always a present, something which speaks from itself, which has and knows everything in itself. We have still to mention Boehme's piety, the element of edification, the way in which the soul is guided in his writings. This is in the highest degree deep and inward, and if one is familiar with his form these depths and this inwardness will be found. But it is a form with which we cannot reconcile ourselves, and which permits no definite conception of details, although we cannot fail to see the profound craving for speculation which existed within this man.

[1] Von göttlicher Beschaulichkeit, chap. i. § 23-39, pp. 1742-1746; chap. ii. § 1-13, 16-30, pp. 1747-1754.

SECTION TWO

Period of the Thinking Understanding

After Neo-Platonism and all that is associated with it is left behind, it is not until Descartes is arrived at that we really enter upon a philosophy which is, properly speaking, independent, which knows that it comes forth from reason as independent, and that self-consciousness is an essential moment in the truth. Philosophy in its own proper soil separates itself entirely from the philosophizing theology, in accordance with its principle, and places it on quite another side. Here, we may say, we are at home, and like the mariner after a long voyage in a tempestuous sea, we may now hail the sight of land; with Descartes the culture of modern times, the thought of modern Philosophy, really begins to appear, after a long and tedious journey on the way which has led so far. It is specially characteristic of the German that the more servile he on the one hand is, the more uncontrolled is he on the other; restraint and want of restraint—originality, is the angel of darkness that buffets us. In this new period the universal principle by means of which everything in the world is regulated, is the thought that proceeds from itself; it is a certain inwardness, which is above all evidenced in respect to Christianity, and which is the Protestant principle in accordance with which thought has come to the consciousness of the world at large as that to which every man has a claim. Thus because the independently existent thought, this culminating point of inwardness, is now set forth and firmly grasped as such, the dead externality of authority is set aside and regarded as out of place. It is only through my own free thought within that thought can however be recognized and ratified by me. This likewise signifies that such free thought is the universal business of the world and of individuals; it is indeed the duty of every man, since everything is based upon it; thus what claims to rank as established in the world man must scrutinize in his own thoughts. Philosophy is thus become a matter of universal interest, and one respecting which each can judge for himself; for everyone is a thinker from the beginning.

On account of this new beginning to Philosophy we find in the old histories of Philosophy of the seventeenth century—*e.g.* that of Stanley—the philosophy of the Greeks and Romans only, and Christianity forms the conclusion. The idea was that neither in Christianity, nor subsequently, any philosophy was to be found, because there was no longer a necessity for it, seeing that the philosophic theology of the Middle Ages had not free, spontaneous thought as its principle (Vol. I. pp. 111, 112). But though it is true that this has now become the philosophic principle, we must not expect that it should be at once methodically developed out of thought. The old assumption is made, that man only attains to the truth through reflection; this plainly is the principle. But the determination and definition of God, the world of the manifold as it appears, is not yet revealed as necessarily proceeding from thought; for we have only reached the thought of a content which is given through ordinary conception, observation, and experience.

On the one hand we see a metaphysic, and, on the other, the particular sciences: on the one hand abstract thought as such, on the other its content taken from experience; these two lines in the abstract stand opposed to one another, and yet they do not separate themselves so sharply. We shall indeed come to an opposition, viz. to that between *a priori* thought—that the determinations which are to hold good for thought must be taken from thought itself—and the determination that we must commence, conclude and think from experience. This is the opposition between rationalism and empiricism; but it is really a subordinate one, because even the metaphysical mode in philosophy, which only allows validity to immanent thought, does not take what is methodically developed from the necessity of thought, but in the old way derives its content from inward or outward experience, and through reflection and meditation renders it abstract. The form of philosophy which is first reached through thought is metaphysics, the form of the thinking understanding; this period has, as its outstanding figures, Descartes and Spinoza, likewise Malebranche and Locke, Leibnitz and Wolff. The second form is Scepticism and Criticism with regard to the thinking understanding, to metaphysics as such, and to the universal of empiricism; here we shall go on to speak of representatives of the Scottish, German, and French philosophies; the French materialists again turn back to metaphysics.

CHAPTER I

THE METAPHYSICS OF THE UNDERSTANDING

METAPHYSICS is what reaches after substance, and this implies that one unity, one thought is maintained in opposition to dualism, just as Being was amongst the ancients. In metaphysics itself we have, however, the opposition between substantiality and individuality. What comes first is the spontaneous, but likewise uncritical, metaphysics, and it is represented by Descartes and Spinoza, who assert the unity of Being and thought. The second stage is found in Locke, who treats of the opposition itself inasmuch as he considers the metaphysical Idea of experience, that is the origin of thoughts and their justification, not yet entering on the question of whether they are absolutely true. In the third place we have Leibnitz's monad—the world viewed as a totality.

A. FIRST DIVISION.

We here encounter the innate ideas of Descartes. The philosophy of Spinoza, in the second place, is related to the philosophy of Descartes as its necessary development only; the method is an important part of it. A method which stands alongside of Spinozism and which is also a perfected development of Cartesianism, is, in the third place, that by which Malebranche has represented this philosophy.

1. DESCARTES.

René Descartes is a bold spirit who re-commenced the

whole subject from the very beginning and constituted afresh the groundwork on which Philosophy is based, and to which, after a thousand years had passed, it once more returned. The extent of the influence which this man exercised upon his times and the culture of Philosophy generally, cannot be sufficiently expressed; it rests mainly in his setting aside all former pre-suppositions and beginning in a free, simple, and likewise popular way, with popular modes of thought and quite simple propositions, in his leading the content to thought and extension or Being, and so to speak setting up this before thought as its opposite. This simple thought appeared in the form of the determinate, clear understanding, and it cannot thus be called speculative thought or speculative reason. There are fixed determinations from which Descartes proceeds, but only of thought; this is the method of his time. What the French called exact science, science of the determinate understanding, made its appearance at this time. Philosophy and exact science were not yet separated, and it was only later on that this separation first took place.

To come to the life of Descartes—he was born in 1596, at La Haye in Touraine, of an ancient and noble race. He received an education of the usual kind in a Jesuit school, and made great progress; his disposition was lively and restless; he extended his insatiable zeal in all directions, pursued his researches into all systems and forms; his studies, in addition to ancient literature, embraced such subjects as philosophy, mathematics, chemistry, physics, and astronomy. But the studies of his youth in the Jesuit school, and those studies which he afterwards prosecuted with the same diligence and strenuous zeal, resulted in giving him a strong disinclination for learning derived from books; he quitted the school where he had been educated, and yet his eagerness for learning was only made the keener through this perplexity and unsatisfied yearning. He went as a young man of eighteen to Paris, and there lived in the great world. But as he here found no satisfaction, he soon left society and returned to his studies. He retired to a suburb of Paris and there occupied himself principally with mathematics, remaining quite concealed from all his former friends. At last, after the lapse of two years, he was discovered by them, drawn forth from his retirement, and again introduced to the great world. He now once more renounced the study of books and threw himself into the affairs of actual life. Thereafter he went to Holland and entered the military service; soon afterwards, in 1619, and in the first year of the Thirty Years' War, he went as a volunteer with the Bavarian troops, and took part in several campaigns under Tilly. Many have found learning unsatisfying; Descartes became a soldier—not because he found in the sciences too little, but because they were too much, too high for him. Here in his winter quarters he studied diligently, and in Ulm, for instance, he made acquaintance with a citizen who was deeply versed in mathematics. He was able to carry out his studies even better in winter quarters at Neuberg on the Danube, where once more, and now most profoundly, the desire awoke in him to strike out a new departure in Philosophy and entirely reconstruct it; he solemnly promised the Mother of God to make a pilgrimage to Loretto if she would prosper him in this design, and if he should now at last come to himself and attain to peace. He was also in the battle at Prague in which Frederick the Elector-Palatine lost the Bohemian crown. Yet since the sight of these wild scenes could not satisfy him, he gave up military service in 1621. He made several other journeys through the rest of Germany, and then proceeded to Poland, Prussia, Switzerland, Italy and France. On account of its greater freedom he withdrew to Holland, in order there to pursue his projects; here he lived in peace from 1629 to 1644—a period in which he composed and issued most of his works, and also defended them against the manifold attacks from which they suffered, and which more especially proceeded from the clergy. Queen Christina of Sweden finally called him to her court at Stockholm, which was the rendezvous for all the most celebrated men of learning of the time, and there he died in 1650.[1]

As regards his philosophic works, those which contain his first principles have in particular something very popular about their method of presentation, which makes them highly to be recommended to those commencing the study of philosophy. Descartes sets to work in a quite simple and childlike manner, with a narration of his reflections as they came to him. Professor Cousin of Paris has brought out a new edition of Descartes in eleven octavo volumes; the greater part consists of letters on natural phenomena. Descartes gave a new impetus to mathematics as well as to philosophy. Several important methods were discovered by him, upon which the most brilliant results in higher mathematics were afterwards built. His method is even now an essential in mathematics, for Descartes is the inventor of analytic geometry, and consequently the first to point out the way in this field of science to modern mathematics. He likewise cultivated physics, optics, and astronomy, and made the most important discoveries in these; we have not, however, to deal with such matters. The application of metaphysics to ecclesiastical affairs, investigations, etc., has likewise no special interest for us.

1. In Philosophy Descartes struck out quite original lines; with him the new epoch in Philosophy begins, whereby it was permitted to culture to grasp in the form

[1] Brucker. Hist. crit. phil. T. IV. P. II. pp. 203-217; Cartes. De Methodo, I-II (Amstelod. 1672, 4), pp. 2-7 (Œuvres complètes de Descartes publiées par Victor Cousin, T. I. pp. 125-133; Notes sur l'éloge de Descartes par Thomas (Œuvres de Descartes publiées par Cousin, T. I), p. 83, et suiv.; Tennemann, Vol. X. pp. 210-216.

of universality the principle of its higher spirit in thought, just as Boehme grasped it in sensuous perceptions and forms. Descartes started by saying that thought must necessarily commence from itself; all the philosophy which came before this, and specially what proceeded from the authority of the Church, was for ever after set aside. But since here thought has properly speaking grasped itself as abstract understanding only, in relation to which the more concrete content still stands over on the other side, the determinate conceptions were not yet deduced from the understanding, but taken up only empirically. In Descartes' philosophy we have thus to distinguish what has, and what has not universal interest for us: the former is the process of his thoughts themselves, and the latter the mode in which these thoughts are presented and deduced. Yet we must not consider the process as a method of consistent proof; it is indeed a deep and inward progress, but it comes to us in an ingenuous and naïve form. In order to do justice to Descartes' thoughts it is necessary for us to be assured of the necessity for his appearance; the spirit of his philosophy is simply knowledge as the unity of Thought and Being. And yet on the whole there is little to say about his philosophy.

a. Descartes expresses the fact that we must begin from thought as such alone, by saying that we must doubt everything (*De omnibus dubitandum est*); and that is an absolute beginning. He thus makes the abolition of all determinations the first condition of Philosophy. This first proposition has not, however, the same signification as Scepticism, which sets before it no other aim than doubt itself, and requires that we should remain in this indecision of mind, an indecision wherein mind finds its freedom. It rather signifies that we should renounce all prepossessions—that is, all hypotheses which are accepted as true in their immediacy—and commence from thought, so that from it we should in the first place attain to some fixed and settled basis, and make a true beginning. In Scepticism this is not the case, for with the sceptics doubt is the end at which they rest.[1] But the doubting of Descartes, his making no hypotheses, because nothing is fixed or secure, does not occur in the interests of freedom as such, in order that nothing should have value except freedom itself, and nothing exist in the quality of an external objective. To him everything is unstable indeed, in so far as the Ego can abstract from it or can think, for pure thought is abstraction from everything. But in consciousness the end is predominant, and it is to arrive at something fixed and objective—and not the moment of subjectivity, or the fact of being set forth, known and proved by me. Yet this last comes along with the other, for it is from the starting point of my thought that I would attain my object; the impulse of freedom is thus likewise fundamental.

In the propositions in which Descartes gives in his own way the ground of this great and most important principle, there is found a naïve and empirical system of reasoning. This is an example: "Because we were born as children, and formed all manner of judgments respecting sensuous things before we had the perfect use of our reason, we are through many preconceived ideas hindered from the knowledge of the truth. From these we appear not to be able to free ourselves in any other way but by once in our lives striving to doubt that respecting which we have the very slightest suspicion of an uncertainty. Indeed it is really desirable to hold as false everything in respect to which we have any doubt, so that we may find more clearly what is most certain and most knowable. Yet this doubt has to be limited to the contemplation of the truth, for in the conduct of our life we are compelled to choose the

[1] Spinoza: Principia philosophiæ Cartesianæ (Benedicti de Spinoza Opera, ed. Paulus. Jenæ, 1802, T. I.), p. 2.

probable, since there the opportunity for action would often pass away before we could solve our doubts. But here, where we have only to deal with the search for truth, we may very reasonably doubt whether any thing sensuous and perceptible exists—in the first place because we find that the senses often deceive us and it is prudent not to trust in what has even once deceived us, and then because every day in dreaming we think we feel or see before ourselves innumerable things which never were, and to the doubter no signs are given by which he can safely distinguish sleeping from waking. We shall hereby likewise doubt everything else, even mathematical propositions, partly because we have seen that some err even in what we hold most certain, and ascribe value to what to us seems false, and partly because we have heard that a God exists who has created us, and who can do everything, so that He may have created us liable to err. But if we conceive ourselves not to derive our existence from God, but from some other source, perhaps from ourselves, we are all the more liable, in that we are thus imperfect, to err. But we have so far the experience of freedom within us that we can always refrain from what is not perfectly certain and well founded."[1] The demand which rests at the basis of Descartes' reasonings thus is that what is recognized as true should be able to maintain the position of having the thought therein at home with itself. The so-called immediate intuition and inward revelation, which in modern times is so highly regarded, has its place here. But because in the Cartesian form the principle of freedom as such is not brought into view, the grounds which are here advanced are for the most part popular.

b. Descartes sought something in itself certain and true,

[1] Cartes. Principia philosophiæ, P. I. § 1–6 (Amstelod. 1672, 4), pp. 1, 2 (Œuvres, T. III. pp. 63–66); cf. Meditationes de prima philosophia, I. (Amstelod. 1685, 4), pp. 5–8 (Œuvres, T. I. pp. 235–245); De Methodo, IV. p. 20 (pp. 156–158).

which should neither be only true like the object of faith without knowledge, nor the sensuous and also sceptical certainty which is without truth. The whole of Philosophy as it had been carried on up to this time was vitiated by the constant pre-supposition of something as true, and in some measure, as in the Neo-Platonic philosophy, by not giving the form of scientific knowledge to its matter, or by not separating its moments. But to Descartes nothing is true which does not possess an inward evidence in consciousness, or which reason does not recognize so clearly and conclusively that any doubt regarding it is absolutely impossible. "Because we thus reject or declare to be false everything regarding which we can have any doubt at all, it is easy for us to suppose that there is no God, no heaven, no body—but we cannot therefore say that we do not exist, who think this. For it is contradictory to say that what thinks does not exist. Hence the knowledge that 'I think, therefore I am,' is what we arrive at first of all, and it is the most certain fact that offers itself to everyono who follows after philosophy in an orderly fashion. This is the best way of becoming acquainted with the nature of spirit and its diversity from body. For if we inquire who we are who can set forth as untrue everything which is different from ourselves, we clearly see that no extension, figure, change of position, nor any such thing which can be ascribed to body, constitutes our nature, but only thought alone; which is thus known earlier and more certainly than any corporeal thing."[1] 'I' has thus significance here as thought, and not as individuality of self-consciousness. The second proposition of the Cartesian philosophy is hence the immediate certainty of thought. Certainty is only knowledge as such in its pure form as self-relating, and this is thought; thus then the unwieldy understanding makes its way on to the necessity of thought.

[1] Cartes. Principia philosophiæ, P. I. § 7, 8, p. 2 (pp. 66, 67).

Descartes begins, just as Fichte did later on, with the 'I' as indubitably certain; I know that something is presented in me. By this Philosophy is at one stroke transplanted to quite another field and to quite another standpoint, namely to the sphere of subjectivity. Presuppositions in religion are given up; proof alone is sought for, and not the absolute content which disappears before abstract infinite subjectivity. There is in Descartes likewise a seething desire to speak from strong feeling, from the ordinary sensuous point of view, just as Bruno and so many others, each in his own fashion, express as individualities their particular conceptions of the world. To consider the content in itself is not the first matter; for I can abstract from all my conceptions, but not from the 'I.' We think this and that, and hence it is—is to give the common would-be-wise argument of those incapable of grasping the matter in point; that a determinate content exists is exactly what we are forced to doubt—there is nothing absolutely fixed. Thought is the entirely universal, but not merely because I can abstract, but because 'I' is thus simple, self-identical. Thought consequently comes first; the next determination arrived at, in direct connection with it, is the determination of Being. The 'I think' directly involves my Being; this, says Descartes, is the absolute basis of all Philosophy.[1] The determination of Being is in my 'I'; this connection is itself the first matter. Thought as Being and Being as thought—that is my certainty, 'I'; in the celebrated *Cogito, ergo sum* we thus have Thought and Being inseparably bound together.

On the one hand this proposition is regarded as a syllogism: from thought Being is deduced. Kant more especially has objected to this that Being is not contained in thinking, that it is different from thinking. This is

[1] Cartes. De Methodo, IV. pp. 20, 21 (p. 158); Spinoza: Principia philosophiæ Cartes, p. 14.

true, but they are still inseparable, or constitute an identity; their difference is not to the prejudice of their unity. Yet this maxim of pure abstract certainty, the universal totality in which everything implicitly exists, is not proved;[1] we must therefore not try to convert this proposition into a syllogism. Descartes himself says: "There is no syllogism present at all. For in order that there should be such, the major premise must have been 'all that thinks exists'"—from which the subsumption would have followed in the minor premise, 'now I am.' By this the immediacy which rests in the proposition would be removed. "But that major premise" is not set forth at all, being "really in the first instance derived from the original 'I think, therefore, I am.'"[2] For arriving at a conclusion three links are required—in this case we ought to have a third through which thought and Being should have been mediated, and it is not to be found here. The 'Therefore' which binds the two sides together is not the 'Therefore' of a syllogism; the connection between Being and Thought is only immediately posited. This certainty is thus the *prius;* all other propositions come later. The thinking subject as the simple immediacy of being-at-home-with-me is the very same thing as what is called Being; and it is quite easy to perceive this identity. As universal, thought is contained in all that is particular, and thus is pure relation to itself, pure oneness with itself. We must not make the mistake of representing Being to ourselves as a concrete content, and hence it is the same immediate identity which thought likewise is. Immediacy is, however, a one-sided determination; thought does not contain it alone, but also the determination to mediate itself with itself, and thereby

[1] Cartes. De Methodo, IV. p. 21 (p. 159); Epistol. T. I. ep. 118 (Amstelod. 1682, 4), p. 379 (Œuvres, T. IX. pp. 442, 443).

[2] Cartes. Responsiones ad sec. objectiones, adjunctæ Meditationibus de prima philosophia, p. 74 (p. 427); Spinoza: Principia philosophiæ Cartes., pp. 4, 5.

—by the mediation being at the same time the abrogation of the mediation—it is immediacy. In thought we thus have Being; Being is, however, a poor determination, it is the abstraction from the concrete of thought. This identity of Being and Thought, which constitutes the most interesting idea of modern times, has not been further worked out by Descartes; he has relied on consciousness alone, and for the time being placed it in the forefront. For with Descartes the necessity to develop the differences from the 'I think' is not yet present; Fichte first applied himself to the deduction of all determinations from this culminating point of absolute certainty.

Other propositions have been set against that of Descartes. Gassendi,[1] for example, asks if we might not just as well say *Ludificor, ergo sum:* I am made a fool of by my consciousness, therefore I exist—or properly speaking, therefore I am made a fool of. Descartes himself recognized that this objection merited consideration, but he here repels it, inasmuch as it is the 'I' alone and not the other content which has to be maintained. Being alone is identical with pure thought, and not its content, be it what it may. Descartes further says: "By thought I, however, understand all that takes place in us within our consciousness, in as far as we are conscious of it; thus will, conception, and even feeling are identical with thought. For if I say 'I see,' or 'I walk out,' and 'therefore I am,' and understand by this the seeing and walking which is accomplished by the body, the conclusion is not absolutely certain, because, as often happens in a dream, I may imagine that I can see or walk even if I do not open my eyes nor move from my place, and I might also possibly do so supposing I had no body. But if I understand it of the subjective feeling or the consciousness of

[1] Appendix ad Cartes. Meditationes, continens objectiones quint. p. 4 (Œuvres, T. II. pp. 92, 93).

seeing or walking itself, because it is then related to the mind that alone feels or thinks that it sees or walks, this conclusion is perfectly certain."[1] "In a dream" is an empirical mode of reasoning, but there is no other objection to it. In willing, seeing, hearing, &c., thought is likewise contained; it is absurd to suppose that the soul has thinking in one special pocket, and seeing, willing, &c., in others. But if I say 'I see,' 'I walk out,' there is present on the one hand my consciousness 'I,' and consequently thought; on the other hand, however, there is present willing, seeing, hearing, walking, and thus a still further modification of the content. Now because of this modification I cannot say 'I walk, and therefore I am,' for I can undoubtedly abstract from the modification, since it is no longer universal Thought. Thus we must merely look at the pure consciousness contained in the concrete 'I.' Only when I accentuate the fact that I am present there as thinking, is pure Being implied; for only with the universal is Being united.

"In this it is implied," says Descartes, "that thought is more certain to me than body. If from the fact that I touch or see the earth I judge that it exists, I must more certainly judge from this that my thought exists. For it may very well happen that I judge the earth to exist, even if it does not exist, but it cannot be that I judge this, and that my mind which judges this does not exist."[2] That is to say, everything which is for me I may assert to be non-existent; but when I assert myself to be non-existent, I myself *assert*, or it is *my* judgment. For I cannot set aside the fact that I judge, even if I can abstract from that respecting which I judge. In this Philosophy has regained its own ground that thought starts from thought as what is certain in itself, and not from something external, not from some-

[1] Cartes. Principia philosophiæ, P. I. § 9, pp. 2, 3 (pp. 67, 68).
[2] Ibid. P. I. § 11, p. 3 (pp. 69, 70).

thing given, not from an authority, but directly from the freedom that is contained in the 'I think.' Of all else I may doubt, of the existence of bodily things, of my body itself; or this certainty does not possess immediacy in itself. For 'I' is just certainty itself, but in all else this certainty is only predicate; my body is certain to *me*, it is not this certainty itself.[1] As against the certainty we feel of having a body, Descartes adduces the empirical phenomenon that we often hear of persons imagining they feel pain in a limb which they have lost long ago.[2] What is actual, he says is a substance, the soul is a thinking substance; it is thus for itself, separate from all external material things and independent. That it is thinking is evident from its nature: it would think and exist even if no material things were present; the soul can hence know itself more easily than its body:[3]

All else that we can hold as true rests on this certainty; for in order that anything should be held as true, evidence is requisite, but nothing is true which has not this inward evidence in consciousness. "Now the evidence of everything rests upon our perceiving it as clearly and vividly as that certainty itself, and on its so entirely depending from, and harmonizing with this principle, that if we wished to doubt it we should also have to doubt this principle likewise" (our *ego*).[4] This knowledge is indeed on its own account

[1] Cartes. Respons. ad sec. object.: Rationes more geometr. dispos., Postulata, p. 86 (pp. 454, 455); Spinoza: Principia philosophiæ, Cartes., p. 13.

[2] Cartes. Princip. philos., P. IV. § 196, pp. 215, 216 (pp. 507-509); Meditation. VI. p. 38 (pp. 329, 330); Spinoza: Principia philos. Cartes., pp. 2, 3.

[3] Cartes. Respons. ad sec. object.: Rat. more geom. dispos., Axiomata V., VI. p. 86 (p. 453), et Propositio IV. p. 91 (pp. 464, 465); Meditationes, II. pp. 9-14 (pp. 246-262).

[4] Cartes. De Methodo, IV. p. 21 (pp. 158, 159); Spinoza: Principia philosoph. Cartes., p. 14.

perfect evidence, but it is not yet the truth; or if we take that Being as truth, it is an empty content, and it is with the content that we have to do.

c. What comes third is thus the transition of this certainty into truth, into the determinate; Descartes again makes this transition in a naïve way, and with it we for the first time begin to consider his metaphysics. What here takes place is that an interest arises in further representations and conceptions of the abstract unity of Being and Thought; there Descartes sets to work in an externally reflective manner. "The consciousness which merely knows itself to be certain now however seeks to extend its knowledge, and finds that it has conceptions of many things—in which conceptions it does not deceive itself, so long as it does not assert or deny that something similar outside corresponds to them." Deception in the conceptions has meaning only in relation to external existence. "Consciousness also discovers universal conceptions, and obtains from them proofs which are evident, *e.g.* the geometric proposition that the three angles of a triangle are together equal to two right angles is a conception which follows incontrovertibly from others. But in reflecting whether such things really exist doubts arise."[1] That there is such a thing as a triangle is indeed in this case by no means certain, since extension is not contained in the immediate certainty of myself. The soul may exist without the bodily element, and this last without it; they are in reality different; one is conceivable without the other. The soul thus does not think and know the other as clearly as the certainty of itself.[2]

Now the truth of all knowledge rests on the proof of the existence of God. The soul is an imperfect substance,

[1] Cartes. Principia philosophiæ, P. I. § 13, pp. 3, 4 (pp. 71, 72).

[2] Cartes. Respons. ad sec. object: Rationes more geom. dispos., Def. I. p. 85 (pp. 451, 452), et Proposit. IV. p. 91 (pp. 464, 465); Meditationes, III. pp. 15-17 (pp. 263-268).

but it has the Idea of an absolute perfect existence within itself; this perfection is not begotten in itself, just because it is an imperfect substance; this Idea is thus innate. In Descartes the consciousness of this fact is expressed by his saying that as long as the existence of God is not proved and perceived the possibility of our deceiving ourselves remains, because we cannot know whether we do not possess a nature ordered and disposed to err (*supra*, p. 226).[1] The form is rather a mistaken one, and it only generally expresses the opposition in which self-consciousness stands to the consciousness of what is different, of the objective; and we have to deal with the unity of both—the question being whether what is in thought likewise possesses objectivity. This unity rests in God, or is God Himself. I shall put these assertions in the manner of Descartes: "Amongst these various conceptions possessed by us there likewise is the conception of a supremely intelligent, powerful, and absolutely perfect Being; and this is the most excellent of all conceptions." This all-embracing universal conception has therefore this distinguishing feature, that in its case the uncertainty respecting Being which appears in the other conceptions, finds no place. It has the characteristic that "In it we do not recognize existence as something merely possible and accidental, as we do the conceptions of other things which we perceive clearly, but as a really essential and eternal determination. For instance, as mind perceives that in the conception of a triangle it is implied that the three angles are equal to two right angles, the triangle has them; and in the same way from the fact that mind perceives existence to be necessarily and eternally implied in the Notion of the most perfect reality, it is forced to conclude that the most

[1] Cartes. Principia philos., P. I. § 20, p. 6 (pp. 76, 77); Meditationes, III. pp. 17-25 (pp. 268-292); De Methodo, IV. pp. 21, 22 (pp. 159-162); Spinoza: Principia philos. Cartes., p. 10.

perfect reality exists."[1] For to perfection there likewise pertains the determination of existence, since the conception of a non-existent is less perfect. Thus we there have the unity of thought and Being, and the ontological proof of the existence of God; this we met with earlier (p. 63, *seq.*) in dealing with Anselm.

The proof of the existence of God from the Idea of Him is in this wise: In this Notion existence is implied; and therefore it is true. Descartes proceeds further in the same direction, in so far as after the manner of empirical axioms he sets forth: (*a*) "There are different degrees of reality or entity, for the substance has more reality than the accident or the mode, and infinite substance has more than finite." (*β*) "In the Notion of a thing existence is implied, either the merely potential or the necessary," *i.e.* in the 'I' there is Being as the immediate certainty of an other-being, of the not-I opposed to the I. (γ) "No thing or no perfection of a thing which really exists *actu* can have the Nothing as original cause of its existence. For if anything could be predicated of nothing, thought could equally well be predicated of it, and I would thus say that I am nothing because I think." Descartes here arrives at a dividing line, at an unknown relationship; the Notion of cause is reached, and this is a thought indeed, but a determinate thought. Spinoza says in his explanation, "That the conceptions contain more or less reality, and those moments have just as much evidence as thought itself, because they not only say that we think, but how we think." These determinate modes as differences in the simplicity of thought, had, however, to be demonstrated. Spinoza adds to this step in advance that "The degrees of reality which we perceive in ideas are not in the ideas in as far as they are considered merely as kinds of thought, but in so far as the one represents a substance and the other a mere mode of substance,

[1] Cartes. Principia philos. P. I., § 14, p. 4 (pp. 72, 73.)

or, in a word, in so far as they are considered as conceptions of things." (δ) "The objective reality of Notions" (*i.e.*, the entity of what is represented in so far as it is in the Notion), "demands a first cause in which the same reality is contained not merely objectively" (that is to say in the Notion); "but likewise formally or even *eminenter*—formally, that is perfectly likewise: *eminenter*, more perfectly. For there must at least be as much in the cause as in the effect." (ε) "The existence of God is known immediately" —*a priori*—"from the contemplation of His nature. To say that anything is contained in the nature or in the Notion of a thing is tantamount to saying that it is true: existence is directly contained in the Notion of God. Hence it is quite true to say of Him that existence pertains of necessity to Him. There is implied in the Notion of every particular thing either a possible or a necessary existence—a necessary existence in the Notion of God, *i.e.* of the absolutely perfect Being, for else He would be conceived as imperfect."[1]

Descartes likewise argues after this manner: "Problem: to prove *a posteriori* from the mere Notion within us the existence of God. The objective reality of a Notion demands a cause in which the same reality is not merely contained objectively" (as in the finite), "but formally" (freely, purely for itself, outside of us) "or *eminenter*" (as original). (Axiom δ.) "We now have a Notion of God, but His objective reality is neither formally nor *eminenter* contained within us, and it can thus be only in God Himself."[2] Consequently we see that with Descartes this Idea is an hypothesis. Now we should say we find this highest Idea in us. If we then ask whether this Idea exists, why, this is

[1] Cartes. Resp. ad sec. obj.: Rat. more geom. disp., Ax. III.-VI., X., Prop. I. pp. 88, 89 (pp. 458-461); Spinoza: Princ. phil. Cart., pp. 14-17.

[2] Spinoza: Princip. philos. Cart., p. 20; Cartesii Resp. ad sec. obj.: Rat. more geom. dispos., Propos. II. p. 89 (pp. 461, 462).

the Idea, that existence is asserted with it. To say that it is only a conception is to contradict the meaning of this conception. But here it is unsatisfactory to find that the conception is introduced thus: 'We have this conception,' and to find that it consequently appears like an hypothesis. In such a case it is not proved of this content in itself that it determines itself into this unity of thought and Being. In the form of God no other conception is thus here given than that contained in *Cogito, ergo sum*, wherein Being and thought are inseparably bound up—though now in the form of a conception which I possess within me. The whole content of this conception, the Almighty, All-wise, &c., are predicates which do not make their appearance until later; the content is simply the content of the Idea bound up with existence. Hence we see these determinations following one another in an empirical manner, and not philosophically proved—thus giving us an example of how in *a priori* metaphysics generally hypotheses of conceptions are brought in, and these become objects of thought, just as happens in empiricism with investigations, observations, and experiences.

Descartes then proceeds: "Mind is the more convinced of this when it notices that it discovers within itself the conception of no other thing wherein existence is necessarily implied. From this it will perceive that that idea of highest reality is not imagined by it; it is not chimerical, but a true and unalterable fact which cannot do otherwise than exist, seeing that existence is necessarily involved in it. Our prejudices hinder us from apprehending this with ease, for we are accustomed to distinguish in all other things the essence" (the Notion) "from the existence." Respecting the assertion that thought is not inseparable from existence, the common way of talking is as follows: 'If what men think really existed, things would be different.' But in saying this men do not take into account that what is spoken of in this way is always a particular content, and that in it the essential nature of the finality of things simply signifies the fact that Notion and Being are separable. But how can one argue from finite things to the infinite? "This Notion," Descartes continues, "is furthermore not made by us." It is now declared to be an eternal truth which is revealed in us. "We do not find in ourselves the perfections which are contained in this conception. Thus we are certain that a first cause in which is all perfection, *i.e.* God as really existent, has given them to us; for it is certain to us that from nothing, nothing arises" (according to Boehme God derived the material of the world from Himself), "and what is perfect cannot be the effect of anything imperfect. From Him we must thus in true science deduce all created things."[1] With the proof of the existence of God the validity of and evidence for all truth in its origin is immediately established. God as First Cause is Being-for-self, the reality which is not merely entity or existence in thought. An existence such as this first cause (which is not what we know as a thing) rests in the Notion of the not-I, not of each determinate thing—since these as determinate are negations—but only in the Notion of pure existence or the perfect cause. It is the cause of the truth of ideas, for the aspect that it represents is that of their Being.

d. Fourthly, Descartes goes on to assert: "We must believe what is revealed to us by God, though we cannot understand it. It is not to be wondered at, since we are finite, that there is in God's nature as inconceivably infinite, what passes our comprehension." This represents the entrance of a very ordinary conception. Boehme on the other hand says (*supra*, p. 212): 'The mystery of the Trinity is ever born within us.' Descartes, however, concludes: "Hence we must not trouble ourselves with investigations respecting the infinite; for seeing that we are finite, it is

[1] Cartes. Principia philosophiæ, P. I. §. 15 16, 18, 24, pp. 4, 5, 7 (pp. 73-75, 78, 79).

absurd for us to say anything about it."[1] This matter we shall not, however, enter upon at present.

"Now the first attribute of God is that He is true and the Giver of all light; it is hence quite contrary to His nature to deceive us. Hence the light of nature or the power of acquiring knowledge given us by God can affect no object which is not really true in as far as it is affected by it" (the power of acquiring knowledge) "*i.e.* as it is perceived clearly and distinctly." We ascribe truth to God. From this Descartes goes on to infer the universal bond which exists between absolute knowledge and the objectivity of what we thus know. Knowledge has objects, has a content which is known; we call this connection truth. The truth of God is just this unity of what is thought by the subject or clearly perceived, and external reality or existence. "Thereby an end is put to doubt, as if it could be the case that what appears quite evident to us should not be really true. We can thus no longer have any suspicion of mathematical truths. Likewise if we give heed to what we distinguish by our senses in waking or in sleeping, clearly and distinctly, it is easy to recognize in each thing what in it is true." By saying that what is rightly and clearly thought likewise is, Descartes maintains that man comes to know by means of thought what in fact is in things; the sources of errors lie on the other hand in the finitude of our nature. "It is certain, because of God's truth, that the faculty of perceiving and that of assenting through the will, if it extends no further than to that which is clearly perceived, cannot lead to error. Even if this cannot be in any way proved, it is by nature so established in all things, that as often as we clearly perceive anything, we assent to it from ourselves and can in no wise doubt that it is true."[2]

[1] Cartes. Principia philosophiæ, P. I. § 24-26, p. 7 (pp. 79, 80).

[2] Ibid. P. I. § 29, 30, 35, 36, 38, 43, pp. 8-11 (pp. 81-86, 89); Meditationes, IV. pp. 25, 26 (pp. 293–297).

All this is set forth very plausibly, but it is still indeterminate, formal, and shallow; we only have the assertion made to us that this is so. Descartes' method is the method of the clear understanding merely. Certainty with him takes the first place; from it no content is deduced of necessity, no content generally, and still less its objectivity as distinguished from the inward subjectivity of the 'I.' At one time we have the opposition of subjective knowledge and actuality, and at another their inseparable union. In the first case the necessity of mediating them enters in, and the truth of God is asserted to be this mediating power. It consists in this, that His Notion contains reality immediately in itself. The proof of this unity then rests solely upon the fact of its being said that we find within us the idea of complete perfection; thus this conception here appears simply as one found ready to hand. With this is compared the mere conception of God which contains no existence within it, and it is found that without existence it would be imperfect. This unity of God Himself, of His Idea, with His existence, is undoubtedly the Truth; in this we find the ground for holding as true what is for us just as certain as the truth of ourselves. As Descartes proceeds further we thus find that in reality everything has truth for him only in so far as it is really an object of thought, a universal. This truth of God has been, as we shall see, expressed even more clearly and in a more concise way by a disciple of Descartes, if one may venture to call him so—I mean Malebranche (who might really be dealt with here),[1] in his *Recherche de la vérité*.

The first of the fundamental determinations of the Cartesian metaphysics is from the certainty of oneself to arrive at the truth, to recognize Being in the Notion of thought. But because in the thought "I think," I am an individual, thought comes before my mind as subjective;

[1] In the Lectures of 1829–1830 the philosophy of Malebranche is inserted here. (Editor's note).

Being is hence not demonstrated in the Notion of thought itself, for what advance has been made is merely in the direction of separation generally. In the second place the negative of Being likewise comes before self-consciousness, and this negative, united with the positive I, is so to speak implicitly united in a third, in God. God, who before this was a non-contradictory potentiality, now takes objective form to self-consciousness, He is all reality in so far as it is positive, *i.e.* as it is Being, unity of thought and Being, the highest perfection of existence; it is just in the negative, in the Notion of this, in its being an object of thought, that Being is contained. An objection to this identity is now old—Kant urged it likewise—that from the Notion of the most perfect existence more does not follow than that *in* thought existence here and now and the most perfect essence are conjoined, but not *outside* of thought. But the very Notion of present existence is this negative of self-consciousness, not out of thought,—but the thought of the 'out of thought.'

2. Descartes accepts Being in the entirely positive sense, and has not the conception of its being the negative of self-consciousness: but simple Being, set forth as the negative of self-consciousness, is extension. Descartes thus separates extension from God, remains constant to this separation, unites the universe, matter, with God in such a way as to make Him its creator and first cause: and he has the true perception that conservation is a continuous creation, in so far as creation as activity is asserted to be separated. Descartes does not, however, trace extension in a true method back to thought; matter, extended substances, stand over against the thinking substances which are simple; in as far as the universe is created by God, it could not be as perfect as its cause. As a matter of fact the effect is less perfect than the cause, since it is that which is posited, if we are to remain at the conception of cause pertaining to the understanding. Hence according to Descartes extension is the

less perfect. But as imperfect the extended substances cannot exist and subsist through themselves or their Notion; they thus require every moment the assistance of God for their maintenance, and without this they would in a moment sink back into nothing. Preservation is, however, unceasing re-production.[1]

Descartes now proceeds to further particulars, and expresses himself as follows: "We consider what comes under consciousness either as things or their qualities, or as eternal truths which have no existence outside our thought"—which do not belong to this or that time, to this or that place. He calls these last something inborn within us, something not made by us or merely felt,[2] but the eternal Notion of mind itself and the eternal determinations of its freedom, of itself as itself. From this point the conception that ideas are inborn (*innatæ ideæ*) hence proceeds; this is the question over which Locke and Leibnitz dispute. The expression "eternal truths" is current even in these modern times, and it signifies the universal determinations and relations which exist entirely on their own account. The word 'inborn' is however a clumsy and stupid expression, because the conception of physical birth thereby indicated, does not apply to mind. To Descartes inborn ideas are not universal, as they are to Plato and his successors, but that which has evidence, immediate certainty, an immediate multiplicity founded in thought itself—manifold conceptions in the form of a Being, resembling what Cicero calls natural feelings implanted in the heart. We would rather say that such is implied in the nature and essence of our mind and spirit. Mind is active and conducts it-

[1] Cartes. Principia philos. P. I. § 22, 23, pp. 6, 7 (pp. 77, 78); Responsiones quartæ, p. 133 (p. 70); Spinoza: Princip. philos. Cart. pp. 30, 31, 36, 38; Buhle: Geschichte der neuern Philosophie, Vol. III. Sec. I. pp. 17, 18.

[2] Cartes. Principia philos. P. I. § 48, p. 12 (p. 92); Meditationes, III. p. 17 (pp. 268, 269).

self in its activity in a determinate manner; but this activity has no other ground than its freedom. Yet if this is the case more is required than merely to say so; it must be deduced as a necessary product of our mind. We have such ideas, for instance, in the logical laws: "From nothing comes nothing," "A thing cannot both be and not be,"[1] as also in moral principles. These are facts of consciousness which Descartes however soon passes from again; they are only present in thought as subjective, and he has thus not yet inquired respecting their content.

As regards things, on which Descartes now directs his attention, the other side to these eternal verities, the universal determinations of things are substance, permanence, order, &c.[2] He then gives definitions of these thoughts, just as Aristotle draws up a list of the categories. But although Descartes laid it down formerly as essential that no hypotheses must be made, yet now he takes the conceptions, and passes on to them as something found within our consciousness. He defines substance thus: "By substance I understand none other than a thing (*rem*) which requires no other something for existence; and there is only one thing, namely God, which can be regarded as such a substance requiring no other thing." This is what Spinoza says; we may say that it is likewise the true definition, the unity of Notion and reality: "All other" (things) "can only exist by means of a concurrence (*concursus*) of God"; what we still call substance outside of God thus does not exist for itself, does not have its existence in the Notion itself. That is then called the system of assistance (*systema assistentiæ*) which is, however, transcendental. God is the absolute uniter of Notion and actuality; other things, finite things which have a limit and stand in dependence,

[1] Cartes. Principia philosophiæ, P. I. § 49, p. 13 (p. 93).

[2] Ibid. P. I. § 48, p. 12 (p. 92).

require something else. "Hence if we likewise call other things substances, this expression is not applicable both to them and to God *univoce*, as is said in the schools; that is to say no definite significance can be given to this word which would equally apply both to God and to the creatures."[1]

"But I do not recognize more than two sorts of things; the one is that of thinking things, and the other that of things which relate to what is extended." Thought, the Notion, the spiritual, the self-conscious, is what is at home with itself, and its opposite is contained in what is extended, spatial, separated, not at home with itself nor free. This is the real distinction (*distinctio realis*) of substances: "The one substance can be clearly and definitely comprehended without the other. But the corporeal and the thinking and creating substance can be comprehended under this common notion, for the reason that they are things which require God's support alone in order to exist." They are universal; other finite things require other things as conditions essential to their existence. But extended substance, the kingdom of nature, and spiritual substance, do not require one another. They may be called substances, because each of them constitutes an entire range or sphere, an independent totality. But because, Spinoza concluded, each side, the kingdom of thought as well as nature, is one complete system within itself, they are likewise in themselves, that is absolutely, identical as God, the absolute substance; for thinking spirit this implicit is thus God, or their differences are ideal.

Descartes proceeds from the Notion of God to what is created, to thought and extension, and from this to the

[1] Cartes. Princip. philosophiæ, P. I. § 51, p. 14 (p. 95).

[2] Ibid. P. I. § 48, pp. 12, 13 (p. 92); § 60, p. 16 (p. 101); § 52, p. 14 (p. 95); Ration. more geometr. dispos., Definit. X. p. 86 (p. 454).

particular. "Now substances have several attributes without which they cannot be thought"—that signifies their determinateness—"but each has something peculiar to itself which constitutes its nature and essence"—a simple universal determinateness—"and to which the others all relate. Thus thought constitutes the absolute attribute of mind," thought is its quality; "extension is" the essential determination of corporeality, and this alone is "the true nature of body. What remains are merely secondary qualities, modes, like figure and movement in what is extended, imagination, feeling and will in thinking; they may be taken away or thought away. God is the uncreated, thinking substance."[1]

Descartes here passes to what is individual, and because he follows up extension he arrives at matter, rest, movement. One of Descartes' main points is that matter, extension, corporeality, are quite the same thing for thought; according to him the nature of body is fulfilled in its extension, and this should be accepted as the only essential fact respecting the corporeal world. We say that body offers resistance, has smell, taste, colour, transparency, hardness, &c., since without these we can have no body. All these further determinations respecting what is extended, such as size, rest, movement, and inertia, are, however, merely sensuous, and this Descartes showed, as it had long before this been shown by the Sceptics. Undoubtedly that is the abstract Notion or pure essence, but to body or to pure existence, there likewise of necessity pertains negativity or diversity. By means of the following illustration Descartes showed that with the exception of extension, all corporeal determinations may be annihilated, and that none can be absolutely predicated. We draw conclusions respecting the solidity and hardness of matter from the resistance which a body offers to our disturbance,

[1] Cartes. Principia philosophiæ, P. I. § 53, 54, p. 14 (pp. 96, 97).

and by means of which it seeks to hold its place. Now if we admit that matter as we touch it always gives way to us like space, we should have no reason for ascribing to it solidity. Smell, colour, taste, are in the same way sensuous qualities merely; but what we clearly perceive is alone true. If a body is ground into small parts, it gives way, and yet it does not lose its nature; resistance is thus not essential.[1] This not-being-for-itself is however a quantitatively slighter resistance only; the resistance always remains. But Descartes desires only to think; now he does not think resistance, colour, &c., but apprehends them by the senses only. Hence he says that all this must be led back to extension as being special modifications of the same. It is undoubtedly to the credit of Descartes that he only accepts as true what is thought; but the abrogation of these sensuous qualities simply represents the negative movement of thought: the essence of body is conditioned through this thought, that is, it is not true essence.

Descartes now makes his way from the Notion of extension to the laws of motion, as the universal knowledge of the corporeal in its implicitude; he shows (*a*) that there is no vacuum, for that would be an extension without bodily substance, *i.e.* a body without body; (*β*) that there are no atoms (no indivisible independent existence), for the same reason, viz., because the essence of body is extension. (*γ*) He further shows that a body is set in motion by something outside of it, but of itself it continues in a condition of rest, and likewise it must, when in a condition of movement, be brought to rest by another outside of it—this is the property of inertia.[2] These are unmeaning propositions, for an abstraction is involved for instance in asserting simple rest and movement in their opposition.

[1] Cartes. Princip. philos., P. I. § 66-74, pp. 19-22 (pp. 107-117); P. II. § 4, p. 25 (pp. 123, 124).

[2] Cartes. Principia philos. P. II. § 16, 20, 37, 38, pp. 29-31, 38, 39 (pp. 133, 134, 137, 138, 152-154).

Extension and motion are the fundamental conceptions in mechanical physics; they represent the truth of the corporeal world. It is thus that ideality comes before the mind of Descartes, and he is far elevated above the reality of the sensuous qualities, although he does not reach so far as to the separation of this ideality. He thus remains at the point of view of mechanism pure and simple. Give me matter (extension) and motion and I will build worlds for you, is what Descartes virtually says.[1] Space and time were hence to him the only determinations of the material universe. In this, then, lies the mechanical fashion of viewing nature, or the natural philosophy of Descartes is seen to be purely mechanical.[2] Hence changes in matter are due merely to motion, so that Descartes traces every relationship to the rest and movement of particles, and all material diversity such as colour, and taste—in short, all bodily qualities and animal phenomena—to mechanism. In living beings processes such as that of digestion are mechanical effects which have as principles, rest and movement. We here see the ground and origin of the mechanical philosophy; but further on we find that this is unsatisfactory, for matter and motion do not suffice to explain life. Yet the great matter in all this is that thought goes forward in its determinations, and that it constitutes from these thought-determinations the truth of nature.

In his consideration of the system of the world and the movement of the heavenly bodies, Descartes has worked out the mechanical view more fully. He thus comes to speak of the earth, the sun, &c., and of his conception of the circling motion of the heavenly bodies in the form of vortices: of metaphysical hypotheses as to how small

[1] Buhle: Geschichte der neuern Philosophie, Vol. III. Sec. I. p. 19; cf. Cartes. Princip. phil., P. III. § 46, 47, p. 65 (pp. 210-212).

[2] Cf. Cartes. Principia philos., P. II. § 64, p. 49 (pp. 178, 179).

particles pass into, out of, and through pores and act on one another; and finally to saltpetre and gunpowder.[1]

Universal reflections should have the first claim on our attention; but on the other hand the transition to the determinate is accomplished in a system of Physics which is the result of observations and experiences, and this is done entirely by means of the understanding. Descartes thus mingles many observations with a metaphysic of this nature, and to us the result is hence obscure. In this philosophy the thinking treatment of empiricism is thus predominant, and a similar method has been adopted by philosophers from this time on. To Descartes and others, Philosophy had still the more indefinite significance of arriving at knowledge through thought, reflection, and reasoning. Speculative cognition, the derivation from the Notion, the free independent development of the matter itself, was first introduced by Fichte, and consequently what is now called philosophic knowledge is not yet separated in Descartes from the rest of scientific knowledge. In those times all the knowledge of mankind was called philosophy; in Descartes' metaphysics we thus saw quite empirical reflection and reasoning from particular grounds, from experiences, facts, phenomena, being brought into play in the naïvest manner, and one has no sense of speculation in the matter. The strictly scientific element here really consisted mainly in the method of proof as it has long been made use of in geometry, and in the ordinary method of the formal logical syllogism. Hence it likewise happens that Philosophy, which ought to form a totality of the sciences, begins with logic and metaphysics; the second part is composed of ordinary physics and mathematics, mingled no doubt with metaphysical speculations, and the third part, ethics, deals

[1] Cartes. Principia philos., P. III. § 5-42, 46 sqq. pp. 51-63, 65 sqq. (pp. 183-208, p. 210 *et suiv.*); P. IV. § 1 sqq., 69, 109-115, p. 137 sqq., 116, 178-180 (p. 330 *et suiv.*, 388, 420-425).

with the nature of man, his duties, the state, the citizen. And this is the case with Descartes. The first part of the *Principia philosophiæ* treats *De principiis cognitionis humanæ*, the second *De principiis rerum materialium*. This natural philosophy, as a philosophy of extension, is, however, none other than what a quite ordinary physics or mechanics might at that time be, and it is still quite hypothetical; we, on the other hand, accurately distinguish empirical physics and natural philosophy, even though the first likewise pertains to thought.

3. Descartes never reached the third part, the philosophy of Mind, for, while he made a special study of physics, in the region of ethics he published one tract only, *De passionibus*. In this reference Descartes treats of thought and human freedom. He proves freedom from the fact of the soul thinking that the will is unrestrained, and of that constituting the perfection of mankind. And this is quite true. In respect to the freedom of the will he comes across the difficulty of how to reconcile it with the divine prescience. As free, man might do what is not ordained of God beforehand—this would conflict with the omnipotence and omniscience of God; and if everything is ordained of God, human freedom would thereby be done away with. Yet he does not solve the contradiction contained in these two different aspects without falling into difficulty. But conformably to the method which he adopts, and which we pointed out above (pp. 238, 239), he says: "The human mind is finite, God's power and predetermination are infinite; we are thus not capable of judging of the relationship in which the freedom of the human soul stands to the omnipotence and omniscience of God—but in self-consciousness we have the certainty of it given us as a fact. And we must hold only to what is certain."[1] When he proceeds

[1] Cartes. Principia philosoph., P. I. § 37, 39-41, pp. 10, 11 (pp. 85-88).

further much appears to him still incapable of explanation; but we see obstinacy and caprice likewise exhibited in his stopping short at the assertion as to the best of his knowledge. The method of knowledge as set forth by Descartes, takes the form of a reasoning of the understanding, and is thus without special interest.

These, then, are the principal points in the Cartesian system. Some particular assertions made by Descartes, which have been specially instrumental in giving him fame, have still to be mentioned—particular forms which have been formerly considered in metaphysics, and likewise by Wolff. For example, in the first place we gather that Descartes regarded animals and other organisms as machines moved by another, and not possessing the principle of the spontaneity of thought within them[1]—a mechanical physiology, a cut and dry thought pertaining to the understanding, which is of no further importance. In the sharp opposition between thought and extension, the former is not considered as sensation, so that the latter can isolate itself. The organic must as body reduce itself to extension; any further development of this last thus only proves its dependence on the first determinations.

In the second place, the relation between soul and body now becomes an important question, that is, the return of the object within itself in such a way that thought posits itself in another, in matter. As to this, many systems are offered to us in metaphysics. One of these is the *influxus physicus,* that the relation of spirit is of a corporeal nature, that the object is related to mind as bodies are to one another—a conception like this is very crude. How does Descartes understand the unity of soul and body? The former belongs to thought, the latter to extension; and thus because both are substance, neither

[1] Cartes. De Methodo, V. pp. 35, 36 (pp. 185-189).

requires the Notion of the other, and hence soul and body are independent of one another and can exercise no direct influence upon one another. Soul could only influence body in so far as it required the same, and conversely—that is, in so far as they have actual relation to one another. But since each is a totality, neither can bear a real relation to the other. Descartes consistently denied the physical influence of one on the other; that would have signified a mechanical relation between the two. Descartes thus established the intellectual sphere in contradistinction to matter, and on it based the independent subsistence of mind; for in his *cogito* 'I' is at first only certain of itself, since I can abstract from all. Now we find the necessity of a mediator to bring about a union of the abstract and the external and individual. Descartes settles this by placing between the two what constitutes the metaphysical ground of their mutual changes, God. He is the intermediate bond of union, in as far as He affords assistance to the soul in what it cannot through its own freedom accomplish, so that the changes in body and soul may correspond with one another.[1] If I have desires, an intention, these receive corporeal realization; this association of soul and body is, according to Descartes, effected through God. For above (p. 239) we saw that Descartes says of God that He is the Truth of the conception: as long as I think rightly and consistently, something real corresponds to my thought, and the connecting link is God. God is hereby the perfect identity of the two opposites, since He is, as Idea, the unity of Notion and reality. In the Idea of Spinoza this is worked out and developed in its further moments. Descartes' conclusion is quite correct; in finite things this identity is imperfect. Only the form employed by Descartes is inadequate; for it implies that in the beginning there are two things, thought or soul and

[1] Cartes. De Methodo, V. p. 29 (173, 174).

body, and that then God appears as a third thing, outside both—that He is not the Notion of unity, nor are the two elements themselves Notion. We must not however forget that Descartes says that both those original elements are created substances. But this expression 'created' pertains to the ordinary conception only and is not a determinate thought; it was Spinoza, therefore, who first accomplished this return to thought.

2. Spinoza.

The philosophy of Descartes underwent a great variety of unspeculative developments, but in Benedict Spinoza a direct successor to this philosopher may be found, and one who carried on the Cartesian principle to its furthest logical conclusions. For him soul and body, thought and Being, cease to have separate independent existence. The dualism of the Cartesian system Spinoza, as a Jew, altogether set aside. For the profound unity of his philosophy as it found expression in Europe, his manifestation of Spirit as the identity of the finite and the infinite in God, instead of God's appearing related to these as a Third—all this is an echo from Eastern lands. The Oriental theory of absolute identity was brought by Spinoza much more directly into line, firstly with the current of European thought, and then with the European and Cartesian philosophy, in which it soon found a place.

First of all we must, however, glance at the circumstances of Spinoza's life. He was by descent a Portuguese Jew, and was born at Amsterdam in the year 1632; the name he received was Baruch, but he altered it to Benedict. In his youth he was instructed by the Rabbis of the synagogue to which he belonged, but he soon fell out with them, their wrath having been kindled by the criticisms which he passed on the fantastic doctrines of the Talmud. He was not, therefore, long in absenting himself from the synagogue, and as the Rabbis were in dread lest his example should have evil consequences, they offered him a yearly allowance of a thousand gulden if he would keep away from the place and hold his tongue. This offer he declined; and the Rabbis thereafter carried their persecution of him to such a pitch that they were even minded to rid themselves of him by assassination. After having made a narrow escape from the dagger, he formally withdrew from the Jewish communion, without, however, going over to the Christian Church. He now applied himself particularly to the Latin language, and made a special study of the Cartesian philosophy. Later on he went to Rhynsburg, near Leyden, and from the year 1664 he lived in retirement, first at Voorburg, a village near the Hague, and then at the Hague itself, highly respected by numerous friends: he gained a livelihood for himself by grinding optical glasses. It was no arbitrary choice that led him to occupy himself with light, for it represents in the material sphere the absolute identity which forms the foundation of the Oriental view of things. Although he had rich friends and mighty protectors, among whom even generals were numbered, he lived in humble poverty, declining the handsome gifts offered to him time after time. Nor would he permit Simon von Vries to make him his heir; he only accepted from him an annual pension of three hundred florins; in the same way he gave up to his sisters his share of their father's estate. From the Elector Palatine, Carl Ludwig, a man of most noble character and raised above the prejudices of his time, he received the offer of a professor's chair at Heidelberg, with the assurance that he would have liberty to teach and to write, because "the Prince believed he would not put that liberty to a bad use by interfering with the religion publicly established." Spinoza (in his published letters) very wisely declined this offer, however, because "he did not know within what limits that philosophic liberty would have to be confined, in order that he might not appear to be interfering with the publicly established religion." He remained in Holland, a country highly interesting in the history of general culture, as it was the first in Europe to show the example of universal toleration, and afforded to many a place of refuge where they might enjoy liberty of thought; for fierce as was the rage of the theologians there against Bekker, for example (Bruck. Hist. crit. phil. T. IV. P. 2, pp. 719, 720), and furious as were the attacks of Voetius on the Cartesian philosophy, these had not the consequences which they would have had in another land. Spinoza died on the 21st of February, 1677, in the forty-fourth year of his age. The cause of his death was consumption, from which he had long been a sufferer; this was in harmony with his system of philosophy, according to which all particularity and individuality pass away in the one substance. A Protestant divine, Colerus by name, who published a biography of Spinoza, inveighs strongly against him, it is true, but gives nevertheless a most minute and kindly description of his circumstances and surroundings—telling how he left only about two hundred thalers, what debts he had, and so on. A bill included in the inventory, in which the barber requests payment due him by M. Spinoza of blessed memory, scandalizes the parson very much, and regarding it he makes the observation: "Had the barber but known what sort of a creature Spinoza was, he certainly would not have spoken of his blessed memory." The German translator of this biography writes under the portrait of Spinoza: *characterem reprobationis in vultu gerens*, applying this description to a countenance which doubtless expresses the melancholy of a profound thinker, but is otherwise mild and benevolent. The *reprobatio* is certainly correct; but it is not a reprobation in the passive sense; it is an active disapprobation on Spinoza's part of the opinions, errors and thoughtless passions of mankind.[1]

[1] Collectanea de vita B. de Spinoza (addita Operibus ed. Paulus

Spinoza used the terminology of Descartes, and also published an account of his system. For we find the first of Spinoza's works entitled "An Exposition according to the geometrical method of the principles of the Cartesian philosophy." Some time after this he wrote his *Tractatus theologico-politicus*, and by it gained considerable reputation. Great as was the hatred which Spinoza roused amongst his Rabbis, it was more than equalled by the odium which he brought upon himself amongst Christian, and especially amongst Protestant theologians—chiefly through the medium of this essay. It contains his views on inspiration, a critical treatment of the books of Moses and the like, chiefly from the point of view that the laws therein contained are limited in their application to the Jews. Later Christian theologians have written critically on this subject, usually making it their object to show that these books were compiled at a later time, and that they date in part from a period subsequent to the Babylonian captivity; this has become a crucial point with Protestant theologians, and one by which the modern school distinguishes itself from the older, greatly pluming itself thereon. All this, however, is already to be found in the above-mentioned work of Spinoza. But Spinoza drew the greatest odium upon himself by his philosophy proper, which we must now consider as it is given to us in his Ethics. While Descartes published no writings on this subject, the Ethics of Spinoza is undoubtedly his greatest work; it was published after his death by Ludwig Mayer, a physician, who had been Spinoza's most intimate friend. It consists of five parts; the first deals with God (*De Deo*). General metaphysical ideas are contained in it, which include the knowledge of God and nature. The second part deals with the nature and origin of mind (*De natura et origine mentis*). We see

Jenæ 1802-1803, T. II.), pp. 593-604, 612-628 (Spinoza Epist. LIII-LIV. in Oper. ed. Paul. T. I. pp. 638-640) 642-665; Spinozæ Oper. ed. Paul. T. II. Præf. p. XVI.

thus that Spinoza does not treat of the subject of natural philosophy, extension and motion at all, for he passes immediately from God to the philosophy of mind, to the ethical point of view; and what refers to knowledge, intelligent mind, is brought forward in the first part, under the head of the principles of human knowledge. The third book of the Ethics deals with the origin and nature of the passions (*De origine et natura affectuum*); the fourth with the powers of the same, or human slavery (*De servitute humana seu de affectuum viribus*); the fifth, lastly, with the power of the understanding, with thought, or with human liberty (*De potentia intellectus seu de libertate humana*).[1] Kirchenrath Professor Paulus published Spinoza's works in Jena; I had a share in the bringing out of this edition, having been entrusted with the collation of French translations.

As regards the philosophy of Spinoza, it is very simple, and on the whole easy to comprehend; the difficulty which it presents is due partly to the limitations of the method in which Spinoza presents his thoughts, and partly to his narrow range of ideas, which causes him in an unsatisfactory way to pass over important points of view and cardinal questions. Spinoza's system is that of Descartes made objective in the form of absolute truth. The simple thought of Spinoza's idealism is this: The true is simply and solely the one substance, whose attributes are thought and extension or nature: and only this absolute unity is reality, it alone is God. It is, as with Descartes, the unity of thought and Being, or that which contains the Notion of its existence in itself. The Cartesian substance, as Idea, has certainly Being included in its Notion; but it is only Being as abstract, not as real Being or as extension (*supra*, p. 241). With Descartes corporeality and the thinking 'I'

[1] Collectanea de vita B. de Spinoza, pp. 629-641; Spinozæ Ethic. (Oper. T. II.) pp. 1, 3 et not., 33.

are altogether independent Beings; this independence of the two extremes is done away with in Spinozism by their becoming moments of the one absolute Being. This expression signifies that Being must be grasped as the unity of opposites; the chief consideration is not to let slip the opposition and set it aside, but to reconcile and resolve it. Since then it is thought and Being, and no longer the abstractions of the finite and infinite, or of limit and the unlimited, that form the opposition (*supra*, p. 161), Being is here more definitely regarded as extension; for in its abstraction it would be really only that return into itself, that simple equality with itself, which constitutes thought (*supra*, p. 229). The pure thought of Spinoza is therefore not the simple universal of Plato, for it has likewise come to know the absolute opposition of Notion and Being.

Taken as a whole, this constitutes the Idea of Spinoza, and it is just what τὸ ὄν was to the Eleatics (Vol. I. pp. 244, 252). This Idea of Spinoza's we must allow to be in the main true and well-grounded; absolute substance is the truth, but it is not the whole truth; in order to be this it must also be thought of as in itself active and living, and by that very means it must determine itself as mind. But substance with Spinoza is only the universal and consequently the abstract determination of mind; it may undoubtedly be said that this thought is the foundation of all true views—not, however, as their absolutely fixed and permanent basis, but as the abstract unity which mind is in itself. It is therefore worthy of note that thought must begin by placing itself at the standpoint of Spinozism; to be a follower of Spinoza is the essential commencement of all Philosophy. For as we saw above (Vol. I. p. 144), when man begins to philosophize, the soul must commence by bathing in this ether of the One Substance, in which all that man has held as true has disappeared; this negation of all that is particular, to which every philosopher must have come, is the liberation of the mind and its absolute foundation. The difference between our standpoint and that of the Eleatic philosophy is only this, that through the agency of Christianity concrete individuality is in the modern world present throughout in spirit. But in spite of the infinite demands on the part of the concrete, substance with Spinoza is not yet determined as in itself concrete. As the concrete is thus not present in the content of substance, it is therefore to be found within reflecting thought alone, and it is only from the endless oppositions of this last that the required unity emerges. Of substance as such there is nothing more to be said; all that we can do is to speak of the different ways in which Philosophy has dealt with it, and the opposites which in it are abrogated. The difference depends on the nature of the opposites which are held to be abrogated in substance. Spinoza is far from having proved this unity as convincingly as was done by the ancients; but what constitutes the grandeur of Spinoza's manner of thought is that he is able to renounce all that is determinate and particular, and restrict himself to the One, giving heed to this alone.

1. Spinoza begins (Eth. P. I. pp. 35, 36) with a series of definitions, from which we take the following.

a. Spinoza's first definition is of the Cause of itself. He says: "By that which is *causa sui*, its own cause, I understand that whose essence" (or Notion) "involves existence, or which cannot be conceived except as existent." The unity of existence and universal thought is asserted from the very first, and this unity will ever be the question at issue. "The cause of itself" is a noteworthy expression, for while we picture to ourselves that the effect stands in opposition to the cause, the cause of itself is the cause which, while it operates and separates an "other," at the same time produces only itself, and in the production therefore does away with this distinction. The establishing of itself as an other is loss or degeneration, and at the same time the negation of this loss; this is a purely speculative Notion, indeed a fundamental Notion in all speculation. The cause in which the cause is identical with the effect, is the infinite cause (*infra*, p. 263); if Spinoza had further developed what lies in the *causa sui*, substance with him would not have been rigid and unworkable.

b. The second definition is that of the finite. "That thing is said to be finite in its kind which can be limited by another of the same nature." For it comes then to an end, it is not there; what is there is something else. This something else must, however, be of a like nature; for those things which are to limit each other must, in order to be able to limit each other, touch each other, and consequently have a relation to each other, that is to say they must be of one nature, stand on a like basis, and have a common sphere. That is the affirmative side of the limit. "Thus a thought is" only "limited by another thought, a body by another body, but thoughts are not limited by bodies nor" conversely "bodies by thoughts." We saw this (p. 244) with Descartes: thought is an independent totality and so is extension, they have nothing to do with one another; they do not limit each other, each is included in itself.

c. The third definition is that of substance. "By substance I understand that which exists in itself and is conceived by itself, *i.e.* the conception of which does not require the aid of the conception of any other thing for its formation (*a quo formari debeat*);" otherwise it would be finite, accidental. What cannot have a conception formed of it without the aid of something else, is not independent, but is dependent upon that something else.

d. In the fourth place Spinoza defines attributes, which, as the moment coming second to substance, belong to it. "By attribute I understand that which the mind perceives as constituting the essence of substance;" and to Spinoza this alone is true. This is an important determination; the attribute is undoubtedly a determinateness, but at the same time it remains a totality. Spinoza, like Descartes, accepts only two attributes, thought and extension. The understanding grasps them as the reality of substance, but the reality is not higher than the substance, for it is only reality in the view of the understanding, which falls outside substance. Each of the two ways of regarding substance—extension and thought—contains no doubt the whole content of substance, but only in one form, which the understanding brings with it; and for this very reason both sides are in themselves identical and infinite. This is the true completion; but where substance passes over into attribute is not stated.

e. The fifth definition has to do with what comes third in relation to substance, the mode. "By mode I understand the affections of substance, or that which is in something else, through the aid of which also it is conceived." Thus substance is conceived through itself; attribute is not conceived through itself, but has a relation to the conceiving understanding, in so far as this last conceives reality; mode, finally, is what is not conceived as reality, but through and in something else.

These last three moments Spinoza ought not merely to have established in this way as conceptions, he ought to have deduced them; they are especially important, and correspond with what we more definitely distinguish as universal, particular and individual. They must not, however, be taken as formal, but in their true concrete sense; the concrete universal is substance, the concrete particular is the concrete species; the Father and Son in the Christian dogma are similarly particular, but each of them contains the whole nature of God, only under a different form. The mode is the individual, the finite as such, which enters into external connection with what is "other." In this Spinoza only descends to a lower stage, the mode is only the foregoing warped and stunted. Spinoza's defect is therefore this, that he takes the third moment as mode alone, as a false individuality. True individuality and subjectivity is not a mere retreat from the universal, not merely something clearly determinate; for, as clearly determinate, it is at the same time Being-for-itself, determined by itself alone. The individual, the subjective, is even in being so the return to the universal; and in that it is at home with itself, it is itself the universal. The return consists simply and solely in the fact of the particular being in itself the universal; to this return Spinoza did not attain. Rigid substantiality is the last point he reached, not infinite form; this he knew not, and thus determinateness continually vanishes from his thought.

f. In the sixth place, the definition of the infinite is also of importance, for in the infinite Spinoza defines more strictly than anywhere else the Notion of the Notion. The infinite has a double significance, according as it is taken as the infinitely many or as the absolutely infinite (*infra*, p. 263). "The infinite in its kind is not such in respect of all possible attributes; but the absolutely infinite is that to whose essence all belongs that expresses an essence and contains no negation." In the same sense Spinoza distinguishes in the nine-and-twentieth Letter (Oper. T. I. pp. 526-532) the infinite of imagination from the infinite of thought (*intellectus*), the actual (*actu*) infinite. Most men, when they wish to strive after the sublime, get no further than the first of these; this is the false infinite, just as when one says "and so on into infinity," meaning perhaps the infinity of space from star to star, or else the infinity of time. An infinite numerical series in mathematics is exactly the same thing. If a certain fraction is represented as a decimal fraction, it is incomplete; $\frac{1}{7}$ is, on the contrary, the true infinite, and therefore not an incomplete expression, although the content here is of course limited. It is infinity in the incorrect sense that one usually has in view when infinity is spoken of; and even if it is looked on as sublime, it yet is nothing present, and only goes ever out into the negative, without being actual (*actu*). But for Spinoza the infinite is not the fixing of a limit and then passing beyond the limit fixed—the sensuous infinity—but absolute infinity, the positive, which has complete and present in itself an absolute multiplicity which has no Beyond. Philosophic infinity, that which is infinite *actu*, Spinoza therefore calls the absolute affirmation of itself. This is quite correct, only it might have been better expressed as: "It is the negation of negation." Spinoza here also employs geometrical figures as illustrations of the Notion of infinity. In his *Opera postuma*, preceding his Ethics, and also in the letter quoted above, he has two circles, one of which lies within the other, which have not, however, a common centre.

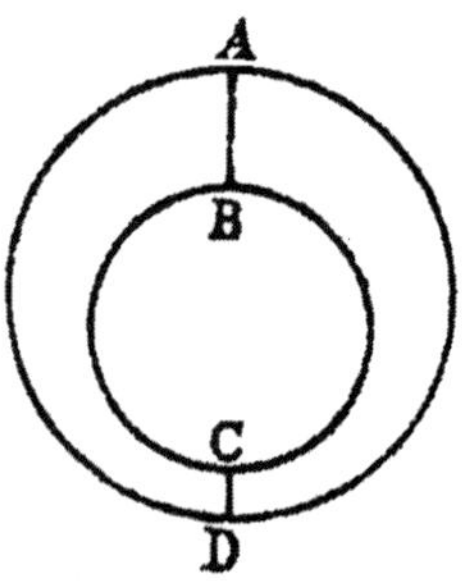

"The inequalities of the space between A B and C D exceed every number; and yet the space which lies between is not so very great." That is to say, if I wish to determine them all, I must enter upon an infinite series. This "beyond" always, however, remains defective, is always affected with negation; and yet this false infinite is there to hand, circumscribed, affirmative, actual and present in that plane as a complete space between the two circles. Or a finite line consists of an infinite number of points; and yet the line is present here and determined; the "beyond" of the infinite number of points, which are not complete, is in it complete and called back into unity. The infinite should be represented as actually present, and this comes to pass in the Notion of the cause of itself, which is therefore the true infinity. As soon as the cause has something else opposed to it—the effect—finitude is present; but here this something else is at the same time abrogated and it becomes once more the cause itself. The affirmative is thus negation of negation, since, according to the well-known grammatical rule, *duplex negatio affirmat*. In the same way Spinoza's earlier definitions have also the infinite already implied in them, for instance in the case of the just mentioned cause of itself, inasmuch as he defines it as that whose essence involves existence (*supra*, p. 258). Notion and existence are each the Beyond of the other; but cause of itself, as thus including them, is really the carrying back of this "beyond" into unity. Or (*supra*, p. 259) "Substance is that which is in itself and is conceived from itself;" that is the same unity of Notion and existence. The infinite is in the same way in itself and has also its Notion in itself; its Notion is its Being, and its Being its Notion; true infinity is therefore to be found in Spinoza. But he has no consciousness of this; he has not recognized this Notion as absolute Notion, and therefore has not expressed it as a moment of true existence; for with him the Notion falls outside of existence, into the thought of existence.

g. Finally Spinoza says in the seventh place: "God is a Being absolutely infinite, *i.e.* a substance consisting of infinite attributes, each of which expresses an eternal and infinite essence." Does substance, one might here ask, possess an infinite number of attributes? But as with Spinoza there are only two attributes, thought and extension, with which he invests God, "infinite" is not to be taken here in the sense of the indeterminate many, but positively, as a circle is perfect infinity in itself.

The whole of Spinoza's philosophy is contained in these definitions, which, however, taken as a whole are formal; it is really a weak point in Spinoza that he begins thus with definitions. In mathematics this method is permitted, because at the outset we there make assumptions, such as that of the point and line; but in Philosophy the content should be known as the absolutely true. It is all very well to grant the correctness of the name-definition, and acknowledge that the word "substance" corresponds with the conception which the definition indicates, but it is quite another question to determine whether this content is absolutely true. Such a question is not asked in the case of geometrical propositions, but in philosophic investigation it is the very thing to be first considered, and this Spinoza has not done. Instead of only explaining these simple thoughts and representing them as concrete in the definitions which he makes, what he ought to have done was to examine whether this content is true. To all appearance it is only the explanation of the words that is given; but the content of the words is held to be established. All further content is merely derived from that, and proved thereby; for on the first content all the rest depends, and if it is established as a basis, the other necessarily follows. "The attribute is that which the understanding thinks of God." But here the question is: How does it come that besides the Deity there now appears the understanding, which applies to absolute substance the two forms of thought and extension? and whence come these two forms themselves? Thus everything proceeds inwards, and not outwards; the determinations are not developed from substance, it does not resolve itself into these attributes.

2. These definitions are followed by axioms and propositions in which Spinoza proves a great variety of points. He descends from the universal of substance through the particular, thought and extension, to the individual. He has thus all three moments of the Notion, or they are essential to him. But the mode, under which head falls individuality, he does not recognize as essential, or as constituting a moment of true existence in that existence; for it disappears in existence, or it is not raised into the Notion.

a. The main point then is that Spinoza proves from these Notions that there is only One Substance, God. It is a simple chain of reasoning, a very formal proof. "Fifth Proposition: There cannot be two or more substances of the same nature or of the same attribute." This is implied already in the definitions; the proof is therefore a useless and wearisome toil, which only serves to render Spinoza more difficult to understand. "If there were several" (substances of the same attribute) "they must be distinguished from one another either by the diversity of their attributes or by the diversity of their affections" (modes). "If they are distinguished by their attributes, it would be directly conceded that there is only one substance having the same attribute." For the attributes are simply what the understanding grasps as the essence of the one substance, which is determined in itself, and not through anything else. "But if these substances were distinguished by their affections, since substance is by nature prior to its affections it would follow that if from substance its affections were abstracted and it were regarded in itself, *i.e.* in its truth, it could henceforth not be regarded as distinct from other substances." "Eighth Proposition: All substance is necessarily infinite. Proof: For otherwise it must be limited by another substance of the same nature, in which case there would be two substances of the same attribute, which is contrary to the fifth proposition." "Every attribute must be conceived for itself," as determination reflected on itself. "For attribute is what the mind conceives of substance as constituting its essence, from which it follows that it must be conceived through itself," *i.e.* substance is what is conceived through itself (see the fourth and third definitions). "Therefore we may not argue from the plurality of attributes to a plurality of substances, for each is conceived by itself, and they have all been, always and at the same time, in substance, without the possibility of the one being produced by the other." "Substance is indivisible. For if the parts retained the nature of the substance, there would be several substances of the same nature, which is contrary to the fifth proposition. If not, infinite substance would cease to exist, which is absurd."[1]

"Fourteenth Proposition: No other substance than God can either exist or be conceived. Proof: God is the absolutely infinite substance, to whom can be denied no attribute which expresses the essence of substance, and He exists necessarily; therefore if there were a substance other than God, it must be explained by means of an attribute of God." Consequently the substance would not have its own being, but that of God, and therefore would not be a substance. Or if it were still to be substance, "then there would necessarily follow the possibility of there being two substances with the same attribute, which according to the fifth proposition is absurd. From this it then follows that the thing extended and the thing that thinks" are not substances, but "are either attributes of God, or affections of His attributes." By these proofs and others like them not much is to be gained. "Fifteenth proposition: What is, is in God, and cannot exist or be conceived without God." "Sixteenth proposition: By the necessity of the divine nature infinite things must follow in infinite modes, *i.e.*, all that can fall under the infinite understanding. God is therefore the absolute First Cause."

Spinoza then ascribes freedom and necessity to God: "God is the absolute free cause, who is determined by nothing outside of Himself, for He exists solely by the necessity of His nature. There is no cause which inwardly or outwardly moves Him to act, except the perfection of His nature. His activity is by the laws of His Being necessary and eternal; what therefore follows from His absolute nature, from His attributes, is eternal, as it follows from the nature of the triangle from eternity and to

[1] Spinoz. Ethices, P. I. Prop. V. VIII. X. et Schol., XIII. pp. 37–39, 41, 42, 45.

[2] Spinoz. Ethices, P. I. Prop. XIV. et Coroll. II. Prop. XV. XVI. et Coroll. I. pp. 46, 51.

eternity that its three angles are equal to two right angles." That is to say, His Being is His absolute power; *actus* and *potentia*, Thought and Being, are in Him one. God has not therefore any other thoughts which He could not have actualized. "God is the immanent cause of all things, not the transient (*transiens*)," *i.e.*, external cause. "His essence and His existence are the same, namely, the truth. A thing which is determined to perform some action, is, since God is cause, necessarily determined thereto by God; and a thing which is thus determined cannot render itself undetermined. In nature nothing is contingent. Will is not a free cause, but only a necessary cause, only a mode; it is therefore determined by another. God acts in accordance with no final causes (*sub ratione boni*). Those who assert that He does so, appear to establish something apart from God, which does not depend on God, and which God in His working keeps in view, as though it were an end. If this view is taken, God is not a free cause, but is subject to fate. It is equally inadmissible to subject all things to the arbitrary pleasure of God, *i.e.*, to His indifferent will."[1] He is determined solely by His own nature; the activity of God is thus His power, and that is necessity. He is then absolute power in contrast to wisdom, which sets up definite aims, and consequently limitations; particular aims, thoughts of what is about to come to pass, and the like are therefore put out of the question. But beyond this universal, no advance is made; for it must be noticed as specially singular, that Spinoza in the fiftieth Letter (Oper. T. I. p. 634) says that every determination is a negation. Moreover, if God is the cause of the world, it is implied that He is finite; for the world is here put beside God as something different from Him.

b. The greatest difficulty in Spinoza is, in the distinc-

[1] Spinoz. Ethices, P. I. Prop. XVII., Coroll. I., II., et Schol., Prop. XVIII., Prop. XX., et Coroll. I. Prop. XXI., XXVI., XXVII., XXIX., XXXII., XXXIII. Schol. II. pp. 51-57, 59, 61, 63, 67, 68.

tions to which he comes, to grasp the relation of this determinate to God, at the same time preserving the determination. "God is a thinking Being, because all individual thoughts are modes which express God's nature in a certain and determinate manner; there pertains therefore to God an attribute the conception of which all individual thoughts involve, and by means of this they also are conceived. God is an extended Being for the same reason." This means that the same substance, under the attribute of thought, is the intelligible world, and under the attribute of extension, is nature; nature and thought thus both express the same Essence of God. Or, as Spinoza says, "The order and system of natural things is the same as the order of the thoughts. Thus, for instance, the circle which exists in nature, and the idea of the existing circle, which is also in God, are one and the same thing" (they are one and the same content), "which is" merely "expressed by means of different attributes. If we therefore regard nature either under the attribute of extension or of thought, or under any other attribute whatever, we shall find one and the same connection of causes, *i.e.*, the same sequence of things. The formal Being of the idea of the circle can be conceived only by means of the mode of thought, as its proximate cause, and this mode again by means of another, and so on infinitely; so that we must explain the order of the whole of nature, or the connection of causes, by the attribute of thought alone, and if things are considered by the attribute of extension, they must be considered only by the attribute of extension, —and the same holds good of other causes."[1] It is one and the same system, which at one time appears as nature, and at another time in the form of thought.

But Spinoza does not demonstrate how these two are

[1] Spinoz. Ethices, P. II. Prop. I., II., VII. et Schol. pp. 78, 79, 82, 83.

evolved from the one substance, nor does he prove why there can only be two of them. Neither are extension and thought anything to him in themselves, or in truth, but only externally; for their difference is a mere matter of the understanding, which is ranked by Spinoza only among affections (Eth. P. I. Prop. XXXI. Demonst. p. 62), and as such has no truth. This has in recent times been served up again by Schelling in the following form: In themselves, the intelligent world and the corporeal world are the same, only under different forms; so that the intelligent universe is in itself the whole absolute divine totality, and the corporeal universe is equally this same totality. The differences are not in themselves; but the different aspects from which the Absolute is regarded are matters external to it. We take a higher tone in saying that nature and mind are rational; but reason is for us no empty word, for it means the totality which develops itself within itself. Again, it is the standpoint of reflection to regard aspects only, and nothing in itself. This defect appears in Spinoza and Schelling in the fact that they see no necessity why the Notion, as the implicit negative of its unity, should make a separation of itself into different parts; so that out of the simple universal the real, the opposed, itself becomes known. Absolute substance, attribute and mode, Spinoza allows to follow one another as definitions, he adopts them ready-made, without the attributes being developed from the substance, or the modes from the attributes. And more especially in regard to the attributes, there is no necessity evident, why these are thought and extension in particular.

c. When Spinoza passes on to individual things, especially to self-consciousness, to the freedom of the 'I,' he expresses himself in such a way as rather to lead back all limitations to substance than to maintain a firm grasp of the individual. Thus we already found the attributes not to be independent, but only the forms in which the understanding grasps substance in its differences; what comes third, the modes, is that under which for Spinoza all difference of things alone falls. Of the modes he says (Ethic. P. I. Prop. XXXII. Demonst. et Coroll. II. p. 63): In every attribute there are two modes; in extension, these are rest and motion, in thought they are understanding and will (*intellectus et voluntas*). They are mere modifications which only exist for us apart from God; therefore whatever refers to this difference and is specially brought about by it, is not absolute, but finite. These affections Spinoza sums up (Ethices, P. I. Prop. XXIX. Schol. pp. 61, 62) under the head of *natura naturata*: "*Natura naturans* is God regarded as free cause, in so far as He is in Himself and is conceived by Himself: or such attributes of substance as express the eternal and infinite essence. By *natura naturata*, I understand all that follows from the necessity of the divine nature, or from any of the attributes of God, all modes of the divine attributes, in so far as they are regarded as things which are in God, and which without God can neither exist nor be conceived." From God proceeds nothing, for all things merely return to the point whence they came, if from themselves the commencement is made.

These then are Spinoza's general forms, this is his principal idea. Some further determinations have still to be mentioned. He gives definitions of the terms modes, understanding, will, and of the affections, such as joy and sadness.[1] We further find consciousness taken into consideration. Its development is extremely simple, or rather it is not developed at all; Spinoza begins directly with mind. "The essence of man consists of certain modifications of the attributes of God"; these modifications are only something related to our understanding. "If we, therefore, say that the human mind perceives this or that,

[1] Spinoz. Ethic. P. I. Prop. XXX-XXXII. pp. 62, 63; P. III. Defin. III. p. 132; Prop. XI. Schol., p. 141.

it means nothing else than that God has this or that idea, not in so far as He is infinite, but in so far as He is expressed by the idea of the human mind. And if we say that God has this or that idea, not in so far as He constitutes the idea of the human mind, but in so far as He has, along with the human mind, the idea of another thing, then we say that the human mind perceives the thing partially or inadequately." Truth is for Spinoza, on the other hand, the adequate.[1] The idea that all particular content is only a modification of God is ridiculed by Bayle,[2] who argues from it that God modified as Turks and Austrians, is waging war with Himself; but Bayle has not a trace of the speculative element in him, although he is acute enough as a dialectician, and has contributed to the intelligent discussion of definite subjects.

The relation of thought and extension in the human consciousness is dealt with by Spinoza as follows: "What has a place in the object" (or rather in the objective) "of the idea which constitutes the human mind must be perceived by the human mind; or there must necessarily be in the mind an idea of this object. The object of the idea which constitutes the human mind is body, or a certain mode of extension. If, then, the object of the idea which constitutes the human mind, is the body, there can happen nothing in the body which is not perceived by the mind. Otherwise the ideas of the affections of the body would not be in God, in so far as He constitutes our mind, but the idea of another thing: that is to say, the ideas of the affections of our body would not be likewise in our mind." What is perplexing to understand in Spinoza's system is, on the one hand, the absolute identity of thought and Being, and, on the other hand, their absolute

[1] Spinoz. Ethices, P. II. Prop. XI. Demonst. et Coroll. pp. 86, 87; Defin. IV. pp. 77, 78.

[2] Dictionnaire historique et critique (édition de 1740, T. IV.), Article Spinosa, p. 261, Note N. No. IV.

indifference to one another, because each of them is a manifestation of the whole essence of God. The unity of the body and consciousness is, according to Spinoza, this, that the individual is a mode of the absolute substance, which, as consciousness, is the representation of the manner in which the body is affected by external things; all that is in consciousness is also in extension, and conversely. "Mind knows itself only in so far as it perceives the ideas of the affections of body," it has only the idea of the affections of its body; this idea is synthetic combination, as we shall immediately see. "The ideas, whether of the attributes of God or of individual things, do not recognize as their efficient cause their objects themselves, or the things perceived, but God Himself, in so far as He is that which thinks."[1] Buhle (Geschichte der neuern Philos. Vol. III. Section II. p. 524) sums up these propositions of Spinoza thus: "Thought is inseparably bound up with extension; therefore all that takes place in extension must also take place in consciousness." Spinoza, however, also accepts both in their separation from one another. The idea of body, he writes (Epistol. LXVI. p. 673), includes only these two in itself, and does not express any other attributes. The body which it represents is regarded under the attribute of extension; but the idea itself is a mode of thought. Here we see a dividing asunder; mere identity, the undistinguishable nature of all things in the Absolute, is insufficient even for Spinoza.

The *individuum*, individuality itself, is thus defined by Spinoza (Ethic. P. II. Prop. XIII. Defin. p. 92): "When several bodies of the same or of different magnitudes are so pressed together that they rest on one another, or when, moving with like or different degrees of rapidity, they communicate their movement to one another in a certain

[1] Spinoz. Ethices, P. II. Prop. XII., XIII. et Schol. Prop. XIV., XXIII., V. pp. 87-89, 95, 102, 80, 81.

measure, we say that such bodies are united to one another, and that all together they form one body or individuum, which by this union distinguishes itself from all the other bodies." Here we are at the extreme limit of Spinoza's system, and it is here that his weak point appears. Individuation, the one, is a mere synthesis; it is quite a different thing from the Ichts or self-hood of Boehme (*supra*, pp. 205-207), since Spinoza has only universality, thought, and not self-consciousness. If, before considering this in reference to the whole, we take it from the other side, namely from the understanding, the distinction really falls under that head; it is not deduced, it is found. Thus, as we have already seen (p. 270) "the understanding in act (*intellectus actu*), as also will, desire, love, must be referred to *natura naturata*, not to *natura naturans*. For by the understanding, as recognized for itself, we do not mean absolute thought, but only a certain mode of thought—a mode which is distinct from other modes like desire, love, etc., and on that account must be conceived by means of absolute thought, *i.e.* by means of an attribute of God which expresses an eternal and infinite essentiality of thought; without which the understanding, as also the rest of the modes of thought, could neither be nor be conceived to be." (Spinoza, Ethices, P. I. Propos. XXXI. pp. 62, 63). Spinoza is unacquainted with an infinity of form, which would be something quite different from that of rigid, unyielding substance. What is requisite is to recognize God as the essence of essences, as universal substance, identity, and yet to preserve distinctions.

Spinoza goes on to say: "What constitutes the real (*actuale*) existence of the human mind is nothing else than the idea of a particular" (individual) "thing, that actually exists," not of an infinite thing. "The essence of man involves no necessary existence, *i.e.* according to the order of nature a man may just as well be as not be." For the human consciousness, as it does not belong to essence as an attribute, is a mode—a mode of the attribute of thought. But neither is the body, according to Spinoza, the cause of consciousness, nor is consciousness the cause of the body, but the finite cause is here only the relation of like to like; body is determined by body, conception by conception. "The body can neither determine the mind to thought, nor can the mind determine the body to motion, or rest, or anything else. For all modes of thought have God as Cause, in so far as He is a thinking thing, and not in so far as He is revealed by means of another attribute. What therefore determines the mind to thought, is a mode of thought and not of extension; similarly motion and rest of the body must be derived from another body."[1] I might quote many other such particular propositions from Spinoza, but they are very formal, and a continual repetition of one and the same thing.

Buhle (Gesch. d. neuern Phil. Vol. III. Section 2, pp. 525-528), attributes limited conceptions to Spinoza: "The soul experiences in the body all the 'other' of which it becomes aware as outside of the body, and it becomes aware of this 'other' only by means of the conceptions of the qualities which the body perceives therein. If, therefore, the body can perceive no qualities of a thing, the soul also can come to no knowledge of it. On the other hand, the soul is equally unable to arrive at the perception of the body which belongs to it; the soul knows not that the body is there, and knows itself even in no other way than by means of the qualities which the body perceives in things which are outside of it, and by means of the conceptions of the same. For the body is an individual thing, determined in a certain manner, which can only gradually, in association with and amidst other individual things, attain to existence, and can preserve itself in existence only as thus connected, combined and associated with others," *i.e.* in

[1] Spinoz. Ethices, P. II. Prop. XI. (Axiom I. p. 78) et Demonstr. Prop. X. pp. 85-87; Prop. VI. p. 81; P. III. Prop. II. pp. 133, 134.

infinite progress; the body can by no means be conceived from itself. "The soul's consciousness expresses a certain determinate form of a Notion, as the Notion itself expresses a determinate form of an individual thing. But the individual thing, its Notion, and the Notion of this Notion are altogether and entirely one and the same thing, only regarded under different attributes. As the soul is nothing else than the immediate Notion of the body and is one and the same thing with this, the excellence of the soul can never be anything else than the excellence of the body. The capacities of the understanding are nothing but the capacities of the body, if they are looked at from the corporeal point of view, and the decisions of the will are likewise determinations of the body. Individual things are derived from God in an eternal and infinite manner" (*i.e.* once and for all), "and not in a transitory, finite and evanescent manner: they are derived from one another merely inasmuch as they mutually produce and destroy each other, but in their eternal existence they endure unchangeable. All individual things mutually presuppose each other; one cannot be thought without the other; that is to say they constitute together an inseparable whole; they exist side by side in one utterly indivisible, infinite Thing, and in no other way whatever.

3. We have now to speak of Spinoza's system of morals, and that is a subject of importance. Its great principle is no other than this, that the finite spirit is moral in so far as it has the true Idea, *i.e.* in so far as it directs its knowledge and will on God, for truth is merely the knowledge of God. It may be said that there is no morality loftier than this, since its only requisite is to have a clear idea of God. The first thing Spinoza speaks of in this regard is the affections: "Everything strives after self-preservation. This striving is the actual essence of the thing, and involves only indefinite time; when referred exclusively to mind, it is termed will; when referred to both mind and body to-

gether, it is called desire. Determination of the will (*volitio*) and Idea are one and the same thing. The sense of liberty rests on this, that men do not know the determining causes of their actions. The affection is a confused idea; the more clearly and distinctly, therefore, we know the affection, the more it is under our control."[1] The influence of the affections, as confused and limited (inadequate) ideas, upon human action, constitutes therefore, according to Spinoza, human slavery; of the passionate affections the principal are joy and sorrow; we are in suffering and slavery in so far as we relate ourselves as a part.[2]

"Our happiness and liberty consist in an enduring and eternal love to God; this intellectual love follows from the nature of mind, in so far as it is regarded as eternal truth through the nature of God. The more a man recognizes God's existence and loves Him, the less does he suffer from evil affections and the less is his fear of death."[3] Spinoza requires in addition the true kind of knowledge. There are, according to him, three kinds of knowledge; in the first, which he calls opinion and imagination, he includes the knowledge which we obtain from an individual object through the senses—a knowledge fragmentary and ill-arranged—also knowledge drawn from signs, pictorial conceptions and memory. The second kind of knowledge is for Spinoza that which we derive from general conceptions and adequate ideas of the properties of things. The third is intuitive knowledge (*scientia intuitiva*) which rises from

[1] Spinoz. Ethices, P. III. Prop. VI.-VIII. Prop. IX. Schol. pp. 139, 140; P. II. Prop. XLIX. Coroll. p. 123; P. III. Prop. II. Schol. p. 136; P. V. Prop. III. Demonst. et Coroll. pp. 272, 273.

[2] Spinoz. Ethices, P. III. Prop. I. p. 132; Prop. III. p. 138; P. IV. Præf. p. 199; P. III. Prop. XI. Schol. pp. 141, 142; P. IV. Prop. II. p. 205; P. III. Prop. III. et Schol. p. 138.

[3] Spinoz. Ethices, P. V. Prop. XXXVI. Schol. Prop. XXXVII. Demonstr., Prop. XXXVIII. et Schol. pp. 293-295.

the adequate idea of the formal essence of certain attributes of God to the adequate knowledge of the essence of things."[1] Regarding this last he then says: "The nature of reason is not to contemplate things as contingent, but as necessary . . . to think of all things under a certain form of eternity (*sub quadam specie æternitatis*);" *i.e.* in absolutely adequate Notions, *i.e.* in God. "For the necessity of things is the necessity of the eternal nature of God Himself. Every idea of an individual thing necessarily includes the eternal and infinite essence of God in itself. For individual things are modes of an attribute of God; therefore they must include in themselves His eternal essence. Our mind, in so far as it knows itself and the body under the form of eternity, has to that extent necessarily the knowledge of God, and knows that it is itself in God and is conceived through God. All Ideas, in so far as they are referable to God, are true."[2] Man must trace back all things to God, for God is the One in All; the eternal essence of God is the one thing that is, the eternal truth is the only thing for man to aim at in his actions. With Spinoza this is not a knowledge arrived at through philosophy, but only knowledge of a truth. "The mind can succeed in tracing back all affections of the body or images of things to God. In proportion as the mind regards all things as necessary, it has a greater power over its affections," which are arbitrary and contingent. This is the return of the mind to God, and this is human freedom; as mode, on the other hand, the spirit has no freedom, but is determined from without. "From the third kind of knowledge there arises the repose of the mind; the supreme good of the mind is to know God, and this is its highest virtue. This knowledgo necessarily produces the intel-

[1] Spinoz. Ethices, P. II. Prop. XL. Schol. II. pp. 113, 114.

[2] Spinoz. Ethices, P. II. Prop. XLIV. et Coroll. II. pp. 117, 118; Prop. XLV. p. 119; P. V. Prop. XXX. p. 289: P. II. Prop. XXXII. p. 107.

lectual love of God; for it produces a joyfulness accompanied by the Idea of God as cause—*i.e.* the intellectual love of God. God Himself loves Himself with an infinite intellectual love."[1] For God can have only Himself as aim and cause; and the end of the subjective mind is to be directed on Him. This is therefore the purest, but also a universal morality.

In the thirty-sixth Letter (pp. 581-582) Spinoza speaks of Evil. The allegation is made that God, as the originator of all things and everything, is also the originator of evil, is consequently Himself evil; in this identity all things are one, good and evil are in themselves the same thing, in God's substance this difference has disappeared. Spinoza says in answer to this: "I assert the fact that God absolutely and truly" (as cause of Himself) "is the cause of everything that has an essential content" (*i.e.* affirmative reality) "be it what it may. Now if you can prove to me that evil, error, crime, etc., are something that expresses an essence, I will freely admit to you that God is the originator of crime and evil and error. But I have elsewhere abundantly demonstrated that the form of evil cannot subsist in anything that expresses an essence, and therefore it cannot be said that God is the cause of evil." Evil is merely negation, privation, limitation, finality, mode—nothing in itself truly real. "Nero's murder of his mother, in so far as it had positive content, was no crime. For Orestes did the same external deed, and had in doing it the same end in view—to kill his mother; and yet he is not blamed," and so on. The affirmative is the will, the intention, the act of Nero. "Wherein then consists Nero's criminality? In nothing else but that he proved himself ungrateful, merciless, and disobedient. But it is certain that all this expresses no essence, and therefore God was

[1] Spinoz. Ethices, P. V. Prop. XIV. p. 280; Prop. VI. p. 275; Prop. XXVII. pp. 287, 288; Prop. XXXII. Coroll.; Prop. XXXV. pp. 291, 292.

not the cause of it, though He was the cause of Nero's action and intention." These last are something positive, but yet they do not constitute the crime as such; it is only the negative element, such as mercilessness, etc. that makes the action a crime. "We know that whatever exists, regarded in itself and without taking anything else into consideration, contains a perfection which extends as widely as the essence of the thing itself extends, for the essence is in no way different therefrom."—"Because then," we find in the thirty-second letter (pp. 541, 543), "God does not regard things abstractly, or form general definitions," (of what the thing ought to be) "and no more reality is required of things than the Divine understanding and power has given and actually meted out to them; therefore it clearly follows that such privation exists only and solely in respect to our understanding, but not in respect to God;" for God is absolutely real. It is all very well to say this, but it does not meet the case. For in this way God and the respect to our understanding are different. Where is their unity? How is this to be conceived? Spinoza continues in the thirty-sixth letter: "Although the works of the righteous (*i.e.* of those who have a clear idea of God, to which they direct all their actions and even their thoughts), and" also the works "of the wicked (*i.e.* of those who have no idea of God, but only ideas of earthly things,"—individual, personal interests and opinions,—"by which their actions and thoughts are directed), and all whatsoever exists, necessarily proceed from God's eternal laws and counsels, and perpetually depend on God, they are yet not distinguished from one another in degree, but in essence; for although a mouse as well as an angel depends on God, and sorrow as well as joy, yet a mouse cannot be a kind of angel, and sorrow cannot be a kind of joy,"—they are different in essence.

There is therefore no ground for the objection that Spinoza's philosophy gives the death-blow to morality; we even gain from it the great result that all that is sensuous is mere limitation, and that there is only one true substance, and that human liberty consists in keeping in view this one substance, and in regulating all our conduct in accordance with the mind and will of the Eternal One. But in this philosophy it may with justice be objected that God is conceived only as Substance, and not as Spirit, as concrete. The independence of the human soul is therein also denied, while in the Christian religion every individual appears as determined to salvation. Here, on the contrary, the individual spirit is only a mode, an accident, but not anything substantial. This brings us to a general criticism of the philosophy of Spinoza, in the course of which we shall consider it from three different points of view.

In the first place Spinozism is asserted to be Atheism—by Jacobi, for instance (Werke, Vol. IV. Section I. p. 216)—because in it no distinction is drawn between God and the world; it makes nature the real God, or lowers God to the level of nature, so that God disappears and only nature is established. But it is not so much God and nature that Spinoza sets up in mutual opposition, as thought and extension; and God is unity, not One made up of two, but absolute Substance, in which has really disappeared the limitation of the subjectivity of thought and nature. Those who speak against Spinoza do so as if it were on God's account that they were interested; but what these opponents are really concerned about is not God, but the finite—themselves. The relationship between God and the finite, to which we belong, may be represented in three different ways: firstly, only the finite exists, and in this way we alone exist, but God does not exist—this is atheism; the finite is here taken absolutely, and is accordingly the substantial. Or, in the second place, God alone exists; the finite has no reality, it is only phenomena, appearance. To say, in the third place, that God exists and we also exist is a false synthetic union, an amicable compromise. It is the popular view of the matter that the one side has as much substantiality as the other; God is honoured and supreme, but finite things also have Being to exactly the same extent. Reason cannot remain satisfied with this "also," with indifference like this. The philosophic requisite is therefore to apprehend the unity of these differences in such a way that difference is not let slip, but proceeds eternally from substance, without being petrified into dualism. Spinoza is raised above this dualism; religion is so also, if we turn its popular conceptions into thoughts. The atheism of the first attitude—when men set up as ultimate the arbitrariness of the will, their own vanity, the finite things of nature, and the world dwells for ever in the mind—is not the standpoint of Spinoza, for whom God is the one and only substance, the world on the contrary being merely an affection or mode of this substance. In the respect that Spinoza does not distinguish God from the world, the finite, it is therefore correct to term his theory atheism, for his words are these: Nature, the human mind, the individual, are God revealed under particular forms. It has been already remarked (pp. 257, 258, 280) that undoubtedly Substance with Spinoza does not perfectly fulfil the conception of God, since it is as Spirit that He is to be conceived. But if Spinoza is called an atheist for the sole reason that he does not distinguish God from the world, it is a misuse of the term. Spinozism might really just as well or even better have been termed Acosmism, since according to its teaching it is not to the world, finite existence, the universe, that reality and permanency are to be ascribed, but rather to God alone as the substantial. Spinoza maintains that there is no such thing as what is known as the world; it is merely a form of God, and in and for itself it is nothing. The world has no true reality, and all this that we know as the world has been cast into the abyss of the one identity. There is therefore no such thing as finite reality, it has no truth whatever; according to Spinoza what is, is God, and God alone. Therefore the allegations of those who accuse

Spinoza of atheism are the direct opposite of the truth; with him there is too much God. They say: If God is the identity of mind and nature, then nature or the individual man is God. This is quite correct, but they forget that nature and the individual disappear in this same identity: and they cannot forgive Spinoza for thus annihilating them. Those who defame him in such a way as this are therefore not aiming at maintaining God, but at maintaining the finite and the worldly; they do not fancy their own extinction and that of the world. Spinoza's system is absolute pantheism and monotheism elevated into thought. Spinozism is therefore very far removed from being atheism in the ordinary sense; but in the sense that God is not conceived as spirit, it is atheism. However, in the same way many theologians are also atheists who speak of God only as the Almighty Supreme Being, etc., who refuse to acknowledge God, and who admit the validity and truth of the finite. They are many degrees worse than Spinoza.

The second point to be considered is the method adopted by Spinoza for setting forth his philosophy; it is the demonstrative method of geometry as employed by Euclid, in which we find definitions, explanations, axioms, and theorems. Even Descartes made it his starting-point that philosophic propositions must be mathematically handled and proved, that they must have the very same evidence as mathematics. The mathematical method is considered superior to all others, on account of the nature of its evidence; and it is natural that independent knowledge in its re-awakening lighted first upon this form, of which it saw so brilliant an example. The mathematical method is, however, ill-adapted for speculative content, and finds its proper place only in the finite sciences of the understanding. In modern times Jacobi has asserted (Werke, Vol. IV. Section I. pp. 217-223) that all demonstration, all scientific knowledge leads back to Spinozism, which alone is a logical method of thought; and because it must lead thither, it is really of no service whatever, but immediate knowledge is what we must depend on. It may be conceded to Jacobi that the method of demonstration leads to Spinozism, if we understand thereby merely the method of knowledge belonging to the understanding. But the fact is that Spinoza is made a testing-point in modern philosophy, so that it may really be said: You are either a Spinozist or not a philosopher at all. This being so, the mathematical and demonstrative method of Spinoza would seem to be only a defect in the external form; but it is the fundamental defect of the whole position. In this method the nature of philosophic knowledge and the object thereof, are entirely misconceived, for mathematical knowledge and method are merely formal in character and consequently altogether unsuited for philosophy. Mathematical knowledge exhibits its proof on the existent object as such, not on the object as conceived; the Notion is lacking throughout; the content of Philosophy, however, is simply the Notion and that which is comprehended by the Notion. Therefore this Notion as the knowledge of the essence is simply one assumed, which falls within the philosophic subject; and this is what represents itself to be the method peculiar to Spinoza's philosophy. Of this demonstrative manner we have already seen these examples: (*a*) The definitions from which Spinoza takes his start—as in geometry a commencement is made with the line, triangle, &c.—concern universal determinations, such as cause of itself, the finite, substance, attribute, mode, and so on, which are solely and simply accepted and assumed, not deduced, nor proved to be necessary; for Spinoza is not aware of how he arrives at these individual determinations. (*β*) He further speaks of axioms, for instance (Ethic. P. I. Ax. I. p. 36): "What is, is either in itself or in another." The determinations "in itself" and "in another" are not shown forth in their necessity: neither is this disjunction proved, it is merely assumed. (γ) The propositions have, as such, a subject and predicate which are not similar. When the predicate is proved of the subject and necessarily combined with it, the discrepancy remains that the one as universal is related to the other as particular: therefore even although the relation is proved, there is present at the same time a secondary relation. Mathematical science, in its true propositions respecting a whole, escapes from the difficulty by proving also the converse of the propositions, in this way obtaining for them a special definiteness by proving each proposition in both ways. True propositions may, therefore, be looked on as definitions, and the conversion is the proof of the proposition in the form in which it is expressed. But this means of escaping the difficulty Philosophy cannot well employ, since the subject of which something is proved is itself only the Notion or the universal, and the proposition form is therefore quite superfluous and out of place. What has the form of the subject is in the form of an existent thing, as contrasted with the universal, the content of the proposition. The existent thing is taken as signifying existent in the ordinary sense; it is the word which we use in every-day life, and of which we have a conception that has nothing of the Notion in it. The converse of a proposition would simply read like this: The Notion is that which is thus popularly conceived. This proof from the usage of language—that we also understand this to be the meaning in every-day life, or in other words that the name is correct—has no philosophic significance. But if the proposition is not one like this, but an ordinary proposition, and if the predicate is not the Notion, but some general term or other, a predicate of the subject, such propositions are really not philosophic: we might instance the statement that substance is one and not several, but only that in which substance and unity are the same. Or, in other words, this unity of the two moments is the very thing which the proof has to demonstrate, it is the Notion or the essence. In this case it looks as if the proposition were the matter of chief importance, the truth. But if in these really only so-called propositions, subject and predicate are in truth not alike, because one is individual and the other universal, their relation is essential, *i.e.* the reason for which they are one. The proof has here a false position indeed, as if that subject were implicit or in itself, whereas subject and predicate are, fundamentally even, moments in separation; in the judgment "God is One," the subject itself is universal, since it resolves itself into unity. On the other side it is implied in this false position that the proof is brought in from outside merely, as in mathematics from a preceding proposition, and that the proposition is not therefore conceived through itself; thus we see the ordinary method of proof take its middle term, the principle, from anywhere it can, in the same way as in classification it takes its principle of classification. The proposition is then, as it were, a secondary affair; but we must ask if this proposition is true. The result as proposition ought to be truth, but is only knowledge. The movement of knowledge, as proof, falls therefore, in the third place, outside of the proposition, which ought to be the truth. The essential moments of the system are really already completely contained in the pre-suppositions of the definitions, from which all further proofs have merely to be deduced. But whence have we these categories which here appear as definitions? We find them doubtless in ourselves, in scientific culture. The existence of the understanding, the will, extension, is therefore not developed from infinite substance, but it is directly expressed in these determinations, and that quite naturally; for of a truth there exists the One into which everything enters, in order to be absorbed therein, but out of which nothing comes. For as Spinoza has set up the great proposition, all determination implies negation (*supra*, p. 267), and as of everything, even of thought in contrast to extension, it may be shown that it is determined and finite, what is essential in it rests upon negation. Therefore God alone is the positive, the affirmative, and consequently the one substance; all other things, on the contrary, are only modifications of this substance, and are nothing in and for themselves. Simple determination or negation belongs only to form, but is quite another thing from absolute determinateness or negativity, which is absolute form; in this way of looking at it negation is the negation of negation, and therefore true affirmation. This negative self-conscious moment, the movement of knowledge, which pursues its way in the thought which is present before us, is however certainly lacking to the content of Spinoza's philosophy, or at least it is only externally associated with it, since it falls within self-consciousness. That is to say, thoughts form the content, but they are not self-conscious thoughts or Notions: the content signifies thought, as pure abstract self-consciousness, but an unreasoning knowledge, into which the individual does not enter: the content has not the signification of 'I.' Therefore the case is as in mathematics; a proof is certainly given, conviction must follow, but yet the matter fails to be understood. There is a rigid necessity in the proof, to which the moment of self-consciousness is lacking; the 'I' disappears, gives itself altogether up, merely withers away. Spinoza's procedure is therefore quite correct; yet the individual proposition is false, seeing that it expresses only one side of the negation. The understanding has determinations which do not contradict one another; contradiction the understanding cannot suffer. The negation of negation is, however, contradiction, for in that it negates negation as simple determination, it is on the one hand affirmation, but on the other hand also really negation; and this contradiction, which is a matter pertaining to reason, is lacking in the case of Spinoza. There is lacking the infinite form, spirituality and liberty. I have already mentioned before this (pp. 93, 94; 129—137) that Lullus and Bruno attempted to draw up a system of form, which should embrace and comprehend the one substance which organizes itself into the universe; this attempt Spinoza did not make.

Because negation was thus conceived by Spinoza in one-sided fashion merely, there is, in the third place, in his system, an utter blotting out of the principle of subjectivity, individuality, personality, the moment of self-consciousness in Being. Thought has only the signification of the universal, not of self-consciousness. It is this lack which has, on the one side, brought the conception of the liberty of the subject into such vehement antagonism to the system of Spinoza, because it set aside the independence of the human consciousness, the so-called liberty which is merely the empty abstraction of independence, and in so doing set aside God, as distinguished from nature and the human consciousness—that is as implicit or in Himself, in the Absolute; for man has the consciousness of freedom, of the spiritual, which is the negative of the corporeal, and man has also the consciousness that his true Being lies in what is opposed to the corporeal. This has been firmly maintained by religion, theology, and the sound common sense of the common consciousness, and this form of opposition to Spinoza appears first of all in the assertion that freedom is real, and that evil exists. But because for Spinoza, on the other hand, there exists only absolute universal substance as the non-particularized, the truly real—all that is particular and individual, my subjectivity and spirituality, has, on the other hand, as a limited modification whose Notion depends on another, no absolute existence. Thus the soul, the Spirit, in so far as it is an individual Being, is for Spinoza a mere negation, like everything in general that is determined. As all differences and determinations of things and of consciousness simply go back into the One substance, one may say that in the system of Spinoza all things are merely cast down into this abyss of annihilation. But from this abyss nothing comes out; and the particular of which Spinoza speaks is only assumed and presupposed from the ordinary conception, without being justified. Were it to be justified, Spinoza would have to deduce it from his Substance; but that does not open itself out, and therefore comes to no vitality, spirituality or activity. His philosophy has only a rigid and unyielding substance, and not yet spirit; in it we are not at home with ourselves. But the reason that God is not spirit is that He is not the Three in One. Substance remains rigid and petrified, without Boehme's sources or springs; for the individual determinations in the form of determinations of the understanding are not Boehme's originating spirits, which energize and expand in one another (*supra*, pp. 202, 203). What we find regarding this particular then is that it is only a modification of absolute substance, which, however, is not declared to be such; for the moment of negativity is what is lacking to this rigid motionlessness, whose single form of activity is this, to divest all things of their determination and particularity and cast them back into the one absolute substance, wherein they are simply swallowed up, and all life in itself is utterly destroyed. This is what we find philosophically inadequate with Spinoza; distinctions are externally present, it is true, but they remain external, since even the negative is not known in itself. Thought is the absolutely abstract, and for that very reason the absolutely negative; it is so in truth, but with Spinoza it is not asserted to be the absolutely negative. But if in opposition to Spinozism we hold fast to the assertion that Spirit, as distinguishing itself from the corporeal, is substantial, actual, true, and in the same way that freedom is not something merely privative, then this actuality in formal thought is doubtless correct, yet it rests only upon feeling; but the further step is that the Idea essentially includes within itself motion and vitality, and that it consequently has in itself the principle of spiritual freedom. On the one hand, therefore, the defect of Spinozism is conceived as consisting in its want of correspondence with actuality; but on the other side it is to be apprehended in a higher sense, I mean in the sense that substance with Spinoza is only the Idea taken altogether abstractly, not in its vitality.

If, in conclusion, we sum up this criticism that we have offered, we would say that on the one hand with Spinoza negation or privation is distinct from substance; for he merely assumes individual determinations, and does not deduce them from substance. On the other hand the negation is present only as Nothing, for in the absolute there is no mode; the negative is not there, but only its dissolution, its return: we do not find its movement, its Becoming and Being. The negative is conceived altogether as a vanishing moment—not in itself, but only as individual self-consciousness; it is not like the *Separator* we met with in Boehme's system (*supra*, p. 206). Self-consciousness is born from this ocean, dripping with the water thereof, *i.e.* never coming to absolute self-hood; the heart, the independence is transfixed—the vital fire is wanting. This lack has to be supplied, the moment of self-consciousness has to be added. It has the following two special aspects, which we now perceive emerging and gaining acceptance; in the first place the objective aspect, that absolute essence obtains in self-consciousness the mode of an object of consciousness for which the "other" exists, or the existent as such, and that what Spinoza understood by the "modes" is elevated to objective reality as an absolute moment of the absolute; in the second place we have the aspect of self-consciousness, individuality, independence. As was formerly the case with respect to Bacon and Boehme, the former aspect is here taken up by the Englishman, John Locke, the latter by the German Leibnitz; in the first case it did not appear as a moment, nor did it in the second appear as absolute Notion. Now while Spinoza only takes notice of these ordinary conceptions, and the highest point of view he reaches in regard to them is that they sink and disappear in the one Substance, Locke on the contrary examines the genesis of these conceptions, while Leibnitz opposes to Spinoza the infinite multiplicity of individuals, although all these monads have one monad as the basis of their Being. Both Locke and Leibnitz therefore came forward as opponents of the abovementioned one-sidedness of Spinoza.

3. Malebranche.

The philosophy of Malebranche is in point of matter entirely identical with that of Spinoza, but it has another, a more religious and more theological form; on account of this form it never encountered the opposition met with by Spinoza, and for the same reason Malebranche has never been reproached with Atheism.

Nicholas Malebranche was born at Paris in 1638. He was sickly and deformed in body, and was hence brought up with great care. He was diffident and loved solitude; in his twenty-second year he entered the *congrégation de l'oratoire*, a sort of spiritual order, and devoted himself to the sciences. In passing a bookseller's shop he happened accidentally to see Descartes' work *De homine*; he read it, and it interested him greatly—so much so that the reading of it brought on severe palpitation and he was forced to cease. This decided his future life; there awoke in him an irrepressible inclination for Philosophy. He was a man of most noble and gentle character, and of the most genuine and unswerving piety. He died at Paris in 1715, and in the seventy-seventh year of his age.[1]

[1] Buhle: Gesch. d. neuern Philosophie, Vol. III. Sec. 2, pp. 430, 431.

His principal work bears the title: *De la recherche de la vérité*. One part of it is entirely metaphysical, but the greater part is altogether empirical. For instance, Malebranche in the first three books treats logically and psychologically of the errors in sight and hearing, in the imagination and understanding.

a. What is most important in this book is his idea of the origin of our knowledge. He says: "The essence of the soul is in thought, just as that of matter is in extension. All else, such as sensation, imagination and will, are modifications of thought." He thus begins with two sides, between which he sets an absolute chasm, and then he follows out in detail the Cartesian idea of the assistance of God in knowledge. His main point is that "the soul cannot attain to its conceptions and notions from external things." For when I and the thing are clearly independent of one another and have nothing in common, the two can certainly not enter into relation with one another nor be for one another. "Bodies are impenetrable; their images would destroy one another on the way to the organs." But further: "The soul cannot beget ideas from itself, nor can they be inborn," for as "Augustine has said, 'Say not that ye yourselves are your own light.'" But how then comes extension, the manifold, into the simple, into the spirit, since it is the reverse of the simple, namely the diverse? This question regarding the association of thought and extension is always an important one in Philosophy. According to Malebranche the answer is, "That we see all things in God." God Himself is the connection between us and them, and thus the unity between the thing and thought. "God has in Him the ideas of all things because He has created all; God is through His omnipresence united in the most intimate way with spirits. God thus is the place of spirits," the Universal of spirit, "just as space" is the universal, "the place of bodies. Consequently the soul knows in God what is in Him," bodies, "inasmuch as

He sets forth" (inwardly conceives) "created existence, because all this is spiritual, intellectual, and present to the soul."[1] Because things and God are intellectual and we too are intellectual, we perceive them in God as they are, so to speak, intellectual in Him. If this be further analyzed it in no way differs from Spinozism. Malebranche indeed in a popular way allows soul and things to subsist as independent, but this independence vanishes away like smoke when the principle is firmly grasped. The catechism says: "God is omnipresent," and if this omnipresence be developed Spinozism is arrived at; and yet theologians then proceed to speak against the system of identity, and cry out about Pantheism.

b. We must further remark that Malebranche also makes the universal, thought, the essential, by placing it before the particular. "The soul has the Notion of the infinite and universal: it knows nothing excepting through the Idea which it has of the infinite; this Idea must hence come first. The universal is not a mere confusion of individual ideas, it is not a union of individual things." According to Locke the individual from which the universal is formed precedes (*infra*, p. 299); according to Malebranche the universal Idea is what comes first in man. "If we wish to think of anything particular we think first of the universal;" it is the principle of the particular, as space is of things. All essentiality precedes our particular conceptions, and this essentiality comes first. "All essential existences (*essences*) come before our ordinary conception; they cannot be such excepting by God's presence in the mind and spirit. He it is who contains all things in the simplicity of His nature. It seems evident that mind would not be capable of representing to itself the universal Notions of

[1] Malebranche: De la recherche de la vérité (Paris, 1736), T. II. L. III. Part I. chap. i. pp. 4–6; T. I. L. I. chap. i. pp. 6, 7; P. II chap. ii. pp. 56–68; chap. iii. p. 72; chap. iv. p. 84; chap. v. p. 92; chap. vi. pp. 95, 96.

species, kind, and suchlike, if it did not see all things comprehended in one." The universal is thus in and for itself, and it does not take its rise through the particular. "Since each existent thing is an individual, we cannot say that we see something actually created when, for example, we see a triangle in general," for we see it through God. "No account can be given of how spirit knows abstract and common truths, excepting through the presence of Him who can enlighten spirit in an infinite way," because He is in and for Himself the universal. "We have a clear idea of God," of the universal: "We can have such only through union with Him, for this idea is not a created one," but is in and for itself. As with Spinoza, the one universal is God, and in so far as it is determined, it is the particular; we see this particular only in the universal, as we see bodies in space. "We already have a conception of infinite Being, inasmuch as we have a conception of Being without regard to whether it is finite or infinite. To know a finite we must limit the infinite; and this last must thus precede. Thus spirit perceives all in the infinite; this is so far from being a confused conception of many particular things that all particular conceptions are merely participations in the universal Idea of infinitude—in the same way that God does not receive this Being from" finite "creatures, but," on the contrary, "all creatures only subsist through Him."[1]

c. As regards the turning of the soul to God, Malebranche says what Spinoza said from his ethical point of view: "It is impossible that God should have an end other than Himself (the Holy Scriptures place this beyond doubt);" the will of God can only have the good, what is without doubt universal as its end. "Hence not only is it essential that our natural love, *i.e.* the emotion which He brings forth in our spirit, should strive after Him"—"the will is

[1] Malebranche: De la recherche de la vérité, T. II. L. III. Part II. chap. vi. pp. 100–102.

really love towards God"—"but it is likewise impossible that the knowledge and the light which He gives to our spirit should make anything else known than what is in Him," for thought only exists in unity with God. "If God were to make a spirit and give it the sun as an idea or as the immediate object of its knowledge, God would have made this spirit and the idea of this spirit for the sun and not for Himself." All natural love, and still more knowledge, and the desire after truth, have God as their end. "All motions of the will as regards the creatures are only determinations of motion as regards the creator." Malebranche quotes from Augustine "that we see God even from the time we first enter upon this life (*dès cette vie*), through the knowledge that we have of eternal truths. The truth is uncreated, unchangeable, immeasurable, eternal above all things; it is true through itself, and has its perfection from no thing. It makes the creator more perfect, and all spirits naturally seek to know it: now there is nothing that has these perfections but God, and thus the truth is God. We perceive these unchangeable and eternal truths, hence we see God." "God indeed sees but He does not feel sensuous things. If we see something sensuous, sensation and pure thought are to be found in our consciousness. Sensation is a modification of our spirit; God occasions this because He knows that our soul is capable of it. The Idea which is bound up with the sensation is in God; we see it, etc. This relation, this union of our mind and spirit with the Word (*Verbe*) of God, and of our will with His love, is that we are formed after the image of God and in His likeness."[1] Thus the love of God consists in relating one's affections to the Idea of God; whoever knows himself and thinks his affections clearly, loves God. We further find sundry empty litanies concerning God, a catechism for children of eight

[1] Malebranche: De la recherche de la vérité, T. II. L. III. P. II. chap. vi. pp. 103–107, 109–111.

years of age respecting goodness, justice, omnipresence, the moral order of the world; in all their lifetime theologians do not get any further.

We have given the principal of Malebranche's ideas; the remainder of his philosophy is composed partly of formal logic, and partly of empirical psychology. He passes to the treatment of errors, how they arise, how the senses, the imagination, the understanding, deceive us, and how we must conduct ourselves in order to effect a remedy. Then Malebranche goes on (T. III. L. VI. P. I. chap. i. pp. 1-3) to the rules and laws for recognizing the truth. Thus here the term Philosophy was even applied to the manner in which reflections on particular objects are drawn from formal logic and external facts.

B.—Second Division.

It was Locke who became the instrument of setting forth this entire manner of thinking in a systematic way, for he worked out Bacon's position more fully. And if Bacon made sensuous Being to be the truth, Locke demonstrated the universal, Thought, to be present in sensuous Being, or showed that we obtained the universal, the true, from experience. From Locke a wide culture proceeds, influencing English philosophers more especially; the forms adopted by this school were various, but the principle was the same; it became a general method of regarding things in a popular way, and calls itself Philosophy, although the object of Philosophy is not to be met with here.

1. Locke.

When experience means that the Notion has objective actuality for consciousness, it is indeed a necessary element in the totality; but as this reflection appears in Locke, signifying as it does that we obtain truth by abstraction from experience and sensuous perception, it is utterly false, since, instead of being a moment, it is made the essence of the truth. It is no doubt true that against the hypothesis of the inward immediacy of the Idea, and against the method of setting it forth in definitions and axioms, as also against absolute substance, the demand that ideas should be represented as results, and the claims of individuality and self-consciousness, assert their rights to recognition. In the philosophy of Locke and Leibnitz, however, these necessities make themselves known in an imperfect manner only; the one fact which is common to both philosophers is that they, in opposition to Spinoza and Malebranche, take for their principle the particular, finite determinateness and the individual. According to Spinoza and Malebranche substance or the universal is the true, the sole existent, the eternal, that which is in and for itself, without origin, and of which particular things are only modifications which are conceived through substance. But hereby Spinoza has done an injury to this negative; he hence arrived at no immanent determination, for all that is determined and individual is merely annihilated in his system. Now, on the contrary, the general inclination of consciousness is to maintain the difference, partly in order to mark itself out as implicitly free in opposition to its object—Being, nature, and God, and partly in order to recognize the unity in this opposition, and from the opposition itself to make the unity emerge. But those who were the instruments of this tendency comprehended themselves but little, they had still no clear consciousness of their task, nor of the manner in which their claims could be satisfied. With Locke, this principle makes its first entrance into Philosophy in a manner so completely at variance with the inflexible undifferentiated identity of the substance of Spinoza, that the sensuous and limited, the immediate present and existent, is the main and fundamental matter. Locke does not get beyond the ordinary point of view of consciousness, viz. that objects outside of us are the real and the true. The finite is thus not grasped by Locke as absolute negativity, *i.e.* in its infinitude; this we shall not find until we come to deal in the third place with Leibnitz. It is in a higher sense that Leibnitz asserts individuality, the differentiated, to be self-existent and indeed objectless, to be true Being. That is to say, it is not according to him finite, but is yet distinguished; thus, each monad is itself the totality. Leibnitz and Locke hence likewise stand in a position of mutual independence and antagonism.

John Locke was born in 1632, at Wrington, in England. He studied for himself the Cartesian philosophy at Oxford, setting aside the scholastic philosophy which was still in vogue. He devoted himself to the study of medicine, which, however, on account of his delicate health, he never really practised. In 1664 he went with an English ambassador for a year to Berlin. After his return to England, he became acquainted with the intellectual Earl of Shaftesbury of that time, who availed himself of his medical advice, and in whose house he lived without requiring to give himself up to practice. When Lord Shaftesbury became Lord Chancellor of England, Locke received an office from him, which, however, he soon lost by a change of ministry. Owing to his dread of falling a prey to consumption, he betook himself in 1675 to Montpellier for the benefit of his health. When his patron came into power again he once more recovered the place he had lost, only to be again deposed on a fresh overthrow of this minister, and he was now compelled to flee from England. "The act by means of which Locke was driven from Oxford" (what post he held there we are not told) "was not an enactment of the University, but of James II., by whose express command, and by the peremptory authority of a written warrant, the expulsion was carried out. From the correspondence that took place, it is evident that the college submitted itself against its will to a measure which it could not resist without compromising the peace and quiet of its members." Locke went to Holland, which was at that time the land wherein all who were obliged to effect their escape from any oppression, whether political or religious, found protection, and in which the most famous and liberal-minded men were to be met with. The Court party persecuted him even here, and by royal warrant he was ordered to be taken prisoner and sent to England; consequently he had to remain hidden with his friends. When William of Orange ascended the English throne, after the Revolution of 1688, Locke returned with him to England. He was there made Commissioner of Trade and Plantations, gave to the world his famous treatise on the Human Understanding, and finally, having withdrawn from public office on account of the delicacy of his health, he spent his remaining years in the country houses of English nobles; he died on the 28th day of October, 1704, in the seventy-third year of his life.[1]

The philosophy of Locke is much esteemed; it is still, for the most part, the philosophy of the English and the French, and likewise in a certain sense of the Germans. To put it in a few words, it asserts on the one hand that truth and knowledge rest upon experience and observation; and on the other the analysis of and abstraction from general determinations is prescribed as the method of knowledge; it is, so to speak, a metaphysical empiricism, and this is the ordinary method adopted in the sciences. In respect of method, Locke thus employs an exactly opposite system to that of Spinoza. In the methods of Spinoza and Descartes an account of the origin of ideas may be dispensed with; they are accepted at once as definitions, such as those of substance, the infinite, mode, extension, etc., all of which constitute a quite incoherent list. But we require to show where these thoughts come in, on what they are founded, and how they are verified. Thus Locke has

[1] Buhle: Geschichte der neuern Philosophie, Vol. IV. Sec. 1, pp. 238-241; Quarterly Review, April, 1817, pp. 70, 71; The Works of John Locke (London, 1812), Vol. I.: The Life of the Author, pp. xix.-xxxix.

striven to satisfy a true necessity. For he has the merit of having deserted the system of mere definitions, which were before this made the starting point, and of having attempted to make deduction of general conceptions, inasmuch as he was, for example, at the pains to show how substantiality arises subjectively from objects. That is a further step than any reached by Spinoza, who begins at once with definitions and axioms which are unverified. Now they are derived, and no longer oracularly laid down, even if the method and manner whereby this authentication is established is not the right one. That is to say, here the matter in question is merely subjective, and somewhat psychological, since Locke merely describes the methods of mind as it appears to us to be. For in his philosophy we have more especially to deal with the derivation of the general conceptions, or ideas, as he called them, that are present in our knowledge, and with their origin as they proceed from what is outwardly and inwardly perceptible. Malebranche no doubt likewise asks how we arrive at conceptions, and thus he apparently has before him the same subject of investigation as has Locke. But firstly, this psychological element in Malebranche is merely the later development, and then to him the universal or God is plainly first, while Locke commences at once with individual perceptions, and only from them does he proceed to Notions, to God. The universal to Locke is, therefore, merely a later result, the work of our minds; it is simply something pertaining to thought, as subjective. Every man undoubtedly knows that when his consciousness develops empirically, he commences from feelings, from quite concrete conditions, and that it is only later on that general conceptions come in, which are connected with the concrete of sensation by being contained therein. Space, for example, comes to consciousness later than the spacial, the species later than the individual; and it is only through the activity of my consciousness that the universal is separated from the particular of conception, feeling, etc. Feeling undoubtedly comes lowest, it is the animal mode of spirit; but in its capacity as thinking, spirit endeavours to transform feeling into its own form. Thus the course adopted by Locke is quite a correct one, but all dialectic considerations are utterly and entirely set aside, since the universal is merely analyzed from the empirical concrete. And in this matter Kant reproaches Locke with reason, the individual is not the source of universal conceptions, but the understanding.

As to Locke's further reflections, they are very simple. Locke considers how the understanding is only consciousness, and in being so is something in consciousness, and he only recognizes the implicit in as far as it is in the same.

a. Locke's philosophy is more especially directed against Descartes, who, like Plato, had spoken of innate ideas. Locke likewise makes special examination of the "inborn impressions (*notiones communes in foro interiori descriptæ*)" which Lord Herbert assumes in his work *De veritate*. In the first book of his work Locke combats the so-called innate ideas, theoretic as well as practical, *i.e.* the universal, absolutely existent ideas which at the same time are represented as pertaining to mind in a natural way. Locke said that we arrive first at *that* which we call idea. By this he understands not the essential determinations of man, but conceptions which we have and which are present and exist in consciousness as such: in the same way we all have arms and legs as parts of our bodies, and the desire to eat exists in everyone. In Locke we thus have the conception of the soul as of a contentless *tabula rasa* which is by-and-by filled with what we call experience.[1] The expression "innate principles" was at that time common, and these

[1] Locke: An Essay concerning human Understanding (The Works of John Locke, Vol. I.), Book I. chap. ii. § 1; chap. iii. § 15, § 22.

innate principles have sometimes been foolishly spoken of. But their true signification is that they are implicit, that they are essential moments in the nature of thought, qualities of a germ, which do not yet exist: only in relation to this last there is an element of truth in Locke's conclusions. As diverse conceptions essentially determined they are only legitimatized by its being shown that they are implied in the essential nature of thought; but as propositions which hold good as axioms, and conceptions which are immediately accepted as laid down in definitions, they undoubtedly possess the form of that which is present and inborn. As they are regarded they are bound to have value in and for themselves; but this is a mere assertion. From the other point of view the question of whence they come is a futile one. Mind is undoubtedly determined in itself, for it is the explicitly existent Notion; its development signifies the coming to consciousness. But the determinations which it brings forth from itself cannot be called innate, for this development must be occasioned by an external, and only on that does the activity of mind react, in order that it may for the first time become conscious of its reality.

The grounds on which Locke refutes innate ideas are empirical. "There is nothing more commonly taken for granted than that there are certain principles, both speculative and practical, universally agreed upon by all mankind: which therefore, they argue, must needs be constant impressions which the souls of men receive in their first Beings."[1] But this universal consent is not to be found. We may instance the proposition, "Whatsoever is, is; and It is impossible for the same thing to be and not to be; which of all others I think have the most allowed title to innate." But this proposition does not hold good for the Notion; there is nothing either in heaven or earth which does not contain Being and non-Being. Many men, "All children and idiots," says Locke, "have not the least apprehension of these propositions." "No proposition can be said to be in the mind which it never yet knew, which it was never yet conscious of. . . . 'Tis usually answered, That all men know and assent to them" (the propositions) "when they come to the use of reason. . . . If it be meant that the use of reason assists us in the knowledge of these maxims, it would prove them not to be innate." Reason is said to be the deriving from principles already known unknown truths. How then should the application of reason be required to discover supposed innate principles? This is a weak objection, for it assumes that by innate ideas we understand those which man possesses in consciousness as immediately present. But development in consciousness is something altogether different from any inherent determination of reason, and therefore the expression innate idea is undoubtedly quite wrong. Innate principles must be found "clearest and most perspicuous nearest the fountain, in children and illiterate people, who have received least impression from foreign opinion." Locke gives further reasons of a similar nature, more especially employing those which are of a practical kind—the diversity in moral judgments, the case of those who are utterly wicked and depraved, devoid of sense of right or conscience.[1]

b. In the second book Locke goes on to the next stage, to the origin of ideas, and seeks to demonstrate this process from experience—this is the main object of his efforts. The reason that the positive point of view which he opposes to any derivation from within, is so false, is that he derives his conceptions only from outside and thus maintains Being-for-another, while he quite neglects the implicit. He says: "Every man being conscious to himself, that he thinks; and that which his mind is applied about, while thinking, being the ideas that are there; 'tis past doubt, that men have in their minds several ideas, such as those expressed in the words, whiteness, hardness, sweetness, thinking,

[1] Locke: An Essay concerning human Understanding (Vol. I.) Book I. chap. ii. § 2-9; § 27; chap. iii. § 1-15.

motion, man, elephant, army, drunkenness, and others." Idea here signifies both the ordinary conception and thought; we understand something quite different by the word idea. "It is in the first place then to be inquired, how he comes by them" (these ideas)? Innate ideas have already been refuted. "Let us then suppose the mind to be, as we say, white paper, void of all characters, without any ideas; how comes it to be furnished? . . . To this I answer in a word, from Experience: in that all our knowledge is founded."[1]

As to the question in point we must in the first place say that it is true that man commences with experience if he desires to arrive at thought. Everything is experienced, not merely what is sensuous, but also what excites and stimulates my mind. Consciousness thus undoubtedly obtains all conceptions and Notions from experience and in experience; the only question is what we understand by experience. In a usual way when this is spoken of the idea of nothing particular is conveyed; we speak of it as of something quite well known. But experience is nothing more than the form of objectivity; to say that it is something which is in consciousness means that it has objective form for consciousness or that consciousness experiences it, it sees it as an objective. Experience thus signifies immediate knowledge, perception, *i.e.* I myself must have and be something, and the consciousness of what I have and am is experience. Now there is no question as to this, that whatever we know, of whatever kind it may be, must be experienced, that rests in the conception of the thing. It is absurd to say that one knows anything which is not in experience. I undoubtedly know men, for instance, from experience, without requiring to have seen them all, for I have, as man, activity and will, a consciousness respecting what I am and what others are. The rational exists, *i.e.* it

[1] Locke: An Essay concerning human Understanding (Vol. I.) Bk. II. chap. i. § 1, 2.

is as an existent for consciousness, or this last experiences it; it must be seen and heard, it must be there or have been there as a phenomenon in the world. This connection of universal with objective is however in the second place not the only form, that of the implicit is likewise absolute and essential—that is, the apprehension of what is experienced or the abrogation of this apparent other-being and the knowledge of the necessity of the thing through itself. It is now quite a matter of indifference whether anything is accepted as something experienced, as a succession of empirical ideas, if one may so say, or conceptions; or whether the succession is a succession of thoughts, *i.e.* implicitly existent.

Locke treats of the various kinds of these ideas imperfectly and empirically merely.

a. According to Locke simple ideas arise partly from outward, and partly from inward experience. For experiences, he says, are in the first place sensations; the other side is reflection, the inward determinations of consciousness.[1] From sensation, from the organs of sight for instance, the conceptions of colour, light, etc., arise; there further arises from outward experience the idea of impenetrability, of figure, rest, motion and such like. From reflections come the ideas of faith, doubt, judgment, reasoning, thinking, willing, etc.; from both combined, pleasure, pain, etc. This is a very commonplace account of the matter.

β. After Locke has pre-supposed experience, he goes on to say that it is the understanding which now discovers and desires the universal—the complex ideas. The Bishop of Worcester made the objection that "If the idea of substance be grounded upon plain and evident reason, then we must allow an idea of substance which comes not in by sensation or reflection." Locke replies: "General ideas

[1] Locke: An Essay concerning human Understanding (Vol. I.), Bk. II. chap. i. § 2-5.

come not into the mind by sensation or reflection, but are the creatures or inventions of the understanding. The mind makes them from ideas which it has got by sensation and reflection." The work of the mind now consists in bringing forth from several simple so-called ideas a number of new ones, by means of its working upon this material through comparing, distinguishing and contrasting it, and finally through separation or abstraction, whereby the universal conceptions, such as space, time, existence, unity and diversity, capacity, cause and effect, freedom, necessity, take their rise. "The mind in respect of its simple ideas is wholly passive, and receives them all from the existence and operation of things, such as sensation or reflection offers them, without being able to make any one idea." But "the mind often exercises an active power in making these several combinations. For it being once furnished with simple ideas it can put them together in several combinations." According to Locke therefore thought itself is not the essence of the soul, but one of its powers and manifestations. He maintains thought to be existent in consciousness as conscious thought, and thus brings it forward as a fact in his experience, that we do not always think. Experience demonstrates dreamless sleep when the sleep is profound. Locke quotes the example of a man who remembered no dream until he had reached his twenty-fifth year. It is as in the Xenien,—[1]

Oft schon war ich, und hab' wirklich an gar nichts gedacht.

That is to say, my object is not a thought. But sensuous perception and recollection are thought, and thought is truth.[2] Locke, however, places the reality of the understanding only in the formal activity of constituting new determinations from the simple con-

[1] v. Schiller's Xenien.

[2] Locke: An Essay concerning human Understanding (Vol. I.), Bk. II., chap. ii. § 2, not.; chap. xii. § 1; chap. xxii. § 2; chap. i. § 10-14.

ceptions received by means of perception, through their comparison and the combination of several into one; it is the apprehension of the abstract sensations which are contained in the objects. Locke likewise distinguishes (Bk. II. chap. xi. § 15-17) beween pure and mixed modes. Pure modes are simple determinations such as power, number, infinitude; in such expressions as causality we reach, on the other hand, a mixed mode.

Locke now explains in detail the manner in which the mind, from the simple ideas of experience, reaches more complex ideas; but this derivation of general determinations from concrete perception is most unmeaning, trivial, tiresome and diffuse; it is entirely formal, an empty tautology. For instance we form the general conception of space from the perception of the distance of bodies by means of sight and feeling.[1] Or in other words, we perceive a definite space, abstract from it, and then we have the conception of space generally; the perception of distances gives us conceptions of space. This however is no deduction, but only a setting aside of other determinations; since distance itself is really space, mind thus determines space from space. Similarly we reach the notion of time through the unbroken succession of conceptions during our waking moments,[2] *i.e.* from determinate time we perceive time in general. Conceptions follow one another in a continual succession; if we set aside the particular element that is present we thereby receive the conception of time. Substance (which Locke does not accept in so lofty a sense as Spinoza), a complex idea, hence arises from the fact that we often perceive simple ideas such as blue, heavy, etc., in association with one another. This association we represent to ourselves as something which so to

[1] Locke: An Essay concerning human Understanding (Vol. I.), Bk. II. chap. xiii. § 2; chap. iv. § 2.

[2] Ibidem (Vol. I.), Bk. II. chap. xiv. § 3.

speak supports these simple ideas, or in which they exist.[1] Locke likewise deduces the general conception of power.[2] The determinations of freedom and necessity, cause and effect, are then derived in a similar way. "In the notice that our senses take of the constant vicissitude of things, we cannot but observe, that several particulars, both qualities and substance, begin to exist; and that they receive this their existence from the due application and operation of some other being. From this observation we get our ideas of cause and effect," for instance when wax is melted by the fire.[3] Locke goes on to say: "Every one, I think, finds in himself a power to begin or forbear, continue or put an end to several actions in himself. From the consideration of the extent of this power of the mind over the actions of the man, which every one finds in himself, arise the ideas of liberty and necessity."[4]

We may say that nothing can be more superficial than this derivation of ideas. The matter itself, the essence, is not touched upon at all. A determination is brought into notice which is contained in a concrete relationship; hence the understanding on the one hand abstracts and on the other establishes conclusions. The basis of this philosophy is merely to be found in the transference of the determinate to the form of universality, but it was just this fundamental essence that we had to explain. As to this Locke confesses of space, for example, that he does not know what it really is.[5] This so-called analysis by Locke of complex conceptions, and his so-called explanation of the same, has, on account of its uncommon clearness and lucidity of expression, found universal acceptance. For what can be clearer than to

[1] Locke: An Essay concerning human Understanding (Vol. II.), Bk. II. chap. xxiii. § 1, 2.

[2] Ibidem (Vol. I.), Bk. II. chap. xxi. § 1.

[3] Ibidem (Vol. II.), Bk. II. chap. xxvi. § 1.

[4] Ibidem (Vol. I.), Bk. II. chap. xxi. § 7.

[5] Ibidem (Vol. I.), Bk. II. chap. xiii. § 17, 18.

say that we have the notion of time because we perceive time, if we do not actually see it, and that we conceive of space because we see it? The French have accepted this most readily and they have carried it further still; their *Idéologie* contains nothing more nor less.

γ. When Locke starts by saying that everything is experience and we abstract for ourselves from this experience general conceptions regarding objects and their qualities, he makes a distinction in respect of external qualities which was before this made by Aristotle (De anima, II. 6), and which we likewise met with in Descartes (*supra*, pp. 245, 246). That is to say, Locke distinguishes between primary and secondary qualities; the first pertain to the objects themselves in truth, the others are not real qualities, but are founded on the nature of the organs of sensation. Primary qualities are mechanical, like extension, solidity, figure, movement, rest; these are qualities of the corporeal, just as thought is the quality of the spiritual. But the determinations of our individual feelings such as colours, sounds, smells, taste, etc., are not primary."[1] In Descartes' case this distinction has however another form, for the second class of these determinations is defined by him in such a way as that they do not constitute the essence of body, while Locke says that they exist for sensation, or fall within existence as it is for consciousness. Locke, however, no doubt reckons figure, etc., as still pertaining to reality, but by so doing nothing is ascertained as to the nature of body. In Locke a difference here appears between the implicit and being 'for-another,' in which he declares the moment of 'for-another' to be unreal—and yet he sees all truth in the relation of 'for-another' only.

c. Since the universal as such, the idea of species, is, according to Locke, merely a product of our mind, which is not itself objective, but relates merely to objects which are

[1] Locke: An Essay concerning human Understanding (Vol. I.), Bk. II. chap. viii. § 9-26.

germane to it, and from which the particular of qualities, conditions, time, place, etc., are separated, Locke distinguishes essences into real essences and nominal essences; the former of these express the true essence of things, while species on the other hand are mere nominal essences which no doubt express something which is present in the objects, but which do not exhaust these objects. They serve to distinguish species for our knowledge, but the real essence of nature we do not know.[1] Locke gives good reasons for species being nothing in themselves—for their not being in nature, or absolutely determined—instancing in exemplification the production of monstrosities (Bk. III. chap. iii. § 17): were species absolute no monster would be born. But he overlooks the fact that since it pertains to species to exist, it thereby likewise enters into relationship with other determinations; thus that is the sphere in which individual things operate upon one another, and may hence be detrimental to the existence of the species. Locke thus argues just as one would who wished to prove that the good does not exist in itself, because there are likewise evil men, that the circle does not exist absolutely in nature, because the circumference of a tree, for example, represents a very irregular circle, or because I draw a circle badly. Nature just signifies the lack of power to be perfectly adequate to the Notion; it is only in spirit that the Notion has its true existence. To say that species are nothing in themselves, that the universal is not the essential reality of nature, that its implicit existence is not the object of thought, is tantamount to saying that we do not know real existence: it is the same litany which has since been so constantly repeated that we are tired of listening to it:

Das Innere der Natur kennt kein erschaffener Geist,

and which goes on until we have perceived that Being-

[1] Locke: An Essay concerning human Understanding (Vol. II.), Bk. III. chap. iii. § 6; § 13, 15.

for-another, perception, is not implicit; a point of view which has not made its way to the positive position that the implicit is the universal. Locke is far back in the nature of knowledge, further back than Plato, because of his insistence on Being-for-another.

It is further noteworthy that from the sound understanding Locke argues (Vol. III. Bk. IV. chap. vii. § 8-11) against universal propositions or axioms such as that A=A, *i.e.* if anything is A it cannot be B. He says they are superfluous, of very little use or of no use at all, for nobody yet has built up a science on a proposition which asserts a contradiction. From such the true may be proved as easily as the false; they are tautological. What Locke has further achieved in respect of education, toleration, natural rights or universal state-right, does not concern us here, but has to do with general culture.

This is the philosophy of Locke, in which there is no trace of speculation. The great end of Philosophy, which is to know the truth, is in it sought to be attained in an empiric way; it thus indeed serves to draw attention to general determinations. But such a philosophy not only represents the standpoint of ordinary consciousness, to which all the determinations of its thought appear as if given, humble as it is in the oblivion of its activity, but in this method of derivation and psychological origination that which alone concerns Philosophy, the question of whether these thoughts and relationships have truth in and for themselves, is not present at all, inasmuch as the only object aimed at is to describe the manner in which thought accepts what is given to it. It may be held with Wolff that it is arbitrary to begin with concrete conceptions, as when our conception of identity is made to take its origin from such things as blue flowers and the blue heavens. One can better begin directly from universal conceptions and say that we find in our consciousness the conceptions of time, cause and effect; these are the later facts of consciousness. This method forms the basis of the Wolffian system of reasoning, only here we must still distinguish amongst the different conceptions those that are to be regarded as most essential; in Locke's philosophy, this distinction cannot really be said to come under consideration. From this time, according to Locke, or in this particular aspect of Philosophy, there is a complete and entire change in the point of view adopted; the whole interest is limited to the form in which the objective, or individual sensations, pass into the form of conceptions. In the case of Spinoza and Malebranche, we undoubtedly likewise saw that it was made a matter of importance to recognize this relation of thought to what is sensuously perceived, and thus to know it as falling into relation, as passing into the relative; the main question hence was: How are the two related? But the question was answered to the effect that it is only this relation for itself that constitutes the point of interest, and this relation itself as absolute substance is thus identity, the true, God, it is not the related parts. The interest does not lie in the related parts; the related parts as one-sided are not the existent, pre-supposed and permanently established, they are accidental merely. But here the related sides, the things and the subject, have their proper value, and they are pre-supposed as having this value. Locke's reasoning is quite shallow; it keeps entirely to the phenomenal, to that which is, and not to that which is true.

There is another question however: Are these general determinations absolutely true? And whence come they not alone into my consciousness, into my mind and understanding, but into the things themselves? Space, cause, effect, etc., are categories. How do these categories come into the particular? How does universal space arrive at determining itself? This point of view, the question whether these determinations of the infinite, of substance, etc., are in and for themselves true, is quite lost sight of.

Plato investigated the infinite and the finite, Being and the determinate, etc., and pronounced that neither of these opposites is of itself true; they are so only as together constituting an identity, wherever the truth of this content may come from. But here the truth as it is in and for itself is entirely set aside and the nature of the content itself is made the main point. It does not matter whether the understanding or experience is its source, for the question is whether this content is in itself true. With Locke, the truth merely signifies the harmony of our conceptions with things; here relation is alone in question, whether the content is an objective thing or a content of the ordinary conception. But it is quite another matter to investigate the content itself, and to ask, "Is this which is within us true? We must not dispute about the sources, for the Whence, the only important point to Locke, does not exhaust the whole question. The interest of the content in and for itself wholly disappears when that position is taken up, and thereby the whole of what is aimed at by Philosophy is given up. On the other hand, when thought is from the beginning concrete, when thought and the universal are synonymous with what is set before us, the question of the relation of the two which have been separated by thought is destitute of interest and incomprehensible. How does thought overcome the difficulties which itself has begotten? Here with Locke none at all have been begotten and awakened. Before the need for reconciliation can be satisfied, the pain of disunion must be excited.

The philosophy of Locke is certainly very comprehensible, but for that very reason it is likewise a popular philosophy to which the whole of the English philosophy as it exists at this day is allied; it is the thinking method of regarding things which is called philosophy carried to its perfection, the form which was introduced into the science which then took its rise in Europe. This is an important moment in culture; the sciences in general and specially the empiric sciences have to ascribe their origin to this movement. To the English, Philosophy has ever signified the deduction of experiences from observations; this has in a one-sided way been applied to physical and economic subjects. General principles of political economy such as free-trade in the present day, and all matters which rest on thinking experience, the knowledge of whatever reveals itself in this sphere as necessary and useful, signifies philosophy to the English (Vol. I. pp. 57, 58). The scholastic method of starting from principles and definitions has been rejected. The universal, laws, forces, universal matter, etc., have in natural science been derived from perceptions; thus to the English, Newton is held to be the philosopher κατ' ἐξοχήν. The other side is that in practical philosophy regarding society or the state, thought applies itself to concrete objects such as the will of the prince, subjects and their ends and personal welfare. Inasmuch as we have an object such as that before us, the indwelling and essential universal is made evident; it must, however, be made clear which conception is the one to which the others must yield. It is in this way that rational politics took their rise in England, because the institutions and government peculiar to the English led them specially and in the first place to reflection upon their inward political and economic relationships. Hobbes must be mentioned as an exemplification of this fact. This manner of reasoning starts from the present mind, from what is our own, whether it be within or without us, since the feelings which we have, the experiences which fall directly within us, are the principles. This philosophy of reasoning thought is that which has now become universal, and through which the whole revolution in the position taken up by mind has come to pass.

2. Hugo Grotius.

Hugo Grotius was studying the laws of nations at the same time as Locke; and in him the very same methods may be found as those already mentioned, inasmuch as he also falls into a quite empirical system of associating nations with one another, combining with that an empirical mode of reasoning. Hugo van Groot, born 1583 at Delft, was a lawyer, fiscal general, and council pensionary; in 1619, however, he was implicated in the Barneveldt trial, and was compelled to fly the country. For a long time he remained in France, but in 1634 he entered the service of Queen Christina of Sweden. In 1635 he was made Swedish ambassador in Paris, and in 1645 he died at Rostock, while on a journey from Stockholm to Holland.[1] His principal work, *De jure belli et pacis*, he composed in 1625; now it is not read, but at one time it exercised a very great and important influence. In it Grotius presented a comparative historical account, the material of which was partly derived from the Old Testament, of the manner in which nations in the various relationships of war and peace have acted towards one another, and what usages they held to be binding. The following may serve as an example of his empirical method of reasoning: Prisoners ought not to be killed; for the object is to disarm the enemy, and if this end be attained nothing further should be done.[2] This empirical way of connecting facts had the effect of bringing general comprehensible and rational principles into consciousness, of making them recognized, and of causing them to be more or less acceptable. Thus we see principles set forth, respecting the righteousness of a king's power for instance; for thought applied itself to everything. We are unsatisfied by such proofs and deductions, but we must not overlook what is thereby accomplished; and this is the establishment of principles which have their ultimate confirmation in the objects themselves, in mind and thought.

[1] Brucker. Histor. critic. philos. T. IV. P. 2, pp. 731-736, 743-745.

[2] Hug. Grot. De jure belli ac pacis, B. III. chap. xi. § 13-16 (Ed. Gronov. Lipsiæ, 1758, 8vo), pp. 900-905; chap. iv. § 10, pp. 792, 793.

3. Thomas Hobbes.

Hobbes, who was celebrated and distinguished on account of the originality of his views, was tutor to the Earl of Devonshiro; he was born in 1588 at Malmesbury, and died in 1679.[1] As a contemporary of Cromwell, he found in the events of that time, in the Revolution which then took place in England, an occasion for reflecting on the principles of state and law, and in fact he succeeded in making his way to quite original conceptions. He wrote much, including a treatise on Philosophy, entitled "The Elements of Philosophy." The first section (*Sectio*) of this work, *De corpore*, appeared in London in 1655; in it he first of all treats of Logic (*Pars* I.), and secondly of *philosophia prima* (*Pars* II.); this last is an ontology and metaphysic. The next sub-division (*Pars* III.), "On the relation between motion and magnitude," is a system of mechanism, a quite popular system of physics; and a study of the human organs. The second section was to treat of the nature of man (*De homine*), and the third of the state (*De cive*), but the intellectual sections of the work Hobbes did not entirely finish. He says in his preface that Copernicus first opened up astronomy, and Galileo physics; before them there was nothing certain in either science. Harvey worked out the science of the human body, and physics generally as well as astronomy were perfected by Keppler. All this was termed Philosophy, in accordance with the point of view which has been already given (p. 313), since in it the reflective understanding desires to know the universal. Hobbes further says concerning the philosophy of the state (*philosophia civilis*), that it only dates from the publication of his book *De cive*.[2] This work, which appeared at Paris

[1] Buhle: Geschichte der neuern Philosophie, Vol. III. Sec. 1, pp. 223, 224, 227.

[2] Hobbes. Epistola dedicatoria ante Elementor. philos. Sectionem primam (Thomæ Hobbesii Opera philosophica, quæ latine scripsit omnia, Amstelod, 1668, 4to), pp. 1, 2.

in 1642,[1] is, like his Leviathan, a much decried book; the second mentioned writing was forbidden to be circulated, and is hence very rare. Both works contain sounder reflections on the nature of society and government than many now in circulation. Society, the state, is to Hobbes absolutely pre-eminent, it is the determining power without appeal as regards law and positive religion and their external relations; and because he placed these in subjection to the state, his doctrines were of course regarded with the utmost horror. But there is nothing speculative or really philosophic in them, and there is still less in Hugo Grotius.

Before this ideals were set before us, or Holy Scripture or positive law was quoted as authoritative. Hobbes, on the contrary, sought to derive the bond which holds the state together, that which gives the state its power, from principles which lie within us, which we recognize as our own. In this way two opposite principles arise. The first is the passive obedience of subjects, the divine authority of rulers, whose will is absolute law, and is itself elevated above all other law. All this is represented in close connection with religion, and proved by examples from the Old Testament, by such stories as those of Saul and David. Criminal and marriage laws, too, for long derived their character from the Mosaic laws, or, speaking generally, from those the provisions of which possessed their value by the fact of being established by express divine command. On the other hand we have in the second place the reasoning wherein we ourselves are the determining agents, and which was called sound reason. In the movement which Cromwell made use of there was allied with this a fanaticism, which from the written letter drew opposite conclusions to the above, and this we see exemplified in the equality of property, for instance. Hobbes,

[1] Cf. Brucker. Histor. crit. philos. T. IV. P. II. p. 154.

it is true, likewise maintained passive obedience, the absolute freedom of the royal will and power; but at the same time he sought to derive the principles of monarchical power, etc., from universal determinations. The views that he adopts are shallow and empirical, but the reasons he gives for them, and the propositions he makes respecting them, are original in character, inasmuch as they are derived from natural necessities and wants.

Hobbes maintained that "The origin of all society is to be found in the mutual fear of all its members;" it is hence a phenomenon in consciousness. "Each association is thus formed in its own interest or for its own renown, that is, from selfish motives." All such matters as security of life, property, and enjoyment, are not to be found outside it. "But men have in all dissimilarity of strength a natural similarity as well." This Hobbes proves by a characteristic reason, viz. that "each individual can make away with the other," each is the ultimate power over the others. "Each can be supreme."[1] Thus their similarity is not derived from the greatest strength; it is not, as in modern times, founded on the freedom of the spirit, or on an equality of merit and independence, but on the equal weakness of mankind; each man is weak as regards others.

b. Hobbes further takes up the position that this natural condition is of such a nature that all possess the desire to rule over one another. "All in their natural condition are possessed of the will to injure others," to tyrannize over other men; each has thus to fear the other. Hobbes looks at this condition in its true light, and we find in him no idle talk about a state of natural goodness; the natural condition is really far more like that of the animals—a condition in which there is an unsubdued individual will. All thus wish to "secure themselves against the pretensions of others, to acquire for themselves advantages and supe-

[1] Hobbes, De cive, chap. i. § 2, 3 (Oper. phil. etc. Amstel. 1668), pp. 3, 4.

rior rights. Opinions, religions, desires, arouse strife; the stronger bears away the victory. The natural condition is consequently a condition of mistrust on the part of all towards all; it is a war of all against all (*bellum omnium in omnes*)," and the endeavour of one to overreach another. The expression nature has a double significance: In the first place the nature of man signifies his spiritual and rational Being; but his natural condition indicates quite another condition, wherein man conducts himself according to his natural impulses. In this way he conducts himself in conformity with his desires and inclinations, while the rational, on the contrary, is the obtaining supremacy over the immediately natural. "In the condition of nature a certain irresistible power grants the right to rule over those who cannot resist; it is absurd to leave those whom we have in our power to become free and strong again." From this Hobbes draws the conclusion that "man must go forth from the natural condition."[1] This is true; the natural condition is not what it should be, and must hence be cast off.

c. Hobbes finally passes to the laws of reason which preserve tranquillity. This condition of law is the subjection of the natural, particular will of the individual to the universal will, which, however, is not that of all individuals, but is the will of the ruler; this is consequently not responsible to individuals, but is directed against this private will, and to it all must be obedient.[2] Thus the whole matter is now placed on quite another footing. But because the universal will is made to reside in the will of one monarch, there nevertheless proceeds from this point of view, which is really correct, a condition of absolute rule, of perfect despotism. The condition of law does not, however, mean

[1] Hobbes, De cive, chap. i. § 4–6, 12–14, pp. 4–8; Leviathan, chap. xiii. (Oper.), pp. 63–66.

[2] Ibidem, chap. v. § 6–12, pp. 37–38; chap. vi. § 12–14, pp. 44–46.

that the arbitrary will of one man constitutes absolute law, for the universal will is no despotism, being rational, inasmuch as it is consistently expressed and determined in laws.

Rixner (Handbuch der Geschichte der Philosophie, Vol. III. p. 30) says: "Law to him is nothing but the sum of the conditions of peace extorted by iron necessity from the original wickedness of mankind." We might add that in Hobbes we at least find this, that the nature and organism of the State is established on the principle of human nature, human desire, &c. The English concerned themselves greatly with that principle of passive obedience, in accordance with which it is said that kings receive their power from God. This, in one aspect, is quite true, but in another it is falsely taken to mean that they have no responsibility, that their blind desires, their merely subjective will, is what must be obeyed.

4. Cudworth. Clarke. Wollaston.

Cudworth wished to revive Plato in England, but to do this after the manner of the demonstrations which we met with in Descartes, and through a trivial metaphysic of the understanding. He wrote a celebrated work: "The true intellectual System of the Universe," but the Platonic ideas expressed are often in a clumsy form and mingled with the Christian conceptions of God and angels—all regarded as particular existent things. What in Plato is mythical, is here taken as reality in the form of existence; this is reasoned about just as we reason respecting a matter of ordinary fact, such as whether it is probable that the French seek to effect a landing in England, and if so, whether they will successfully accomplish it. The Christian intellectual world is dragged down to the form of ordinary actuality, and consequently it is ruined.

The name of Clarke is likewise famous in connection

with his proof of the existence of God. There were quite a number of other English philosophers, whom we do not, however, require to notice; for Clarke, Wollaston, and others carry on their speculations within forms such as belong to a very commonplace metaphysic of the understanding. The manifold systems of moral philosophy which we find taking their rise in England are drawn up from this same mental standpoint; in them the implicitude of mind appears in a form of natural existence, namely, of desires and feelings. Their principles are found in moral sentiments, benevolent desires, sympathy, &c. That form alone is worthy of notice which, on the one hand, represents duty as something which is not foreign, given, commanded, but as clearly belonging to self-consciousness, even while, on the other hand, it represents this property as a natural, unconscious, unspiritual, and irrational existence. Impulse is blind, a solid existence which cannot get beyond itself like thinking self-consciousness. It is indeed true of impulse that its pure activity or its process, and the content, are, as in thought, immediately posited as the same; it has its content in itself, and this is not dead and passive, but self-acting and impelling. But that unity has the form of immediacy only as existent; in the first place it is not a knowledge, it is not necessary, for it is only taken from inward perception; in the second place, it is a determinate which does not abrogate itself, beyond which we cannot get, and which thus is not a universal. Impulse is no more an infinite than is the fixed category of force. Such reasoning takes the impulses in their determinate character from experience, and expresses the appearance of necessity in the same as an inward existence, as a force. For instance, the social instinct is a moment which is found in experience, because man derives all manner of utility from society. Wherein does the necessity of the State, of society, find its basis? In a social desire. This is cause, just as in the physical world a formal interpretation such as this is always to be found. The necessity of any existent fact, such as what pertains to electrical phenomena, finds its basis in a force which brings it forth; it is merely the form of returning from the external to an inward, of passing from the existent to what is thought, which is again in turn represented as an existent. Force is necessitated by reason of the manifestation, we must argue from the latter to the former. On the other hand, the manifestation takes place through the force, for it is the cause of the manifestation; we hence have force in one place as reason, and in another as cause. But in all this there is no realization of the fact that in respect of form there is a transition from the Notion into Being and the other way, while in respect of content there is a perfect contingency of manifestation; we look at electricity in the same way as we look at the fact that men have social instincts, sympathetic inclinations, and so on.

5. Puffendorf.

In the struggle to give to just and equitable relations in the State an independent basis of their own, and to found a judicial system of government, reflective thought put forth its efforts; and this became to it a real interest and concern. And, as in the case of Grotius, it was also true of Puffendorf, that the instinct of mankind—that is, the social instinct, &c.—was made the principle. Samuel von Puffendorf was born in 1632 in Saxony; he studied public law, philosophy, and mathematics at Leipzig and Jena; in 1661, as a professor at Heidelberg, he made natural and civil law for the first time academic studies; in 1668 he became tutor in a Swedish family, which office he later on exchanged for the service of the House of Brandenburg, and in 1694 he died at Berlin as a privy councillor. He wrote several works on political law and history; we must specially mention his work, *De jure naturæ et gentium*, Libr. viii., Londin. Scan. 1672, 4; and also his compendium *De officio hominis*, published at the same place in 1673, 8, and *Elementa jurisprudentiæ universalis.*[1] While the divine right of kings was here still recognized—whereby they rendered account to God alone, or, at all events, were still bound to take counsel of the Church—the impulses and necessities present in mankind were now considered as well. These were regarded as the inward principles for private and political law, and from them the duties both of the government and of rulers were deduced, so that the freedom of mankind might not be interfered with. The basis of the state in Puffendorf's view is the social instinct: the highest end of the state is the peace and security of social life through the transformation of inward duties as prescribed by conscience into external duties as compelled by law.[2]

6. Newton.

The other side is that thought likewise applied itself to nature, and in this connection Isaac Newton is famous by reason of his mathematical discoveries and his work in physics. He was born in 1642 at Cambridge, made a special study of mathematics, and became professor of the same at Cambridge; later on he was made president of the Royal Society in London, and he died in 1727.[3]

Newton was indisputably the chief contributor to the

[1] Buhle: Geschichte der neuern Philosophie, Vol. IV. Sec. 2, pp. 519-523; Rixner: Handbuch der Geschichte der Philosophie, Vol. III. p. 29.

[2] Rixner: Handbuch der Geschichte der Philosophie, Vol. III. p. 31; cf. Puffendorf: De jure naturæ et gent. II. 2, § 5-7 (Francof. ad Moenum, 1706, 4), pp. 157-161; VII. 1, § 3-7, pp. 900-909.

[3] Buhle: Geschichte der neuern Philosophie, Vol. IV. Sec. 1, pp. 107, 108.

popularity of the philosophy of Locke, or the English method of treating of Philosophy, and more especially did he promote its application to all the physical sciences. "Physics, beware of metaphysics," was his maxim,[1] which signifies, Science, beware of thought; and all the physical sciences, even to the present day, have, following in his wake, faithfully observed this precept, inasmuch as they have not entered upon an investigation of their conceptions, or thought about thoughts. Physics can, however, effect nothing without thought; it has its categories and laws through thought alone, and without thought it does not effect any progress. Newton was mainly instrumental in introducing to physics the determinations respecting forces, which pertain to reflection; he raised science to the standpoint of reflection, and set the laws of forces in the place of the laws of phenomena. Regarding matters as he did, Newton derived his conclusions from his experiences; and in physics and the theory of colour-vision, he made bad observations and drew worse conclusions. He passed from experiences to general points of view, again made them fundamental, and from them constructed the individual; this is how his theories are constructed. The observation of things, the discovery of the law immanent therein, and the universal which is found within them, has become the real point of interest. In this way, Newton is so complete a barbarian as regards his conceptions that his case is like that of another of his countrymen who was surprised and rejoiced to learn that he had talked prose all his life, not having had any idea that he was so accomplished. This Newton, like all the Physicists, indeed, never learned; he did not know that he thought in, and had to deal with Notions, while he imagined he was dealing with

[1] Buhle: Geschichte der neuern Philosophie. Vol. IV. p. 115; cf. Newtoni Optices, P. III. (Londini, 1706, 4) p. 314.

physical facts: and he presented the extremest contrast to Boehme, who handled sensuous things as Notions, and, by sheer force of mind, obtained entire possession of their actuality and subjugated them. Instead of this Newton treated Notions like sensuous things, and dealt with them just as men deal with wood and stone. And this is even now the case. In the beginnings of physical science we read of the power of inertia, for instance, of the force of acceleration, of molecules, of centripetal and centrifugal force, as of facts which definitely exist; what are really the final results of reflection are represented as their first grounds. If we ask for the cause of there being no advance made in such sciences, we find that it is because men do not understand that they should apply themselves to Notions, but make up their minds to adopt these determinations without sense or understanding. Hence in Newton's Optics, for instance, there are conclusions derived from his experience which are so untrue and devoid of understanding, that while they are set forth as the finest example of how men can learn to know nature by means of experiments and conclusions derived from experiments, they may also serve as an example of how we should neither experiment nor draw conclusions, of how nothing at all can be learned. A miserable kind of experience like this itself contradicts itself through nature, for nature is more excellent than it appears in this wretched experience: both nature itself and experience, when carried a little further, contradict it. Hence, of all the splendid discoveries of Newton in optics, none now remain excepting one—the division of light into seven colours. This is partly because the conception of whole and part come into play, and partly from an obdurate closing of the eyes to the opposite side. From this empirical method in Philosophy, we shall now pass on to Leibnitz.

C

THIRD SECTION.

The third development of the philosophy of the understanding is that represented by Leibnitz and Wolff. If Wolff's metaphysics is divested of its rigid form, we have as a result the later popular philosophy.

1. LEIBNITZ.

As in other respects Leibnitz represents the extreme antithesis to Newton, so in respect of philosophy he presents a striking contrast to Locke and his empiricism, and also to Spinoza. He upholds thought as against the perception of the English school, and in lieu of sensuous Being he maintains Being for thought to be the essence of truth, just as Boehme at an earlier time upheld implicit Being. While Spinoza asserted the universality, the oneness of substance merely, and while with Locke we saw infinite determinations made the basis, Leibnitz, by means of his fundamental principle of individuality, brings out the essentiality of the opposite aspect of Spinoza's philosophy, existence for self, the monad, but the monad regarded as the absolute Notion, though perhaps not yet as the "I." The opposed principles, which were forced asunder, find their completion in each other, since Leibnitz's principle of individuation completed Spinoza's system as far as outward aspect goes.

Gottfried Wilhelm, Baron von Leibnitz, was born in 1646 at Leipzig, where his father was professor of Philosophy. The subject that he studied in view of a profession was jurisprudence, but first, in accordance with the fashion of the day, he made a study of Philosophy, and to it he devoted particular attention. To begin with, he picked up in Leipzig a large and miscellaneous stock of knowledge, then he studied Philosophy and mathematics at Jena under the mathematician and theosophist Weigel, and took his degree of Master of Philosophy in Leipzig. There also, on the occasion of his graduation as Doctor of Philosophy, he defended certain philosophical theses, some of which discourses are still contained in his works (ed. Dutens, T. II. P. I. p. 400). His first dissertation, and that for which he obtained the degree of doctor of philosophy, was : *De principio individui,*—a principle which remained the abstract principle of his whole philosophy, as opposed to that of Spinoza. After he had acquired a thorough knowledge of the subject, he wished to graduate also as Doctor of Laws. But though he died an imperial councillor, it was his ill fortune to receive from the Faculty at Leipzig a refusal to confer the doctorate upon him, his youth being the alleged reason. Such a thing could scarcely happen nowadays. It may be that it was done because of his over-great philosophical attainments, seeing that lawyers are wont to hold the same in horror. He now quitted Leipzig, and betook himself to Altdorf, where he graduated with distinction. Shortly afterwards he became acquainted in Nürnberg with a company of alchemists, with whose ongoings he became associated. Here he made extracts from alchemistic writings, and studied the mysteries of this occult science. His activity in the pursuit of learning extended also to historical, diplomatic, mathematical and philosophical subjects. He subsequently entered the service of the Elector of Mayence, becoming a member of council, and in 1672 he was appointed tutor to a son of Von Boineburg, Chancellor of State to the Elector. With this young man he travelled to Paris, where he lived for four years. He at this time made the acquaintance of the great mathematician Huygens, and was by him for the first time properly introduced into the domain of mathematics. When the education of his pupil was completed, and the Baron Von Boineburg died, Leibnitz went on his own account to London, where he became acquainted with Newton and other scholars, at whose head was Oldenburg, who was also on friendly terms with Spinoza. After the death of the Elector of Mayence, the salary of Leibnitz ceased to be paid; he therefore left England and returned to France. The Duke of Brünswick-Lüneburg then took him into his service, and gave him the appointment of councillor and librarian at Hanover, with permission to spend as much time as he liked in foreign countries. He therefore remained for some time longer in France, England, and Holland. In the year 1677 he settled down in Hanover, where he became busily engaged in affairs of state, and was specially occupied with historical matters. In the Harz Mountains he had works constructed for carrying off the floods which did damage to the mines there. Notwithstanding these manifold occupations he invented the differential calculus in 1677, on occasion of which there arose a dispute between him and Newton, which was carried on by the latter and the Royal Society of London in a most ungenerous manner. For it was asserted by the English, who gave themselves the credit of everything, and were very unfair to others, that the discovery was really made by Newton. But Newton's *Principia* only appeared later, and in the first edition indeed Leibnitz was mentioned with commendation in a note which was afterwards omitted. From his headquarters in Hanover, Leibnitz, commissioned by his prince, made several journeys through Germany, and also went to Italy in order to collect historical evidence relative to the House of Este, and for the purpose of proving more clearly the relationship between this princely family and that of Brunswick-Lüneburg. At other times he was likewise much occupied with historical questions. Owing to his acquaintance with the consort of Frederick I. of Prussia, Sophia Charlotte, a Hanoverian princess, he was enabled to bring about the foundation of an Academy of Science in Berlin, in which city he lived for a considerable time. In Vienna he also became acquainted with Prince Eugène, which occasioned his being appointed finally an Imperial Councillor. He published several very important historical works as the result of this journey. His death took place at Hanover in 1716, when he was seventy years of age.[1]

It was not only on Philosophy, but also on the most varied branches of science that Leibnitz expended toil and trouble and energy; it was to mathematics, however, that he specially devoted his attention, and he is the inventor of the methods of the integral and differential calculus. His great services in regard to mathematics and physics we here leave out of consideration, and pay attention to his philosophy alone. None of his books can be exactly looked on as giving a complete systematic account of his philosophy. To the more important among them belongs his work on the human understanding (*Nouveaux essais sur l'entendement humain*) in reply to Locke; but this is a mere refutation. His philosophy is therefore scattered through various little treatises which were written in very various connections, in letters, and replies to objections which caused him to bring out one aspect of the question more strongly than another; we consequently find no elaborated systematic whole, superintended or perfected by him. The work which has some appearance of being such, his *Théodicée*, better known to the public than anything else he wrote, is a popular treatise which he drew

[1] La vie de Mr. Leibnitz par Mr. le Chevalier de Jaucourt (Essais de Théodicée, par Leibnitz, Amsterdam, 1747, T. I.), pp. 1-28, 45, 59-62, 66-74, 77-80, 87-92, 110-116, 148-151; Brucker. Hist. crit. phil., T. IV. P. II. pp. 335-368; Leibnitzii Opera omnia (ed. Dutens), T. II., P. I. pp. 45, 46.

up for Queen Sophia Charlotte in reply to Bayle, and in which he took pains not to present the matter in very speculative form. A Würtemberg theologian, Pfaff by name, and others who were correspondents of Leibnitz and were themselves only too well versed in philosophy, brought it as a charge against Leibnitz—a charge which he never denied—that his philosophy was written in popular form.[1] They laughed very much afterwards at Wolff, who had taken them to be quite in earnest; his opinion was that if Leibnitz were not perfectly serious in this sense with his *Théodicée,* yet he had unconsciously written his best therein. Leibnitz's *Théodicée* is not what we can altogether appreciate; it is a justification of God in regard to the evil in the world. His really philosophic thoughts are most connectedly expressed in a treatise on the principles of Grace (*Principes de la Nature et de la Grace*),[2] and especially in the pamphlet addressed to Prince Eugène of Savoy.[3] Buhle (Geschichte der neuern Philosophie, vol. iv. section 1, p. 131) says: "His philosophy is not so much the product of free, independent, original speculation, as the result of well-tested earlier" and later "systems, an eclecticism whose defects he tried to remedy in his own way. It is a desultory treatment of Philosophy in letters."

Leibnitz followed the same general plan in his philosophy as the physicists adopt when they advance a hypothesis to explain existing data. He has it that general conceptions of the Idea are to be found, from which the particular may be derived; here, on account of existing data, the general conception, for example the determination of force or matter furnished by reflection, must have its determinations disposed in such a way that it fits in

[1] Vie de Mr. Leibnitz, pp. 134-143; Brucker. Hist. crit. philos. T. IV. P. II. pp. 385, 389; Tennemann, vol. xi. pp. 181, 182.

[2] Leibnitzii Opera, T. II. P. I. pp. 32-39.

[3] Ibidem, Principia philosophiæ, pp. 20-31.

with the data. Thus the philosophy of Leibnitz seems to be not so much a philosophic system as an hypothesis regarding the existence of the world, namely how it is to be determined in accordance with the metaphysical determinations and the data and assumptions of the ordinary conception, which are accepted as valid [1]—thoughts which are moreover propounded without the sequence pertaining to the Notion and mainly in narrative style, and which taken by themselves show no necessity in their connection. Leibnitz's philosophy therefore appears like a string of arbitrary assertions, which follow one on another like a metaphysical romance; it is only when we see what he wished thereby to avoid that we learn to appreciate its value. He really makes use of external reasons mainly in order to establish relations: "Because the validity of such relations cannot be allowed, nothing remains but to establish the matter in this way." If we are not acquainted with these reasons, this procedure strikes us as arbitrary.

a. Leibnitz's philosophy is an idealism of the intellectuality of the universe; and although from one point of view he stands opposed to Locke, as from another point of view he is in opposition to the Substance of Spinoza, he yet binds them both together again. For, to go into the matter more particularly, on the one hand he expresses in the many monads the absolute nature of things distinguished and of individuality; on the other hand, in contrast to this and apart from it, he expresses the ideality of Spinoza and the non-absolute nature of all difference, as the idealism of the popular conception. Leibnitz's philosophy is a metaphysics, and in sharp contrast to the simple universal Substance of Spinoza, where all that is determined is merely transitory, it makes fundamental the absolute multiplicity of individual substances, which after the example of the ancients he named monads—an expres-

[1] cf. Leibnitz: Essais de Théodicée, T. I. P. I. § 10, p. 86.

sion already used by the Pythagoreans. These monads he then proceeds to determine as follows.

Firstly: "Substance is a thing that is capable of activity; it is compound or simple, the compound cannot exist without the simple. The monads are simple substances." The proof that they constitute the truth in all things is very simple; it is a superficial reflection. For instance, one of Leibnitz's maxims is: "Because there are compound things, the principles of the same must be simple; for the compound consists of the simple."[1] This proof is poor enough; it is an example of the favourite way of starting from something definite, say the compound, and then drawing conclusions therefrom as to the simple. It is quite right in a way, but really it is tautology. Of course, if the compound exists, so does the simple; for the compound means something in itself manifold whose connection or unity is external. From the very trivial category of the compound it is easy to deduce the simple. It is a conclusion drawn from a certain premiss, but the question is whether the premiss is true. These monads are not, however, something abstract and simple in itself, like the empty Epicurean atoms, which, as they were in themselves lacking in determination, drew all their determination from their aggregation alone. The monads are, on the contrary, substantial forms, a good expression, borrowed from the Scholastics (*supra*, p. 71), or the metaphysical points of the Alexandrian School (Vol. II. p. 439); they are the entelechies of Aristotle taken as pure activity, which are forms in themselves (Vol. II. pp. 138, 182, 183). "These monads are not material or extended, nor do they originate or decay in the natural fashion, for they can begin only by a creative act of God, and they can end only by annihila-

[1] Leibnitz: Principes de la nature et la grace, § 1, p. 32 (Recueil de diverses pièces par Des-Maiseaux, T. II. p. 485); Principia philosophiæ, § 1, 2, p. 20.

tion."[1] Thereby they are distinguished from the atoms, which are regarded simply as principles. The expression creation we are familiar with from religion, but it is a meaningless word derived from the ordinary conception; in order to be a thought and to have philosophic significance, it must be much more closely defined.

Secondly: "On account of their simplicity the monads are not susceptible of alteration by another monad in their inner essence; there is no causal connection between them." Each of them is something indifferent and independent as regards the rest, otherwise it would not be an entelechy. Each of them is so much for itself that all its determinations and modifications go on in itself alone, and no determination from without takes place. Leibnitz says: "There are three ways in which substances are connected: (1) Causality, influence; (2) The relation of assistance; (3) The relation of harmony. The relation of influence is a relation pertaining to a commonplace or popular philosophy. But as it is impossible to understand how material particles or immaterial qualities can pass from one substance into another, such a conception as this must be abandoned." If we accept the reality of the many, there can be no transition at all; each is an ultimate and absolutely independent entity. "The system of assistance," according to Descartes, "is something quite superfluous, a *Deus ex machina*, because continual miracles in the things of nature are assumed." If we, like Descartes, assume independent substances, no causal nexus is conceivable; for this presupposes an influence, a bearing of the one upon the other, and in this way the other is not a substance. "Therefore there remains only harmony, a unity which is in itself or implicit. The monad is therefore simply shut up in itself,

[1] Leibnitzii De ipsa natura sive de vi insita actionibusque creaturarum (Oper. T. II. P. II.), § 11, p. 55, Principia philosophiæ, § 3-6, 18, pp. 20-22; Principes de la nature et de la grace, § 2, p. 32.

and cannot be determined by another; this other cannot be set into it. It can neither get outside itself, nor can others get inside it."[1] That is also Spinoza's way of regarding matters: each attribute entirely represents the essence of God for itself, extension and thought have no influence on each other.

In the third place, "however, these monads must at the same time have certain qualities or determinations in themselves, inner actions, through which they are distinguished from others. There cannot be two things alike, for otherwise they would not be two, they would not be different, but one and the same."[2] Here then Leibnitz's axiom of the undistinguishable comes into words. What is not in itself distinguished is not distinguished. This may be taken in a trivial sense, as that there are not two individuals which are alike. To such sensuous things the maxim has no application, it is *prima facie* indifferent whether there are things which are alike or not; there may also be always a difference of space. This is the superficial sense, which does not concern us. The more intimate sense is, however, that each thing is in itself something determined, distinguishing itself from others implicitly or in itself. Whether two things are like or unlike is only a comparison which we make, which falls within our ken. But what we have further to consider is

[1] Leibnitzii Principia philosophiæ, § 7, p. 21; Troisième éclaircissement du système de la communication des substances (Oper. T. II. P. I.), p. 73 (Recueil, T. II. p. 402).

[2] Leibnitzii Principia philosophiæ, § 8, 9, p. 21; Oper. T. II. P. I. pp. 128, 129, § 4, 5: Il n'y a point deux individus indiscernables. Un gentilhomme d'esprit de mes amis, en parlant avec moi en présence de Mad. l'Electrice dans le jardin de Herrenhausen, crut qu'il trouverait bien deux feuilles entièrement semblables. Mad. l'Electrice l'en défia, et il courut longtemps en vain pour en chercher. Deux gouttes d'eau ou de lait regardées par le microscope se trouveront discernables. C'est un argument contre les Atomes (Recueil, T. I. p. 50).—Cf. Hegel's Werke, Vol. IV. p. 45.

the determined difference in themselves. The difference must be a difference in themselves, not for our comparison, for the subject must have the difference as its own peculiar characteristic or determination, *i.e.* the determination must be immanent in the individual. Not only do we distinguish the animal by its claws, but it distinguishes itself essentially thereby, it defends itself, it preserves itself. If two things are different only in being two, then each of them is one; but the fact of their being two does not constitute a distinction between them; the determined difference in itself is the principal point.

Fourthly: "The determinateness and the variation thereby established is, however, an inward implicit principle; it is a multiplicity of modifications, of relations to surrounding existences, but a multiplicity which remains locked up in simplicity. Determinateness and variation such as this, which remains and goes on in the existence itself, is a perception;" and therefore Leibnitz says all monads perceive or represent (for we may translate *perceptio* by representation [Vorstellung]). In other words, they are in themselves universal, for universality is just simplicity in multiplicity, and therefore a simplicity which is at the same time change and motion of multiplicity. This is a very important determination; in substance itself there is negativity, determinateness, without its simplicity and its implicitude being given up. Further, in it there is this idealism, that the simple is something in itself distinguished, and in spite of its variation, that it yet remains one, and continues in its simplicity. An instance of this is found in "I," my spirit. I have many conceptions, a wealth of thought is in me, and yet I remain one, notwithstanding this variety of state. This identity may be found in the fact that what is different is at the same time abrogated, and is determined as one; the monads are therefore distinguished by modifications in themselves, but not by external determinations. These determinations contained in the monads exist in them in ideal fashion; this ideality in the monad is in itself a whole, so that these differences are only representations and ideas. This absolute difference is what is termed the Notion; what falls asunder in the mere representation is held together. This is what possesses interest in Leibnitz's philosophy. Such ideality in the same way pertains to the material, which is also a multiplicity of monads; therefore the system of Leibnitz is an intellectual system, in accordance with which all that is material has powers of representation and perception. As thus representing, the monad, says Leibnitz, possesses activity; for activity is to be different, and yet to be one, and this is the only true difference. The monad not only represents, it also changes; but in doing so, it yet remains in itself absolutely what it is. This variation is based on activity. "The activity of the inner principle, by means of which it passes from one perception to another, is desire (*appetitus*)." Variation in representation is desire, and that constitutes the spontaneity of the monad; all is now complete in itself, and the category of influence falls away. Indeed, this intellectuality of all things is a great thought on the part of Leibnitz: "All multiplicity is included in unity;"[1] determination is not a difference in respect of something else, but reflected into itself, and maintaining itself. This is one aspect of things, but the matter is not therein complete; it is equally the case that it is different in respect of other things.

Fifthly: These representations and ideas are not necessarily conscious representations and ideas, any more than all monads as forming representations are conscious. It is true that consciousness is itself perception, but a higher grade of the same; perceptions of consciousness Leibnitz calls apperceptions. The difference between the merely representing and the self-conscious monads Leibnitz makes one of degrees of clearness. The expression representation

[1] Leibnitzii Principia philosophiæ, § 10-16, pp. 21, 22; Principes de la nature et de la grace, § 2, p. 32.

has, however, certainly something awkward about it, since we are accustomed to associate it only with consciousness, and with consciousness as such; but Leibnitz admits also of unconscious representation. When he then adduces examples of unconscious representations, he appeals to the condition of a swoon or of sleep, in which we are mere monads: and that representations without consciousness are present in such states he shows from the fact of our having perceptions immediately after awakening out of sleep, which shows that others must have been there, for one perception arises only out of others.[1] That is a trivial and empirical demonstration.

Sixthly: These monads constitute the principle of all that exists. Matter is nothing else than their passive capability. This passive capability it is which constitutes the obscurity of the representations, or a confusion which never arrives at distinction, or desire, or activity.[2] That is a correct definition of the conception; it is Being, matter, in accordance with the moment of simplicity. This is implicitly activity; "mere implicitness without actualization" would therefore be a better expression. The transition from obscurity to distinctness Leibnitz exemplifies by the state of swooning.

Seventhly: Bodies as bodies are aggregates of monads: they are mere heaps which cannot be termed substances, any more than a flock of sheep can bear this name.[3] The continuity of the same is an arrangement or extension, but

[1] Leibnitzii Principia philosophiæ, § 19-23, pp. 22, 23; Principes de la nature et de la grace, § 4, pp. 33, 34; Nouveaux essais sur l'entendement humain (Œuvres philosophiques de Leibnitz par Raspe), Bk. II. chap. ix. § 4, p. 90.

[2] Leibnitzii De anima brutorum (Op. T. II. P. I.), § 2-4, pp. 230, 231.

[3] Leibnitzii Oper. T. II. P. I. pp. 214, 215, § 3; De ipsa natura sive de vi insita, § 11, p. 55; Système nouveau de la nature et de la communication des substances (Op. T. II. P. I.), pp. 50, 53.

space is nothing in itself;[1] it is only in another, or a unity which our understanding gives to that aggregate.[2]

b. Leibnitz goes on to determine and distinguish more clearly as the principal moments, inorganic, organic, and conscious monads, and he does it in the following way.

α. Such bodies as have no inner unity, whose elements are connected merely by space, or externally, are inorganic; they have not an entelechy or one monad which rules over the rest.[3] The continuity of space as a merely external relation has not the Notion in itself of the likeness of these monads in themselves. Continuity is in fact to be regarded in them as an arrangement, a similarity in themselves. Leibnitz therefore defines their movements as like one another, as a harmony in themselves;[4] but again, this is as much as saying that their similarity is not in themselves. In fact continuity forms the essential determination of the inorganic; but it must at the same time not be taken as something external or as likeness, but as penetrating or penetrated unity, which has dissolved individuality in itself like a fluid. But to this point Leibnitz does not attain, because for him monads are the absolute principle, and individuality does not annul itself.

β. A higher degree of Being is found in bodies with life and soul, in which one monad has dominion over the rest. The body which is bound up with the monad, of which the one monad is the entelechy or soul, is with this soul named a living creature, an animal. One such entelechy

[1] Leibnitzii Oper. T. II. P. I. pp. 79, 121, 234-237, 280, 295; Nouveaux essais sur l'entendement humain, Bk. II. chap. xiii. § 15, 17, pp. 106, 107.

[2] Leibnitz: Nouveaux essais sur l'entendement humain, Bk. II. chap. xii. § 7, pp. 102, 103; chap. xxi. § 72, p. 170; chap. xxiv. § 1, p. 185.

[3] Leibnitzii Oper. T. II. P. I. p. 39; Nouveaux essais sur l'entendement humain, Bk. III. chap. vi. § 24, p. 278; § 39, p. 290.

[4] Leibnitzii Oper. T. II. P. II. p. 60; Nouveaux essais sur l'entendement humain, Bk. II. chap. xxiii. § 23, p. 181.

rules over the rest, yet not really, but formally: the limbs of this animal, however, are again themselves such living things, each of which has in its turn its ruling entelechy within it.[1] But ruling is here an inappropriate expression. To rule in this case is not to rule over others, for all are independent; it is therefore only a formal expression. If Leibnitz had not helped himself out with the word rule, and developed the idea further, this dominant monad would have abrogated the others, and put them in a negative position; the implicitness of the other monads, or the principle of the absolute Being of these points or individuals would have disappeared. Yet we shall later on come across this relation of the individuals to one another.

γ. The conscious monad distinguishes itself from the naked (material) monads by the distinctness of the representation. But this is of course only an indefinite word, a formal distinction; it indicates that consciousness is the very thing that constitutes the distinction of the undistinguished, and that distinction constitutes the determination of consciousness. Leibnitz more particularly defined the distinction of man as that "he is capable of the knowledge of necessary and eternal truths,"—or that he conceives the universal on the one hand, and on the other what is connected with it; the nature and essence of self-consciousness lies in the universality of the Notions. "These eternal truths rest on two maxims; the one is that of contradiction, the other is that of sufficient reason." The former of these is unity expressed in useless fashion as a maxim, the distinction of the undistinguishable, A=A; it is the definition of thinking, but not a maxim which could contain a truth as content, or it does not express the Notion of distinction as such. The other important principle was, on the other hand: What is not distinguished in thought is not distinguished (p. 333). "The maxim of

[1] Leibnitzii Principia philosophiæ, § 65-71, p. 28; Principes de la nature et de la grace, § 3, 4, pp. 32, 33.

the reason is that everything has its reason,"[1]—the particular has the universal as its essential reality. Necessary truth must have its reason in itself in such a manner that it is found by analysis, *i.e.* through that very maxim of identity. For analysis is the very favourite plan of resolving into simple ideas and principles: a resolution which annihilates their relation, and which therefore in fact forms a transition into the opposite, though it does not have the consciousness of the same, and on that account also excludes the Notion; for every opposite it lays hold of only in its identity. Sufficient reason seems to be a pleonasm; but Leibnitz understood by this aims, final causes (*causæ finales*), the difference between which and the causal nexus or the efficient cause he here brings under discussion.[2]

c. The universal itself, absolute essence, which with Leibnitz is something quite different from the monads, separates itself also into two sides, namely universal Being and Being as the unity of opposites.

a. That universal is God, as the cause of the world, to the consciousness of whom the above principle of sufficient reason certainly forms the transition. The existence of God is only an inference from eternal truths; for these must as the laws of nature have a universal sufficient reason which determines itself as none other than God. Eternal truth is therefore the consciousness of the universal and absolute in and for itself; and this universal and absolute is God, who, as one with Himself, the monad of monads, is the absolute *Monas*. Here we again have the wearisome proof of His existence: He is the fountain of eternal truths and Notions, and without Him no potentiality would have actuality; He has the

[1] Leibnitzii Principia philosophiæ, § 29-31, p. 24; Principes de la nature et de la grace, § 5, p. 34; Essais de Théodicée, T. I. P. I. § 44, p. 115.

[2] Leibnitz: Principes de la nature et de la grace, § 7, p. 35.

prerogative of existing immediately in His potentiality.[1] God is here also the unity of potentiality and actuality, but in an uncomprehending manner; what is necessary, but not comprehended, is transferred to Him. Thus God is at first comprehended chiefly as universal, but already in the aspect of the relation of opposites.

β. As regards this second aspect, the absolute relation of opposites, it occurs in the first place in the form of absolute opposites of thought, the good and the evil. "God is the Author of the world," says Leibnitz; that refers directly to evil. It is round this relation that philosophy specially revolves, but to the unity of which it did not then attain; the evil in the world was not comprehended, because no advance was made beyond the fixed opposition. The result of Leibnitz's Théodicée is an optimism supported on the lame and wearisome thought that God, since a world had to be brought into existence, chose out of infinitely many possible worlds the best possible—the most perfect, so far as it could be perfect, considering the finite element which it was to contain.[2] This may very well be said in a general way, but this perfection is no determined thought, but a loose popular expression, a sort of babble respecting an imaginary or fanciful potentiality; Voltaire made merry over it. Nor is the nature of the finite therein defined. Because the world, it is said, has to be the epitome of finite Beings, evil could not be separated from it, since evil is negation, finitude.[3] Reality and negation remain standing in opposition to one another exactly in the same way as before. That is the principal conception in the Théodicée. But

[1] Leibnitz: Principes de la nature et de la grace, § 8, p. 35; Principia philosophiæ, § 43-46, p. 25.

[2] Leibnitz: Essais de Théodicée, T. I. P. I. § 6-8, pp. 83-85; Principes de la nature et de la grace, § 10, p. 36.

[3] Leibnitz: Essais de Théodicée, T. I. P. I. § 20, pp. 96, 97; § 32, 33, pp. 106, 107; T. II. P. II. § 153, pp. 57, 58; § 378, pp. 256, 257.

something very like this can be said in every-day life. If I have some goods brought to me in the market at some town, and say that they are certainly not perfect, but the best that are to be got, this is quite a good reason why I should content myself with them. But comprehension is a very different thing from this. Leibnitz says nothing further than that the world is good, but there is also evil in it; the matter remains just the same as it was before. "Because it had to be finite" is then a mere arbitrary choice on the part of God. The next question would be: Why and how is there finitude in the Absolute and His decrees? And only then should there be deduced from the determination of finitude the evil which no doubt exists therein.

It is true that Leibnitz has a reply to the above question: "God does not will what is evil; evil comes only indirectly into the results" (blind), "because oftentimes the greater good could not be achieved if evils were not present. Therefore they are means to a good end.' But why does not God employ other means? They are always external, not in and for themselves. "A moral evil may not be regarded as a means, nor must we, as the apostle says, do evil that good may come; yet it has often the relation of a *conditio sine qua non* of the good. Evil is in God only the object of a permissive will (*voluntatis permissivæ*);" but everything that is wrong would be such. "God has therefore among the objects of His will the best possible as the ultimate object, but the good as a matter of choice (*qualemcunque*), also as subordinate; and things indifferent and evils often as means. Evil is, however, an object of His will only as the condition of something otherwise necessary (*rei alioqui debitæ*), which without it could not exist; in which sense Christ said it must needs be that offences come."[1]

[1] Leibnitzii Causa Dei asserta per justitiam ejus (Essais de Théodicée, T. II.), § 34-39, pp. 385, 386.

In a general sense we are satisfied with the answer: "In accordance with the wisdom of God we must accept it as a fact that the laws of nature are the best possible," but this answer does not suffice for a definite question. What one wishes to know is the goodness of this or that particular law; and to that no answer is given. If, for example, it is said that "The law of falling bodies, in which the relation of time and space is the square, is the best possible," one might employ, as far as mathematics are concerned, any other power whatever. When Leibnitz answers: "God made it so," this is no answer at all. We wish to know the definite reason of this law; such general determinations sound pious, but are not satisfying.

γ. He goes on to say that the sufficient reason has reference to the representation of the monads. The principles of things are monads, of which each is for itself, without having influence on the others. If now the Monad of monads, God, is the absolute substance, and individual monads are created through His will, their substantiality comes to an end. There is therefore a contradiction present, which remains unsolved in itself—that is between the one substantial monad and the many monads for which independence is claimed, because their essence consists in their standing in no relation to one another. Yet at the same time, in order to show the harmony that exists in the world, Leibnitz understands the relation of monads to monads more generally as the unity of contrasted existences, namely of soul and body. This unity he represents as a relation without difference, and notionless, *i.e.* as a pre-established harmony.[1] Leibnitz uses here the illustration of two clocks, which are set to the same hour, and keep the same time;[2] in the same way the

[1] Leibnitz: Principes de la nature et de la grace, § 3, p. 33; Premier éclaircissement du système de la communication des substances, p. 70.

[2] Leibnitz: Second et troisième éclaircissemens du système de la communication des substances, pp. 71-73.

movement of the kingdom of thought goes on, determined in accordance with ends, and the movement onward of the corporeal kingdom which corresponds with it, proceeds according to a general causal connection.[1] The case is the same as with Spinoza, that these two sides of the universe have no connection with each other, the one does not influence the other, but both are entirely indifferent to one another; it is really the differentiating relation of the Notion that is lacking. In abstract thought that is without Notion, that determination now receives the form of simplicity, of implicitude, of indifference with regard to what is other, of a self-reflection that has no movement: in this way red in the abstract is in a position of indifference as regards blue, &c. Here, as before, Leibnitz forsakes his principle of individuation; it has only the sense of being exclusively one, and of not reaching to and including what is other; or it is only a unity of the popular conception, not the Notion of unity. The soul has thus a series of conceptions and ideas which are developed from within it, and this series is from the very first placed within the soul at its creation, *i.e.* the soul is in all immediacy this implicit determination; determination is, however, not implicit, but the reflected unfolding of this determination in the ordinary conception is its outward existence. Parallel with this series of differentiated conceptions, there now runs a series of motions of the body, or of what is external to the soul.[2] Both are essential moments of reality; they are mutually indifferent, but they have also an essential relation of difference.

Since now every monad, as shut up within itself, has no influence upon the body and its movements, and yet the infinite multitude of their atoms correspond with one another, Leibnitz places this harmony in God; a better definition

[1] Leibnitzii Principia philosophiæ, § 82, p. 30; Principes de la nature et de la grace, § 11, p. 36.

[2] Leibnitz: Système nouveau de la nature et de la communication des substances, pp. 54, 55.

of the relation and the activity of the Monad of monads is therefore that it is what pre-establishes harmony in the changes of the monads.[1] God is the sufficient reason, the cause of this correspondence; He has so arranged the multitude of atoms that the original changes which are developed within one monad correspond with the changes of the others. The pre-established harmony is to be thought of somewhat in this style; when a dog gets a beating, the pain develops itself in him, in like fashion the beating develops itself in itself, and so does the person who administers the beating; their determinations all correspond with one another, and that not by means of their objective connection, since each is independent.[2] The principle of the harmony among the monads does not consequently belong to them, but it is in God, who for that very reason is the Monad of monads, their absolute unity. We saw from the beginning how Leibnitz arrived at this conception. Each monad is really possessed of the power of representation, and is as such a representation of the universe, therefore implicitly the totality of the whole world. But at the same time this representation is not in consciousness; the naked monad is implicitly the universe, and difference is the development of this totality in it.[3] What develops itself therein is at the same time in harmony with all other developments; all is one harmony. "In the universe all things are closely knit together, they are in one piece, like an ocean: the slightest movement transmits its influence far and wide all around."[4] From a single grain of sand, Leibnitz holds, the whole universe might be comprehended in its entire development—if we

[1] Leibnitzii Principia philosophiæ, § 90, p. 31; Principes de la nature et de la grace, § 12, 13, pp. 36, 37; § 15, pp. 37, 38.

[2] Leibnitzii Oper. T. II. P. I. pp. 75, 76.

[3] Leibnitzii Principia philosoph., § 58-62, p. 27; Oper. T. II. P. I. pp. 46, 47.

[4] Leibnitz: Essais de Théodicée, T. I. P. I. § 9, pp. 85, 86.

only knew the sand grain thoroughly. There is not really much in all this, though it sounds very fine; for the rest of the universe is considerably more than a grain of sand, well though we knew it, and considerably different therefrom. To say that its essence is the universe is mere empty talk: for the fact is that the universe as essence is not the universe. To the sand grain much must be added which is not present; and since thought adds more than all the grains of sand that exist, the universe and its development may in this way certainly be comprehended. Thus according to Leibnitz every monad has or is the representation of the entire universe, which is the same as saying that it is really representation in general; but at the same time it is a determinate representation, by means of which it comes to be this particular monad, therefore it is representation according to its particular situation and circumstances.[1]

The representations of the monad in itself, which constitute its universe, develop themselves from themselves, as the spiritual element in it, according to the laws of their own activity and desire, just as the movements of their outer world do according to laws of bodies; hence liberty is nothing other than this spontaneity of immanent development, but as in consciousness. The magnetic needle, on the contrary, has only spontaneity without consciousness, and consequently without freedom. For, says Leibnitz, the nature of the magnetic needle is to turn to the north; if it had consciousness it would imagine that this was its self-determination; it would thus have the will to move round in accordance with its nature.[2] But it is clear that in the course of conscious representations there is involved no necessary connection, but contingency and want of sequence

[1] Leibnitz: Principes de la nature et de la grace, § 12, 13, pp. 36, 37; Oper. T. II. P. I. p. 337.

[2] Leibnitz: Essais de Théodicée, T. II. P. III. § 291, pp. 184, 185; T. I. P. I. § 50, p. 119.

are to be found, the reason of this according to Leibnitz (Oper. T. II. P. I. p. 75) being "because the nature of a created substance implies that it changes incessantly according to a certain order, which order guides it spontaneously (*spontanément*) in all the circumstances which befall it; so that one who sees all things recognizes in the present condition of substance the past also and the future. The law of order, which determines the individuality of the particular substance, has an exact reference to what takes place in every other substance and in the whole universe." The meaning of this is that the monad is not a thing apart, or that there are two views of it, the one making it out as spontaneously generating its representations, so far as form is concerned, and the other making it out to be a moment of the whole of necessity; Spinoza would call this regarding it from both sides. An organic whole, a human being, is thus for instance the assertion of his aim from out of himself: at the same time the being directed on something else is involved in his Notion. He represents this and that to himself, he wills this and that; his activity employs itself and brings about changes. His inward determination thus becomes corporeal determination, and then change going beyond himself; he appears as cause, influencing other monads. But this Being-for-another is only an appearance. For the other, *i.e.* the actual, in so far as the monad determines it or makes it negative, is the passive element which the monad has in itself: all moments are indeed contained therein, and for that very reason it has no need of other monads, but only of the laws of the monads in itself. But if the Being-for-another is mere appearance, the same may be said of Being-for-self; for this has significance only in reference to Being-for-another.

The important point in Leibnitz's philosophy is this intellectuality of representation which Leibnitz, however, did not succeed in carrying out; and for the same reason this intellectuality is at the same time infinite multiplicity, which has remained absolutely independent, because this intellectuality has not been able to obtain mastery over the One. The separation in the Notion, which proceeds as far as release from itself, or appearance in distinct independence, Leibnitz did not succeed in bringing together into unity. The harmony of these two moments, the course of mental representations and the course of things external, appearing mutually as cause and effect, is not brought by Leibnitz into relation in and for themselves; he therefore lets them fall asunder, although each is passive as regards the other. He moreover considers both of them in one unity, to be sure, but their activity is at the same time not for themselves. Every forward advance becomes therefore incomprehensible when taken by itself, because the course of the representation as through aims in itself, requires this moment of Other-Being or of passivity; and again the connection of cause and effect requires the universal: each however lacks this its other moment. The unity which according to Leibnitz is to be brought about by the pre-established harmony, namely that the determination of the will of man and the outward change harmonize, is therefore brought about by means of another, if not indeed from without, for this other is God. Before God the monads are not to be independent, but ideal and absorbed in Him.

At this point the demand would come in that in God Himself there should be comprehended the required unity of that which before fell asunder; and God has the special privilege of having laid on Him the burden of what cannot be comprehended. The word of God is thus the makeshift which leads to a unity which itself is only hypothetical; for the process of the many out of this unity is not demonstrated. God plays therefore in the later philosophy a far greater part than in the early, because now the comprehension of the absolute opposition of thought and Being is the chief demand. With Leibnitz the extent to which thoughts advance is the extent of the universe; where comprehension ceases, the universe ceases, and God begins: so that later it was even maintained that to be comprehended was derogatory to God, because He was thus degraded into finitude. In that procedure a beginning is made from the determinate, this and that are stated to be necessary; but since in the next place the unity of these moments is not comprehended, it is transferred to God. God is therefore, as it were, the waste channel into which all contradictions flow: Leibnitz's Théodicée is just a popular summing up such as this. There are, nevertheless, all manner of evasions to be searched out—in the opposition of God's justice and mercy, that the one tempers the other; how the fore-knowledge of God and human freedom are compatible—all manner of syntheses which never come to the root of the matter nor show both sides to be moments.

These are the main moments of Leibnitz's philosophy. It is a metaphysic which starts from a narrow determination of the understanding, namely, from absolute multiplicity, so that connection can only be grasped as continuity. Thereby absolute unity is certainly set aside, but all the same it is presupposed; and the association of individuals with one another is to be explained only in this way, that it is God who determines the harmony in the changes of individuals. This is an artificial system, which is founded on a category of the understanding, that of the absoluteness of abstract individuality. What is of importance in Leibnitz lies in the maxims, in the principle of individuality and the maxim of indistinguishability.

WOLFF.

The philosophy of Wolff is directly connected with that of Leibnitz, for really it is a pedantic systematization of the latter, for which reason it is likewise called the Leibnitz-Wolffian system of philosophy. Wolff attained to great distinction in mathematics and made himself famous by his philosophy as well; the latter was for long predominant in Germany. In Wolff, as a teacher dealing with the understanding, we find a systematic exposition of the philosophic element present in human conceptions as a whole. As regards his connection with German culture generally, great and immortal praise is more especially due to him; before all others he may be termed the teacher of the Germans. We may indeed say that Wolff was the first to naturalize philosophy in Germany. Tschirnhausen and Thomasius likewise participated in this honour, for the special reason that they wrote upon Philosophy in the German language. In regard to the matter of the philosophy of Tschirnhausen and Thomasius we have not much to say; it is so-called healthy reason—there is in it the superficial character and the empty universality always to be found where a beginning is made with thought. In this case the universality of thought satisfies us because everything is present there, just as it is present in a moral maxim which has, however, no determinate content in its universality. Wolff, then, was the first to make, not exactly Philosophy, but thoughts in the form of thought, into a general possession, and he substituted this in Germany for mere talk originating from feeling, from sensuous perception, and from the ordinary conception. This is most important from the point of view of culture, and yet it does not really concern us here, excepting in so far as the content in this form of thought has caused itself to be recognized as Philosophy. This philosophy, as a philosophy of the understanding, became the ordinary culture of the day; in it determinate, intelligent thought is the fundamental principle, and it extends over the whole circle of objects which fall within the region of knowledge. Wolff defined the world of consciousness for Germany, and for the world in general, in the same wide sense in which we may say that this was done by Aristotle. What distinguishes him from

Aristotle is that in so doing the point of view that he adopted was that of the understanding merely, while Aristotle treated the subject speculatively. The philosophy of Wolff is hence no doubt built on foundations laid by Leibnitz, but yet in such a manner that the speculative interest is quite eliminated from it. The spiritual philosophy, substantial in a higher sense, which we found emerging first in Boehme, though still in a peculiar and barbarous form, has been quite lost sight of, and has disappeared without leaving any traces or effects in Germany; his very language was forgotten.

The principal events in Christian Wolff's life are these: He was the son of a baker, and was born at Breslau in 1679. He first studied Theology and then Philosophy, and in 1707 he became Professor of Mathematics and Philosophy at Halle. Here the pietistic theologians, and more especially Lange, treated him in the basest manner. Piety did not trust this understanding; for piety, if it is true, embodies a content which is speculative in nature, and which passes beyond the understanding. As his opponents could make no headway by their writings, they resorted to intrigues. They caused it to be conveyed to King Frederick William I., the father of Frederick II., a rough man who took an interest in nothing but soldiers, that according to the determinism of Wolff, free will was impossible, and that soldiers could not hence desert of their own free will, but by a special disposition of God (pre-established harmony)—a doctrine which, if disseminated amongst the military, would be extremely dangerous. The king, much enraged by this, immediately issued a decree that within forty-eight hours Wolff should leave Halle and the Prussian States, under penalty of the halter. Wolff thus left Halle on the 23rd of November, 1723. The theologians added to all this the scandal of preaching against Wolff and his philosophy, and the pious Franke thanked God on his knees in church for the removal of Wolff. But the rejoicings did not last long. Wolff went to Cassel, was there immediately installed first professor in the philosophic faculty at Marburg, and at the same time made a member of the Academies of Science of London, Paris, and Stockholm. By Peter the First of Russia he was made Vice-President of the newly instituted Academy in St. Petersburg. Wolff was also summoned to Russia, but this invitation he declined; he received, however, an honorary post, he was made a Baron by the Elector of Bavaria, and, in short, loaded with public honours which, more especially at that time, though even now it is the case, were very much thought of by the general public, and which were too great not to make a profound sensation in Berlin. In Berlin a commission was appointed to pass judgment on the Wolffian philosophy—for this it had not been possible to eradicate—and it declared the same to be harmless, that is to say, free from all danger to state and religion; it also forbade the theologians to make it a subject of dispute, and altogether put an end to their clamour. Frederick William now issued a recall in very respectful terms to Wolff, who, however, hesitated to comply with it owing to his lack of confidence in its sincerity. On the accession of Frederick II. in 1740 he was again recalled in terms of the highest honour (Lange had meanwhile died), and only then did he comply. Wolff became Vice-Chancellor of the University, but he outlived his repute, and his lectures at the end were very poorly attended. He died in 1754.[1]

Like Tschirnhausen and Thomasius, Wolff wrote a great part of his works in his mother tongue, while Leibnitz for the most part wrote only in Latin or French. This is an important matter, for, as we have already noticed (pp. 114 and 150), it is only when a nation possesses a science in its own language that it can really be said to belong to

[1] Buhle: Geschichte der neuern Philosoph., Vol. IV. Sec. II., pp. 571-582; Tiedemann: Geist der speculativen Philos., Vol. VI. pp. 511-518; Rixner: Handbuch der Geschichte der Philosophie, Vol. III. § 79, pp. 195, 196.

it; and in Philosophy most of all this is requisite. For thought has in it this very moment of pertaining to self-consciousness or of being absolutely its own; when one's own language is the vehicle of expression, as when we talk of "Bestimmtheit" instead of "Determination," and "Wesen" instead of "Essenz," it is immediately present to our consciousness that the conceptions are absolutely its own; it has to deal with these at all times, and they are in no way foreign to it. The Latin language has a phraseology, a definite sphere and range of conception; it is at once taken for granted that when men write in Latin they are at liberty to be dull; it is impossible to read or write what men permit themselves to say in Latin. The titles of Wolff's philosophic works are perpetually of this nature: "Rational thoughts on the powers of the human understanding and their right uses in the knowledge of the truth," Halle, 1712, 8vo; "Rational thoughts on God, the world, and the soul of man, likewise on all things generally," Frankfort and Leipzig, 1719; "On the action and conduct of men," Halle, 1720; "On Social Life," Halle, 1720; "On the operations of Nature," Halle, 1723, and so on. Wolff wrote German and Latin quartos on every department of Philosophy, even on economics—twenty-three thick volumes of Latin, or about forty quartos altogether. His mathematical works make a good many more quartos. He brought into general use the differential and integral calculus of Leibnitz.

It is only in its general content and taken as a whole that Wolff's philosophy is the philosophy of Leibnitz, that is to say, only in relation to the fundamental determinations of monads and to the theodicy—to these he remained faithful; any other content is empiric, derived from our feelings and desires. Wolff likewise accepted in their entirety all the Cartesian and other definitions of general ideas. Hence we find in him abstract propositions and their proofs mingled with experiences, on the indubitable truth of which he builds a large part of his propositions; and he must so build and derive his foundations if a content is to result at all. With Spinoza, on the contrary, no content is to be found excepting absolute substance and a perpetual return into the same. The greatness of Wolff's services to the culture of Germany, which now appeared quite independently and without any connection with an earlier and profounder metaphysical standpoint (*supra*, p. 350), are in proportion to the barrenness and inward contentless condition into which Philosophy had sunk. This he divided into its formal disciplines, spinning it out into determinations of the understanding with a pedantic application of geometric methods; and, contemporaneously with the English philosophers, he made the dogmatism of the metaphysics of the understanding fashionable, that is a philosophizing which determines the absolute and rational by means of self-exclusive thought-determinations and relationships (such as one and many, simple and compound, finite and infinite, causal connection, &c.). Wolff entirely displaced the Aristotelian philosophy of the schools, and made Philosophy into an ordinary science pertaining to the German nation. But besides this he gave Philosophy that systematic and requisite division into sections which has down to the present day served as a sort of standard.

In theoretic philosophy Wolff first treats of Logic purified from scholastic interpretations or deductions; it is the logic of the understanding which he has systematized. The second stage is Metaphysics, which contains four parts: first there is Ontology, the treatment of abstract and quite general philosophic categories, such as Being (ὄν) and its being the One and Good; in this abstract metaphysic there further comes accident, substance, cause and effect, the phenomenon, &c. Next in order is Cosmology, a general doctrine of body, the doctrine of the world; here we have abstract metaphysical propositions respecting the world, that there is no chance, no leaps or bounds in nature—the law of continuity. Wolff excludes natural science and natural history. The third part of the metaphysic is rational psychology or pneumatology, the philosophy of the soul, which deals with the simplicity, immortality, immateriality of the soul. Finally, the fourth is natural theology, which sets forth the proofs of the existence of God.[1] Wolff also inserts (chap. iii.) an empirical psychology. Practical philosophy he divides into the Rights of Nature, Morality, the Rights of Nations or Politics, and Economics.

The whole is propounded in geometric forms such as definitions, axioms, theorems, scholia, corollaries, &c. In mathematics the understanding is in its proper place, for the triangle must remain the triangle. Wolff on the one hand started upon a large range of investigation, and one quite indefinite in character, and on the other, held to a strictly methodical manner with regard to propositions and their proofs. The method is really similar to that of Spinoza, only it is more wooden and lifeless than his. Wolff applied the same methods to every sort of content—even to that which is altogether empirical, such as his so-called applied mathematics, into which he introduces many useful arts, bringing the most ordinary reflections and directions into the geometric form. In many cases this undoubtedly gives his work a most pedantic aspect, expecially when the content directly justifies itself to our conception without this form at all. For Wolff proceeds by first laying down certain definitions, which really rest upon our ordinary conceptions, since these he translated into the empty form of determinations of the under-

[1] Wolf's Vernünftige Gedanken von Gott, der Welt und der Seele des Menschen (Halle, 1741), Pt. I. chap. ii. § 114, 120, pp. 59, 60, 62, 63; chap. iv. § 575-581, 686, pp. 352-359, 425; chap. v. § 742, p. 463; § 926, p. 573; chap. vi. § 928, p. 574, *seq.*

standing. Hence the definitions are merely nominal definitions, and we know whether they are correct only by seeing whether they correspond to conceptions which are referred to their simple thoughts. The syllogism is the form of real importance in this mode of reasoning, and with Wolff it often attains to its extreme of rigidity and formalism.

Under mathematics, which is the subject of four small volumes, Wolff also treats of architecture and military science. One of the propositions in Architecture is this: "Windows must be wide enough for two persons." The making of a door is also propounded as a task, and the solution thereof given. The next best example comes from the art of warfare. The "Fourth proposition. The approach to the fortress must always be harder for the enemy the nearer he comes to it." Instead of saying, because the danger is greater, which would be trivial, there follows the "Proof. The nearer the enemy comes to the fortress, the greater the danger. But the greater the danger the greater the resistance that must be offered in order to defy the attacks, and, so far as may be, avert the danger. Hence the nearer the enemy is to the fort the harder must the approach be made for him. Q.E.D."[1] Since the increase of the danger is given as the reason, the whole is false, and the contrary may be said with equal truth. For if at the beginning all possible resistance is offered to the enemy, he cannot get nearer the fortress at all, and thus the danger cannot become greater. The greater resistance has a real cause, and not this foolish one —namely, that because the garrison is now at closer quarters, and consequently operates in a narrow field, it can offer a greater resistance. In this most trivial way

[1] Wolff's Anfangsgründe aller mathematischen Wissenschaften, Pt. I.: Anfangsgründe der Baukunst, Pt. II. Prop. 8, p. 414; Problem 22, pp. 452, 453; Pt. II.: Anfangsgründe der Fortification, Pt. I. p. 570.

Wolff proceeds with every sort of content. This barbarism of pedantry, or this pedantry of barbarism, represented as it is in its whole breadth and extent, necessarily brought itself into disrepute; and without there being a definite consciousness of the reason why the geometric method is not the only and ultimate method of knowledge, instinct and an immediate consciousness of the foolishness of its applications caused this method to be set aside.

3. The Popular Philosophy of Germany.

Popular philosophy flatters our ordinary consciousness, makes it the ultimate standard. Although with Spinoza we begin with pre-supposed definitions, the content is still profoundly speculative in nature, and it is not derived from the ordinary consciousness. In Spinoza thinking is not merely the form, for the content belongs to thinking itself; it is the content of thought in itself. In the speculative content the instinct of reason satisfies itself on its own account, because this content, as a totality which integrates itself within itself, at once in itself justifies itself to thought. The content in Spinoza is only without ground in so far as it has no external ground, but is a ground in itself. But if the content is finite, a demand for an external ground is indicated, since in such a case we desire to have a ground other than this finite. In its matter the philosophy of Wolff is indeed a popular philosophy, even if in form it still makes thought authoritative. Until the time of Kant the philosophy of Wolff was thus pre-eminent. Baumgarten, Crusius, and Moses Mendelssohn worked each of them independently on the same lines as Wolff; the philosophy of the last-mentioned was popular and graceful in form. The Wolffian philosophy was thus carried on, although it had cast off its pedantic methods: no further progress was however made. The question dealt with was how perfection could be attained—what it is possible to think and what not; metaphysic was reduced to its slightest consistency and to its completest vacuity, so that in its texture not a single thread remained secure. Mendelssohn considered himself, and was considered, the greatest of philosophers, and was lauded as such by his friends. In his "Morgenstunden" we really find a dry Wolffian philosophy, however much these gentlemen endeavoured to give their dull abstractions a bright Platonic form.

The forms of Philosophy which we have considered bear the character which pertains specially to metaphysics, of proceeding from general determinations of the understanding, but of combining therewith experience and observation, or the empiric method in general. One side of this metaphysic is that the opposites of thought are brought into consciousness, and that attention is directed upon the solution of this contradiction. Thought and Being or extension, God and the world, good and evil, the power and prescience of God on the one side, and the evil in the world and human freedom on the other: these contradictions, the opposites of soul and spirit, things conceived and things material, and their mutual relation, have occupied all men's attention. The solution of these opposites and contradictions has still to be given, and God is set forth as the One in whom all these contradictions are solved. This is what is common to all these philosophies as far as their main elements are concerned. Yet we must likewise remark that these contradictions are not solved in themselves, *i.e.* that the nullity of the supposition is not demonstrated in itself, and thereby a true concrete solution has not come to pass. Even if God is recognized as solving all contradictions, God as the solution of these contradictions is a matter of words rather than something conceived and comprehended. If God is comprehended in His qualities, and prescience, omnipresence, omniscience, power, wisdom, goodness justice, &c., are considered as qualities of God Himself, they simply lead to contradictions; and these contradictions, Leibnitz (*supra*, p. 348) sought to remove by saying that the qualities temper one another, *i.e.* that they are combined in such a way that one annuls the other. This, however, is no real comprehension of such contradiction.

This metaphysic contrasts greatly with the old philosophy of a Plato or an Aristotle. To the old philosophy we can always turn again and admit its truth; it is satisfying in the stage of development it has reached—a concrete centre-point which meets all the problems set by thought as these are comprehended. In this modern metaphysic, however, the opposites are merely developed into absolute contradictions. God is indeed given as their absolute solution, but only as an abstract solution, as a Beyond; on this side all contradictions are, as regards their content, unsolved and unexplained. God is not comprehended as the One in whom these contradictions are eternally resolved; He is not comprehended as Spirit, as the Trinity. It is in Him alone as Spirit, and as Spirit which is Three in One, that this opposition of Himself and His Other, the Son, is contained, and with it the resolution of the same; this concrete Idea of God as reason, has not as yet found an entrance into Philosophy.

In order that we may now cast a retrospective glance over the philosophic efforts of other nations, we shall apply ourselves to the further progress of Philosophy. Once more we see Scepticism making its way into this arid philosophy of the understanding. But this time it is, properly speaking, in the form of Idealism, or the determinations are subjective determinations of self-consciousness. In the place of thought we consequently find the Notion now making its appearance. Just as with the Stoics determinateness is held to be an object of thought, we have in modern times this same manifestation of thought as the unmoved form of simplicity. Only here the image or inner consciousness of totality is present, the absolute spirit which the world has before it as its truth and to whose Notion it makes its way—this is another inward principle, another implicitude of mind which it endeavours to bring forth from itself and for itself, so that reason is a comprehension of the same, or has the certitude of being all reality. With the ancients reason (λόγος), as the implicit and explicit Being of consciousness, had only an ethereal and formal existence as language, but here it has certainty as existent substance. Hence with Descartes there is the unity of the Notion and Being, and with Spinoza the universal reality. The first commencement of the Notion of the movement of fixed thoughts in themselves is found in this, that the movement which, as method, simply falls outside its object, comes within it, or that self-consciousness comes within thought. Thought is implicitude without explicitude, an objective mode bearing no resemblance to a sensuous thing; and yet it is quite different from the actuality of self-consciousness. This Notion which we now find entering into thought, has the three kinds of form which we still have to consider; in the first place it has that of individual self-consciousness or the formal conception generally; secondly, that of universal self-consciousness, which applies itself to all objects whether they be objects of thought, determinate conceptions, or have the form of actuality—that is to say it applies itself to what is established in thought, to the intellectual world with the riches of its determinations and looked on as a Beyond, or to the intellectual world in as far as it is its realization, the world here and around us. It is in those two ways, and in those ways alone, that the actual Notion is present in the succeeding chapter; for not as yet is it in the third place to be found as taken back into thought, or as the self-thinking or thought-of Notion. While that universal self-consciousness is, on the whole, a thought which grasps and comprehends, this third kind of thought is the Notion itself recognized as constituting reality in its essence, that is to say as Idealism. These three aspects again divide themselves as before into the three nations which alone count in the civilized world. The empirical and perfectly finite form of Notion pertains to the English; to the French belongs its form as making an attempt at everything, as establishing itself in its reality, abolishing all determination, and therefore being universal, unlimited, pure self-consciousness; and, lastly, to the German pertains the entering into itself of this implicitude, the thought of the absolute Notion.

CHAPTER II

Transition Period

The decadence which we find in thought until the philosophy of Kant is reached, is manifested in what was at this time advocated in opposition to the metaphysic of the understanding, and which may be called a general popular philosophy, a reflecting empiricism, which to a greater or less extent becomes itself a metaphysic; just as, on the other hand, that metaphysic, in as far as it extended to particular sciences, becomes empiricism. As against these metaphysical contradictions, as against the artificialities of the metaphysical synthesis, as against the assistance of God, the pre-established harmony, the best possible world, &c., as against this merely artificial understanding, we now find that fixed principles, immanent in mind, have been asserted or maintained respecting what is felt, intuitively perceived and honoured in the cultured human breast. And in distinction to the assertion that we only find the solution in the Beyond, in God, these concrete principles of a fixed and permanent content form a reconciliation here and now, they adopt a position of independence, and assume an intellectual standing-ground which they find in what has generally been termed the healthy human understanding. Such determinations may indeed be found to be perfectly good and valid if the feelings, intuitions, heart and understanding of man be morally and intellectually fashioned; for in that case better and more noble feelings and desires may rule in men and a more universal content may be expressed in these principles. But when men make what we call sound reason—that which is by nature implanted in man's breast—into the content and the principle, the healthy human understanding discovers itself to be identical with a feeling and knowledge belonging to nature. The Indians who worship a cow, and who expose or slay new-born children, and commit all sorts of barbarous deeds, the Egyptians who pray to a bird, the apis, &c., and the Turks as well, all possess a healthy human understanding similar in nature. But the healthy human understanding and the natural feeling of rude and barbarous Turks, when taken as a standard, result in shocking principles. When we speak of healthy human understanding, however, of natural feelings, we always have before our eyes a cultured mind; and those who make the healthy human reason, the natural knowledge, the immediate feelings and inspirations found in themselves, into a rule and standard, do not know that when religion, morality, and rectitude are discovered to be present in the human breast, this is due to culture and education, which are the first to make such principles into natural feelings. Here natural feelings and the healthy human understanding are thus made the principle; and much may be recognized as coming under these heads. This then is the form taken by Philosophy in the eighteenth century. Taken as a whole, three points of view have to be considered; in the first place, Hume must be regarded on his own account, then the Scottish, and, thirdly, the French philosophy. Hume is a sceptic; the Scottish philosophy opposes the scepticism of Hume, the French philosophy has in the "enlightenment" of Germany (by which expression is indicated that form of German philosophy which is not Wolffian metaphysics) an appendage of a feebler form. Since from the metaphysical God we can make no further progress in the concrete, Locke grounds his content on experience. But that empiricism leads thought to no fixed standpoint, Hume demonstrates by denying every universal; the Scottish philosophers, on the contrary, undoubtedly maintain universal propositions and truths, but not through thought. Hence in empiricism itself the fixed standpoint has now to be adopted; thus the French find the universal in the actuality which they call *réalité*. They do not, however, find its content in and from thought, but as living substance, as nature and matter. All this is a further working out of reflecting empiricism, and some more details respecting it must still be given.

A. Idealism and Scepticism.

Thought generally is simple, universal self-identity, but in the form of negative movement, whereby the determinate abrogates itself. This movement of Being-for-self is now an essential moment of thought, while hitherto it was outside it; and thus grasping itself as movement in itself, thought is self-consciousness—at first indeed formal, as individual self-consciousness. Such a form it has in scepticism, but this distinction marks it off from the older scepticism, that now the certainty of reality is made the starting point. With the ancients, on the contrary, scepticism is the return into individual consciousness in such a way that to it this consciousness is not the truth, in other words that scepticism does not give expression to the results arrived at, and attains no positive significance. But since in the modern world this absolute substantiality, this unity of implicitude and self-consciousness is fundamental—that is, this faith in reality generally—scepticism has here the form of idealism, *i.e.* of expressing self-consciousness or certainty of self as all reality and truth. The crudest form of this idealism is when self-consciousness, as individual or formal, does not proceed further than to say: All objects are our conceptions. We find this subjective idealism in Berkeley,[1] and another form of the same in Hume.

1. Berkeley.

This idealism, in which all external reality disappears, has before it the standpoint of Locke, and it proceeds directly from him. For we saw that to Locke the source of truth is experience, or Being as perceived. Now since this sensuous Being, as Being, has in it the quality of being for consciousness, we saw that it necessarily came to pass that in Locke's case some qualities, at least, were so determined that they were not in themselves, but only for another; and that colour, figure, &c., had their ground only in the subject, in his particular organization. This Being-for-another, however, was not by him accepted as the Notion, but as falling within self-consciousness—i.e. self-consciousness not looked on as universal,—not within mind, but within what is opposed to the implicit.

George Berkeley was born in 1684 at Kilcrin, near Thomastown, in the county of Kilkenny, Ireland: in 1754 he died as an English Bishop.[2] He wrote the "Theory of Vision," 1709; "A Treatise concerning the principles of human knowledge," 1710; "Three Dialogues between Hylas and Philonous," 1713. In 1784 his collected works were published in London in two quarto volumes.

Berkeley advocated an idealism which came very near to that of Malebranche. As against the metaphysic of the

[1] In the lectures of 1825-1826 and 1829-1830 Berkeley was passed over by Hegel; in both courses Hume follows directly after the Scottish and French philosophers, and thus comes immediately before Kant; in the course of 1825-1826 the French philosophy precedes the Scottish also.

[2] Nachrichten von dem Leben und den Schriften des Bischofs Berkeley (in Berkeley's philosoph. Werk. Pt. I. Leipzig, 1781), pp. 1, 45; Buhle: Geschichte der neuern Philosophie, Vol. V. Sect. 1, pp. 86-90.

understanding, we have the point of view that all existence and its determinations arise from feeling, and are constituted by self-consciousness. Berkeley's first and fundamental thought is consequently this: "The Being of whatever is called by us a thing consists alone in its being perceived," *i.e.* our determinations are the objects of our knowledge. "All objects of human knowledge are ideas" (so called by Berkeley as by Locke), "which arise either from the impressions of the outward senses, or from perceptions of the inward states and activities of the mind, or finally, they are such as are constituted by means of memory and imagination through their separation and rearrangement. A union of different sensuous feelings appears to us to be a particular thing, *e.g.* the feeling of colour, taste, smell, figure, &c.; for by colours, smells, sounds, something of which we have a sensation is always understood."[1] This is the matter and the object of knowledge; the knower is the percipient "I," which reveals itself in relation to those feelings in various activities, such as imagination, remembrance, and will.

Berkeley thus indeed acknowledges the distinction between Being-for-self and Other-Being, which in his case, however, itself falls within the "I." Of the matter on which activity is directed, it is no doubt in regard to one portion allowed that it does not exist outside of mind—that is to say, so far as our thoughts, inward feelings and states, or the operations of our imaginary powers are concerned. But in like manner the manifold sensuous conceptions and feelings can only exist in a mind. Locke certainly distinguished extension and movement, for example, as fundamental qualities, *i.e.* as qualities which pertain to the objects in themselves. But Berkeley very pertinently points out inconsistency here from the point of view that

[1] Buhle: Geschichte der neuern Philosophie, Vol. V. pp. 90, 91; The Works of George Berkeley, Prof. Fraser's edition (Dialogues between Hylas and Philonous), Vol. I. p. 264, seq. et passim.

great and small, quick and slow, hold good as something relative; thus were extension and movement to be inherent or implicit, they could not be either large or small, quick or slow; that is, they could not be, for these determinations rest in the conception[1] of such qualities. In Berkeley the relation of things to consciousness is alone dealt with, and beyond this relationship they do not in his view come. From this it follows that it is only self-consciousness that possesses them; for a perception which is not in a conceiving mind is nothing: it is a direct contradiction. There can be no substance, he says, which neither conceives nor perceives, and which is yet the substratum of perceptions and conceptions. If it is represented that there is something outside of consciousness which is similar to the conceptions, this is likewise contradictory; a conception can alone be similar to a conception, the idea to the idea alone.[2]

Thus, while Locke's ultimate point is abstract substance, Being generally with the real determination of a substratum of accidents, Berkeley declares this substance to be the most incomprehensible assumption of all; but the incomprehensibility does not make this Being into an absolute nullity, nor does it make it in itself incomprehensible.[3] For Berkeley brings forward against the present existence of external objects only the inconceivability of the relation of a Being to mind. This inconceivability, however, is destroyed in the Notion, for the Notion is the negative of things; and this moved Berkeley and Leibnitz to shut up the two sides in themselves. There nevertheless remains a relationship of what is "other" to us; these feelings do not develop from us as Leibnitz represents, but

[1] Buhle, Geschichte der neuern Philosophie, Vol. V. Sect. 1, pp. 92, 93; The Works of George Berkeley, Vol. I. p. 279 seq.

[2] Buhle, ibidem, pp. 91, 92; Berkeley, ibidem, pp. 288 seq., 300 seq. et passim.

[3] Buhle, ibidem, pp. 93, 94; Berkeley, ibidem, pp. 289, 308, seq.

are determined through somewhat else. When Leibnitz speaks of development within the monads, it is nothing but empty talk; for the monads as they follow in succession have no inward connection. Each individual is thus determined through another, and not through us; and it does not matter what this external is, since it remains a contingent. Now in relation to the two sides of Leibnitz which are indifferent to one another, Berkeley says that such an "other" is quite superfluous. Berkeley calls the other the objects; but these, he says, cannot be what we call matter, for spirit and matter cannot come together.[1] But the necessity of conceptions directly contradicts this Being-within-self of the conceiver; for the Being-within-self is the freedom of the conceiver; the latter does not, however, produce the conceptions with freedom; they have for him the form and determinateness of an independent "other." Berkeley likewise does not accept idealism in the subjective sense, but only in respect that there are spirits which impart themselves (in the other case the subject forms his own conceptions), and consequently that it is God alone who brings to pass such conceptions; thus the imaginations or conceptions which are produced by us with our individual activity remain separate from these others,[2] *i.e.* from the implicit.

This conception gives an instance of the difficulties which appear in regard to these questions, and which Berkeley wished to escape from in a quite original way. The inconsistency in this system God has again to make good; He has to bear it all away; to Him the solution of the contradiction is left. In this idealism, in short, the common sensuous view of the universe and the separation of actuality, as also the system of thought, of judgments

[1] Buhle: Geschichte der neuern Philosophie, Vol. V. Sect. 1, pp. 94, 95; The Works of George Berkeley, Vol. I. pp. 308, 335.

[2] Buhle, ibidem, pp. 96-99; Berkeley, ibidem, p. 325, seq. et passim.

devoid of Notion, remain exactly as before; plainly nothing in the content is altered but the abstract form that all things are perceptions only.[1] Such idealism deals with the opposition between consciousness and its object merely, and leaves the extension of the conceptions and the antagonisms of the empirical and manifold content quite untouched; and if we ask what then is the truth of these perceptions and conceptions, as we asked formerly of things, no answer is forthcoming. It is pretty much a matter of indifference whether we believe in things or in perceptions, if self-consciousness remains possessed entirely by finalities; it receives the content in the ordinary way, and that content is of the ordinary kind. In its individuality it stumbles about amid the conceptions of an entirely empirical existence, without knowing and understanding anything else about the content: that is to say in this formal idealism reason has no content of its own.

As to what Berkeley further states in respect of the empirical content, where the object of his investigation becomes entirely psychological, it relates in the main to finding out the difference between the sensations of sight and feeling, and to discovering which kind of sensations belong to the one and which to the other. This kind of investigation keeps entirely to the phenomenal, and only therein distinguishes the various sorts of phenomena; or comprehension only reaches as far as to distinctions. The only point of interest is that these investigations have in their course chiefly lighted on space, and a dispute is carried on as to whether we obtain the conception of distance and so on, in short all the conceptions relating to space, through sight or feeling. Space is just this sensuous universal, the universal in individuality itself, which in the empirical consideration of empirical multiplicity invites and leads us on to thought (for it itself is thought), and by it this very sensuous perception and

[1] Cf. Berkeley, ibidem, passim.

reasoning respecting perception is in its action confused. And since here perception finds an objective thought, it really would be led on to thought or to the possession of a thought, but at the same time it cannot arrive at thought in its completion, since thought or the Notion are not in question, and it clearly cannot come to the consciousness of true reality. Nothing is thought in the form of thought, but only as an external, as something foreign to thought.

2. Hume.

We must add to what has preceded an account of the Scepticism of Hume, which has been given a more important place in history than it deserves from its intrinsic nature; its historic importance is due to the fact that Kant really derives the starting point of his philosophy from Hume.

David Hume was born in 1711 at Edinburgh and died there in 1776. He held a librarian's post in that town for some time, then he became secretary to the Embassy in Paris; for quite a long period, indeed, he moved in diplomatic circles. In Paris he came to know Jean Jacques Rousseau and invited him to England, but Rousseau's terribly distrustful and suspicious nature very soon estranged the two.[1] Hume is more celebrated as a writer of history than through his philosophic works. He wrote: "A Treatise of human nature," 3 vols., 1739, translated into German by Jacob, Halle, 1790, 8vo; likewise "Essays and Treatises on several subjects," 2 vols. (Vol. I. containing "Essays moral, political and literary," printed for the first time in Edinburgh, 1742; Vol. II. containing an "Inquiry concerning human understanding," a further development of the Treatise, and first printed separately in London, 1748, 8vo). In his "Essays," which contributed most to

[1] Buhle: Geschichte der neuern Philosophie, Vol. V. Sect. 1, pp. 193-200.

his fame as far as the philosophic side is concerned, he treated philosophic subjects as an educated, thoughtful man of the world would do—not in a systematic connection, nor showing the wide range which his thoughts should properly have been able to attain; in fact in some of his treatises he merely dealt with particular points of view.

We must shortly deal with the main aspects of Hume's philosophy. He starts directly from the philosophic standpoint of Locke and Bacon, which derives our conceptions from experience, and his scepticism has the idealism of Berkeley as its object. The sequence of thought is this: Berkeley allows all ideas to hold good as they are; in Hume the antithesis of the sensuous and universal has cleared and more sharply defined itself, sense being pronounced by him to be devoid of universality. Berkeley does not make any distinction as to whether in his sensations there is a necessary connection or not. Formerly experience was a mixture of the two elements. Hume tells us that all perceptions of the mind may be divided into two classes or species, that of impressions, *i.e.* sensuous perceptions, and thoughts or ideas; the latter are similar in content to the former, but less forcible and lively. All objects of reason are consequently either relations of thoughts such as mathematical axioms, or facts of experience.[1] Since Hume makes these into the content he naturally rejects innate ideas.[2]

Now when Hume goes on to consider more closely what is subsumed under experience, he finds categories of the understanding present there, and more especially the determination of the universal and of universal necessity;

[1] Tennemann's Grundriss der Geschichte der Philosophie von Wendt (Leipzig, 1829), § 370, pp. 439, 440; Hume: Essays and Treatises on several subjects, Vol. III. containing an Inquiry concerning human understanding (London, 1770), Sect. 2, pp. 21, 22; Sect. 4, P. I, p. 42; Tennemann, Vol. XI. pp. 433, 434.

[2] Hume: Essays and Treatises on several subjects, Vol. III. Not. A, pp. 283, 284.

he took under his consideration more particularly the category of cause and effect, and in it set forth the rational element, inasmuch as in this causal relationship necessity is especially contained. Here Hume really completed the system of Locke, since he consistently drew attention to the fact that if this point of view be adhered to, experience is indeed the principle of whatever one knows, or perception itself contains everything that happens, but nevertheless the determination of universality and necessity are not contained in, nor were they given us by experience. Hume has thus destroyed the objectivity or absolute nature of thought-determinations. "Our conviction of the truth of a fact rests on feeling, memory, and the reasonings founded on the causal connection, *i.e.* on the relation of cause and effect. The knowledge of this relation is not attained by reasonings *a priori*, but arises entirely from experience; and we draw inferences, since we expect similar results to follow from similar causes, by reason of the principle of the custom or habit of conjoining different manifestations, *i.e.* by reason of the principle of the association of ideas. Hence there is no knowledge and no metaphysics beyond experience."[1]

The simple thought we have here is exactly what Locke says, that we must receive the conception of cause and effect, and thus of a necessary connection, from experience; but experience, as sensuous perception, contains no necessity, has no causal connection. For in what we term such, that which we properly speaking perceive is merely the fact that something first of all happens and that then something else follows. Immediate perception relates only to a content of conditions or things which are

[1] Tennemann's Grundriss der Geschichte der Philosophie von Wendt, § 370, p. 440; Hume: Essays and Treatises on several subjects, Vol. III. Sect. 4, Pt. I. pp. 43-45; Sect. 5, pp. 66, 67; Buhle: Geschichte der neuern Philosophie, Vol. V. Sect. 1, pp. 204, 205; Tennemann, Vol. XI. pp. 435, 436.

present alongside of and in succession to one another, but not to what we call cause and effect; in time-succession there is thus no relation of cause and effect, and consequently no necessity either.[1] When we say the pressure of the water is the cause of the destruction of this house, that is no pure experience. We have merely seen the water pressing or moving along in this direction, and subsequently the house falling down; and so with other examples. Necessity is thus not justified by experience, but we carry it into experience; it is accidentally arrived at by us and is subjective merely. This kind of universality which we connect with necessity, Hume calls custom. Because we have often seen results to follow we are accustomed to regard the connection as a necessary one; the necessity to him is thus a quite contingent association of ideas, which is custom.

It is the same thing in respect of the universal. What we perceive are individual phenomena and sensations in which we see that this is now one thing and now another. It may likewise be that we perceive the same determination frequently repeated and in manifold ways. But this is still far removed from universality; universality is a determination which is not given to us through experience. It may be said that this is quite a correct remark on Hume's part, if by experience we understand outward experience. Experience is sensible that something exists, but nevertheless the universal is not as yet present in it. Indeed, sensuous existence as such is something which is set forth as indifferent, not differentiated from anything else; but sensuous existence is likewise universal in itself, or the indifference of its determinateness is not its only determinateness. But since Hume regards necessity, the unity of opposites, as resting quite subjectively on custom, we cannot get any deeper in thought. Custom is indeed

[1] Hume: Essays and Treatises on several subjects, Vol. III. Sect. vii. Pt. 1, pp. 102, 103; Pt. 2, pp. 108, 109; Sect. viii. pp. 118, 119.

so far a necessity in consciousness, and to this extent we really see the principle of this idealism in it; but in the second place this necessity is represented as something quite devoid of thought or Notion.

This custom obtains both in our perception which relates to sensuous nature, and in relation to law and morality. The ideas of justice and morality rest upon an instinct, on a subjective, but very often deceptive moral feeling.[1] From a sceptical point of view the opposite may likewise be demonstrated. From this side Hume considers justice, morality, religious determinations, and disputes their absolute validity. That is to say when it is assumed that our knowledge arises from experience, and that we must consider only what we obtain thereby to be the truth, we find indeed in our feeling, the sentiment *e.g.* that the murderer, the thief, &c., must be punished; and because this is likewise felt by others it is universally allowed. But Hume, like the sceptics of former days, appeals to the various opinions of various nations: amongst different nations and in different times various standards of right have been held.[2] There are those who in this case do not have the feeling of wrong-doing in respect of stealing, *e.g.* the Lacedæmonians or the so-called innocent inhabitants of the South Sea Islands. What is by one nation called immoral, shameful and irreligious, is by another not considered so at all. Thus because such matters rest upon experience, one subject has such and such an experience, finds, for instance, in his religious feelings this determination which inclines him to God, while another subject has different experiences altogether. We are in the

[1] Hume: Essays and Treatises on several subjects, Vol. IV. containing an Inquiry concerning the principles of morals, Sect. 1, p. 4; Appendix I. p. 170.

[2] Buhle: Geschichte der neuern Philosophie, Vol. V. Sect. 1, pp. 230, 231; cf. Hume, ibidem, Vol. III. Sect. 12, P. II. p. 221; Vol. IV.; An Inquiry, &c., Sect. 4, pp. 62-65; A dialogue, pp. 235, 236, &c., &c.

habit of allowing one thing to be just and moral, others have another mode of regarding it. Hence if the truth depends upon experience, the element of universality, of objectivity, &c., comes from elsewhere, or is not justified by experience. Hume thus declared this sort of universality, as he declared necessity, to be rather subjectively than objectively existent; for custom is just a subjective universality of this kind. This is an important and acute observation in relation to experience looked at as the source of knowledge; and it is from this point that the Kantian reflection now begins.

Hume (Essays and Treatises on several subjects, Vol. III. Sect. 8, 11) then extended his scepticism to the conceptions and doctrines of freedom and necessity, and to the proofs of the existence of God; and in fact scepticism here possesses a wide field. To such a system of reasoning from thoughts and possibilities another method of reasoning may again be opposed, and this reasoning is no better than the other. What is said to be metaphysically established regarding immortality, God, nature, &c., lacks a real ground for resting upon, such as is professed to be given; for the inferences on which men ground their proofs are subjectively formed conceptions. But where a universality is found, it does not rest in the matter in itself, but is simply a subjective necessity which is really mere custom. Hence the result which Hume arrives at is necessarily astonishment regarding the condition of human knowledge, a general state of mistrust, and a sceptical indecision—which indeed does not amount to much. The condition of human knowledge regarding which Hume so much wonders, he further describes as containing an antagonism between reason and instinct; this instinct, it is said, which embraces many sorts of powers, inclinations, &c., deceives us in many different ways, and reason demonstrates this. But on the other side it is empty, without content or principles of its own;

and if a content is in question at all, it must keep to those inclinations. In itself reason thus has no criterion whereby the antagonism between individual desires, and between itself and the desires, may be settled.[1] Thus everything appears in the form of an irrational existence devoid of thought · the implicitly true and right is not in thought, but in the form of an instinct, a desire.

B. Scottish Philosophy.

In Scotland quite another school of thought developed, and the Scotch are the foremost of Hume's opponents; in German philosophy, on the other hand, we have to recognize in Kant another opposing force to that of Hume. To the Scottish school many philosophers belong; English philosophy is now restricted to Edinburgh and Glasgow, in which places a number of professors belonging to this school succeeded one another. To the scepticism of Hume they oppose an inward independent source of truth for all that pertains to religion and morality. This coincides with Kant, who also maintains an inward source or spring as against external perception; but in the case of Kant this has quite another form than that which it possesses with the Scottish philosophers. To them this inward independent source is not thought or reason as such, for the content which comes to pass from this inwardness is concrete in its nature, and likewise demands for itself the external matter of experience. It consists of popular principles, which on the one hand are opposed to the externality of the sources of knowledge, and, on the other, to metaphysics as such, to abstract thought or reasoning on its own account. This sort of reasoning understanding applied itself to ethics and to politics—sciences which have been much developed by German, French, and above all by Scottish philosophers

[1] Hume: Essays and Treatises on several subjects, Vol. III. Sect. 12, Pt. I. pp. 217, 218; Not. N. pp. 296, 297; Buhle: Geschichte der neuern Philosophie, Vol. V. Sect. 1, p. 210.

(*supra*, p. 320): they regarded morality as cultured men would, and sought to bring moral duties under a principle. Many of their works are translated into German; several of these on ethics or morality are translated by Garve, for instance, who also translated Cicero *De Officiis*, and they are written in a manner similar to that of Cicero when he uses the expression *Insitum est a natura* (Vol. I. p. 93). This moral sentiment and the ordinary human understanding hereafter formed the common principle to a whole succession of Scots, such as Thomas Reid, Beattie, Oswald, and others; in this way they frequently made sagacious observations, but with them speculative philosophy quite disappears. One special characteristic of these Scottish philosophers is that they have sought accurately to define the principle of knowledge; but on the whole they start from the same point as that which was in Germany likewise accepted as the principle. That is to say they represented the so-called healthy reason, or common-sense (*sensus communis*), as the ground of truth. The following are the principal members of this school, each of whom has some special feature distinguishing him from the rest.

1. Thomas Reid.

Thomas Reid, born in 1710, died as a professor in Glasgow in 1796.[1] He maintained the principle of common-sense. His endeavour was to discover the principles of knowledge, and the following are his conclusions: "(a) There are certain undemonstrated and undemonstrable fundamental truths which common-sense begets and recognizes as immediately conclusive and absolute." This hence constitutes an immediate knowledge; in it an inward independent source is set forth which is hereby opposed to religion as revealed. "(b) These immediate truths require

[1] Tennemann's Grundriss der Geschichte der Philosophie von Wendt, § 371, p. 442.

no support from any elaborated science, nor do they submit to its criticism;" they cannot be criticized by philosophy. "(c) Philosophy itself has no root other than that of an immediate, self-enlightening truth; whatever contradicts such truth is in itself false, contradictory, and absurd." This is true for knowledge and "(d) Morality; the individual is moral if he acts in accordance with the perfect principles of the perfection of the whole and with his own duty as it is known to him."[1]

2. James Beattie.

James Beattie, born 1735, was a professor of moral philosophy in Edinburgh and Aberdeen, and died in 1803. He likewise made common-sense the source of all knowledge. "The common-sense of the plain human understanding is the source of all morality, of all religion, and all certainty. The confirmation of common-sense must be added to the testimony of our senses. The truth is what the necessities of my nature call upon me to believe. Belief signifies conviction in the case of truths which are certain, in that of those which are probable, approbation. The truth which is certain is known by means of intuition, the probable truth by means of proofs."[2] Such convictions as are quite certain form the basis of actions.

3. James Oswald.

James Oswald, a Scottish clergyman, made use of an expression which indicates that we have the principles just

[1] Rixner: Handbuch der Geschichte der Philosophie, Vol. III. § 119, p. 259; cf. Thomas Reid; An Inquiry into the human mind on the principles of common sense (Edinburgh, 1810), chap. i. Sect. 4, pp. 19, 20 (translated into German, Leipzig, 1782, pp. 17, 18); chap. vi. Sect. 20, pp. 372-375 (pp. 310, 311), &c.

[2] Rixner: Handbuch der Geschichte der Philosophie, Vol. III. § 120, pp. 261, 262; cf. James Beattie: Essays on the nature and immutability of Truth, &c. (Edinburgh, 1772), Pt. I., chap. i., pp. 18-31 (translated into German, Copenhagen and Leipzig, 1772, pp. 24-42); chap. ii. Sect. 2, pp. 37-42 (pp. 49-55), &c.

mentioned as facts existing within us.[1] "The existence of the Divine Being is (according to him) a fact absolutely raised above all reasoning and all doubt, and immediately certain for the common-sense of morality."[2] The same principle was likewise established in Germany at this time—an inward revelation, a knowledge of the conscience, and specially of God and His Being.

4. Dugald Stewart.

To this school also belong Dugald Stewart, Edward Search,[3] Ferguson, and Hutcheson, most of whom have written on morals. The political economist Adam Smith from this point of view is likewise a philosopher, and the best known of them all. This Scottish philosophy is now given forth in Germany as something new. It is a popular philosophy, which, on the one hand, has the great merit of seeking in man, and in his consciousness, for the source of all that should be held by him as true, the immanence of what should be by him esteemed. The content is at the same time a concrete content; in a certain degree, it is the antithesis of metaphysics proper, of the wandering about in abstract determinations of the understanding. Of these Scots, Dugald Stewart, who is living still,[4] appears to be the last and least significant; in them all there is the same ground-work to be found, the same circle of reflection, namely, an *a priori* philosophy, though not one which is to be pursued in a speculative way. The general idea which pervades their principle is that of the healthy human understanding; to this they have added benevolent desires, sympathy, a moral sense, and from such grounds composed very

[1] Cf. James Oswald: An Appeal of common-sense in behalf of religion (Edinburgh, 1772), Vol. I. Book I. Introduction, p. 12 (translated by Wilmsen, Leipzig, 1774, p. 11).

[2] Rixner, ibidem, § 121, p. 262; cf. James Oswald, ibidem, Vol. II. Book II. chap. i. pp. 50, 51 (pp. 54, 55).

[3] The name assumed by Abraham Tucker.—[Translator's note.]

[4] Lectures of 1825-1826.

excellent moral writings. That is certainly all very well in order to understand approximately, up to a certain degree of culture, what universal thoughts are, in order to narrate their history, to appeal to examples, and to explain them; but further it does not extend.

In more recent times this Scottish philosophy has passed to France, and Professor Royer-Collard, now president of the Second Chamber,[1] as also his disciple, Jouffroy, in conformity with it, pass from the facts of consciousness through cultured reasoning and experience, to a further stage in development. What by the French is called *Idéologie* (*supra*, p. 308) has also its place here; it is abstract metaphysics, in so far as it is an enumeration and analysis of the most simple thought-determinations. They are not treated dialectically, but from our reflection, from our thoughts, the material is derived, and in this the determinations therein contained are demonstrated.

C. French Philosophy.

We pass on to the French philosophy; the relation it bears to metaphysics is this, that while man as a metaphysician stands to himself in the attitude of a layman or outsider, French philosophy does away with the lay or outside position in regard alike to politics, religion, and philosophy. Two forms have to be mentioned which are of the greatest importance in respect to culture—French philosophy and the *Aufklärung*. With the English we saw a certain idealism only: this was either formal, as the mere general translation of Being into Being-for-another, *i.e.* into perceptibility, or else what is implicit in this perceptibility, instincts, impulses, habits, &c.—blind determinate forces; a return into self-consciousness, which itself appears as a physical thing. In that first idealism the whole finitude and extension of appearances, of sensations,

[1] Lectures of 1829-1830.

and likewise of thoughts and determinate fixed conceptions, remain just what they are in the unphilosophic consciousness. The scepticism of Hume makes all that is universal sink into habits and instincts, *i.e.* it consists in a more simple synthesis of the phenomenal world; but these simpler elements, these instincts, impulses, and forces, are just as much a fixed present existence in self-consciousness, unspiritual, and without movement. The French philosophy has more life, more movement, more spirit; it would perhaps be more correct to describe it as full of life and spirit. It is the absolute Notion, which revolts against the whole reigning system of prevalent conceptions and established ideas, which overthrows all that has settled into fixity, and acquires the consciousness of perfect liberty. At the root of this idealistic activity lies the certainty that whatever is, whatever counts for anything in itself, is all a matter of self-consciousness; and as to Notions (individual and isolated existences ruling actual self-consciousness), such as the Notions of good and evil, of power and riches, and the fixed conceptions regarding faith in God and His relation to the world, His mode of government and, further, the duties of self-consciousness towards Him—that all these are not truths in themselves, having validity beyond the bounds of self-consciousness. All these forms, the real implicitude of the actual world and also of the supersensuous world, are therefore set aside in this spirit conscious of itself. It does not trouble itself seriously about those who admit the validity of these conceptions just as they are, and accept them as true, respecting them as independent and free apart from self-consciousness, but it speaks of such conceptions with intelligence and spirit, that is to say, it asserts that self-consciousness by its activity is the first to make anything of them, and to make that a something very different from what they profess to be; for the self-conscious spirit only intellectual relations, these processes of formation and movement by means of its self-consciousness, possess validity and interest. This is the character of the Notion in its actuality; what has reality for this all-perceiving and all-comprehending consciousness is held to be valid.

We must now consider what form existence takes for this absolutely comprehending self-consciousness. In the first place this Notion is fixed as the negative movement of the Notion only; the positive and simple, or existence, falls outside of this movement. There remains to the Notion no distinction, no content; for all determinate content is lost in that negativity. This empty existence is for us pure thought generally, what the French call *être suprême*, or if represented objectively as existent, and as in opposition to consciousness, it is matter. Absolute Being is therefore determined as matter, as empty objectivity, through a Notion which destroys all content and determination, and has as its object this universal alone. It is a Notion which acts only destructively, and does not again construct itself out of this matter or pure thought or pure substantiality. We here see so-called materialism and atheism freely emerge, as the necessary result of the pure comprehending self-consciousness. From one point of view there perishes in this negative movement all determination which represents spirit as something beyond self-consciousness, and more especially all determinations within the spirit, and also those which express it as spirit, indeed all the conceptions formed of it by faith, for which it has validity as an existent self-consciousness beyond self-consciousness—in short, all that is traditional or imposed by authority. There remains only a present, actual Being, for self-consciousness recognizes implicit existence only in the form which it has for self-consciousness, and in which it is actually known to itself; in matter, and matter as actively extending and realizing itself in multiplicity, *i.e.* as nature. In the present I am conscious to myself of my reality, and consequently self-consciousness finds itself as matter, finds the soul to be material, and conceptions to be movements and changes in the inner organ of the brain, which result from external impressions on the senses. Thought is therefore a mode of the existence of matter. The One Substance of Spinoza, to which French materialism as naturalism is parallel, really finds its accomplishment here in this object as in all respects the ultimate; but while in Spinoza this category is a possession which we find ready to hand, here it appears as the result of the abstraction of the understanding proceeding from empiricism.

The other form of the *Aufklärung* is, on the contrary, when absolute Being is set forth as something beyond self-consciousness, so that of itself, of its implicit Being, nothing whatever can be known. It bears the empty name of God. For though God may be determined in any way whatever, all these determinations fall away; He is, like x, the altogether unknown quantity. This view is not therefore to be termed atheism, in the first place because it still employs the empty, meaningless name, and in the second place because it expresses the necessary relations of self-consciousness, duties, &c., not as necessary in an absolute sense, but as necessary through relation to another, namely to the unknown—although there can be no positive relation to an unknown except by abrogating the self as particular. Yet it is not matter, because this simple and empty something is negatively defined as non-existent for self-consciousness. This all comes to the same thing, however, for matter is the universal, and is Being-for-self represented as abrogated. But the true reflection on that unknown is this, that it exists for self-consciousness simply as a negative of the same, *i.e.* as matter, reality, the present; it is this negative for me, this is its Notion. The difference distinguishing this from what appears to be in its entirety something "other," and in which any one side is not permitted to say that what it thinks is such is that particular thing, is the difference which rests on this last abstraction.

Since then the Notion is present only in its negative form, positive extension remains without a Notion; it has the form of nature, of an existent, both in the physical and in the moral sphere. The knowledge of nature remains the ordinary, scientifically unspeculative knowledge, and as to its essence, in so far as it claims to be philosophy, it is a general way of speaking that plays with the words, "forces, relations, manifold connections," but arrives at nothing definite. Similarly, in the spiritual sphere, it is so far true that the metaphysic of the spirit is of such a nature that it is nothing more nor less than a particular organization by means of which the powers which are termed sensation, perception, &c., come into existence; but this is a wearisome way of talking, which can make nothing intelligible, which accepts appearances and perceptions and reasons about them, but none the less reduces their implicit existence to certain determinate forces, of the inward nature of which we know nothing further. The determination and knowledge of the moral sphere has similarly for its object to bring man back to his so-called natural promptings; its essence has the form of a natural impulse, and this natural impulse is termed self-love, selfishness, or benevolence. It is required that man should live in conformity with nature; but this nature does not reach further than general expressions and descriptions, such as the state of nature we find depicted by Rousseau. What is called the metaphysic of ordinary conceptions is the empiricism of Locke, which seeks to show their origin to be in consciousness, in as far as it is individual consciousness; which, when born into the world, emerges out of unconsciousness in order to acquire knowledge as sensuous consciousness. This external origin they confound with the Becoming and Notion of the matter in point. If one were to ask vaguely what is the origin and genesis of water, and the answer were to be given that it comes from the mountains or from rain, this would be a reply in the spirit of the above philosophy. In short, it is only the negative aspect that is interesting, and as for this positive French philosophy, it is out of the question. But even the negative side of it belongs properly to culture mainly, with which we have here nothing to do, and the *Aufklärung* likewise belongs to the same. In the French philosophic writings, which in this respect are of importance, what is worthy of admiration is the astonishing energy and force of the Notion as directed against existence, against faith, against all the power of authority that had held sway for thousands of years. On the one hand we cannot help remarking the feeling of utter rebellion against the whole state of affairs at present prevailing, a state which is alien to self-consciousness, which would fain dispense with it, and in which self-consciousness does not find itself; there is a certainty of the truth of reason, which challenges the whole intellectual world as it stands aloof, and is confident of destroying it. French atheism, materialism, or naturalism has overcome all prejudices, and has been victorious over the senseless hypotheses and assumptions of the positive element in religion, which is associated with habits, manners, opinions, determinations as to law and morality and civil institutions. With the healthy human understanding and earnestness of spirit, and not with frivolous declamations, it has rebelled against the condition of the world as legally established, against the constitution of the state, the administration of justice, the mode of government, political authority, and likewise against art.

Contrasting with this barren content there is the other and fertile side. The positive is in its turn constituted by so-called immediately enlightening truths of the healthy human understanding, which contains nothing except this truth and the claim to find itself, and beyond this form does not pass. But in so doing there arises the endeavour to grasp the absolute as something present, and at the same time as an object of thought and as absolute unity: an endeavour which, as it implies denial of the conception of design both in the natural and in the spiritual sphere—the former involving the idea of life, and the latter that of spirit and freedom—only reaches to the abstraction of a nature undetermined in itself, to sensation, mechanism, self-seeking, and utility. It is this then that we shall have to make evident in the positive side of French philosophy. In their political constitutions the French have, it is true, started from abstractions, but they have done so as from universal thoughts, which are the negative of reality; the English, on the other hand, proceed from concrete reality, from the unwieldy structure of their constitution; just as their writers even have not attained to universal principles. What Luther began in the heart only and in the feelings—the freedom of spirit which, unconscious of its simple root, does not comprehend itself, and yet is the very universal itself, for which all content disappears in the thought that fills itself with itself—these universal determinations and thoughts the French asserted and steadfastly adhered to: they are universal principles, in the form of the conviction of the individual in himself. Freedom becomes the condition of the world, connects itself with the world's history and forms epochs in the same; it is the concrete freedom of the spirit, a concrete universality; fundamental principles as regards the concrete now take the place of the abstract metaphysic of Descartes. Among the Germans we find mere chatter; they would have liked to offer explanations also, but all they have to give is in the form of miserable phenomena and individualism. The French, from their starting-point of the thought of universality, and the German liberty of conscience starting from the conscience which teaches us to "Prove all things," to "hold fast that which is good," have, however, joined hands with one another, or they follow the same path. Only the French, as though they were without conscience, have made short work of everything, and have systematically adhered to a definite thought—the physiocratic system; while the Germans wish to leave themselves a free retreat, and examine from the standpoint of conscience whether a certain course is permissible. The French warred against the speculative Notion with the spirit, the Germans did so with the understanding. We find in the French a deep all-embracing philosophic need, different from anything in the English and Scotch and even in the Germans, and full of vitality: it is a universal concrete view of all that exists, with entire independence both of all authority and of all abstract metaphysics. The method employed is that of development from perception, from the heart; it is a comprehensive view of the entire matter, which keeps the whole ever in sight, and seeks to uphold and attain to it.

This healthy human understanding, this sound reason, with its content taken from the human breast, from natural feeling, has directed itself against the religious side of things in various moments: on the one hand and first of all, as French philosophy, it did so against the Catholic religion, the fetters of superstition and of the hierarchy; on the other hand, in less pronounced form, as the German "illumination," against the Protestant religion, in as far as it has a content which it has derived from revelation, from ecclesiastical authority in general. On the one hand the form of authority in general was challenged, and on the other hand its matter. The content can be easily enough disposed of by this form of thought, which is not what we understand by reason, but which must be termed understanding; it is easy for the understanding to show objections to the ultimate principles of what can be comprehended only by means of speculation. The understanding has thus tried the content of religion by its standard, and has condemned it; the understanding proceeds in the same way against a concrete philosophy. What of religion has in many theologies been very commonly left remaining is what is termed theism, faith in general; this is the same content which is found also in Mohammedanism. But along with this attack upon religion on the part of the reasoning understanding there has been also a movement towards materialism, atheism and naturalism. It is true that we should not make the charge of atheism lightly, for it is a very common occurrence that an individual whose ideas about God differ from those of other people is charged with lack of religion, or even with atheism. But here it really is the case that this philosophy has developed into atheism, and has defined matter, nature, &c., as that which is to be taken as the ultimate, the active, and the efficient. Some Frenchmen, Rousseau for instance, are not, however, to be included with the rest; one of this author's works, "The Confession of Faith of a Vicar,"[1] contains the very same theism which is found in German theologians. Thus French metaphysics finds a parallel not only in Spinoza (*supra*, p. 382) but also in the German metaphysics of Wolff. Other Frenchmen have confessedly gone over to naturalism; among them is specially to be mentioned Mirabaud, to whom the *Système de la Nature* is attributed.

In what has been termed French philosophy, represented by Voltaire, Montesquieu, Rousseau, d'Alembert, Diderot, and in what subsequently appeared in Germany as the *Aufklärung*, and has been also stigmatized as atheism, we may now distinguish three aspects, first, the negative side, to which most exception has been taken; secondly, the positive side; thirdly, the philosophical, metaphysical side.

[1] Emile ou de l'éducation, T. II. (Paris, 1813, éd. stéréotype), Book IV., Profession de foi du vicaire savoyard, p. 215 seq.

1. The Negative Aspect.

Justice must be done even to this negative side, as to everything else; what is substantial in it is the attack of the reasoning instinct against a condition of degeneracy, I may even say of utter and universal falsehood; for instance, against the positive side of a religion that has become wooden and lifeless. What we call religion is firm faith, conviction that there is a God; if this is faith in the doctrines of Christianity, it is more or less abstracted from. But in this attack against religion we have to think of something quite different from the above; in what we find here, the positive of religion is the negative of reason. If we would understand the feeling of indignation to which these writers give utterance, we must keep before our eyes the state of religion in those days, with its might and magnificence, the corruption of its manners, its avarice, its ambition, its luxury, for which nevertheless reverence was claimed—a state of contradiction present and existent. We perceive into what a frightful condition of formalism and deadness positive religion had sunk, as had the bonds of society as well, the means employed for the administration of justice, the power of the state. This French philosophy also attacked the state; it assailed prejudices and superstition, especially the depravity of civic life, of court manners and of Government officials; it laid hold of and brought to light the evil, the ridiculous, the base, and exposed the whole tissue of hypocrisy and unjust power to the derision, the contempt and the hatred of the world at large, and thus brought men's minds and hearts into a state of indifference to the idols of the world and indignation against them. Old institutions, which in the sense of self-conscious freedom and humanity that had developed, no longer found a place, and which had formerly been founded and upheld by mutual good feeling and the obtuseness of a consciousness unconscious of self, institutions which were no longer in harmony with the spirit that had established them, and now, in consequence of the advance that had been made in scientific culture, were bound to make good to reason their claim to be sacred and just,—this was the formalism that those philosophers overthrew. In making their attacks, they wrote sometimes with reasoned argument, sometimes satirically, sometimes in the language of plain common-sense, and they did not wage war on what we call religion; that was left quite unharmed, and its claims were urged with words of choicest eloquence. Those who enforced these views were therefore agents of destruction against that alone which was in itself already destroyed. We place it to our credit when we reproach the French for their attacks upon religion and on the state. We must represent to ourselves the horrible state of society, the misery and degradation in France, in order to appreciate the services that these writers rendered. Hypocrisy and cant, imbecility of mind and the tyranny which sees itself robbed of its prey, may say that attacks were made on religion, on the state, and on manners. But what a religion! Not the religion that Luther purified, but the most wretched superstition, priestly domination, stupidity, degradation of mind, and more especially the squandering of riches and the revelling in temporal possessions in the midst of public misery. And what a state! The blindest tyranny of ministers and their mistresses, wives and chamberlains; so that a vast army of petty tyrants and idlers looked upon it as a right divinely given them to plunder the revenues of the state and lay hands upon the product of the nation's sweat. The shamelessness, the dishonesty were past belief; and morals were simply in keeping with the corruptness of the institutions. We see the law defied by individuals in respect to civil and political life; we see it likewise set at nought in respect to conscience and thought.

In regard to practical politics, the writers in question

never even thought of a revolution, but desired and demanded reforms alone, and that these should be subjective mainly; they called on the Government to sweep away abuses, and appoint honourable men as ministers. The positive recommendations made by them as to the course to be pursued were, for example, that the royal children should receive a good upbringing, that princes should be of frugal habits, &c. The French Revolution was forced on by the stiff-necked obstinacy of prejudices, by haughtiness, utter want of thought, and avarice. The philosophers of whom we are speaking were able to give only a general idea of what ought to be done; they could not indicate the mode in which the reforms were to be carried out. It was the Government's business to make arrangements and carry out reforms in concrete shape; but it did not perceive this. What the philosophers brought forward and maintained as a remedy for this horrible state of disorder was, speaking generally, that men should no longer be in the position of laymen, either with regard to religion or to law; so that in religious matters there should not be a hierarchy, a limited and selected number of priests, and in the same way that there should not be in legal matters an exclusive caste and society (not even a class of professional lawyers), in whom should reside, and to whom should be restricted, the knowledge of what is eternal, divine, true, and right, and by whom other men should be commanded and directed; but that human reason should have the right of giving its assent and its opinion. To treat barbarians as laymen is quite as it should be—barbarians are nothing but laymen; but to treat thinking men as laymen is very hard. This great claim made by man to subjective freedom, perception and conviction, the philosophers in question contended for heroically and with splendid genius, with warmth and fire, with spirit and courage, maintaining that a man's own self, the human spirit, is the source from which is derived all that is to be respected by him. There thus manifests itself in them the fanaticism of abstract thought. We Germans were passive at first with regard to the existing state of affairs, we endured it; in the second place, when that state of affairs was overthrown, we were just as passive: it was overthrown by the efforts of others, we let it be taken away from us, we suffered it all to happen.

In Germany, Frederick II. allied himself with this culture, a rare example in those days. French court manners, operas, gardens, dresses, were widely adopted in Germany, but not French philosophy; yet in the form of wit and jest much of it found its way into this upper world, and much that was evil and barbarous was driven away. Frederick II., without having been brought up on melancholy psalms, without having had to learn one or two of them every day by heart, without the barbarous metaphysics and logic of Wolff (for what did he find to admire in Germany except Gellert?), was well acquainted with the great, although formal and abstract principles of religion and the state, and governed in accordance therewith, as far as circumstances allowed. Nothing else was at that time required in his nation; one cannot ask that he should have reformed and revolutionized it, since not a single person yet demanded representative government and the publicity of courts of justice. He introduced what there was need of, religious tolerance, legislation, improvements in the administration of justice, economy in the revenues of state; of the wretched German law there remained no longer in his states even the merest phantom. He showed what was the object and purpose of the state, and at the same time cast down all privileges, the private rights which pertained to Germans, and arbitrary statute laws. It is foolish when cant and German pseudo-patriotism pounce down upon him now, and try to disparage the greatness of a man whose influence was so enormous, and would even detract from his fame by a charge of vanity and wickedness. What German patriotism aims at should be reasonable.

2. THE POSITIVE ASPECT.

The affirmative content of this philosophy certainly does not satisfy the requirements of profundity. A leading characteristic of its teaching, which is found also with the Scottish philosophers and with ourselves, is the assumption of primitive feelings of justice which man has in himself, as for example benevolence and social instincts which should be cultivated. The positive source of knowledge and of justice is placed in human reason and the common consciousness of mankind, in the healthy human reason, and not in the form of the Notion. It is certainly wonderful to find truths expressed in the form of universal thoughts, respecting which it is of infinite importance that they should be assumptions present in the human mind: that man has in his heart the feeling of right, of love to his fellow-creatures: that religion and faith are not matters of compulsion; that merit, talent, virtue are the true nobility, &c. An important question, especially among the Germans, was what is the end and character of man, by which was meant the nature of his mind and spirit; and certainly, as far as the spiritual is concerned, it is to this point that we must return. But in order to find the nature of spirit, to discover what this determination is, a return was made to perception, observation, experience, to the existence of certain impulses. These are certainly determinations in ourselves, but we have not known them in their necessity. Such an impulse is besides taken as natural, and thus it is here indeterminate in itself, it has its limitation only as a moment of the whole. In regard to knowledge, very abstract thoughts are to be found—though of a truth they are quite as good as ours, and more ingenious—which according to their content ought to be concrete, and also were so. But so superficially were they comprehended that they soon showed themselves far from sufficient for what had to be derived from them. They said, for instance, that Nature is a whole, that all is determined by laws, through a combination of different movements, through a chain of causes and effects, and so on; the various properties, materials, connections of things bring everything to pass. These are general phrases, with which one can fill whole books.

a. Système de la Nature.

To this philosophy belongs the *Système de la Nature*, the leading work on the subject, written in Paris by a German, Baron von Hollbach, who was the central figure of all those philosophers. Montesquieu, d'Alembert, Rousseau, were for a time in his circle; however much these men were moved to indignation at the existing state of things, they were yet in other respects very different from one another. The *Système de la Nature* may very easily be found tiresome to read, because it treats discursively of general conceptions, which are often repeated; it is not a French book, for vivacity is lacking and the mode of presentation is dull.

The great Whole of Nature (*le grand tout de la nature*) is the ultimate: "The universe displays nothing but an immense collection of matter and motion" (as with Descartes), "an unbroken chain of causes and effects, of which causes some directly affect our senses, while others are unknown to us, because their effects, which we perceive, are too remote from their causes. The different qualities of these materials, their manifold connections, and the effects which result therefrom, constitute essences for us. From the diversity of these essences arise the different orders, species, systems, under which things fall, and whose sum total, the great whole, is what we call Nature."[1] It is like what Aristotle (*vide* Vol. I. p. 241) says of Xenophanes, that he gazed into the blue, *i.e.* into Being.

[1] Buhle: Lehrbuch der Geschichte der Philosophie, Pt. VIII. pp. 62, 63: Système de la Nature par Mirabaud (Londres, 1770), T. I. chap. i. p. 10; chap. ii. p. 28.

According to Hollbach all is movement, matter moves itself: beer ferments, the soul is moved by its passions.[1] "The manifold variety of natural phenomena, and their incessant rise and disappearance, have their sole ground in the variety of motions and of their material." Through different combinations and modifications, through a different arrangement, another thing is originated. "Material substances have either a tendency to combine with one another, or else they are incapable of so combining. Upon this are based by physical scientists the forces of attraction and repulsion, sympathy and antipathy, affinity and relation; and the moralists base thereon hatred and love, friendship and enmity." Spirit, the incorporeal, contradicts or opposes itself to motion, to a change of the relations of a body in space.[2]

b. Robinet.

Another work of importance is the still more "dangerous" treatise, *De la Nature*, by Robinet. In it there reigns quite a different and a deeper spirit; one is frequently struck by the depth of earnestness which the writer displays. He begins thus: "There is a God, *i.e.* a cause of the phenomena of that Whole which we call Nature. Who is God? We know not, and we are so constituted that we can never know in what order of things we have been placed. We cannot know God perfectly, because the means of doing so will always be lacking to us. We too might write over the doors of our temples the words which were to be read upon the altar which the Areopagite raised, 'To the unknown God.'" The very same thing

[1] Buhle: Lehrbuch der Geschichte der Philosophie, Pt. VIII. pp. 63, 64. Système de la Nature, T. I. chap. ii. pp. 18, 16, 21, et 15.

[2] Buhle, ibidem, pp. 64, 65, 70; Système de la Nature, T. I. chap. ii. pp. 30, 31; chap. iii. pp. 39, 40; chap. iv. pp. 45, 46; chap. vii. pp. 90, 91.

is said nowadays: there can be no transition from the finite to the infinite. "The order which reigns in the universe is just as little the visible type of His wisdom, as our weak mind is the image of His intelligence." But this First Cause, God, is according to Robinet a creative God, He has brought Nature into existence; so that for him the only possible knowledge is that of Nature. "There is only One Cause. The eternal Cause, who so to speak had sown (*engrainé*) events one in the other, in order that they might without fail follow one upon another as He chose, in the beginning set in motion the endless chain of things. Through this permanent impression the Universe goes on living, moving and perpetuating itself. From the unity of cause there follows the unity of activity, for even it does not appear as something to be more or less admitted. By virtue of this single act all things come to pass. Since man has made Nature his study, he has found no isolated phenomenon, and no independent truth, because there are not and cannot be such. The whole sustains itself through the mutual correspondence of its parts."[1] The activity of Nature is one, as God is One.

This activity, more particularly regarded, signifies that germs unfold themselves in everything: everywhere there are organic Beings which produce themselves; nothing is isolated, everything is combined and connected and in harmony. Robinet here goes through the plants, the animals, and also the metals, the elements, air, fire, water, &c.; and seeks from them to demonstrate the existence of the germ in whatever has life, and also how metals are organized in themselves. "The example of the polypus is convincing as to the animal nature (*animalité*) of the smallest portions of organized matter; for the polypus is a group of associated polypi, each of which is as much a

[1] Robinet: De la Nature (Troisième édition, Amsterdam, 1766), T. I. P. I. chap. iii. iv. pp. 16, 17.

true polypus as the first. It stands proved that from the same point of view the living consists only of the living, the animals of minute animals, every animal in particular of minute animals of the same kind, a dog of dog-germs, man of human germs." In proof of this Robinet states in a "Recapitulation" that "animal sperm swarms with spermatic animalcules." Since he then connects every propagation properly so-called with the co-operation of both sexes, he alleges that every individual is inwardly or also in the external organs a hermaphrodite. Of the minerals he says: "Are we not compelled to regard as organic bodies all those in which we meet with an inward structure such as this? It presupposes throughout a seed, seed-granules, germs, of which they are the development." In the same way the air must have its germ, which does not come to reality until it is nourished by water, fire, &c. "The air, as principle, is only the germ of the air; as it impregnates or saturates itself in varying degrees with water and fire, it will gradually pass through different stages of growth: it will become first embryo, then perfect air."[1] Robinet gives the name of germ to the simple form in itself, the substantial form, the Notion. Although he seeks to prove this too much from the sensuous side, he yet proceeds from principles in themselves concrete, from the form in itself.

He speaks also of the evil and good in the world. The result of his observation is that good and evil balance each other; this equilibrium constitutes the beauty of the world. In order to refute the assertion that there is more good than evil in the world, he says that everything to which we reduce the good consists only in an enjoyment, a pleasure, a satisfaction; but this must be preceded by a want, a lack, a pain, the removal of which constitutes satis-

[1] Robinet: De la Nature, T. I. P. II. chap. ii. pp. 156, 157; chap. vii. pp. 166, 168; chap. ix.-xi.; chap. xv. pp. 202, 203; chap. xix. p. 217.

faction.[1] This is not only a correct thought empirically, but it also hints at the deeper idea that there is no activity except through contradiction.

3. Idea of a Concrete Universal Unity.

The result of the French philosophy is that it insisted on maintaining a general unity, not abstract, but concrete. Thus Robinet now propounded the theory of a universal organic life, and a uniform mode of origination; this concrete system he called Nature, over which God was set, but as the unknowable; all predicates which could be expressed of Him contained something inapplicable. We must admit that grand conceptions of concrete unity are to be found here, as opposed to the abstract metaphysical determinations of the understanding, *e.g.* the fruitfulness of Nature. But, on the other hand, the point of most importance with these philosophers is that what is to be accepted as valid must have presence, and that man in all knowledge must be himself the knower; for, as we may see, those philosophers made war on all external authority of state and church, and in particular on abstract thought which has no present meaning in us. Two determinations found in all philosophy are the concretion of the Idea and the presence of the spirit in the same; my content must at the same time be something concrete, present. This concrete was termed Reason, and for it the more noble of those men contended with the greatest enthusiasm and warmth. Thought was raised like a standard among the nations, liberty of conviction and of conscience in me. They said to mankind, "In this sign thou shalt conquer," for they had before their eyes what had been done in the name of the cross alone, what had been made a matter of

[1] Robinet: De la Nature, T. I. P. I. chap. xxviii. p. 138; chap. xiii. p. 70.

faith and law and religion—they saw how the sign of the cross had been degraded. For in the sign of the cross lying and deceit had been victorious, under this seal institutions had become fossilized, and had sunk into all manner of degradation, so that this sign came to be represented as the epitome and root of all evil. Thus in another form they completed the Reformation that Luther began. This concrete had manifold forms; social instincts in the practical sphere, laws of nature in the theoretical. There is present the absolute impulse to find a compass immanent in themselves, *i.e.* in the human mind. For the human mind it is imperative to have a fixed point such as this, if, indeed, it is to be within itself, if it is to be free in its own world at least. But this striving after really present vitality took forms which as by-paths were themselves one-sided. In this striving after unity, which was, however, concrete unity, the further varieties of the content likewise lie.

On the theoretic side of their philosophy, therefore, the French proceeded to materialism or naturalism, because the requirements of the understanding, as abstract thought, which from a firmly fixed principle allows the most monstrous consequences to be drawn, drove them to set up one principle as ultimate, and that a principle which had at the same time to be present and to lie quite close to experience. Hence they accept sensation and matter as the only truth, to which must be reduced all thought, all morality, as a mere modification of sensation. The unities which the French propounded were in this way one-sided.

a. Opposition of Sensation and Thought.

To this one-sidedness belongs the opposition between *sentir* and *penser*, or else, if you like, their identity, making the latter only a result of the former; there is not, however, any speculative reconciliation of this opposition in God, such as we find in Spinoza and Malebranche. This reduction of all thought to sensation, which in certain respects took place with Locke, becomes a widely extended theory. Robinet (*De la Nature*, T. I. P. IV. chap. iii. pp. 257-259) lights also on this opposition, beyond which he does not get, that mind and body are not separate, but that the manner in which they are united is inexplicable. The *Système de la Nature* (T. I. chap. x. p. 177) is marked by an especially plain reduction of thought to sensation. The leading thought is this: "Abstract thoughts are only modes in which our inmost organ views its own modifications. The words goodness, beauty, order, intelligence, virtue, &c., have no meaning for us if we do not refer and apply them to objects which our senses have shown to be capable of these qualities, or to modes of being and acting which are known to us." Thus even psychology passed into materialism, as for instance we may find in La Mettrie's work *L'homme Machine:* All thought and all conception have meaning only if they are apprehended as material; matter alone exists.

b. Montesquieu.

Other great writers have opposed to the above the feeling in the breast, the instinct of self-preservation, benevolent dispositions towards others, the impulse to fellowship, which last Puffendorf also made the foundation of his system of law (*supra*, p. 321). From this point of view much that is excellent has been said. Thus Montesquieu, in his charming book, *L'Esprit des Lois*, of which Voltaire said it was an *esprit sur les lois*, regarded the nations from this important point of view, that their constitution, their religion, in short, everything that is to be found in a state, constitutes a totality.

c. Helvetius.

This reduction of thought to feeling in the case of Helvetius takes the form that if in man as a moral being a single principle is sought, this ought to be called self-love, and he endeavoured to demonstrate by ingenious analysis that whatever we term virtue, all activity and law and right, has as its foundation nothing but self-love or selfishness, and is resolvable thereinto.[1] This principle is one-sided, although the "I myself" is an essential moment. What I will, the noblest, the holiest, is *my* aim; I must take part in it, I must agree to it, I must approve of it. With all self-sacrifice there is always conjoined some satisfaction, some finding of self; this element of self, subjective liberty, must always be present. If this is taken in a one-sided sense, there may be consequences drawn from it which overthrow all that is sacred; but it is found in equal degree in a morality as noble as any possibly can be.

d. Rousseau.

In connection with the practical side of things this particular must also be noted, that when the feeling of right, the concrete practical mind, and, speaking generally, humanity and happiness were made the principle, this principle, universally conceived, had certainly the form of thought; but in the case of such concrete content derived from our impulse or inward intuition, even though that content were religious, the thought itself was not the content. But now this further phase appeared, that pure thought was set up as the principle and content, even if again there was lacking to this content the true consciousness of its peculiar

[1] Helvetius: De l'esprit (Oeuvres complètes, T. II. Deux-Ponts, 1784), T. I. Discours II. chap. i. pp. 62-64; chap. ii. pp. 65, 68, 69; chap. iv. p. 90; chap. v. p. 91; chap. viii. p. 114; chap. xxiv. pp. 256, 257.

form; for it was not recognized that this principle was thought. We see it emerge in the sphere of will, of the practical, of the just, and so apprehended that the innermost principle of man, his unity with himself, is set forth as fundamental and brought into consciousness, so that man in himself acquired an infinite strength. It is this that Rousseau from one point of view said about the state. He investigated its absolute justification, and inquired as to its foundation. The right of ruling and associating, of the relation of order, of governing and being governed, he apprehends from his own point of view, so that it is made to rest historically on power, compulsion, conquest, private property, &c.[1]

Rousseau makes free-will the principle of this justification, and without reference to the positive right of states he made answer to the above question (chap. iv. p. 12), that man has free-will, because "liberty is the distinguishing feature of man. To renounce his liberty signifies to renounce his manhood. Not to be free is therefore a renunciation of a man's rights as a human being, and even of his duties." The slave has neither rights nor duties. Rousseau therefore says (chap. vi. p. 21): "The fundamental task is to find a form of association which will shield and protect with the power of the whole commonwealth combined the person and property of every one of its members, and in which each individual, while joining this association, obeys himself only, and thus remains as free as before. The solution is given by the Social Contract;" this is the association of which each is a member by his own will. These principles, thus abstractly stated, we must allow to be correct, yet the ambiguity in them soon begins to be felt. Man is free, this is certainly the substantial nature of man; and not only is this liberty not relinquished in the state, but it is actually

[1] Rousseau: Du contrat social (Lyon, 1790), Book I. chap. iii. pp. 8, 9; chap. iv. pp. 10, 11, 13-16.

in the state that it is first realized. The freedom of nature, the gift of freedom, is not anything real; for the state is the first realization of freedom.

The misunderstanding as to the universal will proceeds from this, that the Notion of freedom must not be taken in the sense of the arbitrary caprice of an individual, but in the sense of the rational will, of the will in and for itself. The universal will is not to be looked on as compounded of definitively individual wills, so that these remain absolute; otherwise the saying would be correct: "Where the minority must obey the majority, there is no freedom." The universal will must really be the rational will, even if we are not conscious of the fact; the state is therefore not an association which is decreed by the arbitrary will of individuals. The wrong apprehension of these principles does not concern us. What does concern us is this, that thereby there should come into consciousness as content the sense that man has liberty in his spirit as the altogether absolute, that free-will is the Notion of man. Freedom is just thought itself; he who casts thought aside and speaks of freedom knows not what he is talking of. The unity of thought with itself is freedom, the free will. Thought, as volition merely, is the impulse to abrogate one's subjectivity, the relation to present existence, the realizing of oneself, since in that I am endeavouring to place myself as existent on an equality with myself as thinking. It is only as having the power of thinking that the will is free. The principle of freedom emerged in Rousseau, and gave to man, who apprehends himself as infinite, this infinite strength. This furnishes the transition to the Kantian philosophy, which, theoretically considered, made this principle its foundation; knowledge aimed at freedom, and at a concrete content which it possesses in consciousness.

D

The German Illumination.

The Germans were at this time quietly drifting along in their Leibnitzo-Wolffian philosophy, in its definitions, axioms and proofs. Then they were gradually breathed upon by the spirit of foreign lands, they made acquaintance with all the developments which there came to pass, and took very kindly to the empiricism of Locke; on the other hand they at the same time laid aside metaphysical investigations, turned their attention to the question of how truths can be grasped by the healthy human understanding, and plunged into the *Aufklärung* and into the consideration of the utility of all things—a point of view which they adopted from the French. Utility as the essence of existent things signifies that they are determined as not being in themselves, but for another: this is a necessary moment, but not the only one. The German *Aufklärung* warred against ideas, with the principle of utility as its weapon. Philosophic investigations on this subject had degenerated into a feeble popular treatment of it which was incapable of going deeper; they displayed a rigid pedantry and an earnestness of the understanding, but were unspiritual. The Germans are busy bees who do justice to all nations, they are old-clothesmen for whom anything is good enough, and who carry on their haggling with everyone. Picked up as it was from foreign nations, all this had lost the wit and life, the energy and originality which with the French had made the content to be lost sight of in the form. The Germans, who honestly sift a matter to its root, and who would put rational arguments in the place of wit and vivacity, since wit and vivacity really prove nothing, in this way reached a content which was utterly empty, so much so that nothing could be more wearisome than this profound mode of treatment; such was the case with Eberhard, Tetens, and those like them.

Others, like Nicolai, Sulzer and their fellows, were excellent in their speculations on questions of taste and the liberal sciences; for literature and art were also to flourish among the Germans. But with all this they only arrived at a most trivial treatment of æsthetics—Lessing[1] called it shallow chatter. As a matter of fact, indeed, the poems of Gellert, Weisse and Lessing sank almost, if not quite as much into the same poetic feebleness. Moreover, previous to the philosophy of Kant, the general principle was really the theory of happiness, which we have already met with in the philosophy of the Cyrenaics (Vol. I. p. 477), and the point of view of pleasant or unpleasant sensations held good among the philosophers of that time as an ultimate and essential determination. Of this manner of philosophizing I will quote an example which Nicolai gives in the account of a conversation which he had with Mendelssohn: what is in question is the pleasure in tragic subjects which is held to be awakened even by means of the unpleasant emotions depicted in a tragedy:

HERR MOSES.

"The power of having an inclination for perfections and of shunning imperfections is a reality. Therefore the exercise of this power brings a pleasure with it, which, however, is in nature comparatively less than the displeasure which arises from the contemplation of the object.

I.

Yet even then, when the violence of passion causes us unpleasant sensations, the movement (what else is this movement than the power of loving perfections, &c.?) which it brings with it has still delights for us. It is the

[1] Sämmtliche Schriften, Vol. XXXIX. (Berlin u. Stettin, 1828), pp. 111, 112.

strength of the movement which we enjoy, even in spite of the painful sensations which oppose what is pleasant in the passion, and in a short time obtain the victory.

HERR MOSES.

In a stage play, on the contrary, as the imperfect object is absent, pleasure must gain the upper hand and eclipse the small degree of displeasure.

I.

A passion therefore which is not followed by these results must be altogether pleasant. Of this sort are the imitations of the passions which the tragedy affords."[1]

With such vapid and meaningless drivel they rambled on. In addition to these, the eternity of punishment in hell, the salvation of the heathen, the difference between uprightness and godliness, were philosophic matters on which much labour was expended among the Germans, while the French troubled themselves little about them. Finite determinations were made to hold good against the infinite; against the Trinity it was asserted that One cannot be Three; against original sin, that each must bear his own guilt, must have done his own deeds of himself, and must answer for them; in the same way against redemption, that another cannot take upon himself punishment that is due; against forgiveness of sin, that what is done cannot be rendered undone; to sum up generally, the incommensurability of the human nature with the divine. On the one side we see healthy human understanding, experience, facts of consciousness, but on the other side there was still in vogue the Wolffian metaphysics of the dry, dead understanding; thus we see Mendelssohn take his stand by the healthy human understanding, and make it his rule.

[1] Lessing's Sämmtliche Schriften, Vol. XXIX. pp. 122, 123.

Some movement was brought into this authority, which had settled into perfect peace and security and let no dreams of other matters cross its path, by the chance dispute of Mendelssohn with Jacobi, first as to whether Lessing had been a disciple of Spinoza, and then regarding the doctrines of Spinoza himself. On this occasion it came to light how much Spinoza was really forgotten, and in what horror Spinozism was held. But while Jacobi in this way once more unexpectedly brought to remembrance in connection with Spinozism a quite different content of philosophy, faith, *i.e.* the simply immediate certainty of external, finite things, as well as of the divine (which faith in the divine he called reason) was certainly placed by him, as an independent thinker, in opposition to mediating knowledge, which he apprehended as mere understanding. This continued until Kant gave a new impulse in Germany to philosophy, which had died out in the rest of Europe.

As far as the transition to modern German philosophy is concerned, it is from Hume and Rousseau, as we have said (pp. 369, 374, 402), that it took its start. Descartes opposes extension to thought, as what is simply one with itself. He is charged with dualism, but, like Spinoza and Leibnitz, he did away with the independence of the two sides, and made supreme their unity, God. But, as this unity, God is first of all only the Third; and He is further determined in such a way that no determination pertains to Him. Wolff's understanding of the finite, his school metaphysics generally, his science of the understanding, and his divergence into the observation of nature, after it has grown strong in its conformity with law and in its finite knowledge, turns against the infinite and the concrete determinations of religion, and comes to a standstill with abstractions in his *theologia naturalis;* for the determinate is his domain. But from this time an utterly different point of view is introduced. The infinite is transported into abstraction or incomprehensibility. This is an incomprehensible position to adopt. Nowadays it is looked on as most pious, most justifiable. But as we see the third, the unity of differences, defined as something which cannot be thought or known, this unity is not one of thought, for it is above all thought, and God is not simply thought. Nevertheless this unity is defined as the absolutely concrete, *i.e.* as the unity of thought and Being. Now we have come so far that this unity is a unity simply in thought, and pertaining to consciousness, so that the objectivity of thought—reason—comes forth as One and All. This is dimly conceived by the French. Whether the highest Being, this Being divested of all determination, is elevated above nature, or whether nature or matter is the highest unity, there is always present the establishing of something concrete, which at the same time belongs to thought. Since the liberty of man has been set up as an absolutely ultimate principle, thought itself has been set up as a principle. The principle of liberty is not only in thought but the root of thought; this principle of liberty is also something in itself concrete, at least in principle it is implicitly concrete. Thus far have general culture and philosophic culture advanced. Since what is knowable has now been placed entirely within the sphere of consciousness, and since the liberty of the spirit has been apprehended as absolute, this may be understood to mean that knowledge has entered altogether into the realm of the finite. The standpoint of the finite was at the same time taken as ultimate, and God as a Beyond outside consciousness; duties, rights, knowledge of nature, are finite. Man has thereby formed for himself a kingdom of truth, from which God is excluded; it is the kingdom of finite truth. The form of finitude may here be termed the subjective form; liberty, self-consciousness [Ichheit] of the mind, known as the absolute, is essentially subjective—in fact it is the subjectivity of thought. The more the human reason has grasped itself in itself, the more has it come down from God and the more has it increased the field of the finite. Reason is One and All, which is at the same time the totality of the finite; reason under these conditions is finite knowledge and knowledge of the finite. The question is, since it is this concrete that is established (and not metaphysical abstractions), how it constitutes itself in itself; and then, how it returns to objectivity, or abrogates its subjectivity, *i.e.* how by means of thought God is to be again brought about, who at an earlier time and at the beginning of this period was recognized as alone the true. This is what we have to consider in the last period, in dealing with Kant, Fichte, and Schelling.

SECTION THREE

RECENT GERMAN PHILOSOPHY

IN the philosophy of Kant, Fichte, and Schelling, the revolution to which in Germany mind has in these latter days advanced, was formally thought out and expressed; the sequence of these philosophies shows the course which thought has taken. In this great epoch of the world's history, whose inmost essence is laid hold of in the philosophy of history, two nations only have played a part, the German and the French, and this in spite of their absolute opposition, or rather because they are so opposite. The other nations have taken no real inward part in the same, although politically they have indeed so done, both through their governments and their people. In Germany this principle has burst forth as thought, spirit, Notion; in France, in the form of actuality. In Germany, what there is of actuality comes to us as a force of external circumstances, and as a reaction against the same. The task of modern German philosophy is, however, summed up in taking as its object the unity of thought and Being, which is the fundamental idea of philosophy generally, and comprehending it, that is, in laying hold of the inmost significance of necessity, the Notion (*supra*, p. 360). The philosophy of Kant sets forth, in the first place, the formal aspect of the task, but it has the abstract absoluteness of reason in self-consciousness as its sole result, and, in one respect, it carried with it a certain character of shallowness and want of vigour, in which an attitude of criticism and negativity is retained, and which, as far as any positive element is concerned, adheres to the facts of consciousness and to mere conjecture, while it renounces thought and returns to feeling. On the other hand, however, there sprang from this the philosophy of Fichte, which speculatively grasps the essence of self-consciousness as concrete egoism, but which does not reach beyond this subjective form pertaining to the absolute. From it again comes the philosophy of Schelling, which subsequently rejects Fichte's teaching and sets forth the Idea of the Absolute, the truth in and for itself.

A. JACOBI.

In connection with Kant we must here begin by speaking of Jacobi, whose philosophy is contemporaneous with that of Kant; in both of these the advance beyond the preceding period is very evident. The result in the two cases is much the same, although both the starting point and the method of progression are somewhat different. In Jacobi's case the stimulus was given mainly by French philosophy, with which he was very conversant, and also by German metaphysics, while Kant began rather from the English side, that is, from the scepticism of Hume. Jacobi, in that negative attitude which he preserved as well as Kant, kept before him the objective aspect of the method of knowledge, and specially considered it, for he declared knowledge to be in its content incapable of recognizing the Absolute: the truth must be concrete, present, but not finite. Kant does not consider the content, but took the view of knowledge being subjective; and for this reason he declared it to be incapable of recognizing absolute existence. To Kant knowledge is thus a knowledge of phenomena only, not because the categories are merely limited and finite, but because they are subjective. To Jacobi, on the other hand, the chief point is that the categories are not merely subjective, but that they themselves are conditioned. This is an essential difference between the two points of view, even if they both arrive at the same result.

Friedrich Heinrich Jacobi, born at Düsseldorf in 1743, held office first in the Duchy of Berg, and then in Bavaria. He studied in Geneva and Paris, associating in the former place with Bonnet and in the latter with Diderot. Jacobi was a man of the highest character and culture. He was long occupied with State affairs, and in Düsseldorf he held a public office which was connected with the administration of the finance department in the State. At the time of the French Revolution he was obliged to retire. As a Bavarian official he went to Munich, there became President of the Academy of Sciences in 1804, which office he, however, resigned in 1812; for in the Napoleonic period Protestants were decried as demagogues. He lived at Munich till the end of his life, and died at the same place on the 10th of March, 1819.[1]

In the year 1785, Jacobi published Letters on Spinoza, which were written in 1783, on the occasion of the dispute with Mendelssohn above-mentioned (p. 406); for in none of his writings did Jacobi develop his philosophy systematically, he set it forth in letters only. When Mendelssohn wished to write a life of Lessing, Jacobi sent to ask him if he knew that "Lessing was a Spinozist" (Jacobi's Werke, Vol. IV. Sec. 1, pp. 39, 40). Mendelssohn was displeased at this, and it was the occasion of the correspondence. In the course of the dispute it was made evident that those who held themselves to be professed philosophers and possessed of a monopoly of Lessing's friendship, such as Nicolai, Mendelssohn, &c., knew nothing about Spinozism;

[1] Tenneman's Grundriss von Wendt, § 406, p. 531; Rixner: Handbuch der Geschichte der Philosophie, Vol. III. § 145, p. 317; Jacobi's Werke, Vol. IV. Sec. 1, p. 3.

not only was there manifested in them the superficial character of their philosophic insight, but ignorance as well; with Mendelssohn, for instance, this was shown respecting even the outward history of the Spinozistic philosophy, and much more regarding the inward (Jacobi's Werke, Vol. IV. Sec. 1, p. 91). That Jacobi asserted Lessing to be a Spinozist, and gave a high place to the French—this serious statement came to these good men as a thunderbolt from the blue. They—the self-satisfied, self-possessed, superior persons—were quite surprised that he also made pretensions to knowledge, and of such a "dead dog" as Spinoza (*ibidem*, p. 68). Explanations followed upon this, in which Jacobi further developed his philosophic views.

Mendelssohn is directly opposed to Jacobi, for Mendelssohn took his stand on cognition, placed true existence immediately in thought and conception, and maintained: "What I cannot think as true does not trouble me as doubt. A question which I do not understand, I cannot answer, it is for me as good as no question at all."[1] He continued to argue on these same lines. His proof of the existence of God thus carries with it this necessity of thought, viz that actuality must plainly be in thought, and a thinker must be pre-supposed, or the possibility of the actual is in the thinker. "What no thinking Being conceives as possible is not possible, and what is thought by no thinking creature as actual cannot be actual in fact. If we take away from anything whatsoever the conception formed by a thinking Being that that thing is possible or actual, the thing itself is done away with." The Notion of the thing is thus to man the essence of the same. "No finite Being can think the actuality of a thing in its perfection as actual, and still less can he perceive the possibility and actuality of all present things. There must thus be a thinking Being or an

[1] Jacobi Briefe uber die Lehre des Spinoza (second edition, 1789), pp. 85, 86 (Werke, Vol. IV. Sec. 1, p. 110).

understanding which in the most perfect way thinks the content of all possibilities as possible, and the content of all actualities as actual; *i.e.* there must be an infinite understanding, and this is God."[1] Here on the one hand we see a unity of thought and Being, on the other the absolute unity as infinite understanding—the former is the self-consciousness which is apprehended as finite merely. Actuality, Being, has its possibility in thought, or its possibility is thought; it is not a process from possibility to actuality, for the possibility remains at home in the actuality.

Jacobi maintains against these demands of thought—and this in one view is the chief thought in his philosophy—that every method of their demonstration leads to fatalism, atheism, and Spinozism,[2] and presents God as derived and founded upon something else; for comprehending Him signifies demonstrating His dependence. Jacobi thus asserts that mediate knowledge consists in giving a cause of something which has in its turn a finite effect, and so on; so that a knowledge such as this can all through relate to the finite only.

Jacobi further states upon this subject, in the first place, that "Reason"—later on when he distinguished reason and understanding (of which more hereafter[3]), he altered it to understanding[4]—"can never bring to light more than the conditions of what is conditioned, natural laws and mechanism. We comprehend a thing when we can deduce it from its proximate causes," and not from the remoter causes; the most remote and quite universal cause is always God. "Or" we know the thing if

[1] Buhle: Lehrbuch der Geschichte der Philosophie, Part VIII. pp. 386, 387; Mendelssohn's Morgenstunden (second edition, 1786), pp. 293-296.

[2] Jacobi: Briefe über die Lehre des Spinoza, IV. Prop. pp. 225, 223 (pp. 223, 216).

[3] *Infra*, pp. 418, 419.

[4] Jacobi's Werke, Vol. II. pp. 7 *seq.*; p. 221, note.

we "perceive its immediate conditions as they come in due succession. Thus, for instance, we comprehend a circle when we can clearly represent to ourselves the mechanism of its origination or its physical conditions; we know the syllogistic formulæ when we have actually come to know the laws to which the human understanding is subject in judgment and conclusion, its physical nature and its mechanism. For this reason we have no conceptions of qualities as such, but only intuitions. Even of our present existence we have a feeling only, but no conceptions. Genuine conceptions we have merely of figure, number, position, movement and the forms of thought; qualities are known and understood, if they are traced back to these and objectively annulled." This is undoubtedly really finite knowledge, which is to give the determinate conditions of anything determinate, to demonstrate it as resulting from another cause, in such a way that each condition is again conditioned and finite. Jacobi continues: "The business of reason is really progressive union and connection, and its speculative business is union and connection in accordance with the known laws of necessity, *i.e.* of identity. Everything that reason can bring forth by means of analysis, combination, judgment, conclusion, and re-conception, consists in nothing but things of nature" (*i.e.* finite things), "and reason itself, as a limited existence, belongs to these things. But the whole of nature, the sum of all conditioned existence, cannot reveal more to the investigating understanding than what is contained in it, namely, manifold existence, changes, a succession of forms" (the conditioned), "and not an actual beginning" (of the world), "nor a real principle of any objective existence." [1]

But Jacobi in the second place here accepts reason in a wider sense and says: "If we understand by reason the

[1] Jacobi: Briefe über die Lehre des Spinoza, supplement vii. pp. 419-421, and note (Werke, Vol. IV. Sec. 2, pp. 149-151).

principle of knowledge generally, it is the mind from which the whole living nature of man is constituted; through it man arises; he is a form which it has adopted." With this Jacobi's view of the attempt to know the unconditioned is connected. "I take the whole human being, and find that his consciousness is composed of two original conceptions, the conceptions of the conditioned and the unconditioned. Both are inseparably bound up with one another, and yet in such a way that the conception of the conditioned presupposes the conception of the unconditioned, and can be given in this alone. We are just as certain of its existence as we are of our own conditioned existence, or even more so. Since our conditioned existence rests on an infinitude of mediations, there is opened up to our investigation a vast field which, for the sake of our preservation even, we are forced to work upon." It would, however, be quite another thing to wish to know the unconditioned apart from this practical end. However Jacobi here remarks, "To try to discover the conditions of the unconditioned, to find a possibility for absolute necessity, and to construct this last in order to be able to comprehend it, is what we undertake when we endeavour to make nature an existence comprehensible to us, *i.e.* a merely natural existence, and to bring the mechanism of the principle of mechanism into the light of day. For if everything which can be said to arise and be present in a way comprehensible to us, must arise and be present in a conditioned way, we remain, so long as we continue to comprehend, in a chain of conditioned conditions. Where this chain breaks off, we cease to comprehend, and there the connection which we call nature likewise ceases. The conception of the possibility of the outward existence of nature would thus be the conception of an absolute beginning or origin of nature; it would be the conception of the unconditioned itself in so far as it is a conditioning of nature not naturally connected, *i.e.* a conditioning of nature unconnected and unconditioned for us. Now should a conception of what is thus unconditioned and unconnected, and consequently supernatural, be possible, the unconditioned must cease to be unconditioned, it must itself receive conditions; and absolute necessity must commence to be possibility in order that it may allow itself to be constructed."[1] This is contradictory.

Jacobi then passes on from this point to the second of his main propositions, "The unconditioned is called the supernatural. Now since everything which lies outside the connection of what is conditioned, of what is naturally mediated, also lies outside the sphere of our clear and certain knowledge, and cannot be understood through conceptions, the supernatural cannot be accepted in any other way by us than that in which it is given to us—namely as a fact. It is! This supernatural, this essence of all essence, all tongues join in proclaiming to be God."[2] God as the universal, the true, is here taken in the sense of a spiritual generally, in the sense of power, wisdom, &c. That God is, however, is to Jacobi not absolutely true; for to knowledge pertains His objective absolute existence, but He cannot be said to be known. It is thus merely a fact of my consciousness that God exists independently apart from my consciousness; this, however, is itself maintained through my consciousness; the subjective attitude of thought is thus to Jacobi the element of most importance. The consciousness of God, which is in our consciousness, is, however, of such a nature that along with the thought of God we have immediately associated the fact that He is. The existence of the supernatural and super-sensuous, to which the thought of man regarding the natural and finite passes on, is just as certain to Jacobi as he is himself. This certainty is identical with his self-consciousness; as certainly as I am, so

[1] Jacobi: Briefe über die Lehre des Spinoza, supplement vii. pp. 422-426 (pp. 151-155).

[2] Ibidem, pp. 426, 427 (pp. 155, 156).

certainly is God (Jacobi's Werke, Vol. III. p. 35). Since he thus passes back into self-consciousness, the unconditioned is only for us in an immediate way; this immediate knowledge Jacobi calls Faith, inward revelation (Werke, Vol. II. pp. 3, 4); to this appeal can be made in man. God, the absolute, the unconditioned, cannot, according to Jacobi, be proved. For proof, comprehension, means to discover conditions for something, to derive it from conditions; but a derived absolute, God, &c., would thus not be absolute at all, would not be unconditioned, would not be God (Jacobi's Werke, Vol. III. p. 7). This immediate knowledge of God is then the point which is maintained in the philosophy of Jacobi. The faith of Kant and of Jacobi are, however, different. To Kant it is a postulate of reason, it is the demand for the solution of the contradiction between the world and goodness; to Jacobi it is represented on its own account as immediate knowledge.

Everything which has been written upon God since Jacobi's time, by philosophers such as Fries and by theologians, rests on this conception of immediate intellectual knowledge, and men even call this revelation, though in another sense than the revelation of theology. Revelation as immediate knowledge is in ourselves, while the Church holds revelation to be something imparted from without.[1] In the theological sense, faith is faith in something which is given to us through teaching. It is a sort of deception when faith and revelation are spoken of and represented as if faith and revelation in the theological sense were here in question; for the sense in which they are used, and which may be termed philosophic, is quite a different one, however pious an air may be assumed in using the terms. This is Jacobi's standpoint, and whatever is by philosophers and theologians said against it, this teaching is eagerly accepted and disseminated. And nowhere is there anything to be found but

[1] Cf. Jacobi's Werke, Vol. III. p. 277.

reflections originating from Jacobi, whereby immediate knowledge is opposed to philosophic knowledge and to reason; and people speak of reason, philosophy, &c., as a blind man speaks of colours. It is, indeed, allowed that a man cannot make shoes unless he is a shoemaker, even although he have the measure and foot, and also the hands. But when Philosophy is concerned, immediate knowledge signifies that every man as he walks and stands is a philosopher, that he can dogmatize as he chooses, and that he is completely acquainted with Philosophy.

By reason, however, mediate knowledge merely is on the one hand understood, and on the other the intellectual perception which speaks of facts (*supra*, pp. 413-415). In this respect it is true that reason is the knowledge and revelation of absolute truth, since the understanding is the revelation of the finite (Jacobi's Werke, Vol. II. pp. 8-14, 101). "We maintained that two different powers of perception in man have to be accepted: a power of perception through visible and tangible and consequently corporeal organs of perception, and another kind of power, viz. through an invisible organ which in no way represents itself to the outward senses, and whose existence is made known to us through feeling alone. This organ, a spiritual eye for spiritual objects, has been called by men—generally speaking—reason. He whom the pure feelings of the beautiful and good, of admiration and love, of respect and awe, do not convince that in and with these feelings he perceives something to be present which is independent of them, and which is unattainable by the outward senses or by an understanding directed upon their perceptions alone—such an one cannot be argued with" (Jacobi's Werke, Vol. II. pp. 74, 76). But by faith Jacobi likewise understands all that has immediacy of Being for me: "Through faith we know that we have a body, we become aware of other actual things, and that indeed with the same certainty with which we are aware of ourselves. We obtain all conceptions through the qualities which we receive and accept, and there is no other way of attaining real knowledge; for reason, when it begets objects, begets phantoms of the brain. Thus we have a revelation of nature."[1] Hence the expression faith, which had a deep significance in religion, is made use of for different contents of every kind; this in our own time is the point of view most commonly adopted.

Jacobi here brings faith into opposition with thought. Let us compare the two, and discover whether they are separated by so great a chasm as those who thus oppose them think. On the one hand absolute existence is to faith immediate; believing consciousness feels itself penetrated by this as by its essence: that existence is its life, believing consciousness asserts itself to be in direct unity with it. Thought thinks the absolute existence; such existence is to it absolute thought, absolute understanding, pure thought; but that signifies that it is likewise immediate itself. On the other hand to faith the immediacy of absolute existence has also the significance of a Being: it *is*, and is another than 'I.' And the same is true of the thinker; to him it is absolute Being, actual in itself, and different from self-consciousness or thought as finite understanding, to use the common term. Now what is the reason that faith and thought do not understand one another, and each recognize itself in the other? In the first place faith has no consciousness of being a thought, inasmuch as it asserts absolute consciousness to be identical with it as self-consciousness, and has direct inward knowledge of the same. But it expresses this simple unity; in its consciousness it is only immediacy so to speak in the signification of Being, a unity of its unconscious substance. In the second place Being-for-self is contained in thought; to this faith opposes the immediacy of Being. Thought, on the contrary, has the immediate as absolute potentiality, as

[1] Jacobi: Briefe über die Lehre des Spinoza, pp. 216, 217 (p. 211).

absolutely a thing of thought: and the immediacy belonging to this thing of thought is without the determination of Being, of life. On the heights of this abstraction the two stand opposed to each other, as the *Aufklärung* which asserts absolute existence to be a Beyond of self-consciousness, and as the materialism which makes it so to speak present matter (*supra*, pp. 382, 383). In the one case it is in faith and thought as positive existence or thought, and in the other it is the negative of self-consciousness, which is thus either only determined as negative, as a Beyond, or likewise as existent for self-consciousness. Hence faith and thought are both of them knowledge. We call universal knowledge thought, particular knowledge we call sensuous perception; and we term the introduction of external determinations understanding. The universal element in man is thought, but to it likewise appertains religious feeling for instance; the animal does not possess it, for it has no human feeling; and in so far as this feeling is religious, it is the feeling of a thinker, and what determines this feeling is not the determination of natural desire, &c., but a universal determination. Thus God, even though He is only felt and believed in, is yet the universal taken quite abstractly—even in His personality He is the absolutely universal personality.

As thought and faith are thus one, the same is true of the antithesis between mediated and immediate knowledge. We must, it is true, keep before our eyes the fact that what is revealed in immediate knowledge is the universal. But abstract immediate knowledge is natural, sensuous knowledge; the immediate man in his natural condition, in his desires, does not know this universal. Children, the Esquimaux, &c., know nothing of God; or what the natural man knows of Him is not a real knowledge of Him. Thus the intuitive knowledge of the Egyptians told them that God was an ox or a cat, and the Indians still possess similar sorts of knowledge. On the other hand when man has come so far as to know God as merely an object of the mind, *i.e.* as spiritual, it is easy to perceive that this knowledge which is asserted to be immediate is really a result mediated through instruction, through a long continued culture. It is only by means of being elevated above nature that man arrives at a consciousness of what is higher, and at a knowledge of the universal; there indeed his knowledge is immediate, but he has only arrived at this through mediation. I think, and thus I know the universal immediately, but this very thought is just process in itself, movement and life. All life is process within itself, is mediated, and this is all the more true of spiritual life; for it is the passing from one to the other, that is, from the merely natural and sensuous to the spiritual. It thus indicates a deficiency in the most simple reflection not to know that the universal is not in immediate knowledge, but is a result of the culture, the education, and the self-revelation of the human race. If immediate knowledge is to be allowed, everyone will be responsible merely to himself: this man knows this, another that, and consequently everything is justified and approved, however contrary to right and religion. This opposition between immediacy and mediacy is thus a very barren and quite empty determination; it is a platitude of the extremest type to consider anything like this to be a true opposition; it proceeds from a most wooden understanding, which thinks that an immediacy can be something on its own account, without a mediation within itself. If Philosophy were to result in this it would be a poor affair; these determinations are merely forms, none of which has intrinsic truth. The form into which Philosophy has in Jacobi's case finally fallen, which is that immediacy is grasped as absolute, manifests a lack of all critical faculty, of all logic. The Kantian philosophy is critical philosophy, but from it the fact has been omitted that we cannot constitute the infinite with finite categories—and immediacy is such an one. When we regard this opposition more closely all knowledge may be termed immediate, but all immediate knowledge is likewise mediated in itself. This we know within our consciousness, and we may see it in the most general phenomena. I know, for example, of America immediately, and yet this knowledge is very much mediated. If I stand in America and see its soil, I must first of all have journeyed to it, Columbus must first have discovered it, ships must have been built, &c.; all these discoveries and inventions pertain to it. That which we now know immediately is consequently a result of infinitely many mediations. Likewise when I see a right-angled triangle I know that the squares of the two sides are equal to the square of the hypotenuse: I know this immediately, and yet I have merely learned it and am convinced of it through the mediation of proof. Immediate knowledge is thus everywhere mediated; and Philosophy does nothing but bring this to consciousness—demonstrating the mediation which in point of fact is already present there, *e.g.* in religion, &c.

The philosophy of Jacobi, inasmuch as it says: "Thought cannot proceed further than to the feeling of God," has been accepted *utiliter*; it was more easily arrived at than in the case of Kant. Knowledge, however, is something very different from what Jacobi calls such; against finite knowledge his arguments are quite correct. Immediate knowledge is not knowledge, comprehension, for that implies that the content is determined in itself, *i.e.* is grasped as concrete. But in immediate knowledge it is the case that the only fact known of God is that He exists. For should there be determinations respecting God, they must, according to Jacobi, be grasped as a finite, and the knowledge of them would again merely be a progression from finite to finite. There thus remains only the indeterminate conception of God, an "Above me," an indeterminate Beyond. This gives accordingly the same result as does the *Aufklärung*, viz. that the highest reality is ultimate:

we find the same in French philosophy and in Kant—only here we still have the opinion that this emptiness is the highest philosophy possible. But if each standpoint has an aspect wherein it is justified, there always rests in the proposition that the human mind knows God immediately, the important consideration that we have here a recognition of the freedom of the human spirit: in it we have the source of the knowledge of God, and all externality of authority is thus abrogated in this principle. The principle is hereby gained, but only the principle of freedom of spirit; and the greatness of our time rests in the fact that freedom, the peculiar possession of mind whereby it is at home with itself in itself, is recognized, and that mind has this consciousness within itself. This however is merely abstract, for the next step is that the principle of freedom is again purified and comes to its true objectivity, so that not everything which strikes me or springs up within me must, because it is manifested in me, hold good as true. It is only through thought, which casts off the particular and accidental, that the principle receives this objectivity which is independent of mere subjectivity and in and for itself—though in such a way that the freedom of mind still remains respected. One's own spirit must bear witness to spirit that God is Spirit; the content must be true. But this does not give authenticity to itself by its being revealed with certainty to me. This is the standpoint, and we have thus seen its deficiency and the greatness of the principle which is involved in it.

B. Kant.

The philosophy of Kant, which we have now more parcularly to consider, made its appearance at the same time as the above. While Descartes asserted certainty to be the unity of thought and Being, we now have the consciousness of thought in its subjectivity, *i.e.* in the first place, as determinateness in contrast with objectivity, and then as finitude and progression in finite determinations. Abstract thought as personal conviction is that which is maintained as certain; its contents are experience, but the methods adopted by experience are once more formal thought and argument. Kant turns back to the standpoint of Socrates; we see in him the freedom of the subject as we saw it with the Stoics, but the task in respect of content is now placed on a higher level. An endless aiming at the concrete is required for thought, a filling up in accordance with the rule which completion prescribes, which signifies that the content is itself the Idea as the unity of the Notion and reality. With Jacobi thought, demonstration, does not in the first place reach beyond the finite and conditioned, and in the second place, even when God is likewise the metaphysical object, the demonstration is really the making Him conditioned and finite; in the third place the unconditioned, what is then immediately certain, only exists in faith, a subjectively fixed point of view but an unknowable one, that is to say an undetermined, indeterminable, and consequently an unfruitful one. The standpoint of the philosophy of Kant, on the contrary, is in the first place to be found in the fact that thought has through its reasoning got so far as to grasp itself not as contingent but rather as in itself the absolute ultimate. In the finite, in connection with the finite, an absolute standpoint is raised which acts as a connecting bond; it binds together the finite and leads up to the infinite. Thought grasped itself as all in all, as absolute in judgment; for it nothing external is authoritative, since all authority can receive validity only through thought. This thought, determining itself within itself and concrete, is, however, in the second place, grasped as subjective, and this aspect of subjectivity is the form which from Jacobi's point of view is predominant; the fact that thought is concrete Jacobi has on the other hand for the most part set aside. Both standpoints remain philosophies of subjectivity; since thought is subjective, the capacity of knowing the absolute is denied to it. To Kant God cannot on the one hand be found in experience; He can neither be found in outward experience—as Lalande discovered when he swept the whole heavens and found no God—nor can He be discovered within; though no doubt mystics and enthusiasts can experience many things in themselves, and amongst these God, *i.e.* the Infinite. On the other hand Kant argues to prove the existence of God, who is to him an hypothesis necessary for the explanation of things, a postulate of practical reason. But in this connection another French astronomer made the following reply to the Emperor Napoleon: "*Je n'ai pas eu besoin de cette hypothèse.*" According to this the truth underlying the Kantian philosophy is the recognition of freedom. Even Rousseau represented the absolute to be found in freedom; Kant has the same principle, but taken rather from the theoretic side. The French regard it from the side of will, which is represented in their proverb: "*Il a la tête près du bonnet.*" France possesses the sense of actuality, of promptitude; because in that country conception passes more immediately into action, men have there applied themselves more practically to the affairs of actuality. But however much freedom may be in itself concrete, it was as undeveloped and in its abstraction that it was there applied to actuality; and to make abstractions hold good in actuality means to destroy actuality. The fanaticism which characterized the freedom which was put into the hands of the people was frightful. In Germany the same principle asserted the rights of consciousness on its own account, but it has been worked out in a merely theoretic way. We have commotions of every kind within us and around us, but through them all the German head quietly keeps its nightcap on and silently carries on its operations beneath it.

Immanuel Kant was born at Königsberg in 1724, and there studied theology to begin with; in the year 1755 he entered upon his work as an academic teacher; in 1770 he became professor of logic, and in 1804 he died at Königsberg on the 12th of February, having almost attained his eightieth year (Tennemann's Grundriss der Geschichte der Philosophie by Wendt, § 380, pp. 465, 466), without ever having left his native town.

While to Wolff thought as thought was merely positive self-identity and grasped itself as such, we saw the negative self-moving thought, the absolute Notion, appear in all its power in France; and in the *Aufklärung* it likewise made its way to Germany in such a manner that all existence, all action, was called upon to serve a useful purpose, *i.e.* the implicit was done away with and everything had to be for another; and that for which everything had to be is man, self-consciousness, taken, however, as signifying all men generally. The consciousness of this action in abstract form is the Kantian philosophy. It is thus the self-thinking absolute Notion that passes into itself which we see making its appearance in Germany through this philosophy, in such a way that all reality falls within self-consciousness; it is the idealism which vindicates all moments of the implicit to self-consciousness, but which at first itself remains subject to a contradiction, inasmuch as it still separates this implicit from itself. In other words the Kantian philosophy no doubt leads reality back to self-consciousness, but it can supply no reality to this essence of self-consciousness, or to this pure self-consciousness, nor can it demonstrate Being in the same. It apprehends simple thought as having difference in itself, but does not yet apprehend that all reality rests on this difference; it does not know how to obtain mastery over the individuality of self-consciousness, and although it describes reason very well, it does this in an unthinking empiric way which again robs it of the truth it has. Theoretically the Kantian philosophy is the "Illumination" or *Aufklärung* reduced to method; it states that nothing true can be known, but only the phenomenal; it leads knowledge into consciousness and self-consciousness, but from this standpoint maintains it to be a subjective and finite knowledge. Thus although it deals with the infinite Idea, expressing its formal categories and arriving at its concrete claims, it yet again denies this to be the truth, making it a simple subjective, because it has once for all accepted finite knowledge as the fixed and ultimate standpoint. This philosophy made an end of the metaphysic of the understanding as an objective dogmatism, but in fact it merely transformed it into a subjective dogmatism, *i.e.* into a consciousness in which these same finite determinations of the understanding persist, and the question of what is true in and for itself has been abandoned. Its study is made difficult by its diffuseness and prolixity, and by the peculiar terminology found in it. Nevertheless this diffuseness has one advantage, that inasmuch as the same thing is often repeated, the main points are kept before us, and these cannot easily be lost from view.

We shall endeavour to trace the lines which Kant pursued. The philosophy of Kant has in the first place a direct relation to that of Hume as stated above (p. 370). That is to say, the significance of the Kantian philosophy, generally expressed, is from the very beginning to allow that determinations such as those of universality and necessity are not to be met with in perception, and this Hume has already shown in relation to Locke. But while Hume attacks the universality and necessity of the categories generally, and Jacobi their finitude, Kant merely argues against their objectivity in so far as they are present in external things themselves, while maintaining them to be objective in the sense of holding good as universal and necessary, as they do, for instance, in mathematics and natural science.[1] The fact that we crave for universality

[1] Kant: Kritik der reinen Vernunft (sixth edition, Leipzig, 1818), pp. 4, 11, 13, 93.

and necessity as that which first constitutes the objective, Kant thus undoubtedly allows. But if universality and necessity do not exist in external things, the question arises "Where are they to be found?" To this Kant, as against Hume, maintains that they must be *a priori*, *i.e.* that they must rest on reason itself, and on thought as self-conscious reason; their source is the subject, "I" in my self-consciousness.[1] This, simply expressed, is the main point in the Kantian philosophy.

In the second place the philosophy of Kant is likewise called a critical philosophy because its aim, says Kant, is first of all to supply a criticism of our faculties of knowledge; for before obtaining knowledge we must inquire into the faculties of knowledge. To the healthy human understanding that is plausible, and to it this has been a great discovery. Knowledge is thereby represented as an instrument, as a method and means whereby we endeavour to possess ourselves of the truth. Thus before men can make their way to the truth itself they must know the nature and function of their instrument. They must see whether it is capable of supplying what is demanded of it—of seizing upon the object; they must know what the alterations it makes in the object are, in order that these alterations may not be mixed up with the determinations of the object itself.[2] This would appear as though men could set forth upon the search for truth with spears and staves. And a further claim is made when it is said that we must know the faculty of knowledge before we can know. For to investigate the faculties of knowledge means to know them; but how we are to know without knowing, how we are to apprehend the truth before the truth, it is impossible to say. It is the old story of the σχολαστικός who would not go into the water till he could swim. Thus

[1] Kant: Kritik der reinen Vernunft, pp. 3–5.

[2] Ibidem, Preface, pp. xviii., xix.

since the investigation of the faculties of knowledge is itself knowing, it cannot in Kant attain to what it aims at because it is that already—it cannot come to itself because it is already with itself; the same thing happens as happened with the Jews, the Spirit passes through the midst of them and they know it not. At the same time the step taken by Kant is a great and important one—that is, the fact that he has made knowledge the subject of his consideration.

On the one hand this critique of knowledge applies to the empirical knowledge of Locke, which asserts itself to be grounded on experience, and, on the other hand, it also deals with what claims to be on the whole a more metaphysical kind of philosophy—the Wolffian and German—which had also taken up the line of proceeding on the more empiric method which has been depicted. But this last has at the same time kept itself separate from the merely empiric method, inasmuch as its main efforts have been directed towards making such categories of thought as those of potentiality, actuality, God, &c., have as their foundation categories of the understanding, and then reasoning from them. The Kantian philosophy is in the first instance directed against both. Kant takes away the objective significance of the determinations of the Wolffian metaphysics, and shows how they must be ascribed to subjective thought alone. At the same time Jacobi likewise declared himself against this metaphysic, but since he started more especially from the standpoint of the French and Germans, his point of view was different: he asserts that our finite thought can set forth finite determinations alone, and thus can only consider God and Spirit in accordance with finite relationships. On the practical side there reigned at that time the so-called happiness theory, since man's inherent Notion and the way to realize this Notion was apprehended in morality as a satisfaction of his desires. As against this Kant has very rightly shown that it involves a heteronomy and not an autonomy of reason—a determination through nature and consequently an absence of freedom. But because the rational principle of Kant was formal, and his successors could not make any further progress with reason, and yet morality had to receive a content, Fries and others must still be called Hedonists though they avoid giving themselves the name.

In the third place, as regards the relation of the categories to the material which is given through experience, there is according to Kant already inherent in the subjective determinations of thought, *e.g.* in those of cause and effect, the capacity of themselves to bind together the differences which are present in that material. Kant considers thought as in great measure a synthetic activity, and hence he represents the main question of Philosophy to be this, "How are synthetic judgments *a priori* possible?"[1] Judgment signifies the combination of thought-determinations as subject and predicate. Synthetic judgments *a priori* are nothing else than a connection of opposites through themselves, or the absolute Notion, *i.e.* the relations of different determinations such as those of cause and effect, given not through experience but through thought. Space and time likewise form the connecting element; they are thus *a priori*, *i.e.* in self-consciousness. Since Kant shows that thought has synthetic judgments *a priori* which are not derived from perception, he shows that thought is so to speak concrete in itself. The idea which is present here is a great one, but, on the other hand, quite an ordinary signification is given it, for it is worked out from points of view which are inherently rude and empirical, and a scientific form is the last thing that can be claimed for it. In the presentation of it there is a lack of philosophical abstraction, and it is expressed in the most commonplace way; to say nothing more of the

[1] Kant: Kritik der reinen Vernunft, pp. 8, 9, 75, 77, 15.

barbarous terminology, Kant remains restricted and confined by his psychological point of view and empirical methods.

To mention one example only of his barbarous expressions, Kant calls his philosophy (Kritik der reinen Vernunft, p. 19) a Transcendental philosophy, *i.e.* a system of principles of pure reason which demonstrate the universal and necessary elements in the self-conscious understanding, without occupying themselves with objects or inquiring what universality and necessity are; this last would be transcendent. Transcendent and transcendental have accordingly to be clearly distinguished. Transcendent mathematics signifies the mathematics in which the determination of infinitude is made use of in a pre-eminent degree: in this sphere of mathematics we say, for instance, that the circle consists of an infinitude of straight lines; the periphery is represented as straight, and since the curve is represented as straight this passes beyond the geometric category and is consequently transcendent. Kant, on the contrary, defines the transcendental philosophy as not a philosophy which by means of categories passes beyond its own sphere, but one which points out in subjective thought, in consciousness, the sources of what may become transcendent. Thought would thus be transcendent if the categories of universality, of cause and effect, were predicated of the object, for in this way men would from the subjective element 'transcend' into another sphere. We are not justified in so doing as regards the result nor even to begin with, since we merely contemplate thought within thought itself. Thus we do not desire to consider the categories in their objective sense, but in so far as thought is the source of such synthetic relationships; the necessary and universal thus here receive the significance of resting in our faculties of knowledge. But from this faculty of knowledge Kant still separates the implicit, the thing-in-itself, so that the universality and necessity are all the time a subjective conditionment of knowledge merely, and reason with its universality and necessity does not attain to a knowledge of the truth.[1] For it requires perception and experience, a material empirically given in order, as subjectivity, to attain to knowledge. As Kant says, these form its "constituent parts"; one part it has in itself, but the other is empirically given.[2] When reason desires to be independent, to exist in itself and to derive truth from itself, it becomes transcendent; it transcends experience because it lacks the other constituent, and then creates mere hallucinations of the brain. It is hence not constitutive in knowledge but only regulative; it is the unity and rule for the sensuous manifold. But this unity on its own account is the unconditioned, which, transcending experience, merely arrives at contradictions. In the practical sphere alone is reason constitutive. The critique of reason is consequently not the knowing of objects, but of knowledge and its principles, its range and limitations, so that it does not become transcendent.[3] This is an extremely general account of what we shall now consider in its separate details.

In dealing with this matter Kant adopts the plan of first considering theoretic reason, the knowledge which relates to outward objects. In the second place he investigates the will as self-actualization; and, in the third place, the faculty of judgment, the special consideration of the unity of the universal and individual; how far he gets in this matter we shall likewise see. But the critique of the faculty of knowledge is the matter of main importance.

1. In the first place, as to the theoretic philosophy, Kant in the Critique of Pure Reason sets to work in a psychological manner, *i.e.* historically, inasmuch as he describes

[1] Kant: Kritik der reinen Vernunft, pp. 255, 256.

[2] Ibidem, p. 107.

[3] Ibidem, pp. 497, 498; Kritik der prakt. Vernunft (fourth edition, Riga, 1797), p. 254; Kritik der Urtheilskraft (third edition, Berlin, 1799), Preface, p. v.

the main stages in theoretic consciousness. The first faculty is sensuousness generally, the second understanding, the third reason. All this he simply narrates; he accepts it quite empirically, without developing it from the Notion or proceeding by necessity.

a. The *a priori* fact of sensuous existence, the forms of sensuous existence, constitute the beginning of this transcendentalism. Kant calls the judgment of the same the transcendental æsthetic. Nowadays æsthetic signifies the knowledge of the beautiful. But here the doctrine of intuition or perception is taken from the point of view of its universality, *i.e.* from what in it pertains to the subject as such. Perception, says Kant, is the knowledge of an object given to us through the senses; sensuousness, however, is the capacity of being affected by conceptions as external. Now, according to Kant, in perception there are to be found all manner of contents, and in dealing with this he first of all distinguishes feeling as external, such as redness, colour, hardness, &c., and then as internal, such as justice, wrath, love, fear, pleasurable and religious feelings, &c. He says content such as this forms the one constituent and pertains to feeling; all this is subjective and merely subjective. In this sensuous element there is, however, a universal sensuous element likewise contained, which as such does not belong to feeling in so far as it is immediately determined; in such a content this 'other' consists in the categories of space and time, which of themselves are void and empty. The filling in is performed by the content, by colour, softness, hardness, &c., as regards space; while as regards time, the same content, so soon as it is something transient, or again some other content, and in particular inward feelings are what causes the determination. Space and time are consequently pure, *i.e.* abstract perceptions in which we place outside of us the content of individual sensations, either in time as succeeding one another, or in space as separate from one another. Here we thus meet with the division between subjectivity and objectivity, for if we isolate the 'alongside of' and 'after' we have space and time. It is the act of *a priori* sensuousness to project the content; the forms of intuition or perception constitute this pure perception.[1] Now everything indeed is termed perception, even thought and consciousness; God, who certainly pertains to thought alone, is said to be comprehended by perception or intuition, the so-called immediate consciousness.

Kant further remarks in this regard, (1) "Space is no empirical Notion which has been derived from outward experiences." But the Notion is never really anything empiric: it is in barbarous forms like this that Kant, however, always expresses himself: "For in order that I may relate my sensations to something outside of me, I must presuppose space." Of time Kant speaks in similar terms: "In order that something outside of me may be represented in separate space or time, the conception of space and time must come first, or it cannot be derived from experience, for experience first becomes possible through this antecedent conception." That is to say, time and space which may appear as objective, since their particular filling in certainly belongs to subjective feeling, are not empirical; for consciousness has time and space first of all in itself." (2) "Space is a necessary conception which lies at the basis of all external perceptions. Space and time are conceptions *a priori*, because we cannot represent things without space and time. Time is a necessary basis for all phenomena." As *a priori*, space and time are universal and necessary, that is to say we find this to be the case; but it does not follow that they must be previously present as conceptions. They are fundamental indeed, but they are likewise an external universal. Kant however places the matter somewhat in this fashion: there

[1] Kant: Kritik der reinen Vernunft, pp. 25-27.

are things-in-themselves outside, but devoid of time and space; consciousness now comes, and it has time and space beforehand present in it as the possibility of experience, just as in order to eat it has mouth and teeth, &c, as conditions necessary for eating. The things which are eaten have not the mouth and teeth, and as eating is brought to bear on things, so space and time are also brought to bear on them; just as things are placed in the mouth and between the teeth, so is it with space and time. (3) "Space and time are not general Notions of the relations of things, but pure intuitive perceptions. For we can only represent to ourselves one space; there are not different component parts of space." The same is the case with time. The abstract conception tree, for example, is in its actuality a number of individual and separate trees, but spaces are not such particulars, nor are they parts; for one immediate continuity remains, and hence a simple unity. Ordinary perception has always something individual before it; space or time are always however one only, and therefore *a priori.* It might however be replied to Kant: The nature of space and time undoubtedly involves their being an abstract universal; but there is in like manner only one blue. (4) "Each Notion or conception certainly comprises an infinite number of conceptions under itself, but not within itself; nevertheless this last is the case in space and time, and they are therefore intuitive perceptions and not Notions or conceptions."[1] Space and time, then, are certainly not thought-determinations, if no thoughts are there present, but a Notion, so soon as we have a Notion of them.

From the transcendental point of view it is likewise maintained that this conception of space and time contains synthetic propositions *a priori*, connected with the consciousness of its necessity. Examples of these synthetic propositions are sought in statements such as that of space

[1] Kant: Kritik der reinen Vernunft, pp. 29, 30; 34-36.

having three dimensions, or in the definition of a straight line, that it is the shortest distance between two points, and likewise in the statement that 5 + 7=12.[1] All these propositions are however very analytic. Kant nevertheless in the first place holds that such propositions do not take their rise from experience, or, as we might better express it, are not an individual contingent perception; this is very true, the perception is universal and necessary. In the second place he states that we acquire them from pure sensuous perception, and not through the understanding or Notion. But Kant does not grasp the two together, and yet this comprehension of them is involved in such propositions being immediately certain even in ordinary perception. When Kant then expresses himself (Kritik der reinen Vernunft, p. 49) to the effect that we have many sensations which constitute "the real matter," with which we externally and inwardly "occupy our minds," and that the mind has in itself in space and time "formal conditions of the mode in which we place them" (those manifold feelings) "in our mind," the question of how mind arrives at having just these special forms now forces itself upon us. But what the nature of time and space is, it does not occur to the Kantian philosophy to inquire. To it what space and time are in themselves does not signify 'What is their Notion,' but 'Are they external things or something in the mind?'

b. The second faculty, the understanding, is something very different from sensuousness; the latter is Receptivity, while Kant calls thought in general Spontaneity —an expression which belongs to the philosophy of Leibnitz. The understanding is active thought, I myself; it "is the faculty of thinking the object of sensuous perception." Yet it has thoughts merely without real content: "Thoughts without content are void and empty,

[1] Kant: Kritik der reinen Vernunft, pp. 30, 31, 41; 12, 13, 150.

sensuous perceptions without Notions are blind." The understanding thus obtains from the sensuous its matter, both empirical and *a priori*, time and space; and it thinks this matter, but its thoughts are very different from this matter. Or it is a faculty of a particular kind, and it is only when both occur, when the sensuous faculty has supplied material and the understanding has united to this its thoughts, that knowledge results.[1] The thoughts of the understanding as such are thus limited thoughts, thoughts of the finite only.

Now logic, as transcendental logic, likewise sets forth the conceptions which the understanding has *a priori* in itself and "whereby it thinks objects completely *a priori*." Thoughts have a form which signifies their being the synthetic function which brings the manifold into a unity. *I* am this unity, the transcendental apperception, the pure apperception of self-consciousness. I=I; *I* must 'accompany' all our conceptions.[2] This is a barbarous exposition of the matter. As self-consciousness I am the completely void, general I, completely indeterminate and abstract; apperception is determination generally, the activity whereby I transplant an empirical content into my simple consciousness, while perception rather signifies feeling or conceiving. In order that a content may enter this One, it must be infected by its simplicity; it is thus that the content first becomes my content. The comprehending medium is 'I'; whatever I have to do with must allow itself to be forced into these forms of unity. This is a great fact, an important item of knowledge; what thought produces is unity; thus it produces itself, for it is the One. Yet the fact that I am the one and, as thinking, the simplifier, is not by Kant satisfactorily set forth. The unity may likewise be called relation; for in so far as

[1] Kant: Kritik der reinen Vernunft, pp. 54, 55.

[2] Ibidem, pp. 59, 97-104.

a manifold is pre-supposed, and as this on the one side remains a manifold while on the other side it is set forth as one, so far may it be said to be related.

Now as 'I' is the universal transcendental unity of self-consciousness which binds together the empirical matter of conception generally, there are various modes in this relationship, and here we have the transcendental nature of the categories or universal thought-determinations. But Kant (Kritik der reinen Vernunft, pp. 70, 77) approaches these modes of simplicity by accepting them as they are classified in ordinary logic. For he says that in common logic particular kinds of judgment are brought forward; and since judgment is a special kind of relationship of the manifold, the various functions of thought which 'I' has in it are shown therein. But the following kinds of judgment have been noticed, viz. Universal, Particular and Singular; Affirmative, Negative, Infinite; Categorical, Hypothetical, Disjunctive; Assertoric, Problematic and Apodictic judgments. These particular modes of relationship now brought forward are the pure forms of the understanding. There are thus, according to Kant (Kritik der reinen Vernunft, pp. 75, 76, 78-82), twelve fundamental categories, which fall into four classes; and it is noteworthy, and deserves to be recognized, that each species of judgment again constitutes a triad. (1) The first kind of categories are those of Quantity, viz. Unity, Plurality and Totality. Plurality is negation of the one, the assertion of difference; and the third, the bringing of the other two into one, plurality circumscribed, the indeterminate plurality comprehended as one, is the Totality. (2) In the second series are the categories of Quality: Reality, Negation, Limitation. Limitation is as real or positive as negation. (3) The third series comprises the categories of relation, of connection; and first of all, indeed, the relation of Substantiality, Substance and Accident: then the relation of Causality, the relation of Cause and Effect, and finally Reciprocity. (4) The categories of Modality, of the relation of the objective to our thought, come fourth, viz. Possibility, Existence (actuality) and Necessity. Possibility should come second; in abstract thought, however, the empty conception comes first. It betrays a great instinct for the Notion when Kant says that the first category is positive, the second the negative of the first, the third the synthesis of the two. The triplicity, this ancient form of the Pythagoreans, Neo-Platonists and of the Christian religion, although it here reappears as a quite external *schema* only, conceals within itself the absolute form, the Notion. But since Kant says that a conception can determine itself in me as accidental, as cause, effect, unity, plurality, &c., we thereby have the whole of the metaphysics of the understanding. Kant does not follow up further the derivation of these categories, and he finds them imperfect, but he says that the others are derived from them. Kant thus accepts the categories in an empiric way, without thinking of developing of necessity these differences from unity. Just as little did Kant attempt to deduce time and space, for he accepted them likewise from experience—a quite unphilosophic and unjustifiable procedure.

Thinking understanding is thus indeed the source of the individual categories, but because on their own account they are void and empty, they only have significance through their union with the given, manifold material of perception, feeling, &c. Such connection of sensuous material with categories now constitutes the facts of experience, *i.e.* the matter of sensation after it is brought under the categories; and this is knowledge generally.[1] The matter of perception which pertains to the feelings or sensuous perception is not left in the determination of individuality and immediacy, but I am active in relation to it, inasmuch as I bring it into connection through the

[1] Kant: Kritik der reinen Vernunft, pp. 105-110.

categories and elevate it into universal species, natural laws, &c. The question of whether a completed sensuousness or the Notion is the higher may accordingly be easily decided. For the laws of the heavens are not immediately perceived, but merely the change in position on the part of the stars. It is only when this object of immediate perception is laid hold of and brought under universal thought-determinations that experience arises therefrom, which has a claim to validity for all time. The category which brings the unity of thought into the content of feeling is thus the objective element in experience, which receives thereby universality and necessity, while that which is perceived is rather the subjective and contingent. Our finding both these elements in experience demonstrates indeed that a correct analysis has been made. Kant (Kritik der reinen Vernunft, pp. 119, 120) however connects with this the statement that experience grasps phenomena only, and that by means of the knowledge which we obtain through experience we do not know things as they are in themselves, but only as they are in the form of laws of perception and sensuousness. For the first component part of experience, sensation, is doubtless subjective, since it is connected with our organs. The matter of perception is only what it is in my sensation. I know of this sensation only and not of the thing. But, in the second place, the objective, which ought to constitute the opposite to this subjective side, is itself subjective likewise: it does not indeed pertain to my feeling, but it remains shut up in the region of my self-consciousness; the categories are only determinations of our thinking understanding. Neither the one nor the other is consequently anything in itself, nor are both together, knowledge, anything in itself, for it only knows phenomena—a strange contradiction.

The transition of the category to the empiric is made in the following way: "Pure conceptions of the understanding are quite of a different nature from empiric, indeed from any sensuous perceptions;" we have thus "to show how pure conceptions of the understanding can be applied to phenomena." This is dealt with by the transcendental faculty of judgment. For Kant says that in the mind, in self-consciousness, there are pure conceptions of the understanding and pure sensuous perceptions; now it is the schematism of the pure understanding, the transcendental faculty of the imagination, which determines the pure sensuous perception in conformity with the category and thus constitutes the transition to experience.[1] The connection of these two is again one of the most attractive sides of the Kantian philosophy, whereby pure sensuousness and pure understanding, which were formerly expressed as absolute opposites, are now united. There is thus here present a perceptive understanding or an understanding perception; but Kant does not see this, he does not bring these thoughts together: he does not grasp the fact that he has here brought both sides of knowledge into one, and has thereby expressed their implicitude. Knowledge itself is in fact the unity and truth of both moments; but with Kant the thinking understanding and sensuousness are both something particular, and they are only united in an external, superficial way, just as a piece of wood and a leg might be bound together by a cord. Thus, for example, the conception of substance in the *schema* becomes permanent in time,[2] *i.e.* the pure conception of the understanding, the pure category, is brought into unity with the form of pure sensuous perception.

In as far as we have to deal with our own determinations only and as we do not reach the implicit, the true objective, the Kantian philosophy called itself Idealism. But in this connection Kant (Kritik der reinen Vernunft, pp. 200, 201) brings forward a refutation of empirical or material idealism,

[1] Kant: Kritik der reinen Vernunft, pp. 129-132.
[2] Ibidem, p. 134.

thus: "I am conscious of my existence as determined in time. But all time-determination presupposes something permanent in perception. This permanence cannot be" a sensuous perception "in me." For all the determining grounds of my existence which are met with in me are conceptions, and as such themselves require a constant element different from them, and in relation to which the change taking place in them—consequently "my existence in time," in which they change, "may be determined." Or I am conscious of my existence as of an empirical consciousness which is only capable of being determined in relation to something which is outside of me; *i.e.* I am conscious of something external to me. Conversely it may be said: I am conscious of external things as determined in time and as changing; these hence presuppose something constant which is not in them but outside of them. And this is 'I,' the transcendental ground of their universality and necessity, of their implicitude, the unity of self-consciousness. On another occasion Kant regards it thus (Kritik der reinen Vernunft, p. 101): These moments confuse themselves, because the constant element is itself a category. Idealism, when we regard it as signifying that nothing exists outside of my individual self-consciousness as individual, as also the refutation of this, the assertion that things exist outside of my self-consciousness as individual, are the one as bad as the other. The former is the idealism of Berkeley, in which self-consciousness as individual is alone in question, or the world of self-consciousness appears as a number of limited, sensuous, individual conceptions, which are as completely devoid of truth as though they were called things. The truth or untruth does not rest in their being things or conceptions, but in their limitation and contingency, whether as conceptions or things. The refutation of this idealism is nothing more than calling attention to the fact that this empirical consciousness does not exist in itself—just as those empiric things do not exist in themselves. But the knowing subject does not with Kant really arrive at reason, for it remains still the individual self-consciousness as such, which is opposed to the universal. As a matter of fact there is described in what we have seen only the empirical finite self-consciousness which requires a material from outside, or which is limited. We do not ask whether these facts of knowledge are in and for themselves true or untrue; the whole of knowledge remains within subjectivity, and on the other side there is the thing-in-itself as an external. This subjectivity is however concrete in itself; even the determinate categories of the thinking understanding are concrete, and much more is experience so—the synthesis of the sensation and the category.[1]

c. The third faculty Kant finds in reason, to which he advances from the understanding after the same psychological method; that is to say, he hunts through the soul's sack to see what faculties are still to be found there; and thus by merest chance he lights on Reason. It would make no difference if there had been no Reason there, just as with physicists it is a matter of perfect indifference whether, for instance, there is such a thing as magnetism or not. "All our knowledge begins from the senses, thence proceeds to the understanding, and finishes up with reason; nothing higher than this is to be found in us, for it signifies the working up of the material of perception, and the reducing of it to the highest unity of thought." Reason is therefore, according to Kant, the power of obtaining knowledge from principles, that is, the power of knowing the particular in the universal by means of Notions; the understanding, on the contrary, reaches its particular by means of perception. But the categories are

[1] In the lectures of 1825–1826 the philosophy of Fichte on its theoretic side is interpolated here, while its practical side is only shortly mentioned after an account is given of the Critique of Practical Reason.

themselves particular. The principle of reason, according to Kant, is really the universal, inasmuch as it finds the unconditioned involved in the conditioned knowledge of the understanding. Understanding is hence for him thought in finite relations; reason, on the contrary, is thought which makes the unconditioned its object. Since Kant's time it has become customary in the language of philosophy to distinguish understanding and reason, while by earlier philosophers this distinction was not drawn. The product of reason is, according to Kant, the Idea—a Platonic expression—and he understands by it the unconditioned, the infinite.[1] It is a great step forward to say that reason brings forth Ideas; with Kant, however, the Idea is merely the abstract universal, the indeterminate.

This, the unconditioned, must now be grasped as concrete, and therein lies the main difficulty. For to know the unconditioned means to determine it and to deduce its determinations. Much has been written and said on the subject of knowledge, without a definition of it ever having been offered. But it is the business of Philosophy to see that what is taken for granted as known is really known. Now on this point Kant says that reason has certainly the desire to know the infinite, but has not the power. And the reason which Kant gives for this (Kritik der reinen Vernunft, pp. 277, 278), is on the one hand that no psychologically sensuous intuition or perception corresponds with the infinite, that it is not given in outward or inward experience; to the Idea "no congruent or corresponding object can be discovered in the sensuous world." It depends, however, on how the world is looked at; but experience and observation of the world mean nothing else for Kant than a candlestick standing here, and a snuff-box

[1] Kant: Kritik der reinen Vernunft, pp. 257-259, 264, 267, 268, 273.

standing there. It is certainly correct to say that the infinite is not given in the world of sensuous perception; and supposing that what we know is experience, a synthesis of what is thought and what is felt, the infinite can certainly not be known in the sense that we have a sensuous perception of it. But no one wishes to demand a sensuous proof in verification of the infinite; spirit is for spirit alone. The second reason for considering that the infinite cannot be known, lies in this, that Reason has no part in it except as supplying the forms of thought which we call categories; and these doubtless afford what Kant calls objective determinations, but in such a way that in themselves they are still only subjective. If therefore for the determination of the infinite we employ these categories which are applicable only to phenomena, we entangle ourselves in false arguments (paralogisms) and in contradictions (antinomies); and it is an important point in the Kantian philosophy that the infinite, so far as it is defined by means of categories, loses itself in contradictions. Although reason, says Kant, becomes transcendent by the exhibition of these contradictions, it still retains its claim to trace perception, experience, and knowledge pertaining to the understanding, back to the infinite. This union of the infinite, the unconditioned, with the finite and conditioned as existing in the knowledge given by the understanding, or even in perception, would signify that the acme of concreteness had been reached.

Of this Unconditioned there are several kinds, objects having special features of their own and proceeding from reason, transcendental Ideas; they are thus themselves particular in their nature. The manner in which Kant arrives at these Ideas is again derived from experience, from formal logic, according to which there are various forms of the syllogism. Because, says Kant, there are three forms of the syllogism, categorical, hypothetical, and disjunctive, the Unconditioned is also threefold in its nature: "Firstly, an Unconditioned of the categorical synthesis in a subject."

Synthesis is the concrete; but the expression is ambiguous, since it indicates an external association of independent elements. "In the second place, an Unconditioned of the hypothetical synthesis of the members of a series will have to be looked for; and in the third place, an Unconditioned of the disjunctive synthesis of the parts in a system." We make the first connection, expressed as object of Reason or transcendental Idea, when we conceive "the thinking subject;" the second "is the sum total of all phenomena, the world;" and the third is "the thing which contains the supreme condition of the possibility of all that can be thought, the Being of all Beings," *i.e.* God. When brought to an ultimate point, the question which meets us is whether Reason can bring these objects to reality, or whether they remain confined to subjective thought. Now, according to Kant, Reason is not capable of procuring reality for its Ideas—otherwise it would be transcendent, its limits would be overstepped; it produces only paralogisms, antinomies, and an ideal without reality.[1]

a. "A paralogism is a syllogism false in its form." Since Reason credits with reality that mode of the Unconditioned which constitutes the categorical synthesis in a subject, and therefore the thinking subject, it is termed substance. Now is the thinking ego a substance, a soul, a soul-thing? Further questions are whether it is permanent, immaterial, incorruptible, personal and immortal, and such as to have a real community with the body. The falsity of the syllogism consists in this, that the idea of the unity of the transcendental subject essential to Reason is expressed as a thing; for it is only in this way that the permanency of the same becomes substance. Otherwise I find myself permanent in my thought, of course, but only within perceiving consciousness, not outside of that. The ego is

[1] Kant: Kritik der reinen Vernunft, pp. 261, 262, 274, 275, 284, 288, 289.

therefore the empty, transcendental subject of our thoughts, that moreover becomes known only through its thoughts; but of what it is in itself we cannot gather the least idea. (A horrible distinction! For thought is nothing more or less than the "in-itself" or implicit.) We cannot assert of it any present Being, because thought is an empty form, we have a conception of what thinking Beings are through no outward experience, but only by means of self-consciousness,—*i.e.* because we cannot take the "I" in our hands, nor see it, nor smell it. We therefore know very well that the ego is a subject, but if we pass beyond self-consciousness, and say that it is substance, we go farther than we are entitled to do. I cannot therefore assign any reality to the subject.[1]

We here see Kant fall into contradiction, what with the barbarity of the conceptions which he refutes, and the barbarity of his own conceptions which remain behind when the others are refuted. In the first place, he is perfectly correct when he maintains that the ego is not a soul-thing, a dead permanency which has a sensuous present existence; indeed, were it to be an ordinary thing, it would be necessary that it should be capable of being experienced. But, in the second place, Kant does not assert the contrary of this, namely that the ego, as this universal or as self-thinking, has in itself the true reality which he requires as an objective mode. For he does not get clear of the conception of reality in which reality consists in the possession of a sensuous present existence; accordingly, because the ego is given in no outward experience, it is not real. For self-consciousness, the ego as such, is not, according to Kant, reality; it is only *our* thought, or in other words he regards self consciousness as being itself simply and entirely sensuous. The form which Kant accordingly bestows on Being, thing, substance,

[1] Kant: Kritik der reinen Vernunft, pp. 289-299.

would seem to indicate that these categories of the understanding were too high for the subject, too high to be capable of being predicated of it. But really such determinations are too poor and too mean, for what possesses life is not a thing, nor can the soul, the spirit, the ego, be called a thing. Being is the least or lowest quality that one can assign to spirit, its abstract, immediate identity with itself; Being thus no doubt pertains to spirit, but it must be considered as a determination scarcely worth applying to it.

β. In the second place we have the antinomy, *i.e.* the contradiction in Reason's Idea of the Unconditioned, an Idea applied to the world in order to represent it as a complete summing-up of conditions. That is to say, in the given phenomena Reason demands the absolute completeness of the conditions of their possibility, so far as these constitute a series, so that the unconditioned is contained in the world, *i.e.* the totality of the series. If now this completeness is expressed as existing, an antinomy is alone presented, and Reason is presented only as dialectic: *i.e.* in this object there is on every side a perfect contradiction found.[1] For phenomena are a finite content, and the world is a conjunction of the limited; if this content is now thought by Reason, and therefore subsumed under the unconditioned and the unlimited, we have two determinations, finite and infinite, which contradict each other. Reason demands a perfectly complete synthesis, an absolute beginning; but in phenomena we have, on the contrary, a succession of causes and effects, which never come to an end. Kant here points out four contradictions (Kritik der reinen Vernunft, p. 320), which, however, is not enough; for in each Notion there are antinomies, since it is not simple but concrete, and therefore contains different determinations, which are direct opposites.

[1] Kant: Kritik der reinen Vernunft, pp. 312–314.

αα. These antinomies in the first place involve our making the one determination, limitation, just as valid as non-limitation. "Thesis: The world has a beginning and an end in time, and it is limited in regard to space. Antithesis: It has no beginning and no end in time, and also no limits in space." The one, says Kant, can be proved just as easily as the other; and indeed he does prove each indirectly, though his are not "advocate's proofs."[1] The world, as the universe, is the whole; it is thus a universal idea, and therefore unlimited. The completion of the synthesis in progression as regards time and space is, however, a first beginning of time and space. If therefore the categories of limited and unlimited are applied to the world in order to attain to a knowledge of it, we fall into contradictions, because the categories are not applicable to things-in-themselves.

ββ. The second antinomy is that atoms, from which substance is composed, must necessarily be admitted to exist, therefore simplicity can be proved; but just as easy is it to prove incompleteness, the endless process of division. The thesis is accordingly stated thus: "Every compound substance consists of simple parts," and the antithesis is as follows: "There exists nothing simple."[2] The one is here the limit, a material self-existence, the point which is likewise the enclosing surface; the other is divisibility *ad infinitum*.

γγ. The third antinomy is the opposition between freedom and necessity. The first is the self-determining, the point of view pertaining to infinity: causality according to the laws of freedom is the only causality. The other is: Determinism alone is to be found: everything is determined by means of an external ground or reason.[3]

[1] Kant: Kritik der reinen Vernunft, pp. 317, 318, 328, 329, 332.
[2] Ibidem, pp. 318, 336, 337. [3] Ibidem, pp. 319, 346, 347.

δδ. The fourth antinomy rests on what follows: On the one hand totality completes itself in freedom as a first beginning of action, or in an absolutely necessary Being, as the cause of the world, so that the process is interrupted: but there is opposed to that freedom the necessity of a process according to conditions of causes and effects, and to the necessity of a Being is opposed the consideration that everything is contingent. The absolute necessity of the conditioned world is therefore on the one hand maintained thus: "To the world belongs an absolutely necessary Being." The opposite to this is, "There exists no absolutely necessary Being, either as part of the world or outside of the world."[1]

One of these opposites is just as necessary as the other, and it is superfluous to carry this further here. The necessity of these contradictions is the interesting fact which Kant (Kritik der reinen Vernunft, p. 324) has brought to consciousness; in ordinary metaphysics, however, it is imagined that one of these contradictions must hold good, and the other be disproved. The most important point involved in this assertion of Kant's is, however, unintentional on his part. For he indeed solves these antinomies (Kritik der reinen Vernunft, pp. 385, 386), but only in the particular sense of transcendental idealism, which does not doubt or deny the existence of external things (*supra*, p. 442), but "allows that things are perceived in space and time" (which is the case, whether it allows it or not): for transcendental idealism, however, "space and time in themselves are not things at all," and therefore "do not exist apart from our mind;" *i.e.* all these determinations of a beginning in time, and so on, do not really belong to things, to the implicitude of the phenomenal world, which has independent existence outside of our subjective thought. If such determinations

[1] Kant: Kritik der reinen Vernunft, pp. 319, 354, 355.

belonged to the world, to God, to free agents, there would be an objective contradiction; but this contradiction is not found as absolute, it pertains only to us. Or, in other words, this transcendental idealism lets the contradiction remain, only it is not Being in itself that is thus contradictory, for the contradiction has its source in our thought alone. Thus the same antinomy remains in our mind; and as it was formerly God who had to take upon Himself all contradictions, so now it is self-consciousness. But the Kantian philosophy does not go on to grapple with the fact that it is not things that are contradictory, but self-consciousness itself. Experience teaches that the ego does not melt away by reason of these contradictions, but continues to exist; we need not therefore trouble ourselves about its contradictions, for it can bear them. Nevertheless Kant shows here too much tenderness for things: it would be a pity, he thinks, if they contradicted themselves. But that mind, which is far higher, should be a contradiction—that is not a pity at all. The contradiction is therefore by no means solved by Kant; and since mind takes it upon itself, and contradiction is self-destructive, mind is in itself all derangement and disorder. The true solution would be found in the statement that the categories have no truth in themselves, and the Unconditioned of Reason just as little, but that it lies in the unity of both as concrete, and in that alone.

γ. Kant now goes on to the Idea of God; this third idea is the Being of Beings, which the other ideas presupposed. Kant says (Kritik der reinen Vernunft, pp. 441–452), that according to the definition of Wolff, God is the most real of all Beings; the object then comes to be to prove that God is not only Thought, but that He is, that He has reality, Being. This Kant calls the Ideal of Reason, to distinguish it from the Idea, which is only the sum of all possibility. The Ideal is thus the Idea as existent; just as in art we give the name of ideal to the Idea realized in a sensuous manner. Here Kant takes into consideration the proof of the existence of God, as he asks whether reality can be assigned to this Ideal.

The ontological proof proceeds from the absolute Notion, in order from it to argue up to Being. With Anselm, Descartes, and Spinoza the transition to Being is thus made; and all of them assume in so doing the unity of Being and thought. But Kant says (Kritik der reinen Vernunft, pp. 458–466): To this Ideal of Reason just as little reality can be assigned: there is no transition from the Notion to Being. "Being is not a real predicate," like any other, "a Notion of something which might be added to the Notion of a thing. A hundred real dollars do not contain in the very least more than a hundred possible dollars," they are the same content, *i.e.* the same Notion; they are also a hundred exactly. The one is the Notion, or rather the conception, the other is the object; Being is no new determination of the Notion, otherwise my Notion of a hundred real dollars would contain something different from a hundred real dollars. But "the object, as real, is not contained in my Notion alone; or to my Notion the real hundred dollars are synthetically added." Being cannot therefore be derived from the Notion, because it is not contained therein, but must be added to it. "We must go out of the Notion in order to arrive at existence. With regard to objects of pure thought, there are no means of coming to know of their existence, because it had to be known *a priori;* but our consciousness of all existence belongs entirely to experience." That is to say, Kant does not attain to the comprehension of that very synthesis of Notion and Being, or in other words, he does not comprehend existence, *i.e.* he does not attain to the establishment of it as Notion; existence remains for him something absolutely different from a Notion. The content is no doubt the same for him in what exists and in the Notion: but since Being is not involved in the Notion, the attempt to derive the one from the other is unavailing.

Of course the determination of Being is not found as positive and ready-made in the Notion; the Notion is something different from reality and objectivity. If we therefore abide by the Notion, we abide by Being as something different from the Notion, and adhere to the separation of the two; we then have conception, and not Being at all. That a hundred possible dollars are something different from a hundred actual ones is a reflection of a very popular nature, so much so that no proposition has been so well received as the assertion that no transition can be made from the Notion to Being; for though I imagine to myself a hundred dollars, I do not possess them for all that. But in a like popular fashion it might be said that one must leave off imagining, for that is mere conception: *i.e.* what is merely imaginary is untrue, the hundred imaginary dollars are and remain imaginary. Therefore to believe in them is a proof of an unsound understanding, and is of no manner of use; and he is a foolish fellow who indulges in such fancies and wishes. One possesses a hundred dollars, when they are real only; if a man has therefore so great a desire to possess a hundred dollars, he must put his hand to work in order to obtain them: *i.e.* he must not come to a standstill at the imagination of them, but pass out beyond it. This subjective side is not the ultimate or the absolute; the true is that which is not merely subjective. If I possess a hundred dollars, I have them actually, and at the same time I form a conception of them to myself. But according to Kant's representation we come to a deadlock at the difference; dualism is ultimate, and each side has independent validity as an absolute. Against this false idea of what is to be absolute and ultimate, the healthy human understanding is directed; every ordinary consciousness rises above it, every action aims at setting aside a subjective conception and making it into something objective. There is no man so foolish as that philosophy; when a man feels hungry, he does not call up the imagination of food, but sets about satisfying his hunger. All activity is a conception which does not yet exist, but whose subjectivity is abrogated. Moreover the imaginary hundred dollars become real, and the real ones imaginary: this is a frequent experience, this is their fate; it depends on circumstances entirely outward whether a hundred dollars become my property or not. Of course the mere conception is of no good, if I obstinately hold by it: for I can imagine what I will, but that does not make it exist. The only important point is what I conceive to myself, and then whether I think or comprehend the subjective and Being; by means of this each passes into the other. Thought, the Notion, of necessity implies that the Notion does not remain subjective; this subjective is on the contrary abrogated and reveals itself as objective. Now that unity is expressly affirmed by Descartes solely in reference to the Notion of God, for it is just that which is God; he speaks of no hundred dollars, as these are not an existence which has a Notion in itself. That opposition does away with itself absolutely and entirely, *i.e.* the finite passes away; it holds good only in the philosophy of finitude. If, therefore, there is not a Notion of existence formed, we have in it a notionless, sensuous object of perception; and what is notionless is certainly not a Notion,—therefore sensation, handling, are not Notions. Such existence has of course no Absolute, no real essence: or such existence has no truth, it is only a vanishing moment. This useless thrashing of the empty grainless straw of the common logic is termed philosophizing: it is like Issachar the strong ass, which could not be made to move from the spot where it was (Gen. xlix. 14). People of this kind say: We are good for nothing, and because we are good for nothing, we are good for nothing, and wish to be good for nothing. But it is a very false idea of Christian humility and modesty to desire through one's abjectness to attain to excellence; this confession of one's own nothingness is really inward pride and great self-conceit. But for the honour of true humility we must not remain in our misery, but raise ourselves above it by laying hold of the Divine.

The fact to which Kant clings most strongly (Kritik der reinen Vernunft, p. 467) is this, that Being cannot be extracted from the Notion. The result of this is the proposition that to have the thought of the Infinite is certainly Reason; but that from the Idea of Reason is separated determination in general, and especially the determination which is known as Being. The Ideas of Reason cannot be proved from experience, or obtain from it their verification: if they are defined by means of categories, contradictions arise. If the Idea in general is to be defined as existent only, it is nothing more or less than the Notion; and the Being of the existent is still distinguished from it. This result, however, so highly important with reference to knowledge of the understanding, Kant does not, with reference to Reason, carry further than to say that Reason has on its own account nothing but formal unity for the methodical systematization of the knowledge of the understanding. Abstract thinking is adhered to; it is said that the understanding can only bring about order in things; but order is nothing in and for itself, it is only subjective. There therefore remains nothing for Reason except the form of its pure identity with itself, and this extends no further than to the arranging of the manifold laws and relations of the understanding, the classes, kinds and species which the understanding discovers.[1] I, as Reason or conception, and the things external to me, are both absolutely different from one another; and that, according to Kant, is the ultimate standpoint. The animal does not stop at this standpoint, but practically brings about unity. This is the

[1] Kritik der reinen Vernunft, pp. 497, 498.

critique of theoretical Reason which Kant gives, and in which he states the *a priori* and determinate character of Reason in itself, without bringing it to the determinateness of individuality.[1]

Mention should still be made of the positive philosophy or metaphysics, which Kant sets *a priori* above objective existence, the content of the object of experience, nature; we have here his natural philosophy, which is a demonstration of the universal conceptions of Nature. But this is on the one-hand very scanty and restricted in content, containing as it does sundry general qualities and conceptions of matter and motion, and with regard to the scientific side or the *a priori*, as Kant calls it, it is likewise altogether unsatisfactory. For Kant assumes all such conceptions as that matter has motion and also a power of attraction and repulsion,[2] instead of demonstrating their necessity. The "Principles of Natural Philosophy" have nevertheless been of great service, inasmuch as at the commencement of a philosophy of nature, attention was called to the fact that physical science employs thought-determinations without further investigation; and these determinations constitute the real foundations of its objects. Density, for instance, is looked on by physical science as a variable quantity, as a mere *quantum* in space: instead of this Kant asserted it to be a certain degree of occupation of space, *i.e.* energy, intensity of action. He demands accordingly (Metaphysische Anfangsgründe der Naturwissenschaft, pp. 65-68) a construction of matter from powers and activities, not from atoms; and Schelling still holds to this without getting further. Kant's work is an attempt to think, *i.e.* to demonstrate the determinations of thought, whose product consists of such conceptions as matter; he has

[1] Here there is inserted in the lectures of 1825-1826 an examination of what the philosophy of Jacobi has to say on this point.

[2] Kant: Metaphysische Anfangsgründe der Naturwissenschaft (third edition, Leipzig, 1800), pp. 1, 27.

attempted to determine the fundamental Notions and principles of this science, and has given the first impulse to a so-called dynamic theory of Nature.

"Religion within pure Reason" is also a demonstration of dogmas as aspects of Reason, just as in Nature. Thus in the positive dogmas of religion, which the Aufklärung (the clearing-up)—or the Ausklärung (the clearing-out)—made short work of, Kant called to remembrance Ideas of Reason, asking what rational and, first of all, what moral meaning lies in that which men call dogmas of religion, *e.g.* original sin.[1] He is much more reasonable than the *Ausklärung*, which thinks it beneath its dignity to speak of such matters. These are the principal points in respect to the theoretical part of Kant's philosophy.

2. The second subject of review in Kant's philosophy is the practical sphere, the nature and principle of the will; this subject is dealt with in the Critique of Practical Reason, in which Kant accepted Rousseau's conclusion that the will is absolutely free. Kant's idea of theoretic Reason is that when Reason relates itself to an object, this object must be given to it; but when the object is given by Reason to itself, it has no truth; and Reason in knowlege of this kind does not arrive at independence. As practical, on the contrary, Reason is independent in itself; as a moral Being man is free, raised above all natural law and above all phenomena. As the theoretic Reason had in itself categories, *a priori* distinctions, so practical Reason has in turn the moral law in general, the further determinations of which are constituted by the notions of duty and right, lawful and unlawful; and here Reason disdains all the given material which was necessary to it on the theoretic side. The will determines itself within itself; all that is right and moral rests on freedom; in this man has his absolute

[1] Kant: Die Religion innerhalb der Grenzen der blossen Vernunft (second edition, Königsberg, 1794), pp. 20-48.

self-consciousness.[1] On this side self-consciousness finds essential reality in itself, as theoretical Reason found it in an "other"; and in the first place, indeed, the ego in its individuality is immediate reality, universality, objectivity; in the second place subjectivity strives after reality, but not after sensuous reality such as we had before, for here Reason holds itself to be the real. Here we have the Notion which is sensible of its own deficiency; this theoretic Reason could not be, as in it the Notion had to remain the Notion. Thus we have the standpoint of absoluteness revealed, since there is an infinite disclosed within the human breast. The satisfying part in Kant's philosophy is that the truth is at least set within the heart; and hence I acknowledge that, and that alone, which is in conformity with my determined nature.

a. Kant divides will into lower and higher faculties of desire; this expression is not inapt. The lower faculties of desire are impulses, inclinations, etc.; the higher faculty is the will as such, which has not external, individual aims, but universal. To the question what the principle of will that should determine man in his actions is, all sorts of answers have been given; for instance, self-love, benevolence, happiness, etc. Such material principles of action, Kant now says, are all reducible to impulses, to happiness; but the rational in itself is purely formal, and consists in the maxim that what is to hold good as law, must be capable of being thought of as a law of universal application, without destroying itself. All morality of action now rests upon the conviction that the act is done with consciousness of the law, for the sake of the law and out of respect for the law and for itself, without any regard to what makes for happiness. As a moral Being man has the moral law in himself, the principle of which is freedom and

[1] Kant: Kritik der prakt. Vernunft (fourth edition, Riga, 1797), pp. 3-11, 29-32.

autonomy of the will; for the will is absolute spontaneity. Determinations which are taken from the inclinations are heterogeneous principles as regards the will; or the will is heteronomy if it takes such determinations as its end and aim; for in that case it takes its determinations from something else than itself. But the essence of the will is to determine itself from itself; for practical Reason gives itself laws. But the empirical will is heteronomous, for it is determined by desires; and they belong to our nature, not to the realm of freedom.[1]

It is a highly important point in the Kantian philosophy that what self-consciousness esteems reality, law, and implicit Being, is brought back within itself. While a man is striving after this aim and that, according as he judges the world or history in one way or the other, what is he to take as his ultimate aim? For the will, however, there is no other aim than that derived from itself, the aim of its freedom. It is a great advance when the principle is established that freedom is the last hinge on which man turns, a highest possible pinnacle, which allows nothing further to be imposed upon it; thus man bows to no authority, and acknowledges no obligations, where his freedom is not respected. Great popularity has from one point of view been won for Kantian philosophy by the teaching that man finds in himself an absolutely firm, unwavering centre-point; but with this last principle it has come to a standstill. While the highest pinnacle of the theoretic Reason is abstract identity, because it can furnish only a canon, a rule for abstract classifications,[2] practical Reason, as law-giving, is immediately regarded as concrete; the law which it gives to itself is the moral law. But even if it is stated that it is concrete in itself, there is the further consideration that

[1] Kant: Kritik d. prakt. Vernunft, pp. 40, 41, 56, 126-135, 58, 38, 77.

[2] Kant: Kritik der reinen Vernunft, pp. 62, 500.

this freedom is at first only the negative of everything else; no bond, nothing external, lays me under an obligation. It is to this extent indeterminate; it is the identity of the will with itself, its at-homeness with itself. But what is the content of this law? Here we at once come back to the lack of content. For the sole form of this principle is nothing more or less than agreement with itself, universality; the formal principle of legislation in this internal solitude comes to no determination, or this is abstraction only. The universal, the non-contradiction of self, is without content, something which comes to be reality in the practical sphere just as little as in the theoretical. The universal moral law Kant therefore expresses thus (and the setting up of such a universal form was at all times the demand of the abstract understanding): "Act from maxims" (the law is also to be my particular law), "which are capable of becoming universal laws."[1]

Thus for the determination of duty (for the question which meets us is, what is duty for the free will) Kant has contributed nothing but the form of identity, which is the law of abstract Understanding. To defend one's fatherland, to promote the happiness of another, is a duty, not because of the content, but because it is duty; as with the Stoics, what was thought was true for the very reason that, and in so far as it was thought (Vol. II., pp. 254, 260, 263). The content as such is indeed not what holds good universally in the moral law, because it contradicts itself. For benevolence, for instance, enjoins: "Give your possessions to the poor," but if all give away what they have, beneficence is done away with (Vol. I., pp. 417, 418). Even with abstract identity, however, we do not get a step further, for every content which is put into this form is by being so put freed from self-contradiction. But nothing would be lost if it were not put into this form at all. With regard to property, for

[1] Kant: Kritik d. prakt. Vernunft, pp. 54, 58 (35).

instance, the law of my actions is this: Property ought to be respected, for the opposite of this cannot be universal law. That is correct, but it is quite a formal determination: If property is, then it is. Property is here presupposed, but this determination may also in the same way be omitted, and then there is no contradiction involved in theft: If there is no such thing as property, then it is not respected. This is the defect in the principle of Kant and Fichte, that it is really formal; chill duty is the final undigested lump left within the stomach, the revelation given to Reason.

The first postulate in practical Reason is thus free, independent will which determines itself, but this concrete is still abstract. The second and third are forms which remind us that the will is concrete in a higher sense.

b. The second point is the connection of the Notion of the will with the particular will of the individual; the concrete is here the fact that my particular will and the universal will are identical, or that I am a moral human being. The unity, that man should be moral, is postulated; but beyond the "should" and this talk of morality, no advance is made. It is not said what is moral; and no thought is given to a system of the self-realizing spirit. For really, as theoretic Reason stands opposed to the objective of the senses, so practical Reason stands opposed to the practical sensuousness, to impulses and inclinations. Perfected morality must remain a Beyond; for morality presupposes the difference of the particular and universal will. It is a struggle, the determination of the sensuous by the universal; the struggle can only take place when the sensuous will is not yet in conformity with the universal. The result is, therefore, that the aim of the moral will is to be attained in infinite progress only; on this Kant founds (Kritik der prakt. Vernunft, pp. 219-223) the postulate of the immortality of the soul, as the endless progress of the subject in his morality, because morality itself is incomplete, and must advance into infinitude. The particular will is certainly something other than the universal will; but it is not ultimate or really permanent.

c. The third point is the highest concrete, the Notion of the freedom of all men, or the natural world has to be in harmony with the Notion of freedom. That is the postulate of the existence of God, whom Reason, however, does not recognize. Will has the whole world, the whole of the sensuous, in opposition to it, and yet Reason insists on the unity of Nature or the moral law, as the Idea of the Good, which is the ultimate end of the world. Since, however, it is formal, and therefore has no content on its own account, it stands opposed to the impulses and inclinations of a subjective and an external independent Nature. Kant reconciles the contradiction of the two (Kritik der prakt. Vernunft, pp. 198-200) in the thought of the highest Good, in which Nature is conformed to rational will, and happiness to virtue;—a harmony which does not enter into the question at all, although practical reality consists therein. For happiness is only one's own sensuous consciousness, or the actuality of a particular individual, not universal reality in itself. The unification spoken of itself therefore remains only a Beyond, a thought, which is not actually in existence, but only ought to be. Kant (Kritik der prakt. Vernunft, pp. 205-209) thus agrees entirely with the talk which alleges that in this world it often fares ill with the good, and well with the wicked, and so on; and he postulates further the existence of God as the Being, the causality, through whom this harmony comes to pass, on behalf both of the sanctity of the moral law, and of the rational end to be attained in Nature, but only in infinite progress; which postulate, like that of the immortality of the soul, allows the contradiction to remain as it is all the time, and expresses only in the abstract that the reconciliation ought to come about. The postulate itself is always there, because the Good is a Beyond with respect to Nature; the law of necessity and the law of liberty are different from one another, and placed in this dualism. Nature would remain Nature no longer, if it were to become conformed to the Notion of the Good; and thus there remains an utter opposition between the two sides, because they cannot unite. It is likewise necessary to establish the unity of the two; but this is never actual, for their separation is exactly what is pre-supposed. Kant employs popular language thus: evil ought to be overcome, but yet must not have been overcome. God is to him, therefore, only a faith, an opinion, which is only subjectively, and not absolutely true.[1] This result is also of a very popular character.

These postulates express nothing but the synthesis, devoid of thought, of the different moments which contradict each other on every hand; they are therefore a "nest"[2] of contradictions. For instance, the immortality of the soul is postulated on account of imperfect morality, *i.e.* because it is infected with sensuousness. But the sensuous is implied in moral self-consciousness; the end, perfection, is what really destroys morality as such. Similarly the other aim, the harmony of the sensuous and the rational, to an equal extent abrogates morality; for that consists in this very opposition of Reason to the sensuous. The actuality of the God who produces harmony is of such a character that it does not enter into consciousness at all; it is accepted by consciousness for the sake of harmony, just as children make some kind of scarecrow, and then agree with each other to pretend to be afraid of it. The ground on which God is accepted—that by the conception of a holy law-giver the moral law may acquire additional reverence—contradicts the fact that morality really consists in reverence for the law simply for its own sake.[3] In Practical Reason self-consciousness esteems itself

[1] Kant: Kritik d. prakt. Vernunft, pp. 223-227.
[2] Cf. Kant's Kritik d. reinen Vernunft, p. 471.
[3] Kant: Kritik der prakt. Vernunft, p. 146.

to be implicit Being, as contrasted with theoretic Reason, which assigns implicitude to objective existence, but the one, we see, attains just as little as the other to unity and actuality in itself. It is hard for man to believe that Reason actually exists; but there is nothing real except Reason; it is the absolute power. The vanity of man aspires to have an ideal before him, in order to be able to find fault with everything alike. We possess all wisdom, it is within us, but is not forthcoming. That is the ultimate standpoint; it is a high standpoint, no doubt, but in it the truth is never reached. The absolute Good remains "what ought to be," or without objectivity; and there it has to remain.

3. There is still left for us to consider the third side in Kant's philosophy, the Critique of the Faculty of Judgment, in which the demand for the concrete comes in, the demand that the Idea of unity spoken of before should be established not as a Beyond, but as present; and this side is of special importance. Kant says that the understanding no doubt regulates in the theoretic sphere and produces categories; but these remain mere general determinations, beyond which lies the particular (the other element which belongs to every item of knowledge). The two are distinguished from one another for the understanding; for its distinctions remain in universality. In the practical sphere Reason is certainly the implicit, but its free independence, its law-giving freedom in higher form, is opposed to Nature in its freedom or to Nature's own laws. "In the theoretic sphere Reason can draw conclusions from given laws through syllogisms, only by means of the understanding, and these conclusions never get beyond Nature; it is only in the practical sphere that Reason itself gives laws. Understanding and" (practical) "Reason have two different regulative systems on one and the same ground of experience, without the one being detrimental to the other. For if the Notion of Nature has but little influence on the giving of laws by the Notion of Freedom,

just as little does the latter interfere with the legislation of Nature. The possibility of the existence side by side of the two regulative systems and of the powers belonging to them was proved in the Critique of pure Reason." (! ?) "Now if a unity is not constituted by these two different spheres, which certainly do not put a limit on each other in their regulative action, but do so incessantly in their operations in the sensuous world" (*i.e.* where they encounter each other), "the reason is this, that the Notion of Nature represents its objects in perception, not as things in themselves, but as mere phenomena, while the Notion of Freedom, on the other hand, represents in its object a thing in itself, no doubt, but not in perception. Consequently neither of them can attain to a theoretic knowledge of its object (and even of the thinking subject) as a thing-in-itself, which last would be the supersensuous, an unlimited and inaccessible realm for our whole faculty of knowledge. Now truly there is fixed a gulf over which the eye cannot reach, between the realm of the Notion of Nature, as the sensuous, and the realm of the Notion of Freedom, as the supersensuous, so that it is not possible to pass from the one to the other, since it is just as if there were two different worlds, the first of which could have no influence on the second. Nevertheless the latter is conceived as having an influence on the former, or, in other words, freedom is conceived as having for its mission the realization in the sensuous world of the end indicated by the laws of freedom. Consequently Nature must be so conceived that, while in form it realizes its own laws, there may yet be a possibility of ends being realized in it according to the laws of freedom. Therefore there must surely be some ground for the unity of the supersensuous which lies at the foundation of Nature with that which the Notion of Freedom practically contains, the Notion of which ground of unity, although it attains neither theoretically nor practically to a knowledge of the same, and consequently has no peculiar province, yet makes possible the transition from the mode of thought in accordance with the principles of the one, to the mode of thought in accordance with the principles of the other. Between Understanding and Reason there now comes the Faculty of Judgment, as between the powers of knowledge and desire there come pleasure and its opposite; in this faculty must therefore lie the transition from the province of the Notions of Nature to the province of the Notion of Freedom."[1]

Adaptation to ends has its place here, *i.e.* a particular reality, which is determined only through the universal, the end. The understanding is the ground of this unity of the manifold; the sensuous is therefore here determined by means of the supersensuous. This idea of a universal which implicitly contains the particular is according to Kant the precise object of the faculty of judgment, which he divides as follows:—"If the universal (the rule, principle, law) is given, the faculty of judgment which subsumes the particular under that universal, is determinative,"—the immediate faculty of judgment. But here there is also a particular which is not determined by species. "If, however, only the particular is given, for which the faculty of judgment has to find the universal, it is reflective." The reflective judgment has as its principle the unity of particularity and the abstract universal of the understanding, the idea of a legal necessity which is at the same time free, or of a freedom which is directly one with its content. "This principle can be no other but the fact that since universal laws of Nature have their foundation in our understanding, which prescribes them to nature, although only according to their general conception, the particular, empirical laws, in so far as they are undetermined by universal laws, must

[1] Kant: Kritik der Urtheilskraft (third edition, Berlin, 1799), Einleitung, pp. xvii.-xx. xxiv., xxv.

be viewed as containing that unity which they would contain if they had been given by some intelligence—other, it may be, than our own—with express reference to our cognitive faculties, in order to render possible a system of experience according to particular natural laws. It is not as if such an intelligence must be assumed (for it is only the reflective faculty of judgment to which this idea serves as principle): this faculty gives a law only to itself, not to Nature in addition. Now the conception of an object (if it at the same time contains the ground of the reality of this object), the end, and the harmony of a thing with that quality of things which is only possible in conformity with ends, are termed the adaptation to purpose of the form; therefore the principle of the faculty of judgment in respect to the form of the things of Nature under empirical laws in general is the adaptability to purpose of Nature in its multiplicity. That is to say, Nature is represented by this Notion as if an intelligence contained the ground of the unity in multiplicity of Nature's empirical laws."[1]

Aristotle already regarded Nature as in itself showing this adaptation to end, and as having in itself νοῦς, intelligence, the Universal, so that in undivided unity one element is moment of another (*v.* Vol. II. pp. 156-162). Purpose is the Notion, and immanent; not external form and abstraction as distinguished from a fundamental material, but penetrating, so that all that is particular is determined by this universal itself. According to Kant this is Understanding: no doubt the laws of the Understanding, which it implicitly has in knowledge, leave the objective still undetermined; but because this manifold itself must have a connection in itself, which is yet contingent for human intelligence, "the faculty of judgment must assume as a principle for its own use that what is contingent for us contains a unity, which for us indeed is not knowable, but yet thinkable, in

[1] Kant: Kritik der Urtheilskraft, Introduction, pp. xxv.-xxviii.

the connection of the manifold with an implicitly possible experience."[1] This principle hereby at once falls back again into the subjectivity of a thought, and is only a maxim of our reflection, by which nothing is to be expressed regarding the objective nature of the object,[2] because Being-in-itself is once for all fixed outside of self-consciousness, and the Understanding is conceived only in the form of the self-conscious, not in its becoming another.

Now this principle of the reflective faculty of judgment is in itself a twofold adaptation to end, the formal and the material; the faculty of judgment is thus either æsthetic or teleological: of these the former has to do with subjective, the latter with objective, logical adaptation to end. There are thus two objects of the faculty of judgment—the beautiful in works of art and the natural products of organic life—which make known to us the unity of the Notion of Nature and the Notion of Freedom.[3] The consideration of these works involves the fact, that we see a unity of the Understanding and the particular. But as this consideration is only a subjective manner of representing such products, and does not contain the truth of the same, such things are regarded only according to this unity, and they are not in themselves of this nature; what they are in themselves lies beyond.

a. The Beautiful of the æsthetic faculty of judgment consists in the following: "Pleasure and displeasure are something subjective, which can in no way become a part of knowledge. The object has adaptation to end only to the extent that its conception is directly bound up with the feeling of pleasure; and this is an æsthetic conception. The taking up of forms into the imaginative faculty can never occur

[1] Kant: Kritik der Urtheilskraft, Einleitung, pp. xxvi.-xxxiii.

[2] Ibidem, p. xxxiv.

[3] Ibidem, pp. xlviii.-lii.

without the reflecting faculty of judgment at least comparing them, even unintentionally, by means of its power of relating perceptions to Notions. Now if in this comparison the imaginative faculty (as a faculty of perceptions *a priori?*) "is, by means of a conception given"—something beautiful,—"unintentionally placed in agreement with the Understanding, as the faculty of Notions, and thereby a feeling of pleasure is awakened, the object must then be looked on as in conformity with end for the reflecting faculty of judgment. Such a judgment regarding the adaptability to end of the object, a judgment which is grounded on no previous Notion of the object, and furnishes no Notion of it, is an æsthetic judgment. An object whose form (not the material of its conception as sensation) is judged to be a cause of the pleasure which springs from the conception of such an object, is beautiful,"—the first reasonable thing said about beauty. The sensuous is one moment of the Beautiful, but it must also express the spiritual, a Notion. "The Beautiful is what is conceived without" subjective "interest," but similarly also "without Notions" (*i.e.* determinations of reflection, laws) "as object of a universal pleasure. It is related to no inclination, therefore the subject feels itself quite free therein. It is not beautiful *for me*. The end is the object of a Notion, so far as the latter is looked on as the cause of the former" (the object); "and the causality of a Notion in respect to its object is adaptation to end." To the ideal belongs "the Idea of reason, which makes the aims of humanity, as far as they cannot be sensuously conceived, the principle of judgment of a form through which these aims reveal themselves as their effect in the phenomenon. The ideal we may expect to find revealed only in human form."

The sublime is the effort to give sensuous expression to an Idea in which the inconceivability of the Idea, and the impossibility of finding an adequate expression of it by means of the sensuous, are clearly evidenced.[1] Here in the æsthetic faculty of judgment we see the immediate unity of the universal and the particular; for the Beautiful is this very unity, without Notion and immediate. Because Kant, however, places it in the subject, it is limited, and as æsthetic it also ranks lower, inasmuch as it is not the unity as Notion.

b. The other manner of bringing harmony to pass is the teleological way of regarding Nature, which is found in the objective and material adaptation to end. Here the immediate unity of the Notion and reality is looked upon as objective in the organic products of Nature—this being the purpose of Nature, containing in its universality the particular, in its particularity the species. But such a mode of consideration must be practised not externally, but in conformity with internal teleology. In external adaptation to end one thing has its end in another: "Snow protects the sown crops in cold lands from frost, and facilitates the intercourse of men by permitting of sleighing."[2] Internal adaptation to end signifies, on the contrary, that a thing is in itself end and means, its end is not therefore beyond itself. In the contemplation of the living creature we do not remain at the point of having something sensuous before us, which according to the categories of the Understanding is only brought into relation to something other than itself; for we regard it as cause of itself, as producing itself. This is the self-preservation of the living creature; as an individual it is no doubt perishable, but in living it produces itself, although for that purpose certain conditions are requisite. The end or purpose of Nature is therefore to be sought for in matter, to the extent that matter is an inwardly organized product of

[1] Kant: Kritik der Urtheilskraft, pp. xliii.–xlv., 16–19, 32, 56, 59, 77.

[2] Ibidem, pp. 279–283.

nature, "in which all is end, and all in turn is means;"[1] because all the members of the organism are at the same time means and end, it is an end in itself. That is the Aristotelian Notion—the infinite that returns into itself, the Idea.

Kant at this point calls to mind the following: "We should find no difference between natural mechanism and the technique of Nature, *i.e.* the connection of ends in the same, were our Understanding not of such a kind that it must pass from the universal to the particular, and the faculty of judgment can therefore pronounce no determining sentences, without having a universal law under which it may subsume the particular. Now the particular as such contains a contingent element in regard to the universal, but nevertheless Reason also demands unity in the connection of particular laws of Nature, and consequently a regulative character, which character when found in the contingent is termed adaptation to end: and the derivation of particular laws from universal is, in regard to the element of contingency which those particular laws contain, *a priori* impossible through the determination of the Notion of the object; the Notion of the adaptation to end of Nature in its products becomes thus a Notion necessary for the human faculty of judgment, but not affecting the determination of the objects themselves, and therefore a subjective principle."[2] An organic Being is therefore, according to Kant (Kritik der Urtheilskraft, p. 354) one in which natural mechanism and end are identical. We regard it as if there dwelt in the sensuous a Notion which brings the particular into conformity with itself. In the organic products of Nature we perceive this immediate unity of the Notion and reality; for in a living creature there is perceived in one unity the soul, or

[1] Kant: Kritik der Urtheilskraft, pp. 286–288, 292–296.

[2] Ibidem, pp. 343, 344.

the universal, and existence or particularity, which is not the case with inorganic Nature. Thus there enters into the Kantian philosophy the conception of the concrete, as that the universal Notion determines the particular. But Kant took these Ideas again in a subjective sense only, as guiding thoughts for the faculty of judgment, by which no Being-in-itself can be expressed; and thus, although he expresses the unity of the Notion and reality, he yet lays fresh emphasis on the side of the Notion. He will not therefore throw off his limitations in the moment in which he assumes them as limitations. This is the perpetual contradiction in Kant's philosophy: Kant exhibited the extremes of opposition in their one-sidedness, and expressed also the reconciliation of the contradiction; Reason postulates unity, and this we have also in the faculty of judgment. Kant, however, says (Kritik der Urtheilskraft, pp. 355–363): This is only a mode of our reflecting faculty of judgment, life itself is not so; we are merely accustomed so to regard it. In art it is thus certainly the sensuous mode which gives us the conception of the Idea; reality and ideality are here directly in one. But at this point also Kant says that we must remain at what is one-sided, at the very moment when he is passing out beyond it. The wealth of thought therefore still unfolds itself with Kant in subjective form alone; all fulness, all content, concentrates in conceiving, thinking, postulating. The objective, according to Kant, is only what is in itself; and we know not what Things-in-themselves are. But Being-in-itself is only the *caput mortuum*, the dead abstraction of the "other," the empty, undetermined Beyond.

The reason why that true Idea should not be the truth is therefore that the empty abstractions of an understanding which keeps itself in the abstract universal, and of a sensuous material of individuality standing in opposition to the same, are presupposed as the truth. Kant no doubt expressly advances to the conception of an intuitive or perceiving understanding, which, while it gives universal laws, at the same time determines the particular; and the determination thus given is deep; it is the true concrete, reality determined by the indwelling Notion, or, as Spinoza says, the adequate Idea. For "to knowledge there also belongs intuitive perception, and the possession of a perfect spontaneity of intuition would be a faculty of knowledge" specifically "distinct from the sensuous, and quite independent thereof, and therefore it would be understanding in the most universal sense. Consequently it is possible to think of an intuitive understanding which does not pass from the universal to the particular, and thus proceed through conceptions to the individual—an understanding in which we do not meet with the contingency of the harmony of Nature in her products, according to particular laws, with the understanding, a contingency which makes it so hard for our understanding to bring" together "into the unity of knowledge the manifold of Nature." But that this "*intellectus archetypus*" is the true Idea of the understanding, is a thought which does not strike Kant. Strange to say, he certainly has this idea of the intuitive; and he does not know why it should have no truth—except because our understanding is otherwise constituted, namely such "that it proceeds from the analytic universal to the particular."[1] But absolute Reason and Understanding in itself, as we have already seen (pp. 432, 461), are, in Kant's view, of such a nature that they have no reality in themselves: the Understanding requires material to work upon, theoretic Reason spins cobwebs of the brain, practical Reason has to allow its reality to come to an end with its postulates. In spite of their directly and definitely expressed non-absoluteness, they are yet looked on as true knowledge; and intuitive

[1] Kant: Kritik der Urtheilskraft, pp. 317, 348 (351).

Understanding, which holds Notion and sensuous perception in one unity, is looked on as a mere thought which we make for ourselves.

c. The highest form in which the conception of the concrete comes into Kant's philosophy is this, that the end is grasped in its entire universality; and thus it is the Good. This Good is an Idea; it is my thought; but there exists the absolute demand that it should be realized also in the world, that the necessity of Nature should correspond with the laws of freedom, not as the necessity of an external Nature, but through what is right and moral in human life, through life in the State,—or in other words that the world in general should be good. This identity of the Good and reality is the demand of practical Reason; but subjective Reason cannot realize this. In every good action a man no doubt accomplishes something good, but this is only limited; universal Good, as the final object of the world, can be attained to only through a third. And this power over the world, which has as its final object the Good in the world, is God.[1] Thus the Critique of the Faculty of Judgment also ends with the postulate of God. Now, although the particular laws of Nature, as independent individual relations, have no relation to the Good, Reason consists in having and desiring unity as the essential or substantial in itself. The opposition of these two, the Good and the world, is contrary to that identity; Reason must therefore demand that this contradiction should be abrogated, that there should be a power which is good on its own account, and is a Power over Nature. This is the position which God assumes in Kant's philosophy: no proof is possible, he says, of God's existence, but the demand is there. The deficiency here is the impossibility of proving God's existence, and it consists in this, that if we admit Kant's dualism, it cannot be shown how the Good

[1] Kant: Kritik der Urtheilskraft, pp. 423, 424.

as abstract Idea in itself is the abrogating of its Idea as abstract; and how the world in itself is the abrogating of itself in its externality, and in its diversity from the Good —this being done in order that both may reveal themselves to be their truth, which in respect to them appears as the Third, but is at the same time determined as the First. Thus, therefore, according to Kant (Kritik der Urtheilskraft, pp. 460, 461), God can only be believed in. We associate the faith of Jacobi with this; for in this point Kant agrees with Jacobi.[1]

If now, in accordance with this standpoint of Kant and Jacobi, God is believed in, and we admit this standpoint for an instant, there is certainly a return to the Absolute. But the question remains: What is God? To define Him as supersensuous is not much, nor is it more to say He is universal, abstract, absolute. What then is His determination? Were we here, however, to pass over to determinations of the Absolute, the evil result would follow, as far as this standpoint is concerned, that we should pass over to knowledge; for this signifies knowledge of an object which is in itself concrete, *i.e.* determined. But here the farthest point reached is the general statement that God exists with the determination of being infinite, universal, indeterminate. God cannot be known in this way; for in order to be known He must as concrete possess at least two determinations. In this way mediation would be established, for a knowledge of the concrete is at once a mediate knowledge. But this standpoint lacks mediation, and thus remains at the immediate. Paul, in speaking to the Athenians, appeals to the altar which they had dedicated to the Unknown God, and declares to them what God is; but the standpoint indicated here takes us back to the Unknown God. All the life of Nature, as

[1] What falls under this heading in Jacobi's philosophy is inserted here in the lectures of 1825-1826.

of Spirit, is mediation in itself; and to this mediation the philosophy of Schelling now passed on.

If we sum up the Kantian philosophy, we find on all hands the Idea of Thought, which is in itself the absolute Notion, and has in itself difference, reality. In the theoretic and practical Reason it has only abstract difference, but in the Faculty of Judgment, as the unity of the two, Kant goes so far as to establish the difference as actual, establishing not only particularity, but also individuality. But, to be sure, this Philistine conception proceeds from our human faculty of knowledge, which is valid for him in its empirical form, notwithstanding his statement that it does not know the truth, and his further description of the true idea of the same as being merely a thought which we possess. Therefore actuality counts as something sensuous, empirical, for the comprehension of which Kant takes the categories of the Understanding, giving them the same validity as they have in everyday life. This is a complete philosophy of the Understanding, which renounces Reason: the reason why it became so popular was the negative one, that men were once for all free from the old metaphysic. According to Kant something sensuous is produced, having thought-determinations, which, however, is not the thing, for if a man, for instance, feels something hard, Kant says: "I feel hardness, but I do not feel Something." Kant's philosophy thus ends with a dualism, with the relation which is a plainly essential "ought," with the unreconciled contradiction. It is otherwise with Jacobi's faith; he finds the conception of God as immediate existence, and all mediation is untrue for him. With Kant, therefore, the result is: "We know only phenomena;" with Jacobi, on the other hand, it is: "We know only the finite and conditioned." Over these two results there has been unmingled joy among men, because the sloth of Reason (Heaven be praised!) considered itself liberated from every call to reflect, and now, being saved the trouble of penetrating to its own inward meaning and exploring the depths of Nature and Spirit, it could very well leave itself alone. The further result attending this is the autocracy of the subjective Reason, which, seeing that it is abstract and without knowledge, has only subjective certainty and not objective truth. The second cause of rejoicing was the concession to freedom of a perfect right, which I can neither understand nor justify, and need not do so; my subjective liberty of conviction and certainty holds good all round. The third cause of joy was added by Jacobi, who said that it amounted even to a crime to seek to know the truth, because the infinite was thereby only rendered finite. Truth is in a bad way, when all metaphysic is done away with, and the only philosophy acknowledged is not a philosophy at all!

But besides the general idea of synthetic judgments *a priori*, a universal which has difference in itself, Kant's instinct carried this out in accordance with the scheme of triplicity, unspiritual though that was, in the whole system into which for him the entire universe was divided. This he not only practised in the three critiques, but he also followed it out in most of the sub-divisions under the categories, the ideas of Reason, &c. Kant has therefore set forth as a universal scheme the rhythm of knowledge, of scientific movement; and has exhibited on all sides thesis, antithesis and synthesis, modes of the mind by means of which it is mind, as thus consciously distinguishing itself. The first is existence, but in the form of Other-Being for consciousness; for what is only existence is object. The second is Being-for-self, genuine actuality; here the reverse relation enters in, for self-consciousness, as the negative of Being-in-itself, is itself reality. The third is the unity of the two; the absolute, self-conscious actuality is the sum of true actuality, into which are re-absorbed both the objective and the independently existent subjective.

Kant has thus made an historical statement of the moments of the whole, and has correctly determined and distinguished them: it is a good introduction to Philosophy. The defect of Kant's philosophy consists in the falling asunder of the moments of the absolute form; or, regarded from the other side, our understanding, our knowledge, forms an antithesis to Being-in-itself: there is lacking the negative, the abrogation of the "ought," which is not laid hold of. But thought and thinking had become once for all an absolute requisite that could no longer be set aside. It was consequently in the first place demanded by consistency that particular thoughts should appear as if produced of necessity from the original unity of the ego, and in that way justified. But, in the second place, thought had spread itself over the world, had attached itself to everything, investigated everything, introduced its forms into everything, and systematized everything, so that on every hand thought-determinations had to be followed, instead of any mere feeling or routine or practical common-sense, or what is evidenced in the extraordinary lack of understanding on the part of so-called practical men. And therefore in theology, in governments and their legislation, in the object aimed at by the state, in trades and in mechanics, it is said that men ought to act according to universal determinations, *i.e.* rationally: and men even talk of a rational brewery, a rational brick-kiln, etc. This is the requisite of concrete thought; while in the Kantian result, which is that of phenomenon, an empty thought was alone present. It is verily also the essence of revealed religion to know what God is. There was, therefore, to be found a yearning desire for content, for truth, since man could not possibly return to the condition of a brute, nor yet sink to the form of sensation, so that this yearning was for him the only thing that held good with regard to the higher life. The first requirement—consistency—Fichte sought to satisfy; the other—content—Schelling strove to fulfil.

C. Fichte.

Fichte created a great sensation in his time; his philosophy is the Kantian philosophy in its completion, and, as we must specially notice, it is set forth in a more logical way. He does not pass beyond the fundamentals of Kant's philosophy, and at first regarded his own philosophy as no more than a systematic working out of the other.[1] In addition to these systems of philosophies, and that of Schelling, there are none. Any that pretend to be such merely pick out something from these, and over this they fight and wrangle among themselves. *Ils se sont battus les flancs, pour être de grands hommes.* For in those times there were in Germany many systems of philosophy, such as those of Reinhold, Krug, Bouterweck, Fries, Schulze, &c.; but in them there is only an extremely limited point of view, combined with boastfulness—a strange medley of stray thoughts and conceptions or facts which I find within me. But their thoughts are all derived from Fichte, Kant, or Schelling—that is in so far as there are thoughts there present at all. Or else some slight modification is added, and this for the most part merely consists in making the great principles barren, what points in them were living are destroyed, or else subordinate forms are changed, whereby another principle is said to be set forth, though when we look closer we find that these principles are but the principles of one of those philosophies that have gone before. This may serve as a justification for my not speaking further of all these philosophies; any exposition of them would be no more than a demonstration that everything in them is taken from Kant, Fichte, or Schelling, and that the modification in form is only the semblance of a change, while really it indicates a deterioration in the principles of those philosophies.

[1] Fichte: Grundlage der gesammten Wissenschaftslehre (Leipzig, 1794), Preface, p. xii.

Johann Gottlieb Fichte was born on the 19th of May, 1762, at Rammenau, near Bischoffswerda, in Upper Lusatia. He studied at Jena, and for some time was a private tutor in Switzerland. He wrote a treatise on Religion, termed a "Critique of all Revelation," where the Kantian phraseology is employed throughout—so much so that it was thought to be the work of Kant. After this he was in 1793 summoned to Jena by Goethe as Professor of Philosophy, which appointment he, however, resigned in the year 1799, on account of an unpleasantness which had arisen through his essay "On the ground of our Belief in a Divine Government of the World." For Fichte published a journal in Jena, and a paper in it which was by someone else was regarded as atheistical. Fichte might have kept silence, but he published the above-mentioned essay as an introduction to the article. The authorities wished an investigation to be made into the matter. Then Fichte wrote a letter which contained threats, and respecting it Goethe said that a Government ought not to allow itself to be threatened. Fichte now taught privately for some time in Berlin; in 1805 he became professor at Erlangen, and in 1809 at Berlin, at which place he died on the 27th January, 1814.[1] We cannot here deal more particularly with the details of his life.

In what is termed the philosophy of Fichte a distinction must be made between his properly-speaking speculative philosophy, in which the argument is most consistently worked out, and which is less well known, and his popular philosophy, to which belong the lectures delivered in Berlin before a mixed audience, and, for example, the work termed a "Guidance to a Blessed Life." These last have much in them that is affecting and edifying—many who call them-

[1] Fichte's Leben und Briefwechsel, edited by his son, Pt. I. pp. 3, 6, 24 seq.; 38 seq.; 142, 189; 337, 338, 348, 349, 353, 354, 358–364; Pt. II. pp. 140–142; Pt. I. pp. 370–372, 442–448, 455; 518, 540; 578.

selves the disciples of Fichte know this side alone—and they are expressed in language most impressive to a cultured, religious temperament. In the history of Philosophy, however, such cannot be taken into consideration, although through their matter they may have the highest possible value; the content has to be speculatively developed, and that is done in Fichte's earlier philosophic works alone.[1]

1. The First Principles of Fichte's Philosophy.

As we mentioned above (p. 478), the shortcoming in the Kantian philosophy was its unthinking inconsistency, through which speculative unity was lacking to the whole system; and this shortcoming was removed by Fichte. It is the absolute form which Fichte laid hold of, or in other words, the absolute form is just the absolute Being-for-self, absolute negativity, not individuality, but the Notion of individuality, and thereby the Notion of actuality; Fichte's philosophy is thus the development of form in itself. He maintained the ego to be the absolute principle, so that from it, the direct and immediate certainty of self, all the matter in the universe must be represented as produced; hence, according to Fichte, reason is in itself a synthesis of Notion and actuality. But this principle he once more in an equally one-sided manner set aside; it is from the very beginning subjective, conditioned by an opposite, and its realization is a continual rushing onward in finitude, a looking back at what has gone before. The form in which it is presented has also the disadvantage, and indeed, the real

[1] Fichte's posthumous works, which were not published until after Hegel's death, nevertheless show that the writer in his lectures at the Berlin University likewise worked out scientifically this newly developed point of view in his philosophy; Fichte made a beginning in this regard brocheven in the ure which appeared in 1810: "Die Wissenschaftslehre in ihrem allgemeinen Umrisse" (v. Michelet: Geschichte der letzten Systeme der Philosophie, Pt. I. pp. 441, 442). [Editor's note.]

drawback of bringing the empiric ego ever before one's eyes, which is absurd, and quite distracting to one's point of view.

The claims of Philosophy have advanced so far that in the first place self-consciousness refuses any longer to regard absolute essence as immediate substance which does not in itself possess difference, reality, and actuality. Against this substance self-consciousness ever struggled, for it does not find its explicit Being there, and consequently feels the lack of freedom. But besides this it demanded that this essence, objectively presented, should be personal, living, self-conscious, actual, and not shut up in abstract metaphysical thoughts alone. On the other hand consciousness, for which the other is, demanded the moment of external actuality, Being as such, into which thought must pass, truth in objective existence; and this is what we more especially noticed in connection with the English. This Notion, which is immediately actuality, and this actuality which is immediately its Notion, and that indeed in such a way that there neither is a third thought above this unity, nor is it an immediate unity which does not possess difference, separation, within it, is the ego; it is the self-distinction of opposites within itself. That whereby it distinguishes itself from the simplicity of thought, and distinguishes this other, is likewise immediately for it; it is identical with, or not distinguished from it.[1] Hence it is pure thought, or the ego is the true synthetic judgment *a priori*, as Kant called it. This principle is apprehended actuality, for the taking back of the other-Being into self-consciousness is just apprehension. The Notion of the Notion is from this point of view found in the fact that in what is apprehended self-consciousness has the certainty of itself; what is not apprehended is some-

[1] Fichte: Grundlage der gesammten Wissenschaftslehre, pp. 10-12.

thing foreign to it. This absolute Notion or this absolutely existent infinitude it is which has to be developed in knowledge, and its distinction as the whole distinction of the universe has to be represented from itself, and this has in its distinction to remain reflected within itself in equal absoluteness. Nothing other than the ego anywhere exists, and the ego is there because it is there; what is there is only in the ego and for the ego.[1]

Now Fichte merely set forth this Notion; he did not bring it to a scientific realization from itself. For to him this Notion maintains and asserts itself as this Notion; it has absoluteness for him in so far as it is merely the unrealized Notion, and thus indeed comes once more into opposition with reality. The Fichtian philosophy has the great advantage of having set forth the fact that Philosophy must be a science derived from one supreme principle, from which all determinations are necessarily derived. The important point is this unity of principle and the attempt to develop from it in a scientifically consistent way the whole content of consciousness, or, as has been said, to construct the whole world.[2] Beyond this no progress was made.[3] But the great necessity in Philosophy is to possess one living Idea; the world is a flower which is eternally produced from one grain of seed. Thus Fichte does not, like Kant, throw his work into narrative form because he begins with the ego; but he has proceeded further, inasmuch as he sought to bring about a construction of determinations of knowledge from the ego. The whole extent of knowledge in all the world must be developed, and further this knowledge must be the consequence of the development of determinations; but because Fichte says that what is not

[1] Fichte: Grundlage der gesammten Wissenschaftslehre, pp. 13, 14.

[2] Fichte: Ueber den Begriff der Wissenschaftslehre (Weimar, 1794), p. 12.

[3] Fichte: Grundlage der ges. Wissenschaftsl., Preface, pp. x., xi.

for us does not concern us, he has not grasped this principle of the ego as Idea, but solely in the consciousness of the activity which we exercise in knowing, and consequently it is still laid hold of in the form of subjectivity.

Thus as Kant treats of cognition [Erkennen], so Fichte sets forth real knowledge [Wissen]. Fichte states that the task of Philosophy is to find a theory of knowledge; universal knowledge is both the object and the starting-point of Philosophy. Consciousness knows, that is its nature; the end of philosophic learning is the knowledge of this knowledge. Hence Fichte called his philosophy the Theory of Knowledge (Begriff der Wissenschaftslehre, p. 18), the science of knowledge. That is to say ordinary consciousness as the active ego finds this and that, occupies itself, not with itself, but with other objects and interests, but the necessity that I bring forth determinations, and which determinations—cause and effect, for example,—lies beyond my consciousness: I bring them forth instinctively and cannot get behind my consciousness. But when I philosophize, I make my ordinary consciousness itself my object, because I make a pure category my consciousness: I know what my ego is doing, and thus I get behind my ordinary consciousness. Fichte thus defines Philosophy as the artificial consciousness, as the consciousness of consciousness.[1]

a. Where Fichte in his system has attained the highest degree of determinateness, he begins, as we saw Kant did before (pp. 437, 438), from the transcendental unity of self-consciousness; in it I—as this—am one, this unity is to Fichte the same and the original. Ego is there a fact, says Fichte, but not yet a proposition. As proposition, as principle, the ego must not remain barren, nor be accepted as one, for to a proposition pertains a synthesis. Now Fichte proceeds in his system from the fact that Philosophy

[1] Fichte: Grundlage der gesammten Wissenschaftslehre, pp. 184, 185.

must begin with an absolutely unconditioned, certain principle, with something indubitably certain in ordinary knowledge. "It cannot be proved or defined, because it must be absolutely the first principle."[1] According to Wendt's account (Tennemann's Grundriss, § 393, pp. 494, 495) Fichte gives an exposition of the necessity of such a principle as follows: "Scientific knowledge is a system of cognition obtained through a supreme principle which expresses the content and form of knowledge. The theory of knowledge is the science of knowledge which sets forth the possibility and validity of all knowledge, and proves the possibility of principles in reference to form and content, the principles themselves, and thereby the connection existing in all human knowledge. It must have a principle which can neither be proved from it nor from another science; for it is supreme. If there is a theory of knowledge there also is a system; if there is a system there is also a theory of knowledge and an absolute first principle—and so on through an inevitable circle."[2]

The simple principle of this knowledge is certainty of myself, which is the relation of me to myself; what is in me, that I know. The supreme principle, as immediate and not derived, must be certain on its own account; that is, a determination of the ego only, for it is only from the ego that I cannot abstract.[3] Fichte thus begins, like Descartes, with 'I think, therefore I am,' and he expressly brings this proposition to mind. The Being of the ego is not a dead, but a concrete Being; but the highest Being is thought. Ego, as an explicitly self-existent activity of thought, is thus knowledge, even if it is only abstract knowledge, as in the beginning at least it cannot help being. At the

[1] Fichte: Grundlage der gesammten Wissenschaftslehre, p. 3.

[2] Cf. Fichte: Ueber den Begriff der Wissenschaftslehre, pp. 13-17, 19-39, 50-52.

[3] Fichte: Grundlage der gesammten Wissenschaftslehre, pp. 4, 5.

same time Fichte begins from this absolute certainty with quite other necessities and demands; for from this ego not only Being but also the larger system of thought has to be derived (*supra*, p. 230). According to Fichte, the ego is the source of the categories and ideas, but all conceptions and thoughts are a manifold reduced to a synthesis through Thought. Thus while with Descartes in connection with the ego other thoughts appear which we simply find already in us, such as God, nature, &c., Fichte sought for a philosophy entirely of a piece, in which nothing empiric was to be admitted from without. With this reflection a false point of view was at once introduced, namely that contained in the old conception of knowledge, of commencing with principles in this form and proceeding from them; so that the reality which is derived from such a principle is brought into opposition with it, and hence in truth is something different, *i.e.* it is not derived: or that principle for this same reason expresses only the absolute certainty of itself and not the truth. The ego is certain, it cannot be doubted; but Philosophy desires to reach the truth. The certainty is subjective, and because it is made to remain the basis, all else remains subjective also without there being any possibility of this form being removed. Fichte now analyzes the ego, reducing it to three principles from which the whole of knowledge has to be evolved.

a. The first proposition must be simple, in it predicate and subject must be alike; for were they unlike, their connection—since in accordance with their diversity the determinations are not directly one—would have to be first of all proved by means of a third. The first principle must thus be identical. Fichte now proceeds further to distinguish in this first principle the form and content; but in order that this same may be immediately true through itself, form and content must be again the same, and the principle conditioned by neither. It signifies $A = A$, the abstract undetermined identity; that is the proposition of contradiction, wherein A is an indifferent content. Fichte says, "Thought is by no means essence, but only a particular determination of Being; there are outside of it many other determinations of our Being. I merely remark this, that when 'I am' is overstepped, Spinozism is necessarily reached. Its unity is something which ought to be produced through us, but which cannot be so; it is not anything that is." The first proposition is then that I am identical with myself, Ego = Ego;[1] that undoubtedly is the definition of the ego. The subject and the predicate are the content; and this content of the two sides is likewise their relation, *i.e.* form. Relation requires two sides; the relating and the related are here, however, the same; for on account of the simplicity of the ego, there is nothing but a relation of the ego to the ego. I have knowledge of myself; but in so far as I am consciousness, I know of an object which is different from me, and which is then likewise *mine*. But the ego is in such a way identical with its difference that what is different is immediately the same, and what is identical is likewise different; we have a difference without a difference. Self-consciousness is not dead identity, or non-Being, but the object which is identical with me. This is immediately certain; all else must be as certain to me, inasmuch as it must be my relation to myself. The content must be transformed into the ego, so that in it I have *my* determination alone. This principle is at first abstract and deficient, because in it no difference, or a formal difference only is expressed; whereas the principle should possess a content: a subject and a predicate are indeed distinguished in it, but only for us who reflect upon it, *i.e.* in itself there is no difference, and consequently no true content. In the second place, this principle is indeed the imme-

[1] Grundlage der gesammten Wissenschaftslehre, pp. 23, 5, 15, 17, 8.

diate certainty of self-consciousness, but self-consciousness is likewise consciousness, and in it there is likewise the certainty that other things exist to which it stands in an attitude of opposition. In the third place, that principle has not the truth in it, for the very reason that the certainty of itself possessed by the ego has no objectivity; it has not the form of the differentiated content within it —or it stands in opposition to the consciousness of an "other"

β. Now in order that determination should come to pass, *i.e.* a content and difference, it is essential for Fichte that a second principle should be established, which in regard to form is unconditioned, but the content of which is conditioned, because it does not belong to the ego. This second principle, set forth under the first, is, "I assert a non-ego in opposition to the ego," and in this something other than absolute self-consciousness is set forth.[1] To this pertains the form therein present, relation; but the content is the non-ego, another content from the ego. We might say that through this content the proposition is independent, since the negative therein is an absolute, as truly as the reverse—that it is independent through the form of opposition which cannot be derived from the original. Here, then, we have no more to do with derivation, although this derivation of opposition from the first proposition was all the same demanded. Inasmuch as I posit another in opposition to the ego, I posit myself as not posited; this non-ego is the object generally, *i.e.* that which is opposed to me. This other is the negative of the ego; thus when Fichte called it the non-ego he was expressing himself in a very happy, suitable, and consistent manner. There has been a good deal of ridicule cast on the ego and non-ego; the expression is new, and therefore to us Germans it seems strange at first.

[1] Fichte; Grundlage der ges. Wissenschaftslehre, pp. 17, 19-22.

But the French say *Moi* and *Non-moi*, without finding anything laughable in it. In this principle the positing belongs, however, to the ego; but because the non-ego is independent of the ego, we have two sides, and self-consciousness relates itself to another. This second proposition thus signifies that I posit myself as limited, as non-ego; but non-ego is something quite new to be added. On the one side we thus have before us a field which is merely appropriated from the ego; and in this way we have before us the non-ego as our object.

γ. To these is added yet a third proposition, in which I now make this division into ego and non-ego: it is the synthetic principle, the proposition of ground, which in content is unconditioned, just as in the second was the case in regard to form. This third proposition is the determination of the first two through one another, in such a way that the ego limits the non-ego. "In and through the ego both the ego and the non-ego are posited as capable of being mutually limited by means of one another, *i.e.* in such a way that the reality of the one abrogates the reality of the other." In limitation both are negated, but "only in part"; only thus are synthesis and deduction possible. I posit the non-ego, which is for me, in myself, in my identity with myself; thus I take it from its non-identity, its not-being-I, that is to say I limit it. This limitation of the non-ego Fichte expresses thus: "I place in opposition to the ego," and indeed "to the divisible ego, a divisible non-ego." The non-ego I destroy as a complete sphere, which it was according to the second principle, and posit it as divisible; I likewise posit the ego as divisible in so far as the non-ego is present in it. The whole sphere which I have before me is supposed indeed to be the ego, but in it I have not one but two. The proposition of ground is thus the relation of reality and negation, *i.e.* it is limitation; it contains the ego limited by the non-ego, and the non-ego limited by the ego.[1] Of this synthesis there is nothing, properly speaking, contained in the two earlier propositions. Even this first presentation of the three principles does away with the immanence of real knowledge. Thus the presentation is here also subject to an opposite from the first, as it is with Kant, even if these are two acts of the ego merely, and we remain entirely in the ego.

Now that limitation may take place for me in two different ways: at one time the one is passive, at another time the other is so. In this limitation the ego may posit the non-ego as limiting and itself as limited, in such a way that the ego posits itself as requiring to have an object; I know myself indeed as ego, but determined by the non-ego; non-ego is here active and ego passive. Or, on the other hand, the ego, as abrogating other-being, is that which limits, and non-ego is the limited. I know myself then as clearly determining the non-ego, as the absolute cause of the non-ego as such, for I can think. The first is the proposition of the theoretic reason, of intelligence: the second the proposition of practical reason, of will.[2] The will is this, that I am conscious of myself as limiting the object; thus I make myself exercise activity upon the object and maintain myself. The theoretic proposition is that the object is before me and it determines me. The ego is, since I perceive, a content, and I have this content in me, which is thus outside of me. This is on the whole the same thing as we meet with in the experience of Kant: it comes to the same thing whether it is by matter or the non-ego that the ego is here determined.

b. In the theoretic consciousness the ego, although the assertive generally, finds itself limited by the non-ego.

[1] Fichte: Grundlage der gesammten Wissenschaftslehre, pp. 34, 31, 23, 27-30 (52), 14, 18.

[2] Ibidem, pp. 52-56, 74.

But it is identical with itself; hence its infinite activity ever sets itself to abrogate the non-ego and to bring forth itself. Now the different methods whereby the ego sets forth itself are the different methods of its activity; these we have to understand in their necessity. But since philosophic knowledge is the consideration of consciousness itself (*supra*, p. 483), I can only know knowledge, the act of the ego. Fichte thus appeals to consciousness, postulates ego and non-ego in their abstraction, and since philosophic knowledge is the consciousness of consciousness, it is not sufficient that I should find its determinations in consciousness, for I produce them with consciousness. Common consciousness, indeed, likewise brings forth all the determinations of the ordinary conception and of thought, but without—on the theoretic side at least—having any knowledge of it; for it is the fact of being limited alone that is present to it. Thus, when I see a large square object, such as a wall, my ordinary consciousness accepts these determinations as they are given to it; the object *is*. In so doing I do not think of seeing, but of the object; seeing, however, is my activity, the determinations of my faculty of sensation are thus posited through me.[1] The ego as theoretic is, indeed, aware in philosophic consciousness that it is the ego which posits; but here it posits that the non-ego posits somewhat in me. The ego thus posits itself as that which is limited by the non-ego. I make this limitation mine; thus is it for me in me, this passivity of the ego is itself the activity of the ego. As a matter of fact, all reality which appears in the object for the ego is a determination of the ego,[2] just as the categories and other determinations were in Kant's case. Thus it is here more especially that we should expect Fichte to demonstrate the return of other-Being into absolute consciousness. How-

[1] Fichte's Anweisung zum seligen Leben, pp. 80-82.

[2] Fichte: Grundlage der gesammten Wissenschaftslehre, p. 57.

ever, because after all the other-Being was regarded as unconditioned, as implicit, this return does not come to pass. The ego determines the 'other,' indeed, but this unity is an altogether finite unity; non-ego has thus immediately escaped from determination once more and gone forth from this unity. What we find is merely an alternation between self-consciousness and the consciousness of another, and the constant progression of this alternation, which never reaches any end.[1]

The development of theoretic reason is the following-out of the manifold relationships between the ego and non-ego; the forms of this limitation which Fichte now goes through are the determinations of the object. These particular thought-determinations he calls categories, and he seeks to demonstrate them in their necessity; from the time of Aristotle onwards no one had thought of so doing. The first of these forms is the determination of reciprocity, which we already met with in the third proposition: "By the determination of the reality or negation of the ego, the negation or reality of the non-ego is equally determined;" the two in one is reciprocal action. In the second place, "Causality is the same degree of activity in the one as of passivity in the other." In so far as something is considered as the reality of the non-ego, the ego is considered as passive, and, on the other hand, in so far as 'I' am real, the object is passive; this relation, that the passivity of the object is my activity or reality, and the opposite, is the conception of Causality. "As many parts of negation as the ego posits in itself, so many parts of reality it posits in the non-ego; it therefore posits itself as self-determining in so far as it is determined, and as suffering determination in so far as it determines itself. In so far," in the third place, "as the ego is regarded as embracing the whole absolutely determined realm of all reality, it is substance;

[1] Fichte: Grundlage der gesammten Wissenschaftslehre, pp. 78, 79.

on the other hand when it is posited in a not absolutely determined sphere of this realm, in so far there is an accidence in the ego."[1] That is the first rational attempt that has ever been made to deduce the categories; this progress from one determination to another is, however, only an analysis from the standpoint of consciousness, and is not in and for itself.

The ego is so far the ideal ground of all conceptions of the object; all determination of this object is a determination of the ego. But in order that it may be object, it must be placed in opposition to the ego, *i.e.* the determinations set forth through the ego are another, the non-ego; this placing of the object in opposition is the real ground of conceptions. The ego is, however, likewise the real ground of the object; for it is likewise a determination of the ego that the non-ego as object is set in opposition to the ego. Both, the real ground and the ideal ground of the conception, are thus one and the same.[2] Regarding the ego as ideal principle and the non-ego as real principle, Krug has likewise talked a great deal of nonsense. Regarded from the one point of view, the ego is active and the non-ego purely passive; while from the other side the ego is passive and the object active and operative. But since the ego in the non-philosophic consciousness does not have the consciousness of its activity in the conception of the object, it represents to itself its own activity as foreign, *i.e.* as belonging to the non-ego.

We here see the opposition adopting various forms: ego, non-ego; positing, setting in opposition; two sorts of activity of the ego, &c. The fact that I represent is undoubtedly my activity, but the matter of main importance is the content of the positing and its necessary connection through itself. If one occupies oneself only with this con-

[1] Fichte: Grundlage der gesammten Wissenschaftslehre, pp. 60, 67, 59, 76.

[2] Ibidem, pp. 121, 122.

tent, that form of subjectivity which is dominant with Fichte, and which remains in his opposition, disappears. As the ego is affirmative and determining, there now is in this determination a negative likewise present; I find myself determined and at the same time the ego is like itself, infinite, *i.e.* identical with itself. This is a contradiction which Fichte indeed endeavours to reconcile, but in spite of it all he leaves the false basis of dualism undisturbed. The ultimate, beyond which Fichte does not get, is only an 'ought,' which does not solve the contradiction; for while the ego should be absolutely at home with itself, *i.e.* free, it should at the same time be associated with another. To Fichte the demand for the solution of this contradiction thus adopts the attitude of being a demanded solution only, of signifying that I ever have to destroy the barriers, that I ever have to reach beyond the limitation into utter infinitude, and that I ever find a new limit; a continual alternation takes place between negation and affirmation, an identity with self which again falls into negation, and from this negation is ever again restored. To speak of the bounds of human reason is, however, an unmeaning form of words. That the reason of the subject is limited is comprehensible from the nature of the case, but when we speak of Thought, infinitude is none other than one's own relation to self, and not to one's limit; and the place in which man is infinite is Thought. Infinitude may then be likewise very abstract, and in this way it is also once more finite; but true infinitude remains in itself.

Fichte further deduces the ordinary conception thus: the fact that the ego in going forth at once finds its activity checked by a limitation, and returns once more into itself, brings about two opposite tendencies in me, between which I waver, and which I try to unite in the faculty of imagination. In order that a fixed determination may exist between the two, I have to make the limit a permanent one, and we have that in the understanding. All further determinations of the object are, as categories of the understanding, modes of synthesis; but each synthesis is a new contradiction. New mediations are thus once more necessary, and these are new determinations. Thus Fichte says: I can always continue to determine the non-ego, to make it my conception, *i.e.* to take from it its negation as regards me. I have to deal with my activity alone; but there is always an externality therein present which still remains, and which is not explained by my activity. This Beyond which alone remains to the undetermined ego Fichte calls the infinite check upon the ego, with which it ever has to deal, and beyond which it cannot get; thus the activity which proceeds into infinitude finds itself checked and driven back by this repulsive force, and then it reacts upon itself. "The ego in its self-determination has been considered both as determining and determined; if we reflect on the fact that the absolutely determined determining power must be an absolutely indeterminate, and further, that ego and non-ego are absolutely opposed to one another, in the one case ego is the indeterminate and in the other case non-ego."[1]

Inasmuch as the ego here makes the object its conception and negates it, this philosophy is Idealism, in which philosophy all the determinations of the object are ideal. Everything determinate which the ego possesses it has through its own positing; I even make a coat or a boot because I put them on. There remains only the empty repulsive force, and that is the Kantian Thing-in-itself, beyond which even Fichte cannot get, even though the theoretic reason continues its determination into infinitude. "The ego as intelligence" ever "remains dependent on an undetermined non-ego; it is only through this that it is intelligence."[2] The theoretic side is thus dependent. In

[1] Fichte: Grundlage der gesammten Wissenschaftslehre, pp. 194-197, 204, 221, 222.

[2] Ibidem, p. 228.

it we have not therefore to deal with the truth in and for itself, but with a contingent, because ego is limited, not absolute, as its Notion demands: intelligence is not here considered as spirit which is free. This is Fichte's standpoint as regards the theoretic side.

c. Practical reason comes next; the point of view from which it starts is that "The ego posits itself as determining the non-ego." Now the contradiction has thus to be solved of ego being at home with itself, since it determines its Beyond. The ego is thus infinite activity, and, as ego = ego, the absolute ego, it is undoubtedly abstract. But in order to have a determination, a non-ego must exist; ego is thus activity, causality, the positing of the non-ego. But as with Kant sensuousness and reason remain opposed, the same contradiction is present here, only in a more abstract form, and not in the rude empiricism of Kant. Fichte here turns and twists in all sorts of ways, or he gives the opposition many different forms; the crudest form is that ego is posited as causality, for in it another is necessitated on which it exercises its activity. "The absolute ego has accordingly to be" now "the cause of the non-ego, *i.e.* only of that in the non-ego which remains when we abstract from all demonstrable forms of representation or conception—of that to which is ascribed the check given to the infinitely operative activity of the ego; for the fact that the intelligent ego is, in accordance with the necessary laws of the conception, the cause of the particular determinations of that which is conceived as such, is demonstrated in the theoretic science of knowledge."[1] The limits of intelligence must be broken through, the ego must alone be active; the other side, the infinite repulsion, must be removed, in order that the ego may be liberated.

[1] Fichte: Grundlage der gesammten Wissenschaftslehre, pp. 225, 229, 232.

"According to our hypothesis the ego must now posit a non-ego absolutely, and without any ground, *i.e.* absolutely and without any ground it must limit or in part not posit itself." This, indeed, it already does as intelligent. "It must therefore have the ground of not positing itself" only "in itself." The ego is, however, just the ego, it posits itself, "it must" therefore "have the principle of positing itself within it, and also the principle of not positing itself. Hence the ego in its essence would be contradictory and self-repellent; there would be in it a twofold or contradictory principle, which assumption contradicts itself, for in that case there would be no principle within it. The ego would" consequently "not exist, for it would abrogate itself. All contradictions are reconciled through the further determination of contradictory propositions. The ego must be posited in one sense as infinite, and in another as finite. Were it to be posited as infinite and finite in one and the same sense, the contradiction would be insoluble; the ego would not be one but two. In so far as the ego posits itself as infinite, its activity is directed upon itself and on nothing else but itself. In so far as the ego posits limits, and itself in these limits, its activity is not exercised directly on itself, but on a non-ego which has to be placed in opposition," upon another and again upon another, and so on into infinitude; that is the object, and the activity of the ego "is objective activity."[1] In this way Fichte in the practical sphere also remains at opposition, only this opposition now has the form of two tendencies in the ego, both of which are said to be one and the same activity of the ego. I am called upon to proceed to determine the other in relation to which I am negative, the non-ego, in accordance with my freedom; it has indeed all determinations through the activity of

[1] Fichte: Grundlage der gesammten Wissenschaftslehre, pp. 233, 238, 239.

the ego, but beyond my determination the same non-ego ever continues to appear. The ego clearly posits an object, a point of limitation, but where the limitation is; is undetermined. I may transfer the sphere of my determination, and extend it to an infinite degree, but there always remains a pure Beyond, and the non-ego has no positive self-existent determination.

The last point in respect of the practical sphere is hence this, that the activity of the ego is a yearning or striving [1] —like the Kantian "ought"; Fichte treats this with great prolixity. The Fichtian philosophy consequently has the same standpoint as the Kantian; the ultimate is always subjectivity, as existent in and for itself. Yearning, according to Fichte, is divine; in yearning I have not forgotten myself, I have not forgotten that I possess a superiority in myself; and therefore it is a condition of happiness and satisfaction. This infinite yearning and desire has then been regarded as what is highest and most excellent in the Beautiful, and in religious feelings likewise; and with it is connected the irony of which we have spoken before (Vol. I. pp. 400, 401). In this return the ego is merely an effort, on its side it is fixed, and it cannot realize its endeavours. Striving is thus an imperfect or implicitly limited action. The ultimate result is consequently a "circle" which cannot be broken through, so that "the finite spirit must necessarily posit an absolute outside itself (a thing-in-itself), and yet on the other hand it must recognize that this same is only there for it (a necessary noumenon)." [2] To put it otherwise, we see the ego absolutely determined in opposition only, we see it only as consciousness and self-consciousness which does not get beyond this, and which does not reach so far as to Spirit. The ego is the absolute Notion in so far as it does

[1] Fichte: Grundlage der gesammten Wissenschaftslehre, pp. 302, 246, 247.

[2] Ibidem, p. 273.

not yet reach the unity of thought, or in this simplicity does not reach difference, and in motion does not have rest; that is to say, in so far as positing, or the pure activity of the ego, and setting in opposition, are not by it comprehended as the same. Or the ego does not comprehend the infinite repulsion, the non-ego; self-consciousness determines the non-ego, but does not know how to make this Beyond its own.

The deficiency in the Fichtian philosophy is thus firstly that the ego retains the significance of the individual, actual self-consciousness, as opposed to that which is universal or absolute, or to the spirit in which it is itself a moment merely; for the individual self-consciousness simply signifies standing apart as far as another is concerned. Hence, if the ego was ever called absolute existence, the most terrible offence was given, because really the ego only came before us as signifying the individual subject as opposed to the universal.

In the second place, Fichte does not attain to the idea of Reason as the perfected, real unity of subject and object, or of ego and non-ego; it is only, as with Kant, represented as the thought of a union in a belief or faith, and with this Fichte likewise concludes (Grundlage der gesammten Wissenschaftslehre, p. 301). This he worked out in his popular writings. For because the ego is fixed in its opposition to the non-ego, and *is* only as being opposed, it becomes lost in that unity. The attainment of this aim is hence sent further and further back into the false, sensuous infinitude: it is a progression implying just the same contradiction as that found in Kant, and having no present actuality in itself; for the ego has all actuality in its opposition only. The Fichtian philosophy recognizes the finite spirit alone, and not the infinite; it does not recognize spirit as universal thought, as the Kantian philosophy does not recognize the not-true; or it is formal. The knowledge of absolute unity is apprehended as faith in a moral disposition of the world, an absolute hypothesis in accordance with which we have the belief that every moral action that we perform will have a good result.[1] As in Kant's case, this Idea belongs to universal thought. "In a word, when anything is apprehended it ceases to be God; and every conception of God that is set up is necessarily that of a false God. Religion is a practical faith in the moral government of the world; faith in a supersensuous world belongs, according to our philosophy, to the immediate verities."[2] Fichte thus concludes with the highest Idea, with the union of freedom and nature, but a union of such a nature that, immediately regarded, it is not known; the opposition alone falls within consciousness. This union of faith he likewise finds in the Love of God. As believed and experienced, this form pertains to Religion, and not to Philosophy, and our only possible interest is to know this in Philosophy. But with Fichte it is still associated with a most unsatisfying externality of which the basis is the non-Idea, for the one determination is essential only because the other is so, and so on into infinitude. "The theory of knowledge is realistic—it shows that the consciousness of finite beings can only be explained by presupposing an independent and wholly opposite power, on which, in accordance with their empirical existence, they themselves are dependent. But it asserts nothing more than this opposed power, which by finite beings can merely be *felt* and not known. All possible determinations of this power or of this non-ego which can come forth into infinity in our consciousness, it pledges itself to deduce from the determining faculties of the ego, and it must actually be able to deduce these, so certainly as it is a theory of knowledge. This knowledge, however, is not transcendent but

[1] Fichte: Ueber den Grund unseres Glaubens an eine göttliche Weltregierung (Fichte's Leben, Part II.), p. 111.

[2] Fichte: Verantwortungsschreiben gegen die Anklage des Atheismus, pp. 51, 53.

transcendental. It undoubtedly explains all consciousness from something independent of all consciousness, but it does not forget that this independent somewhat is again a product of its own power of thought, and consequently something dependent on the ego, in so far as it has to be there for the ego. Every thing is, in its ideality, dependent upon the ego; but in its reality even the ego is dependent. The fact that the finite spirit must posit for itself somewhat outside of itself, which last exists only for it, is that circle which it may infinitely extend but never break through." The further logical determination of the object is that which in subject and object is identical, the true connection is that in which the objective is the possession of the ego; as thought, the ego in itself determines the object. But Fichte's theory of knowledge regards the struggle of the ego with the object as that of the continuous process of determining the object through the ego as subject of consciousness, without the identity of the restfully self-developing Notion.

Thirdly, because the ego is thus fixed in its one-sidedness, there proceeds from it, as representing one extreme, the whole of the progress that is made in the content of knowledge; and the deduction of the philosophy of Fichte, cognition in its content and form, is a progression from certain determinations to others which do not turn back into unity, or through a succession of finitenesses which do not have the Absolute in them at all. The absolute point of view, like an absolute content, is wanting. Thus the contemplation of nature, for instance, is a contemplation of it as of pure finitenesses from the point of view of another, as though the organic body were regarded thus: "Consciousness requires a sphere entirely its own for its activity. This sphere is posited through an original,

[1] Fichte: Grundlage der gesammten Wissenschaftslehre, pp. 272-274.

necessary activity of the ego, in which it does not know itself as free. It is a sensuous perception, a drawing of lines; the sphere of activity thereby becomes something extended in space. As quiescent, continuous, and yet unceasingly changing, this sphere is matter, which, as body, has a number of parts which in relation to one another are called limbs. The person can ascribe to himself no body without positing it as being under the influence of another person. But it is likewise essential that I should be able to check this same influence, and external matter is also posited as resisting my influences on it, *i.e.* as a tough, compact matter."[1] These tough matters must further be separated from one another—the different persons cannot hold together like one mass of dough. For "my body is my body and not that of another; it must further operate and be active without my working through it. It is only through the operation of another that I can myself be active and represent myself as a rational being who can be respected by him. But the other being should treat me immediately as a rational being, I should be for him a rational being even before my activity begins. Or my form must produce an effect through its mere existence in space, without my activity, *i.e.* it must be visible. The reciprocal operation of rational beings must take place without activity; thus a subtle matter must be assumed in order that it may be modified by means of the merely quiescent form. In this way are deduced first Light and then Air."[2] This constitutes a very external manner of passing from one step to another, resembling the method of the ordinary teleology, which makes out, for instance, that plants and animals are given for the nourishment of mankind. This is how it is put: Man must eat, and thus there

[1] Fichte: Grundlage des Naturrechts (Jena und Leipzig, 1796), Part I. pp. 55-71.

[2] Ibidem, pp. 78-82.

must be something edible—consequently plants and animals are at once deduced; plants must have their root in something, and consequently the earth is forthwith deduced. What is altogether lacking is any consideration of the object as what it is in itself; it is plainly considered only in relation to another. In this way the animal organism appears as a tough, tenacious matter which is "articulated" and can be modified; light is a subtle matter which is the medium of communication of mere existence, &c.—just as in the other case plants and animals are merely edible. As regards a philosophic consideration of the content there is nothing at all to be found.

Fichte likewise wrote both a Science of Morals and of Natural Rights, but he treats them as sciences pertaining to the understanding only, and his method of procedure is destitute of ideas and carried on by means of a limited understanding. The Fichtian deduction of the conceptions of justice and morality thus remains within the limitations and rigidity of self-consciousness, as against which Fichte's popular presentations of religion and morality present inconsistencies. The treatise on Natural Rights is a special failure, *e.g.* where he, as we have just seen (p. 502), deduces even nature just as far as he requires it. The organization of the state which is described in Fichte's Science of Rights is furthermore as unspiritual as was the deduction of natural objects just mentioned, and as were many of the French constitutions which have appeared in modern times—a formal, external uniting and connecting, in which the individuals as such are held to be absolute, or in which Right is the highest principle. Kant began to ground Right upon Freedom, and Fichte likewise makes freedom the principle in the Rights of Nature; but, as was the case with Rousseau, it is freedom in the form of the isolated individual. This is a great commencement, but in order to arrive at the particular, they have to accept certain hypotheses. The universal is not the spirit, the substance of the whole, but an external, negative power of the finite understanding directed against individuals. The state is not apprehended in its essence, but only as representing a condition of justice and law, *i.e.* as an external relation of finite to finite. There are various individuals; the whole constitution of the state is thus in the main characterized by the fact that the freedom of individuals must be limited by means of the freedom of the whole.[1] The individuals always maintain a cold attitude of negativity as regards one another, the confinement becomes closer and the bonds more stringent as time goes on, instead of the state being regarded as representing the realization of freedom.

This philosophy contains nothing speculative, but it demands the presence of the speculative element. As the philosophy of Kant seeks in unity its Idea of the Supreme Good, wherein the opposites have to be united, so the Fichtian philosophy demands union in the ego and in the implicitude of faith; in this self-consciousness in all its actions makes its starting-point conviction, so that in themselves its actions may bring forth the highest end and realize the good. In the Fichtian philosophy nothing can be seen beyond the moment of self-consciousness, of self-conscious Being-within-self, as in the philosophy of England we find expressed—in just as one-sided a way—the moment of Being-for-another, or of consciousness, and that not as a moment simply, but as the principle of the truth; in neither of the two is there the unity of both—or spirit.

Fichte's philosophy constitutes a significant epoch in Philosophy regarded in its outward form. It is from him and from his methods that abstract thought proceeds, deduction and construction. Hence with the Fichtian philosophy a revolution took place in Germany. The public had penetrated as far as the philosophy of Kant, and until

[1] Fichte: Grundlage des Naturrechts, Part II. p. 21.

the Kantian philosophy was reached the interest awakened by Philosophy was general; it was accessible, and men were curious to know about it, it pertained to the ordinary knowledge of a man of culture (*supra*, p. 218). Formerly men of business, statesmen, occupied themselves with Philosophy; now, however, with the intricate idealism of the philosophy of Kant, their wings droop helpless to the ground. Hence it is with Kant that we first begin to find a line of separation which parts us from the common modes of consciousness; but the result, that the Absolute cannot be known, has become one generally acknowledged. With Fichte the common consciousness has still further separated itself from Philosophy, and it has utterly departed from the speculative element therein present. For Fichte's ego is not merely the ego of the empiric consciousness, since general determinations of thought such as do not fall within the ordinary consciousness have likewise to be known and brought to consciousness; in this way since Fichte's time few men have occupied themselves with speculation. Fichte, it is true, in his later works especially, wrote with a view to meeting the popular ear as we may see in the "Attempt to force the reader into comprehension," but this end was not accomplished. The public was through the philosophy of Kant and Jacobi strengthened in its opinion—one which it accepted *utiliter*—that the knowledge of God is immediate, and that we know it from the beginning and without requiring to study, and hence that Philosophy is quite superfluous.

2. Fichte's System in a Re-constituted Form.

The times called for life, for spirit. Now since mind has thus retreated within self-consciousness, but within self-consciousness as a barren ego, which merely gives itself a content or a realization through finitenesses and individualities which in and for themselves are nothing, the next stage is found in knowing this realization of self-consciousness in itself, in knowing the content in itself as a content which, penetrated throughout by spirit, is self-conscious and spiritual, or a spirit full of content. In his later popular works Fichte thus set forth faith, love, hope, religion, treating them without philosophic interest, and as for a general public: it was a philosophy calculated to suit enlightened Jews and Jewesses, councillors and Kotzebues. He places the matter in a popular form: "It is not the finite ego that is, but the divine Idea is the foundation of all Philosophy; everything that man does of himself is null and void. All existence is living and active in itself, and there is no other life than Being, and no other Being than God; God is thus absolute Being and Life. The divine essence likewise comes forth, revealing and manifesting itself—the world."[1] This immediate unity of the self-conscious ego and its content, or spirit, which merely has an intuition of its self-conscious life and knows it as the truth immediately, manifested itself subsequently in poetic and prophetic tendencies, in vehement aspirations, in excrescences which grew out of the Fichtian philosophy.

3. The more Important of the Followers of Fichte.

On the one hand, in respect of the content which the ego reaches in the philosophy of Fichte, the complete absence of spirituality, the woodenness, and, to put it plainly, the utter foolishness therein evidenced, strike us too forcibly to allow us to remain at his standpoint; our philosophic perception likewise tells us of the one-sidedness and deficiencies of the principle, as also of the evident necessity that the content should prove to be what

[1] Rixner: Handbuch d. Gesch. d. Phil. Vol. III., § 192, p. 416; Fichte: Ueber das Wesen des Gelehrten (Berlin, 1806), pp. 4, 5, 15, 25-27.

it is. But on the other hand self-consciousness was therein posited as reality or essence—not as a foreign, alien self-consciousness, but as ego—a signification which all possess, and which finds an answer in the actuality of all. The Fichtian standpoint of subjectivity has thus retained its character of being unphilosophically worked out, and arrived at its completion in forms pertaining to sensation which in part remained within the Fichtian principle, while they were in part the effort—futile though it was—to get beyond the subjectivity of the ego.

a. Friedrich von Schlegel.

In Fichte's case the limitation is continually re-appearing; but because the ego feels constrained to break through this barrier, it reacts against it, and gives itself a resting-place within itself; this last ought to be concrete, but it is a negative resting-place alone. This first form, Irony, has Friedrich von Schlegel as its leading exponent. The subject here knows itself to be within itself the Absolute, and all else to it is vain; all the conclusions which it draws for itself respecting the right and good, it likewise knows how to destroy again. It can make a pretence of knowing all things, but it only demonstrates vanity, hypocrisy, and effrontery. Irony knows itself to be the master of every possible content; it is serious about nothing, but plays with all forms. The other side is this, that subjectivity has cast itself into religious subjectivity. The utter despair in respect of thought, of truth, and absolute objectivity, as also the incapacity to give oneself any settled basis or spontaneity of action, induced the noble soul to abandon itself to feeling and to seek in Religion something fixed and steadfast; this steadfast basis, this inward satisfaction, is to be found in religious sentiments and feelings. This instinct impelling us towards something fixed has forced many into positive forms of religion, into Catholicism, superstition and miracle working, in order that they may find something on which they can rest, because to inward subjectivity everything fluctuates and wavers. With the whole force of its mind subjectivity tries to apply itself to what is positively given, to bend its head beneath the positive, to cast itself, so to speak, into the arms of externality, and it finds an inward power impelling it so to do.

b. Schleiermacher.

On the other hand the ego finds in the subjectivity and individuality of the personal view of things the height of all its vanity—its Religion. All the various individualities have God within themselves. Dialectic is the last thing to arise and to maintain its place. As this is expressed for philosophic self-consciousness, the foreign intellectual world has lost all significance and truth for ordinary culture; it is composed of three elements, a deity pertaining to a time gone by, and individualized in space and existence, a world which is outside the actuality of self-consciousness, and a world which had yet to appear, and in which self-consciousness would first attain to its reality. The spirit of culture has deserted it, and no longer recognizes anything that is foreign to self-consciousness. In accordance with this principle, the spiritual living essence has then transformed itself into self-consciousness, and it thinks to know the unity of spirit immediately from itself, and in this immediacy to be possessed of knowledge in a poetic, or at least a prophetic manner. As regards the poetic manner, it has a knowledge of the life and person of the Absolute immediately, by an intuition, and not in the Notion, and it thinks it would lose the whole as whole, as a self-penetrating unity, were it not to express the same in poetic form; and what it thus expresses poetically is the intuition of the personal life of self-consciousness.

But the truth is absolute motion, and since it is a motion of forms and figures [Gestalten], and the universe is a kingdom of spirits, the Notion is the essence of this movement, and likewise of each individual form; it is its ideal form [Form] and not the real one, or that of figure [Gestalt]. In the latter case necessity is lost sight of; individual action, life and heart, remain within themselves, and undeveloped; and this poetry vacillates betwixt the universality of the Notion and the determinateness and indifference of the figure; it is neither flesh nor fish, neither poetry nor philosophy. The prophetic utterance of truths which claim to be philosophical, thus belongs to faith, to self-consciousness, which indeed perceives the absolute spirit in itself, but does not comprehend itself as self-consciousness, since it places absolute reality above Knowledge, beyond self-conscious reason, as was done by Eschenmayer and Jacobi. This uncomprehending, prophetic manner of speech affirms this or that respecting absolute existence as from an oracle, and requires that each man should find the same immediately in his own heart. The knowledge of absolute reality becomes a matter pertaining to the heart; there are a number of would-be inspired speakers, each of whom holds a monologue and really does not understand the others, excepting by a pressure of the hands and betrayal of dumb feeling. What they say is mainly composed of trivialities, if these are taken in the sense in which they are uttered; it is the feeling, the gesture, the fulness of the heart, which first gives them their significance; to nothing of more importance is direct expression given. They outbid one another in conceits of fancy, in ardent poetry. But before the Truth vanity turns pale, spitefully sneering it sneaks back into itself. Ask not after a criterion of the truth, but after the Notion of the truth in and for itself; on that fix your gaze. The glory of Philosophy is departed, for it presupposes a common ground of thoughts and principles—which is what science demands—or at least of opinions. But now particular subjectivity was everything, each individual was proud and disdainful as regards all others. The conception of independent thought—as though there could be a thought which was not such (Vol. I. p. 60)—is very much the same; men have, it is said, to bring forth a particularity of their own, or else they have not thought for themselves. But the bad picture is that in which the artist shows himself; originality is the production of what is in its entirety universal. The folly of independent thought is that it results in each bringing forth something more preposterous than another.

c. Novalis.

Subjectivity signifies the lack of a firm and steady basis, but likewise the desire for such, and thus it evermore remains a yearning. These yearnings of a lofty soul are set forth in the writings of Novalis. This subjectivity does not reach substantiality, it dies away within itself, and the standpoint it adopts is one of inward workings and fine distinctions; it signifies an inward life and deals with the minutiæ of the truth. The extravagances of subjectivity constantly pass into madness; if they remain in thought they are whirled round and round in the vortex of reflecting understanding, which is ever negative in reference to itself.

d. Fries, Bouterweck, Krug.

Yet a last form of subjectivity is the subjectivity of arbitrary will and ignorance. It maintained this, that the highest mode of cognition is an immediate knowledge as a fact of consciousness; and that is so far right. The Fichtian abstraction and its hard understanding has a repellent effect on thought; slothful reason allowed itself to be told the result of the philosophy of Kant and Jacobi, and renounced all consistent thought, all construction. This arbitrariness gave itself entire liberty—the liberty of the *Tabagie*—but in doing so it regarded itself from a poetic or prophetic point of view, as we have just seen (pp. 508, 509). Then it was both more sober and more prosaic, and thus brought the old logic and metaphysic once more into evidence, though with this modification that they are made facts of consciousness. Thus Fries turns back to the faith of Jacobi in the form of immediate judgments derived from reason, and dark conceptions incapable of utterance.[1] He wished to improve the critique of pure reason by apprehending the categories as facts of consciousness; anything one chooses can in such a case be introduced. Bouterweck speaks of "The virtue, the living nature of power; the fact that subject and object are regarded as one, that is as absolute virtue. With this absolute virtue we have all Being and action, namely the eternal, absolute and pure unity; in one word we have grasped the world within us and we have grasped ourselves in the world, and that indeed not through conceptions and conclusions, but directly through the power which itself constitutes our existence and our rational nature. To know the All, or indeed to know God in any way, is, however, impossible for any mortal."[2] Krug wrote a "Groundwork of Philosophy," setting forth a "Transcendental Synthesis—that is a transcendental realism and a transcendental idealism inseparably bound together." It is an "original, transcendental synthesis of the real and the ideal, the thinking subject and the corresponding outer world;" this transcen-

[1] Rixner: Handbuch d. Gesch. d. Phil. Vol. III. § 158, pp. 350, 351; Fries: Neue Kritik d. Vernunft (First edition, Heidelberg, 1807), Vol. I. pp. 75, 281, 284, 343; 206.

[2] Rixner: Handbuch d. Gesch. d. Phil. Vol. III. § 156, pp. 347, 348; cf. Bouterweck's Apodiktik (1799), Part II. pp. 206-212.

dental synthesis must "be recognized and asserted without any attempt being made at explaining it."[1]

D. Schelling.

It was Schelling, finally, who made the most important, or, from a philosophic point of view, the only important advance upon the philosophy of Fichte; his philosophy rose higher than that of Fichte, though undoubtedly it stood in close connection with it; indeed, he himself professes to be a Fichtian. Now the philosophy of Schelling from the first admitted the possibility of a knowledge of God, although it likewise started from the philosophy of Kant, which denies such knowledge. At the same time Schelling makes Jacobi's principle of the unity of thought and Being fundamental, although he begins to determine it more closely.[2] To him concrete unity is this, that the finite is no more true than the infinite, the subjective idea no more than objectivity, and that combinations in which both untruths are brought together in their independence in relation to one another, are likewise combinations of untruths merely. Concrete unity can only be comprehended as process and as the living movement in a proposition. This inseparability is in God alone; the finite, on the other hand, is that which has this separability within it. In so far as it is a truth it is likewise this unity, but in a limited sphere, and for that reason in the separability of both moments.

Frederick Wilhelm Joseph Schelling, born on the 27th January, 1775, at Schorndorf,[3] in Würtemberg, studied in

[1] Krug: Entwurf eines neuen Organon der Philosophie (Meissen, 1801), pp. 75, 76; Rixner: Handbuch d. Geschichte d. Philosophie, Vol. III. § 157, p. 349.

[2] Schelling's philosophische Schriften (Landshut, 1809, Vol. I. Vom Ich als Princip der Philosophie, pp. 1-114), pp. 3, 4 (first edition, Tübingen, 1795, pp. 4-7).

[3] His birthplace is usually stated to have been Leonberg, a short distance from Schorndorf.—[Translators' note.]

Leipzig and Jena, where he came to be on terms of great intimacy with Fichte. In the year 1807 he became secretary of the Academy of Science in Munich. We cannot with propriety deal fully with his life, for he is still living.[1]

Schelling worked out his philosophy in view of the public. The series of his philosophic writings also represents the history of his philosophic development and the gradual process by which he raised himself above the Fichtian principle and the Kantian content with which he began. It does not thus contain a sequence of separately worked out divisions of Philosophy, but only successive stages in his own development. If we ask for a final work in which we shall find his philosophy represented with complete definiteness none such can be named. Schelling's first writings are still quite Fichtian, and it is only by slow degrees that he worked himself free of Fichte's form. The form of the ego has the ambiguity of being capable of signifying either the absolute Ego or God, or ego in my particularity;[2] this supplied the first stimulus to Schelling. His first and quite short work of four sheets which he wrote in 1795 at Tübingen, while still at the university, was called, "On the Possibility of any Form of Philosophy"; it contains propositions respecting the Fichtian philosophy only. The next work, "On the Ego as principle of Philosophy, or on the Unconditioned in Human Knowledge" (Tübingen, 1795), is likewise quite Fichtian; in this case, however, it is from a wider and more universal point of view, since the ego is therein grasped as an original identity.[3] We find, however, a summary of the Fichtian principle and the Kantian mode of presentation: "It is only by something being originally set in opposition to the ego, and by the ego being itself

[1] Lectures of 1816-1817. [Translators' note.]

[2] Schelling's philosophische Schriften: Vom Ich als Princip der Philosophie, p. 99 seq. (p. 178 seq.).

[3] Ibidem, pp. 23, 24 (pp. 38-42).

posited as the manifold (in time), that it is possible for the ego to get beyond the unity which belongs to it of merely being posited, and that, for example, it posits the same content on more than one occasion."[1] Schelling then passed on to natural philosophy, adopted Kantian forms and reflective determinations, such as those of repulsion and attraction, from Kant's "Metaphysics of Nature," and likewise dealt with quite empirical phenomena in expressions taken from Kant. All his first works on this subject come under this category, viz.: "Ideas towards a Philosophy of Nature," 1797; "On the World-Soul," 1798, the second edition of which possesses appendices which are entirely inconsistent with what goes before. In the writings of Herder and Kielmeyer[2] we find sensibility, irritability, and reproduction dealt with, as also their laws, such as that the greater the sensibility the less the irritability, &c.—just as the powers or potencies were dealt with by Eschenmayer. It was only later on in relation to these that Schelling first apprehended nature in the categories of thought, and made general attempts of a more definite character in the direction of greater scientific development. It was only through what had been accomplished by these men that he was enabled to come into public notice so young. The spiritual and intellectual side, morality and the state, he represented on the other hand purely in accordance with Kantian principles: thus in his "Transcendental Idealism," although it was written from a Fichtian point of view, he goes no further than Kant did in his "Philosophy of Rights" and his work "On Eternal Peace." Schelling, indeed, later on published a separate treatise on Freedom, deeply speculative in character; this, however, remains isolated and independent, and deals with this one point alone; in Philosophy, however, nothing isolated can be worked out or developed.

[1] Ibidem, p. 83 (p. 150).

[2] Schelling's System des transcendentalen Idealismus, p. 257, not. Zeitschrift für speculative Physik, Vol. II. No. 2, p. 92.

In the various presentations of his views Schelling on each occasion began again from the beginning, because, as we may see, what went before did not satisfy him; he has ever pressed on to seek a new form, and thus he has tried various forms and terminologies in succession without ever setting forth one complete and consistent whole. His principal works in this connection are the "First Sketch of a System of Natural Philosophy," 1799; the "System of Transcendental Idealism," 1800, one of his most carefully thought-out works; "Bruno, a Dialogue on the Divine and Natural Principle of Things," 1802; "Journal of Speculative Physics," 1801; "New Journal of Speculative Physics," 1802 *et seq.* In the second number of the second volume of his "Journal of Speculative Physics," Schelling made the commencement of a detailed treatment of the whole of his philosophy. Here he likewise starts to a certain measure, though unconsciously, from the Fichtian form of construction; but the idea is already present that nature equally with knowledge is a system of reason.

It is not feasible here to go into details respecting what is called the philosophy of Schelling, even if time permitted. For it is not yet a scientific whole organized in all its branches, since it rather consists in certain general elements which do not fluctuate with the rest of his opinions. Schelling's philosophy must still be regarded as in process of evolution, and it has not yet ripened into fruit;[1] we can hence give a general idea of it only.

When Schelling made his first appearance the demands put forward by Philosophy were as follows. With Descartes thought and extension were in some incomprehensible way united in God, with Spinoza it was as motionless substance; and beyond this point of view neither of them ever passed. Later on we saw the form develop, partly in the sciences and partly in the Kantian philosophy. Finally, in the Fichtian

[1] Lectures of 1805-1806.

philosophy, the form was subjectivity on its own account, from which all determinations were held to develop. What is thus demanded is that this subjectivity of infinite form which we saw dying into irony or arbitrariness (pp. 507–510) should be delivered from its one-sidedness in order to be united with objectivity and substantiality. To put it otherwise, the substance of Spinoza should not be apprehended as the unmoved, but as the intelligent, as a form which possesses activity within itself of necessity, so that it is the forming power of nature, but at the same time knowledge and comprehension. This then is the object of Philosophy; it is not the formal union of Spinoza that is demanded, nor the subjective totality of Fichte, but totality with the infinite form. We see this developing in the philosophy of Schelling.

1. In one of his earlier writings, the "System of Transcendental Idealism," which we shall consider first of all, Schelling represented transcendental philosophy and natural philosophy as the two sides of scientific knowledge. Respecting the nature of the two, he expressly declared himself in this work, where he once more adopts a Fichtian starting-point: "All knowledge rests on the harmony of an objective with a subjective." In the common sense of the words this would be allowed; absolute unity, where the Notion and the reality are undistinguished in the perfected Idea, is the Absolute alone, or God; all else contains an element of discord between the objective and subjective. "We may give the name of nature to the entire objective content of our knowledge; the entire subjective content, on the other hand, is called the ego or intelligence." They are in themselves identical and presupposed as identical. The relation of nature to intelligence is given by Schelling thus: "Now if all knowledge has two poles which mutually presuppose and demand one another, there must be two fundamental sciences, and it must be impossible to start from the one pole without being driven to the

other." Thus nature is impelled to spirit, and spirit to nature; either may be given the first place, and both must come to pass. "If the objective is made the chief," we have the natural sciences as result, and "the necessary tendency," the end, "of all natural science thus is to pass from nature to intelligence. This is the meaning of the effort to connect natural phenomena with theory. The highest perfection of natural science would be the perfect spiritualization of all natural laws into laws of intuitive perception and thought. The phenomenal (the material element) must entirely disappear, and laws (the formal element) alone remain. Hence it comes to pass that the more that which is in conformity with law breaks forth in nature itself, the more the outward covering disappears; the phenomena themselves become more spiritual, and finally cease altogether. The perfect theory of nature would be that by which the whole of nature should be resolved into an intelligence. The dead and unconscious products of nature are only abortive attempts on the part of nature to reflect itself, but the so-called dead nature is really an immature," torpid, fossilized "intelligence"; it is implicit only, and thus remains in externality; "hence in its phenomena," even though "still unconsciously, the character of intelligence shines through. Its highest end, which is to become object to itself, is first attained by nature" (instead of nature we should call it the Idea of nature), "through its highest and ultimate reflection, which is none other than man, or, more generally, it is that which we call reason, through which nature for the first time returns completely within itself, and whereby it becomes evident that nature is originally identical with what is known in us as intelligence or the conscious. Through this tendency to make nature intelligent natural science becomes the philosophy of nature." The intelligent character of nature is thus spoken of as a postulate of science. The other point of view is "to give the sub jective the foremost place." Thus here "the problem is how to add an objective element agreeing with it. To start from the subjective as from the first and absolute, and to make the objective arise from it," signifies a new departure; its consideration forms the content of true Transcendental Philosophy, or, as Schelling himself now named this science, "the other science fundamental to Philosophy." The organ of transcendental philosophy is the subjective, the production of inward action. Production and reflection upon this production, the unconscious and conscious in one, is the æsthetic act of the imagination.[1] Thus these two separate processes are as a whole very clearly expressed: the process which leads from nature to the subject, and that leading from the ego to the object. But the true process could only be traced out by means of logic, for it contains pure thoughts; but the logical point of view was what Schelling never arrived at in his presentation of things.

a. In respect of the ego, as principle of the transcendental philosophy, Schelling sets to work in the same way as did Fichte, inasmuch as he begins from the fact of knowledge "in which the content is conditioned through the form, and the form through the content"; this is formal A=A. But does A exist? The ego is "the point where subject and object are one in their unmediated condition"; the ego is just Ego = Ego, subject-object; and that is the act of self-consciousness wherein I am for myself object to myself. In self-consciousness there is not to be found a distinction between me and anything else; what are distinguished are directly identical, and there is so far nothing at all in opposition to this self-consciousness. How the case stands with regard to external objects is the question which must be decided later, in the further course of development. It is only the Notion of the ego which is

[1] Schelling: System des transcendentalen Idealismus, pp. 1-7, 17-21.

to be laid hold of: "The Notion of the ego, that is the act whereby thought in general becomes object to itself, and the ego itself (the object) are absolutely one; independently of this act the ego is nothing." It is the act whereby thought makes itself objective, and wherein the ego is brought into harmony with the objective, with thought; and from this standpoint it had to be demonstrated how the ego makes its way to objectivity. "The ego, as pure act, as pure action, is not objective in knowledge itself, for the reason that it is the principle of all knowledge. If it is to be object of knowledge, this must come to pass through a very different kind of knowledge than the ordinary." The immediate consciousness of this identity is intuition, but inwardly it becomes "intellectual intuition"; it "is a knowledge which is the production of its object: sensuous intuition or perception is perception of such a nature that the perception itself appears to be different from what is perceived. Now intellectual intuition is the organ of all transcendental thought," the act of pure self-consciousness generally. "The ego is nothing else than a process of production which ever makes itself its own object. Science can start from nothing objective," but from "the non-objective which itself becomes object" as an "original duplicity. Idealism is the mechanism of the origination of the objective world from the inward principle of spiritual activity."[1]

On the one hand Schelling's system is related to the philosophy of Fichte, and, on the other hand, he, like Jacobi, makes his principle immediate knowledge—the intelligent intuitive perception which all who wish to philosophize must have. But what comes next is that its content is no longer the indeterminate, the essence of essence, but likewise the Absolute, God, the absolutely self-existent, though expressed as concrete, *i.e.* as mediating

[1] Schelling: System des transcendentalen Idealismus, pp. 24-46, 49-52, 55-58, 63-65.

itself within itself, as the absolute unity or indifference of subjective and objective. Intellectual intuition is the Fichtian imagination oscillating between two different points. We have already spoken above (p. 417) of the *form* of intellectual intuition; it is the most convenient manner of asserting knowledge respecting—anything one likes. But the immediate knowledge of God as spiritual is only in the consciousness of Christian nations, and not for others. This immediate knowledge appears to be still more contingent as the intellectual intuition of the concrete, or the identity of subjectivity and objectivity. This intuition is intellectual indeed, because it is a rational intuition, and as knowledge it is likewise absolutely one with the object of knowledge. But this intuition, although itself knowledge, is not as yet known; it is the unmediated, the postulated. As it is in this way an immediate we must possess it, and what may be possessed may likewise not be possessed. Thus since the immediate pre-supposition in Philosophy is that individuals have the immediate intuition of this identity of subjective and objective, this gave the philosophy of Schelling the appearance of indicating that the presence of this intuition in individuals demanded a special talent, genius, or condition of mind of their own, or as though it were generally speaking an accidental faculty which pertained to the specially favoured few. For the immediate, the intuitively perceived, is in the form of an existent, and is not thus an essential; and whoever does not understand the intellectual intuition must come to the conclusion that he does not possess it. Or else, in order to understand it, men must give themselves the trouble of possessing it; but no one can tell whether he has it or not—not even from understanding it, for we may merely think we understand it. Philosophy, however, is in its own nature capable of being universal; for its ground-work is thought, and it is through thought that man is man. Schelling's principle is thus indeed clearly a universal; but if a definite intuition, a definite consciousness is demanded, such as the consciousness or intuition of the identity of subjective and objective, this determinate particular thought is not as yet to be found in it.

It was, however, in this form of knowledge of the absolute as concrete, and, further, in the form of unity of subjective and objective, that Philosophy as represented by Schelling more especially marked itself off from the ordinary conceiving consciousness and its mode of reflection. Even less than Fichte did Schelling attain to popularity (*supra*, pp. 504, 505), for the concrete in its nature is directly speculative. The concrete content, God, life, or whatever particular form it has, is indeed the content and object of natural consciousness; but the difficulty lies in bringing what is contained in the concrete into concrete thought in accordance with its different determinations, and in laying hold of the unity. It pertains to the standpoint of the understanding to divide and to distinguish, and to maintain the finite thought-determinations in their opposition; but Philosophy demands that these different thoughts should be brought together. Thought begins by holding apart infinite and finite, cause and effect, positive and negative; since this is the region of reflecting consciousness, the old metaphysical consciousness was able to take part in so doing: but the speculative point of view is to have this opposition before itself and to reconcile it. With Schelling the speculative form has thus again come to the front, and philosophy has again obtained a special character of its own; the principle of Philosophy, rational thought in itself, has obtained the form of thought. In the philosophy of Schelling the content, the truth, has once more become the matter of chief importance, whereas in the Kantian philosophy the point of interest was more especially stated to be the necessity for investigating subjective knowledge. This is the standpoint of Schelling's philosophy in its general aspects.

b. Since in further analysis the distinction between subject and object comes into view and is accepted, there follows the relationship of the ego to its other; with Fichte that forms the second proposition, in which the self-limitation of the ego is posited. The ego posits itself in opposition to itself, since it posits itself as conditioned by the non-ego; that is the infinite repulsion, for this conditionment is the ego itself. Schelling, on the one hand, says: "The ego is unlimited as the ego only in so far as it is limited," as it relates to the non-ego. Only thus does consciousness exist, self-consciousness is a barren determination; through its intuition of self the ego becomes finite to itself. "This contradiction only allows itself to be dissolved by the ego becoming in this finitude infinite to itself, *i.e.* by its having an intuitive perception of itself as an infinite Becoming." The relation of the ego to itself and to the infinite check or force of repulsion is a constant one. On the other hand it is said: "The ego is limited only in so far as it is unlimited;" this limitation is thus necessary in order to be able to get beyond it. The contradiction which we find here remains even if the ego always limits the non-ego. "Both activities—that which makes for infinitude, the limitable, real, objective activity, and the limiting and ideal, mutually pre-suppose one another. Idealism reflects merely on the one, realism on the other, transcendental idealism on both."[1] All this is a tangled mass of abstractions.

c. "Neither through the limiting activity nor through the limited does the ego arrive at self-consciousness. There consequently is a third activity, compounded from the other two, through which the ego of self-consciousness arises; this third is that which oscillates between the two—the struggle between opposing tendencies." There is essential relation only, relative identity; the difference

[1] Schelling: System des transcendentalen Idealismus, pp. 69, 70, 72-79.

therein present thus ever remains. "This struggle cannot be reconciled by one such action, but only by an infinite succession of such," *i.e.* the reconciliation of the opposition between the two tendencies of the ego, the inward and the outward, is, in the infinite course of progression, only an apparent one. In order that it may be complete, the whole inward and outward nature must be presented in all its details: but Philosophy can only set forth the epochs which are most important. "If all the intermediate links in sensation could be set forth, that would necessarily lead us to a deduction of all the qualities in nature, which last is impossible." Now this third activity, which contains the union directly in itself, is a thought in which particularity is already contained. It is the intuitive understanding of Kant, the intelligent intuition or intuitively perceiving intelligence; Schelling, indeed, definitely names this absolute unity of contradictions intellectual intuition. The ego here is not one-sided in regard to what is different; it is identity of the unconscious and the conscious, but not an identity of such a nature that its ground rests on the ego itself.[1]

This ego must be the absolute principle: "All philosophy starts from a principle which as absolute identity is non-objective." For if it is objective, separation is at once posited and it is confronted by another; but the principle is the reconciliation of the opposition, and therefore in and for itself it is non-objective. "Now how should a principle such as this be called forth to consciousness and understood, as is required if it is the condition attached to the comprehension of all philosophy? That it can no more be comprehended through Notions [Begriffe] than set forth, requires no proof." Notion to Schelling signifies a category of the ordinary understanding; Notion is, however, the concrete thought which in itself is infinite. "There thus remains

[1] Schelling: System des transcendentalen Idealismus, pp. 85, 86, 89, 98, 442-444.

nothing more than that it should be set forth in an immediate intuition. If there were such an intuition which had as object the absolutely identical, that which in itself is neither subjective nor objective, and if for such, which," however, "can be an intellectual intuition only, one could appeal to immêdiate experience," the question would be: "How can this intuition be again made objective, *i.e.* how can it be asserted without doubt that it does not rest on a subjective deception, if there is not a universal objectivity in that intuition, which is recognized by all?" This intellectual principle in itself should thus be given in an experience so that men may be able to appeal to it. "The objectivity of intellectual intuition is art. The work of art alone reflects to me what is otherwise reflected through nothing—that absolute identical which has already separated itself in the ego itself." The objectivity of identity and the knowledge of the same is art; in one and the same intuition the ego is here conscious of itself and unconscious.[1] This intellectual intuition which has become objective is objective sensuous intuition—but the Notion, the comprehended necessity, is a very different objectivity.

Thus a principle is presupposed both for the content of philosophy and for subjective philosophizing: on the one hand it is demanded that the attitude adopted should be one of intellectual intuition, and, on the other hand, this principle has to be authenticated, and this takes place in the work of art. This is the highest form of the objectivization of reason, because in it sensuous conception is united with intellectuality, sensuous existence is merely the expression of spirituality. The highest objectivity which the subject attains, the highest identity of subjective and objective, is that which Schelling terms the power of imagination. Art is thus comprehended as what is inmost and highest, that which produces the intellectual and real

[1] Schelling: System des transcendentalen Idealismus, pp. 471, 472, 475.

in one, and philosophizing is conceived as this genius of art. But art and power of imagination are not supreme. For the Idea, spirit, cannot be truly given expression to in the manner in which art expresses its Idea. This last is always a method pertaining to intuitive perception; and on account of this sensuous form of existence the work of art cannot correspond to the spirit. Thus because the point last arrived at is designated as the faculty of imagination, as art, even in the subject this is a subordinate point of view, and thus in itself this point is not the absolute identity of subjectivity and objectivity. In subjective thought, rational, speculative thought is thus indeed demanded, but if this appears false to you nothing further can be said than that you do not possess intellectual intuition. The proving of anything, the making it comprehensible, is thus abandoned; a correct apprehension of it is directly demanded, and the Idea is thus assertorically pre-established as principle. The Absolute is the absolute identity of subjective and objective, the absolute indifference of real and ideal, of form and essence, of universal and particular; in this identity of the two there is neither the one nor the other. But the unity is not abstract, empty, and dry; that would signify logical identity, classification according to something common to both, in which the difference remains all the while outside. The identity is concrete: it is subjectivity as well as objectivity; the two are present therein as abrogated and ideal. This identity may easily be shown in the ordinary conception: the conception, we may for example say, is subjective; it has, too, the determinate content of exclusion in reference to other conceptions; nevertheless, the conception is simple—it is one act, one unity.

What is lacking in Schelling's philosophy is thus the fact that the point of indifference of subjectivity and objectivity, or the Notion of reason, is absolutely pre-supposed, without any attempt being made at showing that this is the truth.

Schelling often uses Spinoza's form of procedure, and sets up axioms. In philosophy, when we desire to establish a position, we demand proof. But if we begin with intellectual intuition, that constitutes an oracle to which we have to give way, since the existence of intellectual intuition was made our postulate. The true proof that this identity of subjective and objective is the truth, could only be brought about by means of each of the two being investigated in its logical, *i.e.* essential determinations; and in regard to them, it must then be shown that the subjective signifies the transformation of itself into the objective, and that the objective signifies its not remaining such, but making itself subjective. Similarly in the finite, it would have to be shown that it contained a contradiction in itself, and made itself infinite; in this way we should have the unity of finite and infinite. In so doing, this unity of opposites is not asserted beforehand, but in the opposites themselves it is shown that their truth is their unity, but that each taken by itself is one-sided—that their difference veers round, casting itself headlong into this unity—while the understanding all the time thinks that in these differences it possesses something fixed and secure. The result of thinking contemplation would in this former case be that each moment would secretly make itself into its opposite, the identity of both being alone the truth. The understanding certainly calls this transformation sophistry, humbug, juggling, and what-not. As a result, this identity would, according to Jacobi, be one which was no doubt conditioned and of set purpose produced. But we must remark that a one-sided point of view is involved in apprehending the result of development merely as a result; it is a process which is likewise mediation within itself, of such a nature that this mediation is again abrogated and asserted as immediate. Schelling, indeed, had this conception in a general way, but he did not follow it out in a definite logical method, for with him it remained an immediate truth, which can only be verified by means of intellectual intuition. That is the great difficulty in the philosophy of Schelling. And then it was misunderstood and all interest taken from it. It is easy enough to show that subjective and objective are different. Were they not different, nothing could be made of them any more than of A=A; but they are in opposition *as one*. In all that is finite, an identity is present, and this alone is actual; but besides the fact that the finite is this identity, it is also true that it is the absence of harmony between subjectivity and objectivity, Notion and reality; and it is in this that finitude consists. To this principle of Schelling's, form, or necessity, is thus lacking, it is only asserted. Schelling appears to have this in common with Plato and the Neo-Platonists, that knowledge is to be found in the inward intuition of eternal Ideas wherein knowledge is unmediated in the Absolute. But when Plato speaks of this intuition of the soul, which has freed itself from all knowledge that is finite, empirical, or reflected, and the Neo-Platonists tell of the ecstasy of thought in which knowledge is the immediate knowledge of the Absolute, this definite distinction must be noticed, viz., that with Plato's knowledge of the universal, or with his intellectuality, wherein all opposition as a reality is abrogated, dialectic is associated, or the recognized necessity for the abrogation of these opposites; Plato does not begin with this, for with him the movement in which they abrogate themselves is present. The Absolute is itself to be looked at as this movement of self-abrogation; this is the only actual knowledge and knowledge of the Absolute. With Schelling this idea has, however, no dialectic present in it whereby those opposites may determine themselves to pass over into their unity, and in so doing to be comprehended.

2. Schelling begins with the idea of the Absolute as identity of the subjective and objective, and accordingly there evinced itself in the presentations of his system which followed, the further necessity of proving this idea;

this he attempted to do in the two Journals of Speculative Physics. But if that method be once adopted, the procedure is not immanent development from the speculative Idea, but it follows the mode of external reflection. Schelling's proofs are adduced in such an exceedingly formal manner that they really invariably presuppose the very thing that was to be proved. The axiom assumes the main point in question, and all the rest follows as a matter of course. Here is an instance: "The innermost essence of the Absolute can only be thought of as identity absolute, altogether pure and undisturbed. For the Absolute is only absolute, and what is thought in it is necessarily and invariably the same, or in other words, is necessarily and invariably absolute. If the idea of the Absolute were a general Notion" (or conception), "this would not prevent a difference being met with in it, notwithstanding this unity of the absolute. For things the most different are yet in the Notion always one and identical, just as a rectangle, a polygon and a circle are all figures. The possibility of the difference of all things in association with perfect unity in the Notion lies in the manner in which the particular in them is combined with the universal. In the Absolute this altogether disappears, because it pertains to the very idea of the Absolute that the particular in it is also the universal, and the universal the particular; and further that by means of this unity form and existence are also one in it. Consequently, in regard to the Absolute, from the fact of its being the Absolute, there likewise follows the absolute exclusion from its existence of all difference, and that at once." [1]

In the former of the two above-named works, the "Journal of Speculative Physics," Schelling began by again bringing forward the Substance of Spinoza, simple, absolute Existence, inasmuch as he makes his starting-point

[1] Schelling: Neue Zeitschrift für speculative Physik, Vol. I. Part I. pp. 52, 53.

the absolute identity of the subjective and objective. Here, like Spinoza, he employed the method of geometry, laying down axioms and proving by means of propositions, then going on to deduce other propositions from these, and so on. But this method has no real application to philosophy. Schelling at this point laid down certain forms of difference, to which he gave the name of potencies, adopting the term from Eschenmayer, who made use of it (p. 514);[1] they are ready-made differences, which Schelling avails himself of. But philosophy must not take any forms from other sciences, as here from mathematics. With Schelling, the leading form is that which was brought into remembrance again by Kant, the form of triplicity as first, second, and third potency.

Schelling, like Fichte, begins with I = I, or with the absolute intuition, expressed as proposition or definition of the Absolute, that "Reason is the absolute indifference of subject and object": so that it is neither the one nor the other, for both have in it their true determination; and their opposition, like all others, is utterly done away with. The true reality of subject and object is placed in this alone, that the subject is not posited in the determination of subject against object, as in the philosophy of Fichte; it is not determined as in itself existent, but as subject-object, as the identity of the two; in the same way the object is not posited according to its ideal determination as object, but in as far as it is itself absolute, or the identity of the subjective and objective. But the expression "indifference" is ambiguous, for it means indifference in regard to both the one and the other; and thus it appears as if the content of indifference, the only thing which makes it concrete, were indifferent. Schelling's next requirement is

[1] Kritisches Journal der Philosophie, published by Schelling and Hegel, Vol. I. Part I. p. 67; Schelling: Zeitschrift für speculative Physik, Vol. II. No. II. Preface, p. xiii.

that the subject must not be hampered with reflection; that would be bringing it under the determination of the understanding, which, equally with sensuous perception, implies the separateness of sensuous things. As to the form of its existence, absolute indifference is with Schelling posited as A = A; and this form is for him the knowledge of absolute identity, which, however, is inseparable from the Being or existence of the same.[1]

Thus, therefore, opposition, as form and reality or existence, no doubt appears in this Absolute, but it is determined as a merely relative or unessential opposition: "Between subject and object no other than quantitative difference is possible. For no qualitative difference as regards the two is thinkable," because absolute identity "is posited as subject and object only as regards the form of its Being, not as regards its existence. There is consequently only a quantitative difference left," *i.e.* only that of magnitude: and yet difference must really be understood as qualitative, and must thus be shown to be a difference which abrogates itself. This quantitative difference, says Schelling, is the form *actu*: "The quantitative difference of subjective and objective is the basis of all finitude. Each determined potency marks a determined quantitative difference of the subjective and objective. Each individual Being is the result of a quantitative difference of subjectivity and objectivity. The individual expresses absolute identity under a determined form of Being:" so that each side is itself a relative totality, A = B, and at the same time the one factor preponderates in the one, and the other factor in the other, but both remain absolute identity.[2] This is insufficient, for there are other determinations; difference

[1] Schelling: Zeitschrift für speculative Physik, Vol. II. No. II. § 1, pp. 1, 2; § 4, p. 4; § 16-18, pp. 10-12.

[2] Ibidem, § 22-24, pp. 13-15; § 37, 38, pp. 22, 23; § 40-42, pp. 25, 26.

is undoubtedly qualitative, although this is not the absolute determination. Quantitative difference is no true difference, but an entirely external relation; and likewise the preponderance of subjective and objective is not a determination of thought, but a merely sensuous determination.

The Absolute itself, in so far as the positing of difference is taken into account, is defined by Schelling as the quantitative indifference of subjective and objective: in respect to absolute identity no quantitative difference is thinkable. "Quantitative difference is only possible outside of absolute identity, and outside of absolute totality. There is nothing in itself outside of totality, excepting by virtue of an arbitrary separation of the individual from the whole. Absolute identity exists only under the form of the quantitative indifference of subjective and objective." Quantitative difference, which appears outside of absolute identity and totality, is therefore, according to Schelling, in itself absolute identity, and consequently thinkable only under the form of the quantitative indifference of the subjective and objective. "This opposition does not therefore occur in itself, or from the standpoint of speculation. From this standpoint A exists just as much as B does; for A like B is the whole absolute identity, which only exists under the two forms, but under both of them alike. Absolute identity is the universe itself. The form of its Being can be thought of under the image of a line," as shown by the following scheme:

$$\frac{\overset{+}{A}=B \qquad\qquad A=\overset{+}{B}}{A=A}$$

"in which the same identity is posited in each direction, but with A or B preponderating in opposite directions."[1]

[1] Schelling: Zeitschrift für speculative Physik, Vol. II. No. II. § 25, 26, 28, 30-32, pp. 15-19; § 44, 46, pp. 27-29.

If we go into details, the main points from an elementary point of view are the following.

The first potency is that the first quantitative difference of the Absolute, or "the first relative totality is matter. Proof: A=B is not anything real either as relative identity or as relative duplicity. As identity A=B, in the individual as in the whole, can be expressed only by the line," —the first dimension. "But in that line A is posited throughout as existent," *i.e.* it is at the same time related to B. "Therefore this line presupposes A=B as relative totality throughout; relative totality is therefore the first presupposition, and if relative identity exists, it exists only through relative totality,"—this is duplicity, the second dimension. "In the same way relative duplicity presupposes relative identity. Relative identity and duplicity are contained in relative totality, not indeed *actu*, but yet *potentia*. Therefore the two opposites must mutually extinguish each other in a third" dimension. "Absolute identity as the immediate basis of the reality of A and B in matter, is the force of gravitation. If A preponderates we have the force of attraction, if B preponderates we have that of expansion. The quantitative positing of the forces of attraction and expansion passes into the infinite; their equilibrium exists in the whole, not in the individual."[1] From matter as the first indifference in immediacy Schelling now passes on to further determinations.

The second potency (A^2) is light, this identity itself posited as existent; in so far as A=B, A^2 is also posited. The same identity, "posited under the form of relative identity," *i.e.* of the polarity which we find appearing "in A and B, is the force of cohesion. Cohesion is the impression made on matter by the self-hood" of light "or by

[1] Schelling: Zeitschrift für speculative Physik, Vol. II. No. II. § 50, Note 1, § 51, pp. 34-36; § 54, p. 40; § 56, Appendix 2, § 57 and note, pp. 42-44.

personality, whereby matter first emerges as particular out of the universal identity, and raises itself into the realm of form." Planets, metals and other bodies form a series which under the form of dynamic cohesion expresses particular relations of cohesion, in which on the one hand contraction preponderates, and on the other hand expansion. These potencies appear with Schelling as north and south, east and west polarity: their developments further appear as north-west, south-east, &c. He counts as the last potency Mercury, Venus, the Earth, &c. He continues: "Cohesion outside of the point of indifference I term passive. Towards the negative side" (or pole) "fall some of the metals which stand next to iron, after them the so-called precious metals," then the "diamond, and lastly carbon, the greatest passive cohesion. Towards the positive side, again, some metals fall, in which the cohesive nature of iron gradually diminishes," *i.e.* approaches disintegration, and lastly "disappears in nitrogen." Active cohesion is magnetism, and the material universe is an infinite magnet. The magnetic process is difference in indifference, and indifference in difference, and therefore absolute identity as such. The indifference point of the magnet is the "neither nor" and the "as well as"; the poles are potentially the same essence, only posited under two factors which are opposed. Both poles depend "only upon whether + or − preponderates"; they are not pure abstractions. "In the total magnet the empirical magnet is the indifference point. The empirical magnet is iron. All bodies are mere metamorphoses of iron—they are potentially contained in iron. Every two different bodies which touch each other set up mutually in each other relative diminution and increase of cohesion. This mutual alteration of cohesion by means of the contact of two different bodies is electricity; the cohesion-diminishing factor +E is the potency of hydrogen, −E is the potency of oxygen.

"The totality of the dynamic process is represented only by the chemical process."[1]

"By the positing of the dynamic totality the addition of light is directly posited as a product. The expression, the total product, therefore signifies light combined with the force of gravitation; by the positing of the relative totality of the whole potency, the force of gravity is directly reduced to the mere form of the Being of absolute identity." This is the third potency (A^3), the organism.[2] Schelling launched out into too many individual details, if he desired to indicate the construction of the whole universe. On the one hand, however, he did not complete this representation, and on the other hand, he has confined himself mainly to implicit existence, and has mixed therewith the formalism of external construction according to a presupposed scheme. In this representation he advanced only as far as the organism, and did not reach the presentation of the other side of knowledge, *i.e.* the philosophy of spirit. Schelling began time after time, in accordance with the idea implied in this construction, to work out the natural universe, and especially the organism. He banishes all such meaningless terms as perfection, wisdom, outward adaptability; or, in other words, the Kantian formula, that a thing appears so and so to our faculty of knowledge, is transformed by him into this other formula, that such and such is the constitution of Nature. Following up Kant's meagre attempt at demonstrating spirit in nature, he devoted special attention to inaugurating anew this mode of regarding nature, so as to recognize in objective

[1] Schelling: Zeitschrift für spec. Phys., Vol. II. No. II. § 62-64, pp. 47, 48; § 92, 93, pp. 59, 60; § 67-69, pp. 49, 50; § 95, pp. 64-68; (Neue Zeitschrift für speculative Physik, Vol. I. Part II. pp. 92, 93, 98, 117-119; Erster Entwurf eines Systems der Natur-philosophie, p. 297); § 76-78, p. 53; § 83 and Appendix, p. 54; § 103, Note, p. 76; § 112. p. 84.

[2] Ibidem, § 136, 137, pp. 109, 110; § 141, Appendix I. p. 112.

existence the same schematism, the same rhythm, as is present in the ideal. Hence nature represents itself therein not as something alien to spirit, but as being in its general aspect a projection of spirit into an objective mode.

We have further to remark that Schelling by this theory became the originator of modern Natural Philosophy, since he was the first to exhibit Nature as the sensuous perception or the expression of the Notion and its determinations. Natural Philosophy is no new science; we met with it continually—in the works of Aristotle, for instance, and elsewhere. English Philosophy is also a mere apprehension in thought of the physical; forces, laws of Nature, are its fundamental determinations. The opposition of physics and Natural Philosophy is therefore not the opposition of the unthinking and the thinking view of Nature; Natural Philosophy means, if we take it in its whole extent, nothing else than the thoughtful contemplation of Nature; but this is the work of ordinary physics also, since its determinations of forces, laws, &c., are thoughts. The only difference is that in physics thoughts are formal thoughts of the understanding, whose material and content cannot, as regards their details, be determined by thought itself, but must be taken from experience. But concrete thought contains its determination and its content in itself, and merely the external mode of appearance pertains to the senses. If, then, Philosophy passes beyond the form of the understanding, and has apprehended the speculative Notion, it must alter the determinations of thought, the categories of the understanding regarding Nature. Kant was the first to set about this; and Schelling has sought to grasp the Notion of Nature, instead of contenting himself with the ordinary metaphysics of the same. Nature is to him nothing but the external mode of existence as regards the system of thought-forms, just as mind is the existence of the same system in the form of consciousness. That for which we have to thank

Schelling, therefore, is not that he brought thought to bear on the comprehension of Nature, but that he altered the categories according to which thought applied itself to Nature; he introduced forms of Reason, and applied them—as he did the form of the syllogism in magnetism, for instance—in place of the ordinary categories of the understanding. He has not only shown these forms in Nature, but has also sought to evolve Nature out of a principle of this kind.

In the "Further Exposition of the System of Philosophy" which the "New Journal for Speculative Physics" furnishes, Schelling chose other forms; for, by reason of incompletely developed form and lack of dialectic, he had recourse to various forms one after another, because he found none of them sufficient. Instead of the equilibrium of subjectivity and objectivity, he now speaks of the identity of existence and form, of universal and particular, of finite and infinite, of positive and negative, and he defines absolute indifference sometimes in one and sometimes in another form of opposition, just according to chance. All such oppositions may be employed; but they are only abstract, and refer to different stages in the development of the logical principle itself. Form and essence are distinguished by Schelling in this way, that form, regarded on its own account, is the particular, or the emerging of difference, subjectivity. But real existence is absolute form or absolute knowledge immediately in itself, a self-conscious existence in the sense of thinking knowledge, just as with Spinoza it had the form of something objective or in thought. Speculative Philosophy is to be found in this assertion, not that it asserts an independent philosophy, for it is purely organization; knowledge is based on the Absolute. Thus Schelling has again given to transcendental Idealism the significance of absolute Idealism. This unity of existence and form is thus, according to Schelling, the Absolute; or if we regard reality as the universal, and form as the particular, the

Absolute is the absolute unity of universal and particular, or of Being and knowledge. The different aspects, subject and object, or universal and particular, are only ideal oppositions; they are in the Absolute entirely and altogether one. This unity as form is intellectual intuition, which posits Thinking and Being as absolutely alike, and as it formally expresses the Absolute, it becomes at the same time the expression of its essence. He who has not the power of imagination, whereby he may represent this unity to himself, is deficient in the organ of Philosophy. But in this consists the true absoluteness of all and each, that the one is not recognized as universal, and the other as particular, but the universal in this its determination is recognized as unity of the universal and particular, and in like manner the particular is recognized as the unity of both. Construction merely consists in leading back everything determined and particular into the Absolute, or regarding it as it is in absolute unity; its determinateness is only its ideal moment, but its truth is really its Being in the Absolute. These three moments or potencies—that of the passing of existence (the infinite) into form (the finite), and of form into existence (which are both relative unities), and the third, the absolute unity, thus recur anew in each individual. Hence Nature, the real or actual aspect, as the passing of existence into form or of the universal into the particular, itself again possesses these three unities in itself, and in the same way the ideal aspect does so; therefore each potency is on its own account once more absolute. This is the general idea of the scientific construction of the universe—to repeat in each individual alike the triplicity which is the scheme of the whole, thereby to show the identity of all things, and in doing so to regard them in their absolute essence, so that they all express the same unity.[1]

[1] Schelling: Neue Zeitschrift für speculative Physik, Vol. I. Part I. pp. 1-77; Part II. pp. 1-38.

The more detailed explanation is extremely formal: "Existence passes into form—this taken by itself being the particular (the finite)—by means of the infinite being added to it; unity is received into multiplicity, indifference into difference." The other assertion is: "Form passes into existence by the finite being received into the infinite, difference into indifference." But passing into and receiving into are merely sensuous expressions. "Otherwise expressed, the particular becomes absolute form by the universal becoming one with it, and the universal becomes absolute existence by the particular becoming one with it. But these two unities, as in the Absolute, are not outside of one another, but in one another, and therefore the Absolute is absolute indifference of form and existence," as unity of this double passing-into-one. "By means of these two unities two different potencies are determined, but in themselves they are both the exactly equal roots of the Absolute."[1] That is a mere assertion, the continual return after each differentiation, which is perpetually again removed out of the Absolute.

"Of the first absolute transformation there are copies in phenomenal Nature; therefore Nature, regarded in itself, is nothing else than that first transformation as it exists in the absolute (unseparated from the other). For by means of the infinite passing into the finite, existence passes into form; since then form obtains reality only by means of existence, existence, when it has passed into form without form having (according to the assumption) similarly passed into existence, can be represented only as potentiality or ground of reality, but not as indifference of possibility and actuality. But that which may be described thus, namely as existence, in so far as that is mere ground of reality, and therefore has really passed into form, although form has not in turn passed into it, is what presents itself as Nature.—

[1] Schelling: Ibidem, Vol. I. Part II. p. 39.

Existence makes its appearance in form, but in return form also makes its appearance in existence; this is the other unity," that of mind. "This unity is established by the finite being received into the infinite. At this point form, as the particular, strikes into existence, and itself becomes absolute. Form which passes into existence places itself as absolute activity and positive cause of reality in opposition to the existence which passes into form, and which appears only as ground. The passing of absolute form into existence is what we think of as God, and the images or copies of this transformation are in the ideal world, which is therefore in its implicitude the other unity."[1] Each of these two transformations, then, is the whole totality, not, however, posited and not appearing as totality, but with the one or the other factor preponderating; each of the two spheres has, therefore, in itself again these differences, and thus in each of them the three potencies are to be found.

The ground or basis, Nature as basis merely, is matter, gravity, as the first potency; this passing of form into existence is in the actual world universal mechanism, necessity. But the second potency is "the light which shineth in darkness, form which has passed into existence. The absolute unification of the two unities in actuality, so that matter is altogether form, and form is altogether matter, is organism, the highest expression of Nature as it is in God, and of God as He is in Nature, in the finite." On the ideal side "Knowledge is the essence of the Absolute brought into the daylight of form; action is a transformation of form, as the particular, into the essence of the Absolute. As in the real world form that is identified with essence appears as light, so in the ideal world God Himself appears in particular manifestation as the living form which has emerged in the passing of form into essence, so that in every respect the ideal and real world

[1] Schelling: Ibidem, Vol. I. Part II. pp. 39-41.

are again related as likeness and symbol. The absolute unification of the two unities in the ideal, so that material is wholly form and form wholly material, is the work of art; and that secret hidden in the Absolute which is the root of all reality comes here into view, in the reflected world itself, in the highest potency and highest union of God and Nature as the power of imagination." On account of that permeation art and poetry therefore hold the highest rank in Schelling's estimation. But art is the Absolute in sensuous form alone. Where and what could the work of art be, which should correspond to the Idea of the spirit? "The universe is formed in the Absolute as the most perfect organic existence and the most perfect work of art: for Reason, which recognizes the Absolute in it, it possesses absolute truth; for the imagination, which represents the Absolute in it, it possesses absolute Beauty. Each of these expresses the very same unity," regarded "from different sides; and both arrive at the absolute indifference point in the recognition of which lies both the beginning and the aim of real knowledge."[1] This highest Idea, these differences, are grasped as a whole in a very formal manner only.

3. The relation of Nature to Spirit, and to God, the Absolute, has been stated by Schelling elsewhere, *i.e.* in his later expositions, as follows: he defines the existence of God as Nature—in so far as God constitutes Himself its ground or basis, as infinite perception—and Nature is thus the negative moment in God, since intelligence and thought exist only by means of the opposition of one Being. For in one of his writings, directed on some particular occasion against Jacobi, Schelling explains himself further with regard to the nature of God and His relation to Nature. He says: "God, or more properly the existence which is God, is ground: He is ground of Himself as a moral Being,

[1] Schelling, Ibidem, Vol. I. Part II. pp. 41-50.

But" then "it is ground that He makes Himself"—not cause. Something must precede intelligence, and that something is Being—"since thought is the exact opposite of Being. That which is the beginning of an intelligence cannot be in its turn intelligent, since there would otherwise be no distinction; but it cannot be absolutely unintelligent, for the very reason that it is the potentiality of an intelligence. It will accordingly be something between these, *i.e.* it will operate with wisdom, but as it were with an innate, instinctive, blind, and yet unconscious wisdom; just as we often hear those who are under a spell uttering words full of understanding, but not uttering them with comprehension of their meaning, but as it were owing to an inspiration." God, therefore, as this ground of Himself, is Nature—Nature as it is in God; this is the view taken of Nature in Natural Philosophy.[1] But the work of the Absolute is to abrogate this ground, and to constitute itself Intelligence. On this account Schelling's philosophy has later been termed a Philosophy of Nature, and that in the sense of a universal philosophy, while at first Natural Philosophy was held to be only a part of the whole.

It is not incumbent on us here to give a more detailed account of Schelling's philosophy, or to show points in the expositions hitherto given by him which are far from satisfactory. The system is the latest form of Philosophy which we had to consider, and it is a form both interesting and true. In the first place special emphasis, in dealing with Schelling, must be laid on the idea that he has grasped the true as the concrete, as the unity of subjective and objective. The main point in Schelling's philosophy thus is that its interest centres round that deep, specula-

[1] Schelling: Denkmal der Schrift von den göttlichen Dingen, pp. 94, 85, 86 (Philosophische Untersuchungen über das Wesen der menschlichen Freiheit in den Philosophischen Schriften, Vol. I. Landshut, 1809, p. 429), 89-93.

tive content, which, as content, is the content with which Philosophy in the entire course of its history has had to do. The Thought which is free and independent, not abstract, but in itself concrete, comprehends itself in itself as an intellectually actual world; and this is the truth of Nature, Nature in itself. The second great merit possessed by Schelling is to have pointed out in Nature the forms of Spirit; thus electricity, magnetism, &c., are for him only external modes of the Idea. His defect is that this Idea in general, its distinction into the ideal and the natural world, and also the totality of these determinations, are not shown forth and developed as necessitated in themselves by the Notion. As Schelling has not risen to this point of view, he has misconceived the nature of thought; the work of art thus becomes for him the supreme and only mode in which the Idea exists for spirit. But the supreme mode of the Idea is really its own element; thought, the Idea apprehended, is therefore higher than the work of art. The Idea is the truth, and all that is true is the Idea; the systematizing of the Idea into the world must be proved to be a necessary unveiling and revelation. With Schelling, on the other hand, form is really an external scheme, and his method is the artificial application of this scheme to external objects. This externally applied scheme takes the place of dialectic progress; and this is the special reason why the philosophy of Nature has brought itself into discredit, that it has proceeded on an altogether external plan, has made its foundation a ready-made scheme, and fitted into it Nature as we perceive it. These forms were potencies with Schelling, but instead of mathematical forms or a type of thought like this, by some other men sensuous forms have been taken as basis, just as were sulphur and mercury by Jacob Boehme. For instance, magnetism, electricity, and chemistry have been defined to be the three potencies in Nature, and thus in the organism reproduction has been termed chemistry;

irritability, electricity; and sensibility, magnetism.[1] In this way there has crept into Natural Philosophy the great formalism of representing everything as a series, which is a superficial determination without necessity, since instead of Notions we find formulas. Brilliant powers of imagination are displayed, such as were exhibited by Görres. This mistake of applying forms which are taken from one sphere of Nature to another sphere of the same has been carried a long way; Oken, for example, calls wood-fibres the nerves and brain of the plant, and is almost crazy on the subject. Philosophy would in this way become a play of mere analogical reflections; and it is not with these but with thoughts that we have to do. Nerves are not thoughts, any more than such expressions as pole of contraction, of expansion, masculine, feminine, &c. The formal plan of applying an external scheme to the sphere of Nature which one wishes to observe, is the external work of Natural Philosophy, and this scheme is itself derived from the imagination. That is a most false mode of proceeding; Schelling took advantage of it to some extent, others have made a complete misuse of it. All this is done to escape thought; nevertheless, thought is the ultimate simple determination which has to be dealt with.

It is therefore of the greatest importance to distinguish Schelling's philosophy, on the one hand, from that imitation of it which throws itself into an unspiritual farrago of words regarding the Absolute; and, on the other hand, from the philosophy of those imitators, who, owing to a failure to understand intellectual intuition, give up comprehension, and with it the leading moment of knowledge, and speak from so-called intuition, *i.e.* they take a glance at the thing in question, and having fastened on it some superficial analogy or definition, they fancy they have expressed its

[1] Cf. Schelling's Erster Entwurf der Natur-philosophie, p. 297.

whole nature, while in point of fact they put an end to all capacity for attaining to scientific knowledge. This whole tendency places itself, in the first place, in opposition to reflective thought, or to progress in fixed, steadfast, immovable Notions. But instead of remaining in the Notion and recognizing it as the unresting ego, they have lighted on the opposite extreme of passive intuition, of immediate Being, of fixed implicitude; and they think that they can make up for the lack of fixity by superficial observation, and can render this observation intellectual by determining it once more by some fixed Notion or other; or they bring their minds to bear on the object of consideration by saying, for instance, that the ostrich is the fish among birds, because he has a long neck—fish becomes a general term, but not a Notion. This whole mode of reasoning, which has forced its way into natural history and natural science, as well as into medicine, is a miserable formalism, an irrational medley of the crudest empiricism with the most superficial ideal determinations that formalism ever descended to. The philosophy of Locke is not so crude as it is, for it is not a whit better in either its content or its form, and it is combined with foolish self-conceit into the bargain. Philosophy on this account sank into general and well-deserved contempt, such as is for the most part extended to those who assert that they have a monopoly of philosophy. Instead of earnestness of apprehension and circumspection of thought, we find in them a juggling with idle fancies, which pass for deep conceptions, lofty surmises, and even for poetry: and they think they are right in the centre of things when they are only on the surface. Five-and-twenty years ago[1] the case was the same with poetic art; a taste for ingenious conceits took possession of it, and the effusions of its poetic inspiration came forth blindly from itself, shot out as

[1] From the lectures of 1805-1806.

from a pistol. The results were either crazy ravings, or, if they were not ravings, they were prose so dull that it was unworthy of the name of prose. It is just the same in the later philosophies. What is not utterly senseless drivel about the indifference-point and polarity, about oxygen, the holy, the infinite, &c., is made up of thoughts so trivial that we might well doubt our having correctly apprehended their meaning, in the first place because they are given forth with such arrogant effrontery, and in the second place because we cannot help trusting that what was said was not so trivial as it seems. As in the Philosophy of Nature men forgot the Notion and proceeded in a dead unspiritual course, so here they lose sight of spirit entirely. They have strayed from the right road; for by their principle, Notion and perception are one unity, but in point of fact this unity, this spirit, itself emerges in immediacy, and is therefore in intuitive perception, and not in the Notion.

E. Final Result.

The present standpoint of philosophy is that the Idea is known in its necessity; the sides of its diremption, Nature and Spirit, are each of them recognized as representing the totality of the Idea, and not only as being in themselves identical, but as producing this one identity from themselves; and in this way the identity is recognized as necessary. Nature, and the world or history of spirit, are the two realities; what exists as actual Nature is an image of divine Reason; the forms of self-conscious Reason are also the forms of Nature. The ultimate aim and business of philosophy is to reconcile thought or the Notion with reality. It is easy from subordinate standpoints to find satisfaction in modes of intuitive perception and of feeling. But the deeper the spirit goes within itself, the more vehement is the opposition, the more abundant is the wealth without; the depth is to be measured by the greatness of the craving with which spirit seeks to find itself in what lies outside of itself. We saw the thought which apprehends itself appearing; it strove to make itself concrete within itself. Its first activity is formal; Aristotle was the first to say that νοῦς is the thought of thought. The result is the thought which is at home with itself, and at the same time embraces the universe therein, and transforms it into an intelligent world. In apprehension the spiritual and the natural universe are interpenetrated as one harmonious universe, which withdraws into itself, and in its various aspects develops the Absolute into a totality, in order, by the very process of so doing, to become conscious of itself in its unity, in Thought. Philosophy is thus the true theodicy, as contrasted with art and religion and the feelings which these call up—a reconciliation of spirit, namely of the spirit which has apprehended itself in its freedom and in the riches of its reality.

To this point the World-spirit has come, and each stage has its own form in the true system of Philosophy; nothing is lost, all principles are preserved, since Philosophy in its final aspect is the totality of forms. This concrete idea is the result of the strivings of spirit during almost twenty-five centuries of earnest work to become objective to itself, to know itself:

Tantæ molis erat, se ipsam cognoscere mentem.

All this time was required to produce the philosophy of our day; so tardily and slowly did the World-spirit work to reach this goal. What we pass in rapid review when we recall it, stretched itself out in reality to this great length of time. For in this lengthened period, the Notion of Spirit, invested with its entire concrete development, its external subsistence, its wealth, is striving to bring spirit to perfection, to make progress itself and to develop from spirit. It goes ever on and on, because spirit is progress alone. Spirit often seems to have forgotten and lost itself, but inwardly opposed to itself, it is inwardly working ever forward (as when Hamlet says of the ghost of his father, "Well said, old mole! canst work i' the ground so fast?" [1]), until grown strong in itself it bursts asunder the crust of earth which divided it from the sun, its Notion, so that the earth crumbles away. At such a time, when the encircling crust, like a soulless decaying tenement, crumbles away, and spirit displays itself arrayed in new youth, the seven league boots are at length adopted. This work of the spirit to know itself, this activity to find itself, is the life of the spirit and the spirit itself. Its result is the Notion which it takes up of itself; the history of Philosophy is a revelation of what has been the aim of spirit throughout its history; it is therefore the world's history in its innermost signification. This work of the human spirit in the recesses of thought is parallel with all the stages of reality; and therefore no philosophy oversteps its own time. The importance which the determinations of thought possessed is another matter, which does not belong to the history of Philosophy. These Notions are the simplest revelation of the World spirit: in their more concrete form they are history.

We must, therefore, in the first place not esteem lightly what spirit has won, namely its gains up to the present day. Ancient Philosophy is to be reverenced as necessary, and as a link in this sacred chain, but all the same nothing more than a link. The present is the highest stage reached. In the second place, all the various philosophies are no mere fashionable theories of the time, or anything of a similar nature; they are neither chance products nor the blaze of a fire of straw, nor casual eruptions here and there, but a spiritual, reasonable, forward advance; they are of necessity one Philosophy in its development, the revelation of God, as He knows Himself to be. Where several

[1] Hamlet, Act I. Scene V.

philosophies appear at the same time, they are different sides which make up one totality forming their basis; and on account of their one-sidedness we see the refutation of the one by the other. In the third place we do not find here feeble little efforts to establish or to criticize this or that particular point; instead of that, each philosophy sets up a new principle of its own, and this must be recognized.

If we glance at the main epochs in the whole history of Philosophy, and grasp the necessary succession of stages in the leading moments, each of which expresses a determinate Idea, we find that after the Oriental whirl of subjectivity, which attains to no intelligibility and therefore to no subsistence, the light of thought dawned among the Greeks.

1. The philosophy of the ancients had the absolute Idea as its thought; and the realization or reality of the same consisted in comprehending the existing present world, and regarding it as it is in its absolute nature. This philosophy did not make its starting-point the Idea itself, but proceeded from the objective as from something given, and transformed the same into the Idea; the Being of Parmenides.

2. Abstract thought, *νοῦς*, became known to itself as universal essence or existence, not as subjective thought; the Universal of Plato.

3. In Aristotle the Notion emerges, free and unconstrained, as comprehending thought, permeating and spiritualizing all the forms which the universe contains.

4. The Notion as subject, its independence, its inwardness, abstract separation, is represented by the Stoics, Epicureans and Sceptics: here we have not the free, concrete form, but universality abstract and in itself formal.

5. The thought of totality, the intelligible world, is the concrete Idea as we have seen it with the Neo-Platonists.

This principle is ideality generally speaking, which is present in all reality, but not the Idea which knows itself: this is not reached until the principle of subjectivity, individuality, found a place in it, and God as spirit became actual to Himself in self-consciousness.

6. But it has been the work of modern times to grasp this Idea as spirit, as the Idea that knows itself. In order to proceed from the conscious Idea to the self-conscious, we must have the infinite opposition, namely the fact that the Idea has come to the consciousness of being absolutely sundered in twain. As spirit had the thought of objective existence, Philosophy thus perfected the intellectuality of the world, and produced this spiritual world as an object existing beyond present reality, like Nature,—the first creation of spirit. The work of the spirit now consisted in bringing this Beyond back to reality, and guiding it into self-consciousness. This is accomplished by self-consciousness thinking itself, and recognizing absolute existence to be the self-consciousness that thinks itself. With Descartes pure thought directed itself on that separation which we spoke of above. Self-consciousness, in the first place, thinks of itself as consciousness; therein is contained all objective reality, and the positive, intuitive reference of its reality to the other side. With Spinoza Thought and Being are opposed and yet identical; he has the intuitive perception of substance, but the knowledge of substance in his case is external. We have here the principle of reconciliation taking its rise from thought as such, in order to abrogate the subjectivity of thought: this is the case in Leibnitz's monad, which possesses the power of representation.

7. In the second place, self-consciousness thinks of itself as being self-consciousness; in being self-conscious it is independent, but still in this independence it has a negative relation to what is outside self-consciousness. This is infinite subjectivity, which appears at one time as the critique of thought in the case of Kant, and at another

time, in the case of Fichte, as the tendency or impulse towards the concrete. Absolute, pure, infinite form is expressed as self-consciousness, the Ego.

8. This is a light that breaks forth on spiritual substance, and shows absolute content and absolute form to be identical; —substance is in itself identical with knowledge. Self-consciousness thus, in the third place, recognizes its positive relation as its negative, and its negative as its positive,—or, in other words, recognizes these opposite activities as the same, *i.e.* it recognizes pure Thought or Being as self-identity, and this again as separation. This is intellectual perception; but it is requisite in order that it should be in truth intellectual, that it should not be that merely immediate perception of the eternal and the divine which we hear of, but should be absolute knowledge. This intuitive perception which does not recognize itself is taken as starting-point as if it were absolutely presupposed; it has in itself intuitive perception only as immediate knowledge, and not as self-knowledge: or it knows nothing, and what it perceives it does not really know,—for, taken at its best, it consists of beautiful thoughts, but not knowledge.

But intellectual intuition is knowledge, since, in the first place, in spite of the separation of each of the opposed sides from the other, all external reality is known as internal. If it is known according to its essence, as it is, it shows itself as not existing of itself, but as essentially consisting in the movement of transition. This Heraclitean or Sceptical principle, that nothing is at rest, must be demonstrated of each individual thing; and thus in this consciousness—that the essence of each thing lies in determination, in what is the opposite of itself—there appears the apprehended unity with its opposite. Similarly this unity is, in the second place, to be recognized even in its essence; its essence as this identity is, in the same way, to pass over into its opposite, or to realize itself, to become for itself something different; and thus the opposition in it is brought about by itself. Again, it may be said of the opposition, in the third place, that it is not in the Absolute; this Absolute is existence, the eternal, &c. This is, however, itself an abstraction in which the Absolute is apprehended in a one-sided manner only, and the opposition is apprehended only as ideal (*supra*, p. 536); but in fact it is form, as the essential moment of the movement of the Absolute. This Absolute is not at rest, and that opposition is not the unresting Notion; for the Idea, unresting though it is, is yet at rest and satisfied in itself. Pure thought has advanced to the opposition of the subjective and objective; the true reconciliation of the opposition is the perception that this opposition, when pushed to its absolute extreme, resolves itself; as Schelling says, the opposites are in themselves identical—and not only in themselves, but eternal life consists in the very process of continually producing the opposition and continually reconciling it. To know opposition in unity, and unity in opposition—this is absolute knowledge; and science is the knowledge of this unity in its whole development by means of itself.

This is then the demand of all time and of Philosophy. A new epoch has arisen in the world. It would appear as if the World-spirit had at last succeeded in stripping off from itself all alien objective existence, and apprehending itself at last as absolute Spirit, in developing from itself what for it is objective, and keeping it within its own power, yet remaining at rest all the while. The strife of the finite self-consciousness with the absolute self-consciousness, which last seemed to the other to lie outside of itself, now comes to an end. Finite self-consciousness has ceased to be finite; and in this way absolute self-consciousness has, on the other hand, attained to the reality which it lacked before. This is the whole history of the world in general up to the present time, and the history of Philosophy in particular, the sole work of which is to depict this strife. Now, indeed, it seems to have reached its goal, when this absolute self-consciousness, which it had the work of representing, has ceased to be alien, and when spirit accordingly is realized as spirit. For it becomes such only as the result of its knowing itself to be absolute spirit, and this it knows in real scientific knowledge. Spirit produces itself as Nature, as the State; nature is its unconscious work, in the course of which it appears to itself something different, and not spirit; but in the State, in the deeds and life of History, as also of Art, it brings itself to pass with consciousness; it knows very various modes of its reality, yet they are only modes. In scientific knowledge alone it knows itself as absolute spirit; and this knowledge, or spirit, is its only true existence. This then is the standpoint of the present day, and the series of spiritual forms is with it for the present concluded.

At this point I bring this history of Philosophy to a close. It has been my desire that you should learn from it that the history of Philosophy is not a blind collection of fanciful ideas, nor a fortuitous progression. I have rather sought to show the necessary development of the successive philosophies from one another, so that the one of necessity presupposes another preceding it. The general result of the history of Philosophy is this: in the first place, that throughout all time there has been only one Philosophy, the contemporary differences of which constitute the necessary aspects of the one principle; in the second place, that the succession of philosophic systems is not due to chance, but represents the necessary succession of stages in the development of this science; in the third place, that the final philosophy of a period is the result of this development, and is truth in the highest form which the self-consciousness of spirit affords of itself. The latest philosophy contains therefore those which went before; it embraces in itself all the different stages thereof;

it is the product and result of those that preceded it. We can now, for example, be Platonists no longer. Moreover we must raise ourselves once for all above the pettinesses of individual opinions, thoughts, objections, and difficulties; and also above our own vanity, as if our individual thoughts were of any particular value. For to apprehend the inward substantial spirit is the standpoint of the individual; as parts of the whole, individuals are like blind men, who are driven forward by the indwelling spirit of the whole. Our standpoint now is accordingly the knowledge of this Idea as spirit, as absolute Spirit, which in this way opposes to itself another spirit, the finite, the principle of which is to know absolute spirit, in order that absolute spirit may become existent for it. I have tried to develop and bring before your thoughts this series of successive spiritual forms pertaining to Philosophy in its progress, and to indicate the connection between them. This series is the true kingdom of spirits, the only kingdom of spirits that there is—it is a series which is not a multiplicity, nor does it even remain a series, if we understand thereby that one of its members merely follows on another; but in the very process of coming to the knowledge of itself it is transformed into the moments of the one Spirit, or the one self-present Spirit. This long procession of spirits is formed by the individual pulses which beat in its life; they are the organism of our substance, an absolutely necessary progression, which expresses nothing less than the nature of spirit itself, and which lives in us all. We have to give ear to its urgency—when the mole that is within forces its way on—and we have to make it a reality. It is my desire that this history of Philosophy should contain for you a summons to grasp the spirit of the time, which is present in us by nature, and—each in his own place—consciously to bring it from its natural condition, *i.e.* from its lifeless seclusion, into the light of day.

I have to express my thanks to you for the attention

with which you have listened to me while I have been making this attempt; it is in great measure due to you that my efforts have met with so great a measure of success. And it has been a source of pleasure to myself to have been associated with you in this spiritual community; I ought not to speak of it as if it were a thing of the past, for I hope that a spiritual bond has been knit between us which will prove permanent. I bid you a most hearty farewell.

(The closing lecture of the series was given on the 22nd March, 1817; on the 14th March, 1818; on the 12th August, 1819; on the 23rd March, 1821; on the 30th March, 1824; on the 28th March, 1828; and on the 26th March, 1830.)

INDEX

CORRIGENDA IN VOLS. I. & II.

VOL. I.

Page xii., line 32, *for* "never . . . completely" *read* "never have emptiness and conceit swum so persistently on the surface."

" 12, " 26, *for* "is in" *read* "is not in."

" 56, " 9, *for* "sound" *read* "found."

" 60, " 17, *for* "wherever, etc." *read* "be this positive character derived from whence it may."

" 70, " 29, *for* "And Mind . . . implicit," *read* "And Mind is implicitly not that."

" 71, " 2, *for* "Finality" *read* "Finiteness."

" 72, " 7, *for* "involve" *read* "involves"; line 22, *omit* "through"; line 24 *omit* "of."

" 73, " 26, *for* "and" *read* "all."

" 81, " 11, *for* "What . . . evidence" *read* "The essential truth contained in the testimony."

" 82, " 9, *for* "symbolism" *read* "his *Symbolik*."

" 85, " 36, *omit* "the."

" 86, " 3, *omit* "the."

" 90, " 29, *for* "thought—determination" *read* "thought-determination."

" 112, " 24, *for* "Tiedmann" *read* "Tiedemann"; line 30, *for* "Plato of Brucker" *read* "Bipontine edition of Plato."

" 113, " 21, *for* "overthrown by" *read* "converted into;" line 27, *for* "a correct" *read* "a more correct."

" 114, lines [illegible] and 8, *for* "Aft" *read* "Ast;" line 18, *for* "Rirner" *read* "Rixner"; line 33, *for* "and hence . . . philosophers" *read* "giving also biographical sketches of the principal philosophers."

" 117, line 9, *for* "East" *read* "West"; line 20, *for* "and approximates" to end of sentence *read* "which is very liable to be taken for Philosophy, and we must indicate the main reason why the Oriental idea of religion is so liable to be regarded as a religious philosophy."

" 118, " 10, *for* "Civa" *read* "Siva"; line 16, *for* "Zeroane" *read* "Zervane."

" 119, " 6, *for* "lawlessness" *read* "absence of individual rights"; line 20, *for* "To that . . . substance" *read* "This finite can only come to be true when absorbed in substance."

" 120, " 16, *for* "last" *read* "arise"; line 26, *for* "Liebnitz" *read* "Leibnitz."

Page 122, line 6, *for* "sensuous" *read* "thoughtful."
„ 123, „ 32, „ „ „ „
„ 135, „ 11, „ „ „ „
„ 128, „ 23, *for* "very extensive" *read* "widely diffused."
„ 129, „ 5, *for* "it must . . . again" *read* "it must be separated from nature in order that it may not come back."
„ 154, „ 5, *for* "connoisseurs" *read* "masters."
„ 169, „ 4, *for* "of" *read* "in."
„ 173, „ 5, *for* "; and it carries . . . weight" *read* "with a very important air."
174, „ 2, *for* "for he speaks . . . them" *read* "; he speaks of them in general terms for the most part."
„ 176, „ 6, *for* "Tiedmann" *read* "Tiedemann."
„ 181, „ 9, „ „ „ „
„ 183, „ 29, „ „ „ „
„ 214, „ 15, *for* "posited as" *read* "added to"; line 16, *for* "as" *read* "to."
„ 231, lines 32 and 33, *for* "solar corpuscles" *read* "motes."
„ 244, line 19, *for* "Spinozaism" *read* "Spinozism."
„ 249, „ 23, *for* "Thætetus," *read* "Theætetus."
„ 280, „ 23, *for* "if" *read* "even though;" line 24, *omit* "also"; line 34, *for* "until modern time" *read* "until a late period of antiquity."
„ 281, „ 8, *for* "knowledge of language" *read* "philological learning."
„ 323, „ 18, *for* "we find, it held among" *read* "as we have seen, was held by."
„ 359, „ 23, *for* "we have a desire to go on" *read* "let us go on."
„ 384, „ 25, *for* "For a mental turning-point . . . thought" *read* "For there exhibited itself in him a turning-point of spirit in the guise of philosophic thought."
„ 388, „ 24, *for* "yield itself up . . . that" *read* "make concessions, and therefore achieved no substantial result by its study, praised Socrates as he has often enough been praised since, in that."
„ 390, „ 33, *for* "maintaining that it was given" *read* "but succeeded in having it given."
„ 393, „ 31, *for* "every" *read* "that."
„ 394, „ 1, *omit* "alone."
„ 406, „ 7, *omit* comma after "that."
„ 427, „ 9, *for* "happy" *read* "frivolous"; line 18, *for* "refute" *read* "establish."
„ 429, „ 31, *for* "suprem" *read* "supreme"; line 35, *for* "execratione" *read* "execration."
„ 472, „ 33, *for* "that . . . other" *read* "in this way that one stone would not be sitting on another."
„ 478, „ 26, *for* "the Ptolemies" *read* "by the Ptolemy."

VOL. II.

Page 59, line 1, *omit* "either of."
„ 98, „ 16, *for* "to be" *read* "as."
„ 160, lines 13 and 14, *for* "In the Kantian philosophy . . . have" *read* "Not until we come to the Kantian philosophy have we."
„ 204, line 27, *for* "virtue" *read* "reason."